THE GREAT WHITE FLOOD
RACISM IN AUSTRALIA

AAR

American Academy of Religion
Cultural Criticism Series

Number 2

THE GREAT WHITE FLOOD

RACISM IN AUSTRALIA

by
Anne Pattel-Gray

THE GREAT WHITE FLOOD
RACISM IN AUSTRALIA

Critically Appraised from an Aboriginal
Historico-Theological Viewpoint

by
Anne Pattel-Gray

Scholars Press
Atlanta, Georgia

THE GREAT WHITE FLOOD
RACISM IN AUSTRALIA

Critically Appraised from an Aboriginal
Historico-Theological Viewpoint

by
Anne Pattel-Gray

A thesis submitted in fulfilment of the requirements for the degree of Doctor of Philosophy
University of Sydney, School of Studies in Religion, 1994

Copyright © 1998 by the American Academy of Religion

Unless otherwise noted, all Bible verses are taken from the New Revised Standard Version, copyright © 1989 by the National Council of the Churches of Christ in the U.S.A. Used by permission.

Library of Congress Cataloging in Publication Data
Pattel-Gray, Anne.
    The great white flood ; critically appraised from an Aboriginal historico-theological viewpoint / by Anne Pattel-Gray.
        p.   cm. — (American Academy of Religion cultural criticism series ; no. 2)
    Includes bibliographical references.
    ISBN 0-7885-0132-1 (alk. paper). — ISBN 0-7885-0133-X (pbk. : alk. paper)
    1. Australian aborigines—Race identity. 2. Australian aborigines—Government policy. 3. Australian aborigines—Social conditions. 4. Racism—Government policy—Australia. 5. Racism—Australia—Religious aspects—Christianity. 6. Australia—Race relations. I. Title. II. Series.
GN666.P236   1995
305.89'915—dc20   95-9379
                                            CIP

Printed in the United States of America
on acid-free paper

TABLE OF CONTENTS

ABSTRACT..xi

ACKNOWLEDGEMENTS...xiii

ABBREVIATIONS..xv

"The Great White Flood," by Lyndel Robb...xviii

INTRODUCTION..1

1. RACE AND RACISM..3

Race

Stereotype

Prejudice

Ethnocentrism

Racism

    Definitions

    White Racism

Racist Ideology

Forms of Racism

    Individual Racism

    Institutional Racism

    Scientific Racism

    "Christian" Racism

Racist Violence

Summary

2. RACISM IN AUSTRALIAN SOCIETY..15

Background: White Australian Society Contributes to Racism.....................15

    The Myths of *Terra Nullius* and "No Sovereignty"

    History—Continuing the Lie

    Amalgamation and "Non-Slavery" Slavery

    Segregation

    "Protection"

    "White Australia"

        Federation: The Institutionalization of Australian Racism

        White Australia Policy

    "Assimilation"

        Assimilation Practice

        Assimilation Policy

        Assimilation Background

v

Progress?!
Practice: Australian Society *Still* Contributes to Racism 40
Multiculturalism 40
    Multiculturalism For All?
    True Multiculturalism Begins at Home
    The Myth of Australian Multiculturalism
Governments Contribute to Racism 42
    Still No Land Rights and Still No Justice
    Disregard for Genocide
    Flawed Structures
    Myth and Mismanagement
    Failures to Sign (and Act Upon) International Instruments
    Exclusions from National and International Arenas
    Biased & Xenophobic Immigration Policies
Politicians Contribute to Racism 56
Business Community Contributes to Racism 61
    Contempt for Aboriginal People, Culture and Rights
    Continuing Violations of Aboriginal Lands and Sacred Sites
    Anaemic Support of Aboriginal Employment
    Environmental Racism
Legal, Police and Prison Systems Contribute to Racism 67
    Who Really Makes (and Enforces) the Laws?
    Extremely High Rates of Imprisonment
    High Rates of Aboriginal Deaths in Custody
    Intimidation and Violence against Minorities
    Contempt by Officials
Health and Medical Systems Contribute to Racism 79
    No Clean Water
    Inadequate Services
    Severely Under-Resourced Services
    Continuing Inaction
    Complete Failure to Implement the National Aboriginal Health
      Strategy
Academic World Contributes to Racism 84
    Distorting the Facts
    Ignoring the Evidence of Over 60,000 Years
    Exercising Control Over "History," but with "Skeletons" in the Closet
    Legitimizing Racism

Educational System Contributes to Racism...90
    Using Flawed Textbooks
    Perpetuating Lies
    Reinforcing Stereotypes
    Allowing Racist Role Models
    Omitting Facts
    Omitting People—Keeping Aboriginals Out
    Failing to "Self-Examine"
    Aboriginal Action and Change
Media Contribute to Racism 102
    One-Sided Reporting
    Offensive Language
    Inflammatory Rhetoric
    Irresponsible Supervision
    Excusing Racism
Society Contributes to Racism... 105
    Self-Image vs. Reality
    Right-Wing and Racist Groups
    Case Study: Native Title (Mabo) Judgement and Act
Summary 116
3. RACISM IN THE AUSTRALIAN CHURCH... 117
Background: The Australian Church Contributed to Racism.................... 118
    Australian Racism's Roots in European Society and Church
    Australian Church Racism Was Heretical
        Theology
        Christology
        Biblical Exegesis and Hermeneutics
        Ecclesiology
        Missiology
        Discourse and Praxis
    Theological Imperialism
    Hypocrisy
    Hypocrisy in the Extreme
    Collusion with the Government
    Institutionalizing Racism
        Racist Institutions
        Racist Individuals
        The Violence of Racist Theology and Teachings

Practice: The Australian Church *Still* Contributes to Racism 148
    Still No Land Rights
        Church Greed
        Questionable Remorse
        Questionable Actions
    Crises in Leadership and Theological Education
        Shortage of Indigenous Leaders
        Inadequate Theological Education
    Distorted Memory
    Continual Self-Justification
    Ambivalence in Statements
    Failures to Stand
    Exemptions?
    Ignoring the Problem
    Slaves to the Sin of Racism
An Aboriginal Womanist Critique of Australian Church Feminism 162
    Flawed Assumptions
        Social Origins
        Epistemology
        Experience/History
        Slavery and Servitude from 1788
        Brutality
        From Segregation to "So-Called" Protection
        Assimilation
    Aboriginal Women Tell Their Stories
    Feminist Theological Assumptions
        Flawed Methodology: Conspicuous By Our Absence
        Splitting the Movement
    Australian Feminist Theology as Racist
        In History
        Today
    No Self-Criticism
    Conclusion

4. THE LEGACY OF RACISM 187
The Sin of Racism 187
    Naming the Problem
    Tracing the Problem
The Psychology of Racism 189
    Uncontrolled Sexual and Aggressive Drives

Contents   ix

Unresolved Oedipal Complex
A Flawed Superego
A Non-Autonomous Ego
The Racism of the "Normal"
The Workings of Racism 196
Exploitation
Genocide
Dependency
A State of Illusion
White Australians as Racist
Solving the Wrong Problem
Wrong Methods
Confronting the Truth
Reports on Racism and Deaths in Custody
Individual Racism
So the Legacy Lives On
Privileges and Rewards
Malice and Slander
The Impact of Racism 212
Internalized Oppression
Racist Doctrine
Liberation and Freedom

5. RECONCILIATION: A FACSIMILE OF JUSTICE 219
A Euro-Australian Dream, An Aboriginal Nightmare 219
Trick or Treaty?
Federal Government Provision for Reconciliation
What Does The Church Say About Reconciliation? 227
1988, the *March for Justice, Freedom and Hope* and "Covenanting"
Posturing About Their Aboriginal Enclaves
Freedom From Oppression 231
Liberation as a Precondition to Reconciliation
Christ the Reconciler and Liberator
Christ Condemns the Religious Leaders
Australia's Original Sin

BIBLIOGRAPHY 241

LIST OF DIAGRAMS
1. The Downward Spiral of Racism 13
2. The Wheel of Discrimination 14
3. Australian Social Hierarchy 165

LIST OF TABLES

1. Aboriginal "Protection" Legislation..26
2. Representative Listing of Legislation (Negatively) Affecting
      Aboriginal People (1900–1967) 36
3. Real Median Annual Incomes, Aboriginal and Total Population
      Aged 15 and Over (1980–81 Dollars) 64
4. Australian and International Imprisonment Rates....................70
5. Examples of Racist Names Currently Used
      in Australian Geography...96

ACKNOWLEDGEMENTS

The author wishes to acknowledge Kevin Gilbert for permission to quote from his writings.

Sections of this work have been published elsewhere, and appreciation is due to the editors and publishers of various books and journals. These include the following:

Chapters

"Australia: The Struggle for Land Rights of the Indigenous People of Australia." *Land Is Our Life, The Earth Is The Lord's: Integrity of Creation, Justice and Peace, Global Consultation, Landrights, Darwin, Australia.* Geneva: World Council of Churches, 1989. [Translated into, and published in, French, German, Russian and Spanish.]

"The Text of the Land Rights Plenary." *PCR Information: Between Two Worlds: Report of a WCC Team Visit to Aboriginal Communities in Australia.* Geneva: World Council of Churches, Programme to Combat Racism, 1991, pp. 81–97.

"The Australian Educational System Contributes to Racism." In *Aboriginal Studies: A National Priority,* ed. by Damian Coghlan, Rhonda Craven and Nigel Parbury. Sydney: Aboriginal Studies Association, 1993, pp. 355–365.

"Aboriginal People, Multiculturalism and Immigration." In *Immigration,* ed. by Catherine Hannon. Sydney: Australian Catholic Social Justice Council, 1994.

Articles

"Come Holy Spirit—Renew Your Whole Creation." *Youth* 14,2 (June 1990): 6.

"1993: Year of the Half Hearted?" *Ministry* 3,3 (Autumn 1993): 19–21.

"Australian Churches and Native Title." *In Unity* 41,1 (May 1994): 3.

"One Mob, One Land: Australian Aboriginals Die Fighting for Land Rights." *PCR Information: Women Under Racism and Casteism—Global Gathering.* Geneva: World Council of Churches, Programme to Combat Racism, 1994.

(with Garry W. Trompf, Ph.D.) "Styles of Australian Aboriginal and Melanesian Theology." *International Review of Mission* 82,326 (April 1993): 159–181.

Acknowledgement is made to authors, editors and publishers of various works cited in this book. They include selected extracts from the following works.

*from *Dismantling Racism,* by Joseph Barndt, copyright © 1991 by Augsburg Fortress [Publishers].

Abbreviations

ABC	Australian Broadcasting Commission
ABCEAT	The Archbishops and Bishops of the Church of England in Australia and Tasmania
ABS	Australian Bureau of Statistics
ACC	Australian Council of Churches
ACT	Australian Capital Territory
ACG	Aboriginal Consultative Group
AIBCA	Aboriginal and Islander Baptist Council of Australia
AIC	Aboriginal & Islander Commission (of the ACC)
AJN	*Australian Jewish News* [Newspaper]
ALP	Australian Labor Party
ALR	Australian Law Reports
ALJR	Australian Law Journal Reports
ALS	Aboriginal Legal Service
AMIC	Australian Mining Industry Council
ANU	Australian National University
APG	Aboriginal Provisional Government
ATSIC	Aboriginal and Torres Strait Islander Commission
ATSISJC	Aboriginal and Torres Strait Islander Social Justice Commission
CAR	Council for Aboriginal Reconciliation
CLR	Commonwealth Law Reports
CoA	Commonwealth of Australia
CoA-DFAT	Commonwealth of Australia, Department of Foreign Affairs and Trade
CoA-MT	Commonwealth of Australia, Minister for Territories
CSW/ACC/NSW	Commission on the Status of Women, Australian Council of Churches, New South Wales State Council
DAA	Department of Aboriginal Affairs (Federal)
DPMC-RAC	Department of Prime Minister and Cabinet, Resources Assessment Commission
DTM	*Daily Telegraph Mirror* [Newspaper]
EARC/Q	Electoral and Administrative Review Commission (Queensland)
FAB	Federal Aborigines Board (of the Churches of Christ)

FAIRA	Foundation for Aboriginal and Islander Research and Action
F&F	*Faith and Freedom* [Journal]
FLR	Federal Law Reports
FS	*Final Submission on behalf of Aboriginal Groups and Individuals [to the Royal Commission into British Nuclear Tests in Australia]*, 16 September 1985.
HRA	*Human Rights Australia* [Newsletter]
HREOC	Human Rights and Equal Opportunity Commission
IDC	Interdepartmental Committee on International Environmental Issues [established by the Australian Federal Cabinet]
ILO	International Labor Organization
KM	*Koori Mail* [Newspaper]
LRN	*Land Rights News* [Newspaper]
MP	Member of Parliament
NAAG	National Aboriginal Anglican Council
NAHSWP	National Aboriginal Health Strategy Working Party
NATSICC	National Aboriginal and Torres Strait Islander Catholic Council
NCDBR	National Committee to Defend Black Rights
NEB	New English Bible
NGO	Non-Governmental Organization
NLC	Northern Land Council
NSW	New South Wales
NSWALC	New South Wales Aboriginal Land Council
NSWDOEDSP	N.S.W. Department of Education, Directorate of Special Programmes
NSWPS	N.S.W. Police Service
NT	Northern Territory
OCCR	Office of the Commissioner for Community Relations
OT	Oral Testimony
PCR	Programme to Combat Racism of the World Council of Churches
QC	Queen's Counsel
RCADC	Royal Commission into Aboriginal Deaths in Custody
RSL	Returned Services League
SBS	Special Broadcast Service

SCWA	Select Committee Appointed to Inquire into Native Welfare Conditions in the Laverton-Warburton Range Area, Western Australia (12 December 1956)
SMH	*Sydney Morning Herald* [Newspaper]
TIB	Thursdays in Black
UAICC	Uniting Aboriginal and Islander Christian Congress
UCA	Uniting Church in Australia
UN	United Nations
UNCED	United Nations Conference on Environment and Development
URM-CCA	Urban Rural Mission-Christian Conference of Asia
WA	Western Australia
WCC	World Council of Churches

THE GREAT WHITE FLOOD
Lyndel Robb (Kairi)

The torture, the pain that would be caused
by a captain with a fleet of ships
but I suppose I should move ahead
I should forget that my grandmother was whipped.

Terra Nullius was declared
but, Aboriginals are now moving ahead.
Perhaps I'll record this for you
Then you can judge whether my history is dead too.

An educated white guy once said to me
"Look there's no real need to worry
Aboriginal people have barely been made citizens
re-adjustment doesn't happen in a hurry"!

So I left feeling rather elated
knowing this man knew his facts
but then my feelings were deflated
as I saw the written racist attack.

I had left my friend in the city
I saw a sign as I left him there
it's awesome blood red writing
for all white Australians to bear.

Abo's go home, Abo's go back home!
Was this what I had read?
The lettering all running down the wall
probably the same way my Ancestors' blood was shed.

You tell me white Australia
that I should move ahead
but here in this century and times
I can still feel my Ancestors' deaths.

I cannot help but reflect upon
that sign I told you about
for ignorant white Australia was it you?
Or perhaps it was that infamous "Great Australian Lout".

Let me welcome every Indigenous nation
that has ever shed their blood
for here, yet again is another white invasion
Or yet another...............GREAT WHITE FLOOD!

INTRODUCTION

In the following study, I have tried to highlight racist government legislation and policies over the last two hundred years and their impact upon the Indigenous People of Australia. Australian racism is rooted in the long relationship between government and church. Australian societal behaviour came out of their corrupt relationship. Today, both entities need to create illusions for the rest of the world about their humanitarian and human rights stances. They invaded the country on the lie of *terra nullius,* waged untold wars, committed unrecorded massacres, enslaved the Indigenous People, forced segregation and more. Yet, today, Australians will not even face the historical research that uncovers these facts; nor will they acknowledge their own continuing denial of the human rights of the Indigenous People of Australia. The children of the invaders say that they cannot be held responsible or be considered guilty for the sins of their parents. Yet they have continued to benefit from those structures established by their forebears, and they are maintaining their privileged status and "rewards"—like the slave-owner whose child inherits the slaves, and says "I cannot be guilty because I did not enslave them," and continues to exploit them and profiteer off them.

Racism is alive and well in Australia. It is firmly entrenched in Australian society, rearing its ugly head in every area, from government to schools to courts to churches. It is an endemic and chronic problem that must be addressed and, more importantly, solved.

The methodology of this work attempts: 1) to present the elements of this reality by defining terminology, and clarifying some of the language and concepts of racism; and, 2) to address this reality by reviewing the historical and contemporary expressions of Australian racism in society and in the church; by presenting the legacy of racism; and by assessing both the concept and the recent process of reconciliation in Australia.

The work will include as much oral-historical investigation as possible. There is an enormous gap in the literary world in relation to the original and primary sources being recognized as having academic credibility. Most literature written about Aboriginal People usually is based on secondary sources, which raises questions about authenticity. Therefore, in my research, the primary materials sought were those written by

1

Aboriginal authors—autobiographies, histories (social, traditional, cultural, political, etc.), and others. This is not to discount some major works done by certain non-Aboriginal academics who have made significant contributions to several fields by unmasking the history of the colonial rule and the destruction within the Aboriginal societies. I have undertaken detailed research into church archives, seeking the relevant documents regarding churches' theologies, ecclesiologies and missiologies. I have inquired into the churches' true intent in "Christianizing" the Indigenous People. How much of a role did the churches play in the socializing of the Indigenous People as well as the non-indigenous people within Australia? How much of an influence did the church have?

During the research, much work by non-Aboriginals critiquing racism from many different perspectives was found, but these failed to identify the hidden element within Australia of the socializing process that takes place not only for the oppressor but also for the oppressed. If we are going to address the issue of racism and its power, and how it emerges, we then need to take a serious look at the hidden elements and the source in which racism is embedded. Most Australians would say that they are non-racist. It is clear, however, that they should re-evaluate this position after reading the present study because they would find that they too were consciously and unconsciously "cloned" to be racist and to believe in their own "superiority," without even realizing that the process was happening.

The scope of this work is focused on Australian Aboriginal People. It does not refer—explicitly—to any other Peoples, including Torres Strait Islanders, non-Aboriginal minorities, migrants, refugees, etc. This is in no way an expression that these groups do not face racism in Australia; rather, it is a result of the limits of the scope of this work.

In what follows, I have identified the Indigenous People of Australia as "Aboriginals," and in some cases as "blacks." The term "Euro-Australians" has also been used, in reference to the British invaders and their descendants today.

CHAPTER 1
RACE AND RACISM

There are many words which are used to describe the relationships that exist between people. Some positive and uplifting ones include: justice, equality, respect, acceptance and harmony. Some inherently neutral words include: Aboriginal, black and indigenous. Some decidedly more negative and destructive ones include: apartheid, assimilation, classism, discrimination, ethnocentrism, genocide, ideology, integration, paternalism, prejudice, racism, segregation, sexism and stereotype. The purpose of this chapter is to highlight some of the terminology that describes historical as well as contemporary social relationships between Aboriginal and white Australia. In so doing, it will identify the downward spiral in which human relationships are, or can be, determined. It also will attempt to highlight some of the negative facets of white Australia's social and racial interaction over the past two hundred years, in order to provide the grounding for understanding an Aboriginal perspective of black and white Australia.

Race

"Race" is a word that has been used in many different ways by many different people. Its use has been affected by various factors such as the period of history, and the specific social, political, economic and other contexts. So as we begin, it is important for us to note the changing meanings and uses of this word.

> The term "race" was first used (around the beginning of the 16th Century) synonymously with "group", "category" or "class", although it was commonly used to refer to groups or categories of people. . . .
>
> Over a period of some 200 years, then, the idea of race was progressively refined by western society, from initially being simply a term for a group of people with something in common with one another, to being a concept which was used to explain human culture, and cultural inferiority and superiority, as the necessary consequence of biological differences between separate sub-groupings of the human species. It is a concept which has been used to justify oppression, to deny human rights (and indeed humanity) to millions of people, and to direct the attempted or actual genocide of millions of people. . . .

3

The idea of race was used as a prop to support processes of imperial and colonial expansion, to justify the invasion of many lands by European societies, and to support claims that people of European (or white) descent were superior to all other peoples, and so had a right to conquer and control the whole world. . . .

The use of the concept of race to justify these kinds of beliefs has become known as racism. (McConnochie et al. 1989:7, 15–16, 21)

Race, itself, is "an abstraction" (Benedict 1942:53). Yet, as history clearly shows us, the use of the word "race" changed from innocuous description to dehumanizing weapon. The change can be seen and described in the following words and concepts: stereotype, prejudice, ethnocentrism and racism.

Stereotype

A word can be value-neutral—used as a descriptive category, to set out facts, without judgement. When a word is not value-neutral, it can become a "stereotype." Gordon W. Allport has defined a "stereotype" as "an exaggerated belief associated with a category. Its function is to justify (rationalize) our conduct in relation to that category" (1958:187, in Kelsey 1965:43).

Throughout history, it is not too often that the word "race" has been value-neutral; rather, it has been used to stereotype Peoples, especially black Peoples, and thus to exclude them from equality and justice. Kelsey writes of stereotypes as

the articles of faith of the racist ideology. . . . A stereotype may be favorable or unfavorable. If it purports to describe the in-race, it is always favorable. If it purports to describe the out-race, it is always unfavorable. . . . Stereotypes, of course, justify the existing power arrangements. (1965:43–44)

When applied to human beings, then, certain words can be extremely "value-laden," and can become stereotypes. These, in turn, can lead to prejudices.

Prejudice

Saint Thomas Aquinas wrote, "Prejudice is thinking ill of others without sufficient cause" (McConnochie et al. 1989:21). This succinct definition of "prejudice" describes one of the most enduring and destructive characteristics of human beings. We have an absolute propensity to "jump to conclusions" about people. We do this about what others are thinking, and what they are going to say or do, and it usually gets us into trouble. We get into a categorically more serious level of "trouble," however, when we jump to negative conclusions about *who other people are*. In the words of Lorna Lippman,

> prejudice is part of the normative order of the society and the normative order of any society is part of the culture. There is a significant and growing body of theory which suggests that societies like the Australian one operate in ways that feed the historic injustice done to minority groups, particularly this applies to aborigines [*sic*], so as to reinforce and maintain their lower status and lesser awards, e.g. unequal educational opportunities will lead to poor jobs or to unemployment. This leads to a continuation in poverty so the cycle continues. (Rollason [1980]:24)[1]

In some cases, because of the strong link between "who other people are" and what race they are, prejudice is often directly related to culture and ethnicity.

Ethnocentrism

"Ethnocentrism" refers

> to the belief that one's own culture is superior to the cultures of other people, that members of one's own culture are superior to members of other cultures, and that these beliefs provide justification for discriminating against people from other cultures on those grounds of perceived cultural superiority. (McConnochie et al. 1989:23)

Ethnocentrism is a step beyond prejudice, from "thinking ill" to "acting ill" based on a belief in *cultural* superiority.

However, ethnocentric beliefs

> leave open the possibility of conversion [*sic*]. Culture is assumed to be learned, and so can be re-learned . . . by changing . . . values, beliefs and attitudes, and so becoming assimilated into the other cultural or ethnic group" (McConnochie et al. 1989:31)

In other cases, because of the strong link between culture and race, ethnocentrism is often directly related to race.

Racism

Definitions

Beyond stereotype, prejudice and ethnocentrism, there is "racism." This view:

---

[1] The "cycle of poverty" concept is quite limited, so the "wheel of discrimination" concept, described below, will be used instead.

takes the process of ethnocentrism a step further. . . . racism involves an additional set of beliefs: that the perceived cultural superiority is based on genetic superiority. That is, racists argue that:
* Their culture is superior to that of others,
* this cultural superiority is based on genetic, or racial superiority, and
* this racial superiority provides justification for discrimination.
(McConnochie et al. 1989:30–31; cf. Kelsey 1965:28–30; Vincent 1970:18)

Racism is a corruption of biological realities—"a biological heresy" (Vincent 1970:19; cf. Montagu 1972:10–11, 118–20). Racism is not the same as prejudice or ethnocentric hostility (Wellman 1993:4). In fact, a distinct difference between ethnocentrism and racism is that

Racist beliefs do not leave open this possibility [for change or assimilation into the other cultural or ethnic group]. If you are presumed inferior because you have inferior genes, then there is nothing that can be done about it. The concept of assimilation is then considered not only impossible, but actually dangerous to the "superior" genes of the racist society because of the possibility of the race being "weakened" by the "inferior" genes of the victims of racism. (McConnochie et al. 1989:31–32)

Another perspective that moves us toward what racism is, and how it can be expressed, can be found in a 1970 statement by the United States Commission on Civil Rights.

Racism is any attitude, action or institutional structure which subordinates a person or group because of their color. . . . Racism is not just a matter of attitudes: actions and institutional structures can also be a form of racism. (Skelton and Kerr 1989:13)

Racism involves having the power to enforce prejudice. To put it more simply, "Racial Prejudice + Power = Racism" (Skelton and Kerr 1989:13; cf. Kelsey 1965:46; NEA 1973:12).

White Racism

Oppressors often use racism to blame the oppressed—the people who are usually somehow "different" in origin, language, culture or religious belief, and suffer some kind of injustice because of their particular form of "being." Racism, however, does not *originate* with indigenous or minority Peoples, especially Peoples of colour.

Most racist discrimination is discrimination by the one-eighth of the world's whites against the other seven-eighths. We must, therefore, speak of *white* racism . . . . (Vincent 1970:19)

The World Council of Churches, in the Report of the Assembly Committee on Church and Society at the Uppsala Assembly in 1968, defined "white racism" as follows.

> By *white racism* is meant the conscious or unconscious belief in the inherent superiority of persons of European ancestry (particularly those of Northern European origin), which entitles all white peoples to a position of dominance and privilege, coupled with the belief in the innate inferiority of all darker peoples . . . which justifies their subordination and exploitation. (Vincent 1970:19)

Professor David T. Wellman, of the Institute for the Study of Social Change at the University of California, Berkeley, adds to this definition the elements of cultural and structural acceptance. He writes that

> Racism can mean *culturally sanctioned* beliefs which, regardless of the intentions involved, defend the advantages *whites* have because of the subordinated position of racial minorities. (1993:xi, emphasis added)

Indeed, many argue this line quite clearly stating that "racism is a white problem" (Chambers and Pettman 1986:8; cf. Kovel 1970:9–11; Katz 1982:10; Keirl 1992:24).

White racism is a plague on the human scene. It is a destructive presence in many societies around the world, to the specific detriment of many of the world's Peoples, and to the general detriment of the human race.

> Almost every aspect of civilization—science, religion, law, economics, politics, etiquette and art—have been infected with *white racism*. (WCC 1975:3, emphasis added)

History reveals, and the life experiences of countless Aboriginal People confirm, that Australian society has been infected with white racism. Indeed, if anyone has a case to develop and practice "reverse racism," it is the Aboriginal and non-English speaking peoples of Australia who have suffered untold horrors due to its presence. Yet, these groups continually refuse to participate in the "payback" mode of reverse racist behaviour. Take for example a recent interview with Mandawuy Yunupingu, the lead singer of the renowned Aboriginal band *Yothu Yindi*. Mr. Yunupingu— himself a leader of the Yolngu community who took the Australian Commonwealth Government to the High Court in the famous Yirrkala (Gove) Land Rights Case—once was asked for his "Best white-person joke." His response: "Racism is not part of my agenda" (Casimir and Holmes 1992:2s).

Amazingly, just five weeks after this interview and in what became a national racism scandal with extensive media coverage, Mandawuy Yunupingu was thrown out of a Melbourne restaurant for "being Aboriginal."[2] Clearly, racism was part of *another Australian's* agenda.

Subsequently, Mr. Yunupingu was named "Australian of the Year for 1993"—a proud moment for Australia, especially during the United Nations International Year for the World's Indigenous People (MacKinolty 27 January 1993:3). But, within hours of the awards ceremony, a racist attack on a commercial radio programme labelled his winning as "tokenism" (Sider and Wright 1993:7). It seems that Australian Aboriginal People cannot win; no matter how talented, or productive, or illustrious we are, we face Australian white racism. In Australia, it is very clear that the racist agenda continues.

Racist Ideology

The use of racism and/or racist concepts to deny rights to certain racial and ethnic groups is racist *ideology*. It is not a natural concept, but rather one created by human beings. Chambers and Pettman have noted that, "Racism as an ideology is . . . an historical and social *construct*" (1986:6, emphasis added; cf. Flynn 1980:5; Niles 1992:170). Even a recent Vatican study by the Pontifical Commission "Iustitia et Pax" agrees, declaring that a "racist ideology, opposed to the teaching of the church, was *forged*" (1988:13, emphasis added).

In other words, we are not born racist, we are *taught* to be racist. Racist ideology is something artificially *created* and maintained to keep privileges for some people while systematically oppressing other people. In a great many societies around the world, racist ideology has been used as a socio-political tool, to keep white-skinned peoples "over and above" black-skinned peoples and other peoples of colour—by force and often by violence.

> . . . racist ideology produces cohesion within white society. At this point, the ideology is a call to vigilance, and if need be, to attack. (Kelsey 1965:42)

---

[2] Newspaper coverage was quite extensive: NLC 1992:1; Dow 1992:3; *Australian* 6 March 1992:1; Skulley 1992:2; Binnie, Ballantine, Champness and Alberici 1992:1–2; Viscovich 1992:12; *Herald-Sun* 6 March 1992:12; SMH 7 March 1992:5; SMH 7 March 1992:47. Other coverage included lead stories on both radio (e.g., JJJ- and MMM-National Networks) and television (e.g., ABC, Seven-, Nine- and Ten-National Networks), and even some editorial cartoons (e.g., Knight 1992:10).

This is the case in Australia. Racist ideology in Australia is described by Lorna Lippman, a former Victorian State Director of the Commissioner for Community Relations, in the following way.

> There is in Australia a broadly accepted ideology of white supremacy and superiority, that we expect to see whites in positions of authority and power and we have a suspicion that white is alright. (Rollason [1980]:24)

Thus racism becomes racist ideology, and racist ideology becomes engrained in our very consciousness and is reinforced in our very social structures.

Forms of Racism

Racism appears in many different forms in our human societies, including individual, institutional, scientific, direct, indirect, and so on. Each is just as destructive as any other. Sadly, it seems that all over the world we are faced with the same persistent problem: racism.

Individual Racism

> Individual racism refers to the expression of racist attitudes in the behaviour of individual people in face-to-face situations. It is based on the attitudes of individual people and has typically been studied by psychologists, interested in personality and attitudes. (McConnochie et al. 1989:32)

Individual racism is what a person encounters from another person. It is experienced by people every day, from family members, teachers, employers, shopkeepers, restaurateurs, journalists, broadcasters, club-goers, athletes, policemen, solicitors, judges and many more; indeed, it is even present in so-called "Christians."

Kovel writes of three kinds of individual racists. The first, the *dominative* racist, he describes as follows.

> The true white bigot expresses a definitive ambition through all his activity: he openly seeks to keep the black man down, and he is willing to use force to further his ends. (Kovel 1970:54)

The second, the *aversive* racist, he explains in these terms.

> The type who believes in white race superiority and is more or less aware of it, but does nothing overt about it. . . . the person tends to behave in ways that avoid the issue: [s/]he tries to ignore the existence of black people, tries to avoid contact with them, and at most to be polite, correct and cold in whatever dealings are necessary between the races. (Kovel 1970:54–55)

The third he does not give a name, but rather describes as one, who does not reveal racist tendencies at all—except as the unconscious persistence of what may be considered mass fantasies. (Kovel 1970:55)

These three descriptions present to us individual racism. The reality of their embodiments are evident throughout the complex history of race relations.

Institutional Racism

Institutional racism . . . is rather more complex, and refers to the ways in which racist beliefs or values have been built into the operations of social institutions in such a way as to discriminate against, control and oppress various minority groups. Institutional racism is more likely to be studied by sociologists, historians or anthropologists. (McConnochie et al. 1989:32)

Institutional racism is what a person encounters from another person *in an organization*. It is experienced by people every day in the family, at school, on the job, at shops, in restaurants, at home reading newspapers or watching television, in clubs, at sporting events, in courts and prisons, and yes at church (cf. WCC 1975:9–10).

Both individual and institutional forms of racism are destructive, and have plagued our human history. Yet both rest on the unsteady pillars of very questionable pseudo-science (cf. Snyder 1962:10).

Scientific Racism

In the enlightened era, science has made an increasingly powerful impact on many different expressions of human thought. In the 1800s, some extremely questionable "scientific" research contributed to the development of what came to be known as scientific racism. Advances in the biological sciences were expanding human understanding of the animal world. Darwin's theories of evolution (and especially his concept of "survival of the fittest"), for example, became popular and indeed gained worldwide recognition (cf. Desmond and Moore 1992). These theories, however, were taken up improperly by social scientists and mistakenly applied to human sciences; this began blurring human understanding of itself. Darwinian scientific theory became Social Darwinism, based on racist notions of the superiority of the white race (cf. Tinker 1993:99–100). Social Darwinism held to a hierarchized system, with "superior" beings (the white, Western race) at the top and "inferior" entities (the black, non-Western races) at the bottom of a theoretical scale of development (cf. H. Spencer 1874). Social Darwinism spawned other "questionable sciences" such as "phrenology," which claimed that a person's character and abilities could be determined by certain measurements of the skull, using such tools as sand and marbles (Reynolds 1989:79–81). Further, it provided grounding for more "respectable sciences" such as anthropology, which harboured a hidden history of greed, murder and racism.[3]

In time pseudo-science became the backbone of scientific racism and Social Darwinism, which "justified genocide, dispossession and neglect" (Parbury 1986:81), and laid the groundwork for the colonial era. By and large, white communities around the world accepted these pseudo-scientific theories without question, because they had been produced by men (and a few women) of science.[4] After all, if they could not be trusted, then who could? Amazingly, the church, often savagely critical of scientific cosmogony, not only absorbed but also defended various elements of scientific racism and implemented practices and policies based on it. Thus the state, with the cooperation of a church blinded by greed, accepted the pillar of scientific racism, and this simple action had a profoundly negative impact, not only upon Western culture, but also upon the church (Kovel 1970:122).

"Christian" Racism

Perhaps one of the most controversial forms of racism known is so-called "Christian racism."[5] Though an apparent oxymoron, "Christian" racism has been with us for millennia. Kelsey indicates that

> The immediate background of modern racial alienation is the *religious intolerance* of the Middle Ages. . . . as Christianity and Islam became increasingly embroiled in religious rivalry, with each succeeding crusade, intolerance increased between the two faiths. . . . For each religious community, the human race was divided into two groups—"we" and "they." "We" and "they" meant believers and unbelievers. The unbeliever was considered a fit subject for *conquest and enslavement.* (1965:21, emphasis added)

---

[3] Cf. Chapter Two below. Details of this horrific history are revealed in Monaghan 1991:31–34, 38; Beatson 1991:37; and, the documentary film *Darwin's Body-Snatchers,* aired in Britain on 8 October 1991.

[4] Indeed, "such theses had considerable resonance *in Germany.* It is well known that the *National-Socialist totalitarian party* made a racist ideology the basis of its insane programme, aimed at the physical elimination of those it deemed belonging to 'inferior races'"; Pontifical Commission "Iusticia et Pax" 1988:14.

[5] For the sake of clarity, we mean religious racism to include all forms of racism linked with the broad parameters of religion, including people, beliefs, doctrine, etc."

Religion, specifically Christianity, became inextricably entwined with an unceasing and unquenchable European lust for political power and territorial expansion, and began to transmutate into racism (cf. esp., Kovel 1970:122–38). Indeed, the lines of demarcation between Christianity and racism virtually disappeared. "Christian" racism came to be part of the socio-politico-religious order, and "rationalized" the European colonization, missionization and enslavement of much of the globe.

In many parts of the world, racism is explicitly linked with the Christian faith, or rather, with this theological error in the Christian faith.

> . . . behind every discriminative action, if accepted and justified as a Christian mode of behaviour, there lies some hidden *heresy*. (WCC 1975:15, emphasis added)

It has been stated that, "Racism is a faith . . . a form of idolatry" (Kelsey 1965:9). It even has been written that, "Racism is the new *Calvinism*" (Benedict 1942:2, emphasis added).

No matter what the form—individual, institutional, "Christian" or another—the witness of history makes it abundantly clear that racism moves toward exploitation and violence (cf. Kelsey 1965:33; Kovel 1970:123).

Racist Violence

Racist violence is

> a specific *act* of violence, intimidation or harassment carried out against an individual, group or organisation (or their property) on the basis of:
> * race, colour, descent, or national or ethnic origin; and/or
> * support for non-racist policies. (HREOC 1991:14, emphasis added)

Racist violence moves beyond what we think and feel to what we do (or, in many cases, have done in the past). Lippman notes that in Australia, racist violence has been present since the arrival of European convicts and their jailers.

> The history of black/white contact began with forced entry and conquest, it was followed by economic exploitation, political control, cultural control and all of this was accompanied by a self-justifying ideology. Through it all Australian society as a whole has declared its devotion to justice and equality on many occasions and to the Christian principle of loving one's neighbour. Yet at an early stage aborigines [*sic*] were placed by force on reserves and church missions, they were governed and controlled. (Rollason [1980]:25)

The Indigenous People of Australia have known and experienced violence based on white racism for over 200 years.

Summary

Race is a word which has been used and misused for centuries. It is intimately related to other words such as prejudice, ethnocentrism and racism, each of which shows an increasing level of negative connotation and impact. Perhaps the easiest way to show this is through Diagram 1.

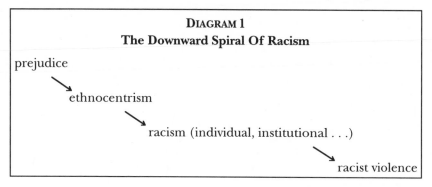

DIAGRAM 1
The Downward Spiral Of Racism

prejudice

      ethnocentrism

           racism (individual, institutional . . .)

                 racist violence

Diagram 2 is most helpful in illustrating the complex interrelationships between many of these issues (McConnochie et al. 1988:38).

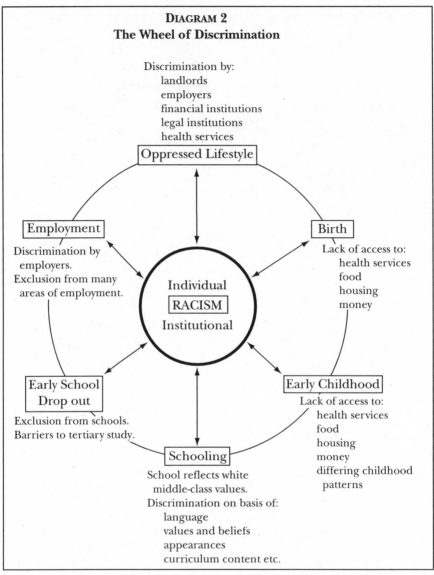

DIAGRAM 2
The Wheel of Discrimination

Discrimination by:
    landlords
    employers
    financial institutions
    legal institutions
    health services

Oppressed Lifestyle

Employment

Discrimination by
  employers.
Exclusion from many
  areas of employment.

Individual
RACISM
Institutional

Birth

Lack of access to:
    health services
    food
    housing
    money

Early School
Drop out

Exclusion from schools.
Barriers to tertiary study.

Early Childhood

Lack of access to:
    health services
    food
    housing
    money
    differing childhood
    patterns

Schooling

School reflects white
  middle-class values.
Discrimination on basis of:
    language
    values and beliefs
    appearances
    curriculum content etc.

Whatever the particular expression, racism seems to be present with
humanity all around the world. Indeed, some have indicated that, "racism
is a 'growth industry'" (Bailey 1992:315). What follows is the story of
racism in every part of Australian society, from the government to the
church.

CHAPTER 2

RACISM IN AUSTRALIAN SOCIETY

In 1770, James Cook wrote in his Journal,

> from what I have seen in the Natives of New Holland they may appear to some
> to be the most wretched People on Earth . . . . (J. Cook, cited in Reynolds
> 1989:98)

On this racist lie was built modern Australian society. For over 200 years, the Australian social structure has contributed to racism and, amazingly, continues such actions today. This chapter traces the multifaceted historical and contemporary manifestations of racism in Australian society.

Background: White Australian Society Contributes to Racism

The Myths of *Terra Nullius* and "No Sovereignty"

In 1768, Lieutenant James Cook had been instructed,

> You are . . . *with the consent of the natives* to take possession of convenient
> situations in the country in the name of the King of Great Britain, or, if you
> find the country uninhabited take possession for His Majesty by setting up
> proper marks and inscriptions as first discoverers and possessors. (M. Dodson
> 1993:50)

Yet, in 1770, Cook attempted several landings all along the eastern coast of Australia. More than once, his landing parties were repelled by Aboriginal People (cf. Parbury 1986:44; Reynolds 1987b:76–80). Though very well-documented, this side of the first contact between the Indigenous People of Australia and the invading British colonizers has been forgotten—or, more accurately, romanticized into the myths of *terra nullius* and "no sovereignty."

Nothing has been the same for Aboriginal People after the "arrival" of Cook on the Australian continent. From the very beginning of British contact with Australia, they declared it *terra nullius,* or "empty land,"[1] and proceeded to make three separate declarations of British sovereignty (in

---

[1] Such is the case with the invasion of other areas of the world, such as Latin America; cf. Dussel 1981:38.

1788, 1824 and 1829) upon Aboriginal land (Reynolds 1989:183). From then on, the Aboriginal Nations—which had existed uninterrupted for tens of thousands of years—were supposed to "be no more" (cf. *The Secret Country*). *Terra nullius* was—and still is—*a deliberate social construction designed to enable settlement without compensation* (cf. Dunn 1975:42–43). It enabled dispossession of the Australian Aboriginal People, "parcel by parcel, to make way for expanding colonial settlement" (M. Dodson 1993:33).

> The loss of their land is also the primary consequence for the Aborigine of white colonisation; in the landless and poverty stricken situation of the Aborigine and the wealth of the white Australian society, the whole essence of colonialism is brought into focus. It is important to bear in mind that the present poverty and dependence of the Aborigines results directly from the appropriation of their land, their economic and cultural base. (WCC 1971b:28)
>
> More important than direct slaughter was the land robbery which not only deprived the native of their living resources but destroyed the religious and social organisations that were so closely linked with the territory of each tribe. (Price 1949, quoted in WCC 1971b:28; cf. Reynolds 1989:98)

Terra nullius stems from absolute ignorance of true Aboriginal society, and from racist English and Anglo-centric views of alleged superiority. The invaders simply "closed their eyes" to the facts of history.

The British *refused* to recognize the existence of the Aboriginal Nations, Aboriginal native title and Aboriginal sovereignty (cf. Gilbert 1990; S. Harris 1979:1; M. Dodson 1993:32–34; OT: Gilbert 1991). They refused to formally engage with the Aboriginal Peoples that were in Australia—to "seek consent" (M. Dodson 1993:50), or to declare war on any of the Aboriginal Nations (Rowley 1972a:29; *Special Treatment* 1991), or to pay compensation or otherwise to make any kind of restitution for the lands which they stole from our ancestors (Reynolds 1989:86–88). Their actions had nothing to do with the correct application of British law or international law; for that matter, it did not even follow historical precedent.

> Cook's action was supported by the British Authorities. Their approval was in *sharp contrast,* however, to British policy in New Zealand, Papua New Guinea, Canada and the American colonies. There, treaties were made which *recognised native title* to their land. . . . Thus in 1763, just 7 years *before* Cook claimed possession of Eastern Australia, George the Third declared the right of the Canadian Indians to "the undisturbed use of their traditional lands." Cook and his superiors therefore had *no legal excuse* for omitting to negotiate a treaty with the Aborigines, or at least making future provision to do so. (Carne 1980:72)

Aboriginal People have never signed any kind of treaty with any Australian Government (cf. Neate 1989:2; *Special Treatment* 1991). Aboriginal People did *not* become "instant subjects of the King" of England (Reynolds 1987a:4; Reynolds 1989:182–83). Indeed, Australian Aboriginal People have *never* given up their sovereignty (cf. Gilbert 1990; Mansell 1989:4–6). Whether or not it is recognized, comprehensively, in white Australian law, the undebatable facts of history remain: the sovereign Aboriginal People have been on the Australian continent from time immemorial. Thus, the myths of *terra nullius* and "no sovereignty," which were the foundation stones of white Australian society, were based upon pure fiction.

History—Continuing the Lie

As far back as 1832, George A. Robinson, Chief Protector of Aborigines at Port Phillip, wrote:

> I am at a loss to conceive by what tenure we hold this country, for it does not appear to be that we either hold it by conquest or by right of purchase. (Reynolds 1987b:back cover)

Even today, some (very few) whites recognize the clear illegality of British actions—not to mention their appalling arrogance. Associate Professor Henry Reynolds, noted historian and author, writes:

> If the extravagance of the British claim impressed an eminent twentieth century jurist [Sir Kenneth Roberts-Wray, who found it "startling" and "incredible"] it would have seemed even more extraordinary to the resident Aborigines had they known of the proceedings. As many as *half a million people,* living in *several hundred tribal groupings,* in occupation of even the most inhospitable corners of the continent, had in a single instant, been dispossessed. From that apocalyptic moment forward they were technically trespassers on Crown land even though many of them would not see a white man for another thirty, another fifty years. Even the sons and daughters of those dispossessed might not meet their expropriators until middle age. English legal witchcraft was so powerful that it had wiped out all tenure, all rights to land which had been occupied for *40,000 years,* for *1600 generations and more.* The white man's technology had brought him to the southern continent. His jurisprudence delivered the ownership of a *million and a half square miles* of someone else's land and it could be received with a clear conscience in the belief that the dispossessed would respond to the "amity and kindness" of the first settlers.
>
> It was a stunning takeover. It would have dazzled even the lions of the modern business world, their financial power and electronic wizardry notwithstanding. (Reynolds 1987b:8–9, emphasis added)

Aboriginal sovereignty was never recognized because English law, and then—until very recently—white Australian law, considered the continent to be *terra nullius*. Australia never came to terms with its history of dispossession of the Indigenous People—and the lie was continued.

Amalgamation and "Non-Slavery" Slavery

Even from before they arrived to "settle" Australia, the British *spoke* of justice. Writing in Britain, in 1787, Governor Arthur Phillip stated:

> The laws of this country will, of course, be introduced in [New] South Wales, and there is one that I would wish to take place from the moment his Majesty's forces take possession of the country: That there can be no slavery in a free land, and consequently no slaves. (A. Phillip 1892:53)

Yet, subsequent actions by the British betrayed their true beliefs and feelings. It appears that the reference to "in a free land" did not include Aboriginal People, who were to be "civilized." Ominously, another statement by Phillip reveals a deeper layer of meaning and intent.

> Even before he arrived in Australia Phillip determined that he would "endeavour to persuade" the Aborigines to "settle near us" in order that they could be furnished "with every thing that can tend to civilize [the Aborigines]." (1990:85–86)

Another prominent colonial figure spoke of a "unique" kind of *rapprochement* between the Europeans and the indigenous Australians.

> South Australia's Governor Hindmarsh addressed the clans around Adelaide in the following manner:
> "Black Men,
> We wish to make you happy. But you cannot be happy unless you *imitate white men*. Build huts, wear clothes, work and be useful.
> Above all things you cannot be happy unless you love God who made heaven and earth and men and all things.
> Love white men. Love other tribes of black men. *Learn to speak English.*"
> (Reynolds 1990:86, emphasis added)

As Reynolds points out, however, there seemed to be a blurring of lines between cultural interchange and cultural imperialism.

> Amalgamation, then, could only occur in one way: black would imitate white. The arrogance was vast, the cultural self-confidence quite invincible. (1990:86)
> [The European] hierarchical view of the world allowed them to advocate amalgamation without thinking that Aborigines would ever be their equals. (1990:100; cf. Bolton 1992:3)

In the early decades of the nineteenth century, there was continual "confusion" between amalgamation and slavery. Aboriginal People were "taken into service" by everyone from clergymen such as the Rev. Samuel Marsden and Richard Johnson, to "the pioneer of settlement at Port Phillip," John Batman (Reynolds 1990:165–66).

> ... what was good enough for Samuel Marsden was good enough for many other settlers in all parts of the Australian colonies throughout the nineteenth century. Europeans kidnapped black children, or received them, with remarkably clear consciences. (Reynolds 1990:165)

Europeans from all walks of life—from clergymen to government officials to farmers, pastoralists, miners and seafarers—enjoyed the "services" of Aboriginal People. It appears that virtually no one stopped to ask questions about how the services were "attained." The colonists did not seem to worry about the use of force—often violent force—against the Indigenous Peoples, for there was a greater "Christian" and civil good being dispensed. White Australia saw slavery as the "school for civilization" (cf. W. L. Rose 1982:77).

The British, it seems, did not worry about the Indigenous Peoples—or any of their attendant "rights"—because they did not consider the Aboriginals to be human beings at all. Rather, they considered them to be "animals" (cf. McCall 1957:34) and "savages" (cf. Reynolds 1987a:108–9; M. Dodson 1993:44). They considered them non-human and, therefore, ignored them as Sovereign Nations. This ideology provided the philosophical and pragmatic grounding for their denial of Aboriginal human, social, political and other rights, in the rapacious advance of European colonization (cf. Rousseau 1973:97).

Thus, Aboriginal People were given no rights at all and, quite the contrary, were literally enslaved. While the actual word "slavery" was not used very often (at least not by whites), the actual practice was basically a white-initiated slave economy based on the forced labours of the Aboriginal People and of the imported European convicts (cf. Dunn 1975). The horrific nature of this behaviour was well known; as far back as 1834, the renowned British anti-slavery leader Thomas Fowell Buxton wrote of the situation of the Australian Aboriginal People.

> My attention has been drawn of late to the wickedness of our proceedings as a nation, towards the ignorant and barbarous natives of countries of which we seize. *What have we Christians done for them?* We have usurped their lands, kidnapped, *enslaved* and murdered themselves. The greatest of their crimes is

that they sometimes trespass into the lands of their forefathers. (Reynolds 1987b:83, emphasis added)

The example of these so-called "leaders" set a two-fold precedent (ideological and pragmatic) for slavery, which—depending upon your perspective—can be described as follows. During the "settlement" of Australia, it became socially acceptable for Europeans to both "receive" disadvantaged Aboriginal men, women and children, and to train them in the "virtues" of "Christian service." To put it another way, early on in Australian history, racist Euro-Australian colonists laid the religious and secular foundations for the kidnapping, enslavement and continuing oppression of Aboriginal People. In even more direct parlance, from the beginning of Aboriginal-European contact, invading whites laid down the ideological framework for the physical and cultural genocide of Indigenous blacks.

No matter how the precedent is described, the fact remains that it held firm. Abhorrent racist ideas became engrained in white Australian society and, in the years that followed, the enslavement of the Aboriginal People—as well as other such dehumanizing practices—increased in strength. The first hundred years after the arrival of Europeans saw the *geometric* increase in the enslavement of Aboriginal People. Minutes of Evidence given before the South Australian Select Committee of the Legislative Council on the *Aborigines Bill 1899*, recorded the following information:

> Following the initial impact of settlement it was obvious that Aborigines had succumbed to *a virtual state of peonage* and that "they were treated just as any other chattel would be . . . used when (they) were required and sent about their business (when) they were not." Natives were attracted away from their tribal country by varying devices to resettle on the pastoralists' runs, but once having been taken away from his home country "the black (could) not get away" and the new employer practically made "a *slave* of him". (F. Stevens 1981:16, emphasis added)

Aboriginal People had no rights in European eyes. They were lured— or forcibly taken—away from their families and lands, and placed onto white farms, stations, reserves or missions (cf. Elkin 1959:27). Once there, they were not allowed to leave; indeed, in many cases, they *could not* leave because they were *physically chained* to the beds and *locked* into the rooms at night (cf. Gilbert 1977). If they tried to go home, they would be hunted down like wild animals. In fact, many natives (were) shot in the back for no other cause than that they were running away from their *slave* masters. (F. S. Stevens 1981:15, emphasis added; cf. P. Wilson 1985:83)

Incredibly, such practices continued into the second century of contact, and,

until *1971*, it was an offence under the Queensland Act for an Aborigine to "escape" from a "Reserve". (OCCR 1979:28, emphasis added)

So, high ideals of justice in the colonies that were set in faraway England remained just that—"high ideals" and "faraway." Australian social practice was actually "non-slavery slavery."

Segregation

In the early decades of the nineteenth century, Australian government and churches collaborated in establishing mission stations and reserves for Aboriginal People. All across the continent, Aboriginal People were "placed" in these institutions. This effectively separated them from outside influences. History reveals, however, that "placement" was one of the white euphemisms for forcible displacement of black Peoples away from white living areas. Over time, ". . . *racist* and *ethnocentric* attitudes led to social policies such as segregation, protectionism and assimilation" (CAR 1993a:14, emphasis added).

In other words, Aboriginal People were ripped from their traditional lands, their sacred sites, their families, and their food and water sources. They were forcibly herded into holding camps, to keep them away from the sight of the white colonists. White colonial thinking fairly well mastered the myth that there were not supposed to be any Indigenous People in Australia. It just seems to have taken longer for them to grasp the concept that the continuing presence of Aboriginal People in and around white cities and settlements betrayed the lie of *terra nullius,* and therefore the lie of "peaceful settlement" of this "unoccupied" land. So, white people removed as many black people as they could, following the idea of, "Out of (public) sight, out of (public) mind."

At times, British segregation became quite ridiculous. In 1816, for example, a proclamation *written in English* by Governor Lachlan Macquarie, stipulated the following.

1. Armed Aborigines were not to appear within one mile of any British settlement. . . .

2. No more than 6 unarmed Aborigines to lurk or loiter near any farm in the interior, on the pain of being considered enemies, and treated accordingly.

> 3. Aborigines were not to assemble in large numbers to fight and attack each other on the plea of inflicting punishment of a transgressor of their own customs. This "barbarous custom was not to be practised, even in remote parts of the land. . . ."
>
> 4. Any Aborigine who wished the *protection* of the British government . . . could obtain a *"Passport* or Certificate" signed by the governor . . . . (Brook and Kohen 1991:32, emphasis added)

How were thousands of Aboriginal People of the area supposed to *read* a document *written* in *English?* Would Indigenous People from an oral tradition care about such words, even if they were to read them? It is ludicrous to think that Aboriginal People, who had been gathering on and travelling across these areas of *their own land* for tens of thousands of years, would cease to do so because a few white newcomers *wrote* so!

Yet, British colonial arrogance firmly believed it could make such assumptions of power. It continued to fuel the enactment of segregationist laws and policies, which caused further deterioration of peaceful relations between blacks and whites.

It is important to note, however, that European segregation of the Indigenous People was specific and selective. Not all Aboriginal People were placed so far out of reach that they could not be exploited, for it is clear that in white, colonial Australia, segregation walked hand in hand with slavery. All Aboriginal People were to be kept away from white settlements, except, of course, for forced labourers such as young Aboriginal girls made to serve as domestics, and young Aboriginal boys made to work as stockmen or drovers or cane-cutters—those performing work that whites considered to be "denigrating," somehow "menial" or "manual" (cf. Evans, Saunders and Cronin 1975:109–10). Aboriginal People were never meant to be brought "into economic competition with the white worker" (Evans, Saunders and Cronin 1975:110; Rowley 1970). They could not be near whites, except when performing the services of slaves.

But the aftermath of dispossession and mental and physical abuse came back to haunt white colonists in a way they never dreamed. Whites thought nothing of the negative impact of slavery and social and economic exploitation of the Aboriginals—that is, until these had the unexpected result of causing Aboriginal People to begin gathering and sleeping on the fringes of white towns, farms and other settlements (cf. CoA-MT 1959:3–4; CoA-MT 1960:20–21). The "advance" of white "civilization" "removed" the Aboriginal People off their own traditional lands; it destroyed their sacred sites; and, it killed the means for their sustenance. Worse, it introduced foreign diseases such as tuberculosis, measles and whooping cough; it brought foreign vices such as alcohol; and, it made them dependent upon white rations and handouts of sugar, flour, tea, and blankets. Where were these Indigenous People supposed to go? They could not *go* home, for they already *were* home. They were on the land where they were born, where their parents had lived all their lives, where their ancestors had hunted and fished for generations, where their People, culture, language and religion had existed for millennia.

Aboriginal People were on their own land. They could not leave, even though every passing year of white European invasion only brought them worsening social conditions. On a larger scale they faced cultural upheaval, a massive reduction in population, and what Reynolds calls a "catastrophic fall" in their birth rate (1981:125); on a smaller scale, they were confronted with daily hunger, severe physical illnesses, social revilement and racism. They were deprived of every form of right— human or otherwise.

The problem for white Europeans, however, was not that this shameful state of affairs caused them to feel contrition, but rather contempt. The aggrieved reality of Aboriginal existence in colonial Australia simply made whites try to hide the problems even further by institutionalizing the blacks—far, far away (cf. Cannon 1993:257).

White Australian society was determined that Aboriginals were to be locked away from sight, and who better to enforce this than the white Australian church? Claiming a "higher calling," the church—with the full support of the government and society—institutionalized not just the people, but segregation itself.

The establishment of institutions appeared to be the most effective way of keeping the blacks away from the white working class and at the same time inculcating habits of order, *obedience* and industry. The Rev. Robert Cartwright proposed such an institution to Governor Macquarie in 1819, the object of which was *"to keep these black Natives entirely separate from our own people"* (Reynolds 1990:103, emphasis added).

It did not take long for these factors to begin taking their toll. Direct genocidal practices such as mass poisonings of water holes, rations and blankets already had wiped out entire Aboriginal tribes. Now Europeans began a slower process, but it was genocide just the same. Aboriginal children were taken from their mothers and fathers, and Aboriginal families were split into institutions far distant from each other.[2]

---

[2] Vast literature exists documenting the devastating effects of this segregation; cf.,

Aboriginal languages and ceremonies were forbidden, and subsequently forgotten. The very special Aboriginal relationships to land were disrupted, and in many cases the land itself was farmed or mined into oblivion. All in all, a slow process of cultural genocide began to take a devastating toll upon Aboriginal being and identity.

For Aboriginal People, the beginning of segregation was the beginning of destruction. Whites began the systematic establishment of what might today be called "concentration camps." Places such as Palm Island and Yarrabah,

> were set aside as repositories for those Aborigines deemed to have no useful place in the developing white Queensland democracy. In these communities, the Aboriginal residents were controlled by a white colonial administration and for seventy years placed in an institutionalised limbo. (Loos 1982:xvii)

Yarrabah, near Cairns, is an example of such an "institutionalised limbo." Accessible only by sea, Yarrabah was proclaimed a reserve and an Anglican Mission in 1892 (J. Thomson 1989:1). In 1986, the "Yarrabah Council received the Deeds of Grant in Trust for their land from the Queensland government" (J. Thomson 1989:xv). Yet, today, over 100 years after the government and church institutions were founded, the Aboriginal People of Yarrabah still have no *binding* legal title over the land there.

Beyond being "repositories," these places became literal prisons for Aboriginal People. Palm Island is an example.

> The island was first established by the people of the Hull River Settlement in 1918. In that year a cyclone had destroyed the new settlement at Hull River, so the "Protector" decided that Palm Island would be their new home. It was considered to be an ideal place to confine "problem cases" and "uncontrollables", mostly children. Thus Palm Island became known as a *penal* settlement. (Rosser 1978:2, emphasis added)

Even worse, when Aboriginal People became terminally ill, they were not sent back to the mainland for treatment, but rather were shipped off to nearby (and appropriately named) Phantom Island, to die.

Though now not technically a penal settlement, Palm Island still is very much a place of confinement for Aboriginal People. A comment, written sixty years after the establishment of the settlement, shows that contemporary social reality still limits the hopes of the Aboriginal People there.

---

e.g., Cummings 1990; Edwards and Read 1989; Maushart 1993; S. L. Gilbert 1992.

Unbelievable oppression and exploitation are taking place on Palm Island. And it is getting worse! (Rosser 1978:3)

Forty miles out to sea off the eastern coast of North Queensland, Palm Island is very easily seen as a paradigm of this "Out-of-Sight Policy." Many other such isolated institutions were established, as segregation had become common practice in white Australian society.[3]

"Protection"

Throughout the nineteenth century, a worldwide movement put pressure on many nations to end slavery.[4] By 1833, slavery had been abolished—*officially*, at least. "The Empire" had established a House of Commons Select Committee on the Native Inhabitants of British Settlements by 1837 (Reynolds 1989:183), as well as a Royal Society for the Protection of Aborigines by 1838 (Parbury 1986:65). Public opinion about "the rights" of Indigenous Peoples was changing.

In an effort to keep up *appearances* in the eyes of the world—and especially in the eyes of its British "parent"—Australia was forced to change its ways. And, Australia did change them. The country embarked on a campaign of "protection" of the "natives." All across the country, policies and laws began to give substance to various theories and methods of "protection" (cf. Elkin 1958:2; Elkin 1959:6). The legislations varied from state to state, but the intention was basically the same.

> The first government policy towards the Aborigines was intended to "protect" him [*sic*] from the effects of contact with; or "to smooth the dying pillow" as it has been otherwise described. This was a "humane" attempt to facilitate the extinction of the Aborigines which complacent administrators considered inevitable as a result of Darwinistic ideas about competition with superior species. "Protection" involved separating the Aborigines as far as possible from contact with the white man [*sic*] and providing them with sufficient flour, tea and sugar to stave off *immediate* starvation (since colonisation had made it largely impossible for the Aborigines to continue their hunting/gathering life style). (WCC 1971a:1, emphasis added; cf. Prentis 1988:87; Duguid 1963)

---

[3] The critically important role of the church is seen in that, as late as *1910*, the Archbishops and Bishops of the Church of England published a Pastoral Letter indicating that, ". . . [i]n view of the [A]boriginal character, experience seems to show that the only effectual way of treating the *problem* is on the principle of *segregation*" (ABCEAT 1910:6, emphasis added).

[4] For U.S. literature on this, cf., e.g., W. L. Rose 1964; W. L. Rose 1982; Stampp 1956; S. M. Elkins 1959; et al.

"Protection" was merely a new and (publicly) more "humane" synonym for the "segregation" with which Aboriginal People already were so familiar. It quickly became clear, at least to the Aboriginal People, that "protection" simply meant further dispossession and dehumanization. Indeed, Rowley describes protection as involving "isolation, which also conformed with *white settler prejudice*" (1972:239, emphasis added). Thus, a "change of ways" was simply a shift from outright extermination (cf. McCall 1957:35) and enslavement towards more subtle and less obvious forms of repression.

Australia established the so-called "Protectorate" system, with activity located all across Australia (cf. Reynolds 1989:186; Cannon 1993:7–28, 123–36, 179–98). In the late 1830s, the Aboriginal Protectorate in Port Phillip was established, and George Augustus Robinson named Chief Protector of Aborigines (Reynolds 1987b:78–79; cf. Rae-Ellis 1988). Other states followed and throughout the rest of the century, governments jumped on the bandwagon and put in place a flurry of laws and related policies (see Table 1).

TABLE 1
ABORIGINAL "PROTECTION" LEGISLATION

Year	State	Legislation	Sources
1844	New South Wales	*Protection of Aboriginal Children Act*	P
1844	South Australia	*Aboriginal Orphans (Ordinance No 12 of 1844)*	M
1869	Victoria	*Aborigines Protection Act*	H
1886	Victoria	*Aborigines Protection Act (Amendment) Act*	H
1886	Western Australia	*Aborigines Protection Act*	H
1889	Western Australia	*Aborigines Act*	H
1890	Victoria	*Aborigines Act*	H
1892	Western Australia	*Aborigines Protection Act (Amendment) Act*	H
1897	Queensland	*The Aboriginals Protection and Restriction of the Sale of Opium Act, 1897*	H
1897	Queensland	*An Act to make Provision for the better Protection and Care of the Aboriginal Half-Caste Inhabitants of the Colony*	H

Sources: H=Hanks and Keon-Cohen 1984:267–303, 354–56; M=Mattingley and Hampton 1988:157, 45; P=Pattel-Gray 1991a:18, 156.

British policy of the day meant for the Australian Protectorate system to do some actual good. There seems to have been a problem, however, along the journey from British mandate to Australian colonial enactment.

For [Thomas Fowell] Buxton, in England, the Protectors were to see the indigenes weren't cheated out of their land. *In Australia their role was seen as controlling the Aboriginal "nuisance"* and limiting the spread of frontier violence. It's not that the settlers didn't understand what the Imperial authorities wanted. They understood only too well. Aborigines could have "protection", they couldn't have land. (Reynolds 1987b:151, emphasis added)

The laws gave so-called "Protectors" and "Assistant Protectors" vast powers over the lives of Aboriginal People (cf. Thomson 1989:9). Private citizens, government employees, humanitarians, clergymen and missionaries, and—ominously—policemen were named to these positions. They became virtual "masters" over such facets of Aboriginal existence as the specific composition of the family unit, the availability of education, the possibility of employment, the determination and location of wages, the specificity of marriage partners, the frequency of travel, even the actual chronology of daily life.

Many of these laws stayed in force for decades. For example, Queensland's "legislation . . . remained virtually intact until *1965*" (Reynolds 1989:195–96, emphasis added; cf. Loos 1982:xvii). Yet, despite their existence, the laws did not actually protect Aboriginal People from the violent racism of white colonists in many places across Australia. Quite the opposite, formal and established policies and laws of "protection" were just as savagely oppressive as slavery, their legacy just the same (OT: Iles 1989; Rosendale 1990; cf. Tucker 1977; West 1984; Rintoul 1993). Consider, for example, the words of three Aboriginal People who "lived" that protection. One man states:

It seems that the "Protection" Board on some reserves appoints men to torture us mentally with bullying tactics. This, with the wrecking of our physical condition through inadequate food supply, has only one object— Extermination. (Patten 1938:1)

Vi Stanton remembers:

Our legislators! That terrible legislation, the ordinance! In those days there were such restrictions on Aboriginals that you were just naturally a ward of the state. You had virtually no freedoms whatsoever. It was put out in the 1950s that if you dared identify as an Aborigine you would come under the Protector of Aboriginals. It's invidious, but people thought they *were* being protected. Protected! Do you know what protection was? The police could go into your home . . . into a tribal or non-tribal Aboriginal's home without a warrant and search it any time they felt like it. And the police used this to the extent where in 1968 I had to tape a conversation between a policeman and a woman and threaten police with it. (quoted in Gilbert 1977:8–9)

And, Elizabeth Pearce recalls:

> Everyone who elected to come out from this ordinance of the time was not, in future, to claim they were Aboriginals. Therefore they were no longer to be protected. They were virtually free. Now my father and others who had some dignity refused to be "protected." The authorities to this day say to tribal people that when the choice was given to such people—that's us—that we chose not to be known as Aboriginals. It's not true! They were saying that for their own purpose! It was all caused by that repressive ordinance! (quoted in Gilbert 1977:9)

Thus, the change from segregation to protection was simply an exercise in semantics. Aboriginal People continued to suffer injustice—in many cases, at the hands of their "protectors."

The great financial expense, the lack of successful "protection," the many complaints received by London by the British Secretary of State, and perhaps more centrally the refusal of white Australians to recognize their cynicism and insincerity in establishing the Protectorate in the first place—all led to the demise of the system.

> ... the Protectorate was saddled with most of the blame for the failure of Aboriginal-European relations. Protectors were a convenient scapegoat: the more public money they spent in trying to overcome a deteriorating situation, the easier it was to claim that all such humanitarian efforts were useless. (Cannon 1993:179)

In 1841, the Governor of New South Wales, George Gipps, wrote to London, declaring that his

> hopes of any advantage being derived from the employment of the Protectors are every day diminishing. (Cannon 1993:124)

It did not take long for his fears to be confirmed. A mere seven years later, the next Governor of New South Wales, Charles FitzRoy, received a report from C. J. La Trobe, first Superintendent (chief government officer) of the Port Phillip district, that

> the government had spent a total of £61,000 on native welfare in thirteen years of white settlement in Port Phillip.
> ... The result of all this outlay may be stated in few words. ... Every one of these plans ... has either *completely failed,* or shows at this date most undoubted signs of failure. ... If no such establishment [as the Protectorate] had existed, the state of the Aboriginal native within the District would not have differed very greatly from what it now is. (Cannon 1993:4, 197, emphasis added; cf. Rowley 1972:239–40)

It must be admitted that certain Protectors did do *some* good (cf. Cannon 1993:256); nevertheless, overwhelming evidence makes it clear that the Protectorate system was an abysmal failure (Reynolds 1989:10; Parbury 1986:65). Indeed, its policies, "are to be condemned for undermining their own supposed aims, by crushing Aboriginal initiative" (Prentis 1988:83). Further, the particularly Australian implementation of British Protection policies and legislation somehow "removed" provisions pertaining to the "rights" of the Aboriginal People, and thus obliterated any semblance of justice.

> The colonists were able to *rob* the imperial reforms of their central driving force—the concern for Aboriginal *rights to land* and for *compensation* from the settlers. (Reynolds 1987b:151–52, emphasis added)

In the end, the Australian Protectorate system was abandoned. Aboriginal People were "on their own."

"White Australia"

In many ways, the federation, in 1901, of the six Australian colonies into one interrelated system of government marked a turning point in race relations—from "protection" to formal "White Australia" and Assimilation policies.

Federation: The Institutionalization of Australian Racism

The *Commonwealth of Australia Constitution Act 1900* gave former "colonists" opportunity to rejoice at the birth of "their" brand new "nation" on 1 January 1901. Not all the people of Australia celebrated, however, as the Aboriginal People were never asked about their opinions on the matter, were never included in the vote and, indeed, were not included in the nation itself. Section 127 of the Australian Constitution read,

> 127—In reckoning the numbers of the people of the Commonwealth, or of a State or other part of the Commonwealth, *Aboriginal natives shall not be counted.* (CoA 1901:s.127, emphasis added)

The fact is that the Aboriginal People that had been a part of the land from time immemorial were *specifically excluded* from the actual text of the Federation document.

White Australia Policy

It is important to note, from the very outset, that "There is no White Australia Act" (Palfreeman 1971:136).

There never has been one—in law (cf. Immigration Reform Group 1962:140). Yet, a White Australia Policy has existed, and operated, for almost a century as "an unwritten administrative procedure" (Palfreeman 1971:136).

Australia, it seems, was founded to be the domain of white people, and the new Australian Government acted on this right from the start. Some scholars indicate that "the demand for a white Australia . . . was a *principal* factor in the federation of the Australian colonies" (Encel 1971:32). Further, in the words of Ron Castan, QC,

> The Australian Constitution was avowedly racist when adopted. A *principal* motivation for Federation was the institution of an effective White Australia Policy, to prevent a further influx of Chinese, and of Pacific Islander natives (known as Kanakas).
>
> The Aborigines were not people whose existence mattered, and there was no need for any national policy to be adopted, or for any notice to be taken of the "remnant" which was still to remain.
>
> Both racist themes manifested themselves in the Constitution. . . . This was the framework for *the two pillars of racism upon which Australia was founded, the White Australia Policy, and the denial of the humanity of the Aboriginal People.* (APG June 1993:11–12, emphasis added)

Before federation, and right up to the turn of the century, Australia society had already begun to "tire" of its "duty" to "protect" Aboriginal People. The high ideals of egalitarianism had clashed with the harsh realities of so-called frontier life. The Aboriginals were *not* dying out (cf. Duguid 1963)—as had been predicted (cf. Commonwealth of Australia 1937:16); the economic burden of protection was ever-increasing; indeed, many sectors were at a loss as to how to deal with "the native problem." Eventually, these pressures began to take their toll in a new and more devastating manner.

The Australian Government was already in collusion with the churches, establishing and running missions for Aboriginal People all across the country. Yet the Australian Government was not to be praised for these actions—its behaviour was morally and socially irresponsible in the extreme. Protection, yes, but not if it cost money. As late as 1937, the Federal Minister of the Interior stated publicly,

> Up to the present the Government has not considered that it is its responsibility to pay missions for the care of the aged, infirm and sick aborigines on the stations, nor to provide missions with medical supplies. It is contended that, as the missions encourage aborigines to come to the stations, primarily for religious purposes, the responsibility for attending to the medical

requirements of such aborigines rests with the missions. (National Missionary Conference 1937:21)

Both government and church began to look for scapegoats. Since white Australians could not seem to "solve" the "native problem," and since they believed themselves to be so vastly superior to the black-skinned peoples, there must—they believed—be some other explanation for the impasse. They reasoned that they were not at fault and that the cause(s) must lie somewhere outside the white power structures. Who to blame—who better than the Aboriginal People themselves?

> *Blaming the victims* . . . for what befell them characterized the *racist* attitudes towards Aborigines, which were to develop and become a fundamental rationale of white Australian society towards the end of the nineteenth century. (Reid 1990:13)

After federation the Australian Government again refined its policies by completely reversing its position on Aboriginals. It moved from its stances of "segregation" and "protection"—with all their ensuing problems and costs—to developing official and national practices and policies of "assimilation."

"Assimilation"

Assimilation Practice

Operative during the same time-frame as the White Australia Policy was the practice/policy of "Assimilation." This—*theoretically*—worked towards the goal of "one nation" where all nationalities and races in Australia would see themselves as one people,[5] and was supposed to establish true justice for all people of the country (cf. CoA 1937).

In reality, however, assimilation practices complemented the "White Australia" policies that institutionalized racism at federation. They "solidified" and, with time, themselves became institutionalized. At the 1936 Premier's Conference

> it was decided that "there should be a conference of Chief Protectors and boards controlling Aborigines in the States and the Northern Territory. (Hasluck 1988:66)

---

[5] It is most curious that this "One Nation" language was used again by the Labour Party in its 1992 national and community programs; some Aboriginal People believe that this indicates a continuing, rather more sophisticatedly disempowering, Assimilation Policy.

In April 1937, the Aboriginal Welfare Conference gathered Commonwealth and State officials from all across Australia—except Tasmania—and ". . . sought such goals as uniformity of legislation and agreement on general principles while leaving details of administration to each State" (Hasluck 1988:66; cf. Commonwealth of Australia 1937:1). The result was the establishment of a "Policy of Assimilation" (Hasluck 1966:69).

> In official government circles the era of "protection" of a disappearing people was replaced in 1937 by one of "assimilation," but this did not become effective until 1951. In 1965 the official definition of the policy was altered to recognize that assimilation did not mean the surrender of identity, customs and culture. (Engel 1970:297; cf. Howe 1977:30–35)

If the black-skinned race could not be destroyed, or separated, then they might just be "absorbed." The theory stressed that Aboriginal People were to be treated *exactly the same* as all other Australians—with no special privileges, no unique social benefits, no material or financial compensation for white dispossession—that is, with no "special treatment" of any kind. To some people, the words sounded like justice; to others, they sounded like cultural genocide all over again. This new position, then, became the driving socio-political force in Australia, held in place right throughout much of this century. (Some believe it still strongly influences white attitudes towards Aboriginals today.)

Assimilation Policy

The 1937 meeting of federal and state government officials involved in Aboriginal affairs was followed by other, similar meetings. In 1951, federal and state Ministers joined the meeting process, and some significant steps were taken. First, the Commonwealth of Australia adopted the official "Assimilation Policy" (Commonwealth of Australia 1951:3; cf. WCC 1971b:26);[6] and second, the Native Welfare Conference was formed (CoA-MT 1962:[10]). Though "an" Assimilation policy had been in place and functioning for years, it never had been formalized until then. In January 1961, the Commonwealth and State Ministers again gathered and "reviewed the results of, and reaffirmed their adherence to, the policy of assimilation" (CoA-MT 1961:10). Paul Hasluck, then Commonwealth

---

[6] It is important to note that Hasluck ". . . did not originate the idea nor . . . introduce the word into the discussion of policy" (Hasluck 1988:70), and that the government was simply following the lead taken by the churches, since the policy of assimilation both was developed and supported strongly by the church.

Minister for Territories, described the formal "Policy of Assimilation" in a statement in the House of Representatives in April of that year.

> The policy of assimilation means in the view of all Australian governments that all Aborigines and part Aborigines are expected eventually to attain the *same manner of living* as other Australians and to live as members of a single Australian community, enjoying the *same rights and privileges,* accepting the *same responsibilities,* observing the *same customs* and influenced by the *same beliefs and hopes* as other Australians. (Hasluck 1961:1, emphasis added)

The international community was not impressed with Australian policy initiatives. A World Council of Churches study describes the effects of the change in policy this way.

> This replaced the "protectionist" policies which had concentrated on separating the Aborigines from the rest of the Australian community. In fact, an option had always been present to allow an Aborigine who could overcome the barriers which faced him, to move into white society. . . . At no time however was there any possibility of the Aborigines being allowed to develop as a community within Australian society, sharing the wealth of that society.
>
> Early definitions of "assimilation" show a clear intent to eliminate the Aborigines as an independent race and culture. (WCC 1971b:26; cf. F. Stevens 1971:v.2, 114)

It was clear, at least to people outside Australia, that assimilation did not make positive or constructive changes.

Assimilation Background

During the first half of the twentieth century the world experienced a number of major financial crises. Severe economic depression caused great strain on national and state budgets. Taking this factor into account has led some scholars to support the idea—long known by Aboriginal People—that the Australian Government Policy of Assimilation was developed, not to pursue some morally correct goal of social responsibility, but rather to relieve the ever increasing financial burden of maintaining numerous missions across the country, especially during the times of economic depression (cf. Gale and Brockman 1975:60; Reid 1990:12; and, especially, Gsell 1955:154).

> The result of the past policy of segregating Aborigines on reserves had been to make them into dependent paupers, controlled and administered by a separate department in each State. This was an expensive and totally unsuccessful policy. Such procrastination in facing the real issues merely made the problems greater. (Gale and Brockman 1975:67–68)

The change in policy direction could, in fact, be seen as morally reprehensible as it was the height of cynicism to attempt to "assimilate" people into the "mainstream culture" because they are beginning to cost too much money to "protect" as a valuable and culturally distinct indigenous population.

Indeed, the assimilation policies did not recognize the distinct cultural differences between white Australians and the Aboriginal Nation. *Its real purpose was to make Aboriginal People white.* Very many publications of the day confirm this intent.

> In its simplest terms assimilation means that, to *survive* and prosper, the aborigines [*sic*] must *live* and *work* and *think as white Australians do* . . . . (CoA-MT 1958a:1, emphasis added)

An international assessment of the policy and its implications put it this way.

> Assimilation implies that an individual will change his [*sic*] self-identity to that of the dominant society and will adopt the same manner of living, values and beliefs. In itself, as it still dominates official dogma, it is the most subtle and pernicious aspect of Australia's *institutional racism.* (WCC 1971a:2)

If Aboriginal People could not be destroyed outright, and could not be enslaved or segregated due to international and economic pressures, then perhaps they could simply be "absorbed" into oblivion.

Assimilation Policies came to define the very substance of life itself for Aboriginal and immigrant peoples. The policies became an actively pursued ideology (F. S. Stevens 1971:3; Tatz [1971]:2).

> . . . Australian policy not only attempts to decide that Aborigines *shall be assimilated* into our [white] culture, but it also attempts to decide how fast and by what process [this] will be accomplished. We offer Aborigines theoretically at least, one basic freedom—the *freedom to conform.* (Pittock 1965:5, emphasis added)

In recent times, this unilateral imposition has become more sophisticated.

> Subsequent criticism has resulted in this definition [above] being somewhat modified so as not to appear to dictate so obviously and arrogantly what the pattern of development should be for the Aborigines. The policy now "seeks" rather than "means" that the Aborigines "will choose to attain" rather than "are expected eventually to attain" what is essentially a white way of life.* But apparently, this has been no more than an exercise in semantics.
> . . . If any meaning is to be deduced from the policy statements, it is that the Aborigines have much the same choice as they ever had. They can accept the

directions imposed on them by the white administration or remain in their present poverty. (WCC 1971b:26–27; F. S. Stevens 1971:114)

Sociologists, anthropologists and other scholars have constantly made reference to the fact that Aboriginal People did not live in cities until the 1950s, making the implicit assumption that they did not *want* to (Gale and Brockman 1975:3). What scholars such as these neglect to state is that, by Australian law, *segregation* (the name of protection) was maintained for decades. That is, by law, Aboriginal People were not allowed off the missions and reserves, and they would be punished severely if found associating with white people in a white community. Aboriginal People *could not* live in cities, even if they wanted to.

Even though "assimilation" is no longer in effect as The Official Policy of Australian governments, it is, nevertheless, The Official Attitude and the social setting by which Aboriginal People are continually judged. Assimilation still is the "un-official" policy, and possibly the hidden agenda, upon which white society determines its interaction with the Indigenous Peoples.

But assimilation is more than semantics; it has a destructive impact on people's very lives and it never has been acceptable to the Aboriginal People. Table 2 provides just a brief listing of Australian legislative measures that have had a destructive effect upon Aboriginal People and rights.

The Rev. Canon Pearson, Secretary for Aborigines of the Church Missionary Council of Australia and a key architect of the National Missionary Council of Australia's Statements on the assimilation of Aboriginal People, once noted that:

> [Aboriginal People] have a right to decide for themselves where they will live, and whether or not they want to accept the civilising influences and aids which we offer to them. The idea of confining people to certain areas or settlements cannot be accepted—it would be like the policy of Apartheid in South Africa. (Pearson 1964:3)

This statement is interesting, and more relevant than at first may appear, for there were very significant socio-political ties between Australia and South Africa.

TABLE 2
Representative Listing of Legislation (Negatively) Affecting
Aboriginal People (1900–1967)

Year	Type	Legislation
1900	Commonwealth	*Commonwealth of Australia Constitution Act*
1901	Commonwealth	*Post and Telegraph Act*
1902	Commonwealth	*Commonwealth Franchise Act*
1908	Commonwealth	*Invalid and Old-Age Pensions Act*
1910	Commonwealth	*Emigration Act*
1912	Commonwealth	*Maternity Allowance Act*
1923	Commonwealth	*Removal of Prisoners (Territories) Act*
1941	Commonwealth	*Child Endowment Act*
1951	Commonwealth	*National Service Act*
1958	Commonwealth	*Migration Act*
1959	Commonwealth	*Social Services Act*
1967	Commonwealth	*Constitution Alteration (Aboriginals) Act*
1909	N.S.W.	*Aborigines Protection Act*
1936	N.S.W.	*Aborigines Protection (Amendment) Act*
1927	Queensland	*Aboriginals Protection and Restriction of the Sale of Opium Act of 1927*
1939	Queensland	*Aboriginals Preservation and Protection Act*
1957	Queensland	*Commonwealth Aluminium Corporation Pty Ltd Agreement Act of 1957*
1967	Queensland	*Aboriginal Relics Preservation Act of 1967*
1910	South Australia	*Northern Territory Aborigines Act*
1934	South Australia	*Aborigines Act*
1912	Tasmania	*Cape Barren Island Reserve Act*
1910	Victoria	*Aborigines Act*
1958	Victoria	*Aborigines Act*
1905	Western Australia	*Aborigines Act*
1963	Western Australia	*Native Welfare Act*
1918	Northern Territory	*Aboriginals Ordinance*
1923	Northern Territory	*Aboriginals Ordinance*
1954	Australian Capital Terr.	*Aborigines Welfare Ordinance*

(Source: H=Hanks and Keon-Cohen 1984:267–303, 354–56.)

Borrowing Policies from South Africa

In the late decades of the nineteenth century, Australia was consumed by concern over invasions from the Asians to the north (especially the

Chinese and Japanese) (cf. Johanson 1962:1; Hall 1971:130–32), and the White Australia policies were pushed to new "moral lows." Colonial governments attempted to ward off these "invasions" through various legal and legislative measures, spurred on by xenophobia and racism. Perennially concerned for their public image, however, the colonies pursued White Australia policies carefully. Some argued that blatantly racist policies were not a good idea and, therefore, White Australia policies must never be written into law.

> ... the *machinery* of exclusion needed to be racially neutral. (Palfreeman 1971:137)

Other more complex pressures, however, forced some action to be taken immediately. The *Coloured Races Restriction and Regulation Bill of 1896,* for example, had the full support of the then-Premier of New South Wales, George Reid (Yarwood 1971:152). Though this particular attempt failed, others did not. Queensland's discrimination against Japanese citizens, for instance, already had created years of diplomatic tension between the Australian colonies and Japan. It was so bad that even the British got involved, making very interesting suggestions.

> The [British] Secretary of State for the Colonies recommended ... action on the lines of Natal's *Immigration Restriction Act of 1897,* which required a modest standard of literacy in a European language. (Yarwood 1971:153)

Eventually, British pressure pushed Australian colonies to import South African tactics of "population regulation." In Australia,

> it was decided to *borrow* the dictation test method of *exclusion* from the *South African Natal Act of 1897,* together with exemption certificates and deportation procedure as the methods of *control.* (Palfreeman 1971:137)
>
> Western Australia, New South Wales and Tasmania did so in 1897 and 1898. The Commonwealth followed their lead in 1901 with the *Immigration Restriction Act,* establishing a dictation test in any European language chosen by the administering officer that was to prove capable of excluding any immigrant to whom it was applied. (Yarwood 1991:153; cf. Palfreeman 1971:137)

Thus, one of the very first actions of the newly created Commonwealth of Australia was to enact the *Immigration Restriction Act of 1901,* which "became the means by which all 'coloured persons' could be excluded from a white Australia" (McConnochie et al. 1989:71; cf. Johanson 1962:13).

> During the 1901 debate in Parliament on the Immigration Restriction Bill, it became quite clear that the overwhelming majority of members wanted the complete exclusion of non-Europeans from permanent settlement in

Australia. . . . Parliamentary opinion was almost unanimously in favour of exclusion. (Palfreeman 1971:137)

The Immigration Act also severely limited the entry of Melanesians and, indeed, deported many already in the country (HREOC 1991:50). In conjunction with the Commonwealth's *Pacific Islands Labourer's Act of 1906,* the non-white Pacific peoples had slim chances of entering, or remaining, in Australia (Yarwood 1971:151; Palfreeman 1971:136). So, Australia followed the example of South Africa and began, "legally," to exclude certain peoples—mostly those of colour.

It is important to note that the policies also travelled in the other direction (cf. Tatz 1971). There is *ample* evidence documenting the fact that Australian policies also went to South Africa (OT: Mosala 1993). For example,

> the native regulations of Queensland . . . provided guidance in South Africa *for the establishment of the Apartheid system* in the early 1950s. (M. Dodson 1993:17, emphasis added)

Amazingly, the Australian Immigration Act "remained in force until 1959 when it was entirely replaced by the Migration Act" (Palfreeman 1971:137). Many people—including many people of colour—in Australia argue that such discriminatory policies and practices continue even today.[7]

Genocidal Aboriginal Assimilation policies, coupled with racist immigration policies, combined to build an almost impenetrable wall around "Fortress White Australia." The attempted conquest of Australia by the white-skinned peoples of Europe was truly underway.

Progress?!

Since the 1780s, white Australian society "progressed" through various stages of "development"—including the myths of *Terra Nullius* and "no sovereignty," an historical continuation of The Lies, Amalgamation and "Non-Slavery" Slavery, Segregation, "Protection," practices and policies of "White Australia" and Assimilation and ultimately immigration policies from South Africa. The realities of Aboriginal existence in Australia, however, indicate clearly that in no way can the movement through these stages be called "progress."

---

[7] Interestingly, Australia has become a major destination for white South Africans fleeing socio-political changes in that country; cf. Perlez 1987:4.

The extent of racial discrimination against Aboriginal People in this country is illustrated by the fact that they were not even counted in the National Census until 1967! This is despite the fact that, as citizens, Aboriginal People fought alongside non-Aboriginal Australians in both World Wars, the Korean War, and the Vietnam War (cf. CoA-MT 1961:30; Jackomos and Fowell 1991).

> My father had a big influence on me as a kid. He fought for his country in the Second World War. I think the thing that hurt him most was that when he came back to Australia he had to go through the indignity of getting a citizenship rights card so as to be able to walk into a hotel to have a drink with the same men he fought side by side with. That really got his pride. (Gloria Brennan, quoted in Gilbert 1977:79)

> Such are the often bizarre twists of fortune during war that when the Japanese launched their first raid, some Aborigines were languishing in Darwin's Fannie Bay jail. They had been sentenced to 20 years for murdering five Japanese trepangers on the coast of Arnhem Land in 1932. They couldn't believe their luck—or white man's logic—when authorities released them 10 years later and told them to kill more Japanese. (Leser 1992:41)[8]

Racial discrimination against Aboriginal People in this country has existed for decades, despite the fact that this denial of full participation violated all or parts of *numerous* Articles of at least six major internationally accepted instruments—*all* of which were in force *before* 1967![9]

The 1967 referendum is seen by Aboriginal People as a callous and cynical ploy by the Australian government to make direct gains in political power, and as a means for it to undermine Aboriginal sovereignty, and any present and future claim for a treaty.

The nation's history makes it clear, then, that Australia's social background is saturated with racism. From the myths of *terra nullius* to the

---

[8] It is critically important to note that the Aboriginal men killed the Japanese because the latter had assaulted a number of Aboriginal women, and indeed spared the life of one Japanese man who had not assaulted Aboriginal women; cf. Berndt and Berndt 1953.

[9] Non-recognition of comprehensive Aboriginal citizenship violates *at least:* Article 15 of the *Universal Declaration of Human Rights* (1948); Articles 3 and 32 of the *Convention relating to the Status of Stateless Persons* (1954); Articles 1, 5, and 9 of the *Convention on the Reduction of Statelessness* (1961); Articles 1, 2, 3, 4, 5, 6, and 11 of the *United Nations Declaration on the Elimination of All Forms of Racial Discrimination* (1963); Articles 1, 2, 3, 5, and 6 of the *International Convention on the Elimination of All Forms of Racial Discrimination* (1965); Articles 16, 24 and 26 of the *International Covenant on Civil and Political Rights* (1966); United Nations 1988:4, 25–28, 53–56, 58–61, 273–294; emphasis added.

policies and practices of segregation, "protection," "White Australia," and assimilation, it is evident that racism has affected the Australian identity— both Aboriginal and non-Aboriginal. Far from being part of the past as a "lesson learned," however, racism persists in contemporary Australian society. We now turn to current social practice, and will assess racism in a number of areas of modern Australian life.

Practice: Australian Society *Still* Contributes to Racism

Australia constantly tells the world and itself about the justice to be found in this country for all peoples, yet it continually fails in the areas of human rights for its own Indigenous population (Einfeld 1996). These failures are to be found in every area of Australian social practice. Australian racism comes from many different sources, including the Australian Government and politicians, Australian society, the business community, the legal, police and prison systems, the academic world, the educational system, the media, and yes—the churches. The following section will give details of each.

Multiculturalism

Multiculturalism For All?

White Australia has moved from a position of overt land theft ("justified" by the concept of *terra nullius*), blatant oppression, and outright murder to a much more sophisticated form of institutional racism and violence. The language commonly now used by public officials is that of social and ethnic "pluralism." The Australian reality, however, is one of social, racial, and ethnic exclusion and disenfranchisement, especially of the Indigenous People. The most common term used today is "multiculturalism." But, is it possible that Australian multiculturalism is really "white multiculturalism"? That it is defined by, and implemented for the benefit of, "whites only," or "non-Aboriginals only"?

Aboriginal People are at a loss as to what multiculturalism is in a true sense within Australia. Often when we hear the expression multiculturalism, it is used in reference to express different races, languages, cultures and faiths or to establish an ideal goal (e.g., policy). In this definition, we have yet to see where Aboriginal culture, tradition, language, people and religion fit in, because within my life span of being committed to the struggles of my people, I fail to see the full meaning and actualization of this word and ideal expressed in this country.

Aboriginal People are still being excluded from a great deal of modern-day Australian society. We have been simply excluded from housing, health, safety, education, employment, law and justice, positive media, politics, development and free religious expression.

In the words of an Aboriginal person,

> I was not born with an inferiority complex. I did not acquire one. I had one *forced upon me* and was made (by law) to accept this complex as my just lot. (Cooper 1968:[20], cited in WCC 1971a:13, emphasis added)

Australia today is composed of Aboriginal People, as well as invaders, immigrants, migrants and refugees. This latter group also is excluded from many areas of social, economic and political participation. This incredibly diverse group does not, however, make up a community of Australians. There are significant problems to address. The next section deals with some of these issues.

True Multiculturalism Begins At Home

Multiculturalism implies the exclusion of Aboriginal People in this country. How can Australia be "multi"-cultural when it has so miserably failed to become "bi"-cultural—when it has failed to come to terms with its own true history and its horrific treatment towards Aboriginal People?

Its failure is seen clearly in its rejection of a treaty agreement between the Indigenous People and the newcomers (Neate 1989: 2; Cunneen, in *Special Treatment* 1991). Before Australia can even consider multicultural relationships, it has to begin with bi-cultural relationships. First and foremost, it has to right its relationship with the Indigenous People of this land.[10]

Racism is the basis of the denial of so many rights to the Indigenous People of this land. The recent *National Inquiry into Racist Violence in Australia* by the Human Rights and Equal Opportunity Commission delivered 18 major findings, among them:

> Racist violence, intimidation and harassment against Aboriginal and Torres Strait Islander people are social problems *resulting from racism in our society*, rather than isolated acts of maladjusted individuals.
>
> Racist violence is an *endemic* problem for Aboriginal and Torres Strait Islander people in *all* Australian States and Territories. (HREOC 1991:387)

---

[10] This idea was expanded in my address: "Aboriginality and the Great White Flood," Plenary Address delivered at the 6th Annual Conference of the Australian Association for the Study of Religion, Sydney, Australia, July 1991.

Even official Australian government bodies recognise racism and racist violence are serious problems affecting Aboriginal People today.

The Myth of Australian Multiculturalism

Beginning with the European invasion of Australia, all non-Anglo-Celtic peoples who have come to the Australian continent have had to give up their own identity in order to gain some kind of mythical, romanticised "Australian" identity. They have had to give up their own languages, cultures, social structures and organizations and so on, so that they might gain entry on political, social, and other grounds. But Australia, the so-called "lucky country," is not so lucky a place to be for these arrivals.

Multiculturalism is a myth in Australia today. Non-white immigrants, refugees and others encounter racism, exclusion and oppression instead of the haven and new life they seek. And things may be getting worse. In 1992, the Leader of the Federal Opposition, Dr. John Hewson, told a Liberal Party gathering in Perth that multiculturalism was, ". . . absolutely a fundamental mistake."[11] If this quotation is any indication of the future, then Australian multiculturalism—mythical or not—is well and truly an "endangered" concept.

Australian racism comes from many different sources—the Government and politicians, Australian society, the business community, the legal, police and prison systems, the academic world, the educational system, the media, and yes, the churches.

Governments Contribute to Racism

Australian Governments, Parliamentarians and bureaucrats at all levels contribute to racism. This is evident in their failure to grant land rights and facilitate justice for Aboriginal People, their complete disregard for Aboriginal charges of genocide, their failure to sign (and act upon) relevant international instruments, their exclusion of Aboriginal People in national and international arenas and their xenophobic and protectionist immigration policies.

---

[11] John Hewson, quoted by Brian Toohey on the television program *Face The Press,* 2 September 1992; Office of Philip Ruddock, M.P., "Transcript: Face the Press: Coalition Immigration and Ethnic Affairs Policy," Media Release, 4 September 1992, p. 1.

Still No Land Rights and Still No Justice

Federal Level

The Australian Federal Government has been promising land rights and justice for Aboriginal People for years but has failed to grant land rights and to facilitate justice due to its racism. In 1967, the federal government held a referendum in which Aboriginal People were counted in the National Census for the first time (Commonwealth of Australia Bureau of Census and Statistics 1968:66). While this may seem to have earth-shattering consequences, a few simple facts are commonly overlooked and conveniently forgotten. It does not seem to matter (and is certainly never remembered) that:

1) Aboriginal People have, to this day, never given up their *sovereignty*.

2) Aboriginal People were *never asked* whether or not they *wanted* to be counted in the Census.

3) Aboriginal People were not able to, and did not, vote then, and *still have not voted* now, on whether or not they want to be counted in the Census of the Commonwealth of Australia.

4) Even internal Federal Cabinet documents admit that a major result of the 1967 referendum was the *redistribution of electorates* in a way that was *definitely favourable* to the party in power at the time (cf. SMH 1 January 1994:6).

A more racist and dehumanizing action is difficult to imagine, yet the story continues.

In 1972, the Federal Labour party came to power on a platform of land rights, yet took no actions in this area. In 1975, then-Prime Minister Gough Whitlam promised land rights, began to take action and promptly got sacked by the Governor-General. In June of 1988, then-Prime Minister Bob Hawke signed the Barunga Statement promising to engage in a process that would lead to a treaty by the end of the year, but took no action (LRN 1988:26). The 1990s have already seen two Ministers for Aboriginal Affairs propose their own institutional projects for justice—Gerry Hand with the Aboriginal and Torres Strait Islander Commission (ATSIC) (ATSIC 1988:12),[12] and now Robert Tickner with the Council for Aboriginal Reconciliation (CAR) (KM 18 December 1991:1). Neither ATSIC nor CAR have power to create or enforce legislation. Taken together, all are just talk—Aboriginal People in Australia still do not have

---

[12] ATSIC came into being under the *Aboriginal and Torres Strait Islander Commission Act 1988* 1988:1–2. It replaced the Department of Aboriginal Affairs and the Aboriginal Development Corporation, and began operating in March 1990.

land rights and they do not have justice. To this day, Australia is the only former British colony never to have signed a treaty with the Indigenous People of the land (WCC 1971a:11; Pattel-Gray 1991a:58). Indeed, it has been stated that racist and restrictive Australian policies served as a model to South Africa, which for years used the name of Australia to defend its apartheid policies (cf. Immigration Reform Group 1962:152). If these are the words and deeds of the Australian Government at the Federal level, the very top of non-Aboriginal Australian authority, what can we expect of the rest of Australian society?

State Level

Australian State Governments have fared no better than the Federal Government in the areas of land rights and justice for Aboriginal People. Former Australian Prime Minister, Gough Whitlam, has stated that:

> We have made for too little progress in Aboriginal Affairs, primarily because the States oppose it. (July 1992)

All across the country, Australian State Governments have developed an abysmal record. Queensland, for example, has been compared to South Africa, and described as

> . . . a "regime based on white leadership, white trusteeship, white guardianship, and white tutelage." The Queensland Aborigines and Torres Strait Islanders Affairs Act of 1965 gave the state powers of detention, separate Aboriginal courts and gaols, restricted drinking rights, and control of movement. It also removes the rights of Aborigines to their property and wages. (Tatz 1968:12, cited in WCC 1971a:5)

In Western Australia,

> there is nearly a complete and separate Aboriginal government administration within the state administration which . . . is synonymous with Welfare and the concept of welfare "is consistent with maintaining a human zoo. . . ." (WCC 1971a:5)

In New South Wales, some believe that the State Government recently changed the Aboriginal Land Rights Act as a carefully orchestrated political ploy to hijack the N.S.W. Aboriginal Land Council's $10 million investment fund in order to pay for its massive State Government deficit (now $1.5 billion) (cf. Bray 1992:27; Coultan 28 March 1992:7; Coultan 8 April 1992:3).

The Australian Federal Government has the power to make and enforce State Government compliance with minimum standards in many areas of Aboriginal People's lives. It has the power, but not the political will.

Disregard for Genocide

We often see that our claims of genocide are summarily discarded by the Australian Government not only in the courts, but also as a part of a political ploy illegally to gain rights to our land, which has a strategic value to their "national security,"[13] and an "economic value" to the GNP (Gross National Product) through the profits gained from its exploitation. In 1983/84, for example, there were $461 million in after-tax profits for the mining companies and $505 million in dividends for investors in mining companies,[14] with little or no benefits for the Aboriginal People.

In a more traditional interpretation, Aboriginal land is being exploited for the "strategic defense" of the country. Australia is mining uranium, not mostly some benign life-giving nutrient like salt.[15] In addition, vast areas of Aboriginal traditional land are being leased from the Australian Government to the United States Government for use as nuclear missile bases.[16]

Knowing the difficulty of the "burden of proof," the Australian Government can simply brush aside any charges of either genocide or apartheid. They can then move in on Aboriginal Sacred Sites, where tremendously rich oil and mineral deposits have been found, and "take-out" whatever is in the way—including Aboriginal People, who have nowhere else to go.

---

[13] "National security" language is commonly used by élites such as the Latin American oligarchy to "justify" all manner of unspeakable crimes ("disappearances," torture, political killings, etc.) against people—all-too-often Indigenous and poor people. See chapter five of Míguez Bonino 1983:65–78. See also, especially, Comblin 1979.

[14] Even these are outdated figures (1983/84) taken directly from a mining industry source: AMIC [1984]:[2].

[15] "Australia is a major producer of heavy mineral sands concentrates, and is the world's largest exporter of rutile and zircon." Rutile is further processed into titanium metal—"The predominant consumer of titanium metal is the *aerospace industry,* particularly in Europe and the USA." Zircon is further processed into zirconium metal—"The demand for zirconium metal is closely linked to the *nuclear industry* . . ."; Department of Resources and Energy, Bureau of Resource Economics 1987:72, 98–100; emphasis added.

[16] "Australia's Nuclear Connections: Uranium, Reactors, Facilities, Bases," Carlton South, Victoria: Pax Christi Australia, (December) 1984, as cited in *Aboriginal Film & Video Guide* 1988:10.

When the Aboriginal people are reduced to a drunken, brawling race—a picture that is constantly fed to white citizens—it is much easier to treat them as inferior beings. They are therefore not worthy of assistance, power or human empathy. Just as the Nazis found that degrading Jews made mass murder less terrible to the murderers, so too does white Queensland find that the degradation of black people assists in rationalising our paternalism and indifference, and the immorality of assimilationist policies. (P. Wilson 1985:83; cf. S. Elkins:1959).[17]

As the World Council of Churches investigative team stated:

In their policy, the government is still pursuing a paternalistic line based on the superiority of white Australian culture. . . . the Aborigines were theoretically given the right to choose to be Australian but at a practical level it prevents choices, such as ownership of land like white Australians, being made. In essence the policy of eliminating the Aboriginal problem by eliminating the Aborigines remains—*cultural genocide.* (WCC 1971a:3, emphasis added)

Flawed Structures

Another racist, and perhaps one of the most offensive, element of the Australian Government is its continual imposition of unwanted organizational structures. A case in point is the Aboriginal and Torres Strait Islander Commission (or ATSIC as it is known), formed by act of Parliament in 1988 (*Aboriginal and Torres Strait Islander Commission Act 1988*). Though it did receive support from some Aboriginal People, the ATSIC proposal had significant problems and was *not* supported by the majority of Aboriginal People, organizations and communities. One of the most persistent criticisms of ATSIC is that it is not representative of the grassroots.

Even the recently established Aboriginal and Torres Strait Islander Social Justice Commission (ATSISJC) is problematical. Developed as a part of the Human Rights and Equal Opportunity Commission, the ATSISJC is one the the Australian Federal Government's responses to the Royal Commission into Aboriginal Deaths in Custody. Particular elements of the way in which it has been set up, however, present serious questions as to its integrity and effectiveness. In the words of its first Commissioner, Michael Dodson,

    . . . subsection (1) provides for appointment by the Governor-General. In blunt terms the office of Aboriginal and Torres Strait Islander Social Justice

---

[17] Wilson draws from Des Pres 1976.

Commissioner is the gift of the Queen's representative in Australia acting on the advice of the Commonwealth Government of the day.

[And,] . . . it was not necessary for me to be an Aboriginal person or a Torres Strait Islander. (1993:2–3)

Thus, arguably the two most important Aboriginal structures within the Australian Government have very serious flaws.

Myth and Mismanagement

The Australian Federal Government continually makes grandiose claims to be dealing effectively with "its Aboriginal people." Often such statements reduce to nothing more than media hype. Consider, for example, two Government statements relating to how much money the Australian Government spends on Aboriginals.

The first statement, from July 1959, was made by the then-Federal Minister for Territories, the Hon. Paul Hasluck, M.P.

At a rough estimate Australian governments are spending up to *£4 million a year* on services solely for the benefit of aborigines [*sic*], quite apart from the provision in which aborigines [*sic*] can share with the rest of the community. (1959:1, emphasis added; cf. Roberton 1959)

The second statement, from January 1991, was made in an address by the then-Prime Minister, the Hon. R. J. L. Hawke, at the Official Opening of the World Council of Churches 7th Assembly, held in Canberra.

. . . the Australian Government will provide almost *one billion dollars* on specific programmes for Aboriginals and Torres Strait Islanders this financial year. . . . On a per capita basis, this is a larger sum than is spent by any other country on special programmes for indigenous people. (1991, emphasis added)

Though uttered over three decades apart, the statements reveal an amazing similarity, and smack of nothing more than public posturing and glory-seeking by those responsible for the continuing disadvantage of Aboriginal People. If so much money has been spent previously, and is being spent today, then why is there still a problem?

Not surprisingly, the Aboriginal community sees through the hype and is not deceived. In response to the second statement by the then-Prime Minister, the Head of the National Federation of Land Councils, Geoff Clarke, stated:

You can throw another *$10 billion* at it, but it will not solve the problem. (1991, emphasis added)

Indeed, even the international community is not deceived. In his response to Mr. Hawke, one of the then-Presidents of the World Council of Churches, Metropolitan Dr. Paulos Mar Gregorios, of the Malankara Orthodox Syrian Church of India, said:

> I'm so thrilled that the government has put such a very generous sum of money at the disposal of those who are trying to remedy this imbalance, but may I say, Sir, that money cannot solve this problem, though money is important. The most important thing, Sir, it seems to me as one who comes from outside, but has devoted some attention to this problem, is that the *dominating* community has to be educated to change its attitudes towards the Aboriginal People. Unfortunately in most of the pluralistic, multicultural societies that now exist, one culture dominates over the other cultures. (1991)

Upon just a little scrutiny, it becomes apparent that the projected image is just that—projection, fantasy and myth. Australia is racist—the condition its Aboriginal People are kept in shows it. Dr. Janice Love, reporting on behalf of the Official WCC Team Visits to Aboriginal Communities, stated at a Media Conference at the World Council of Churches 7th Assembly that:

> A week ago today, two teams . . . were privileged to meet with the women and men of two Aboriginal communities—Wilcannia (New South Wales) and Mornington Island (Queensland). What we witnessed needs to be reported today. . . . The impact of *racism* by Australians on the Aboriginal people in this nation is not just horrific, but *genocidal,* and must be addressed. (WCC 1991a, emphasis added)

Australia can try to deny and hide its abhorrent behaviour towards Aboriginal People, but its actions continually reveal racism. Speaking in 1977, Alice Briggs (an Aboriginal woman from New South Wales) put it this way:

> I always think it's quite a joke when I hear how many thousands have been allocated to Aborigines. These thousands that they rave on about are allocated, huh, but not for the benefit of Aborigines. Most of the money from this goes into people likes of anthropologists and other whites that think they know best for Aborigines. By the time the rest of the money gets to Aboriginals there isn't a fraction of the money there to do anything. So, you know, we're being ripped off all the time. I see this happening, specifically, in Canberra where I was absolutely amazed to find out that the anthropologists' department, which means nothing to us, is being funded by the Department of Aboriginal Affairs. (quoted in Gilbert 1977:52).[18]

---

[18] The Department of Aboriginal Affairs is now the Aboriginal and Torres Strait

The Australian Government's "truth-in-advertising" practice is severely lacking truth. In the words of Eric Kerr, of Queensland:

> As for saying that Aborigines are getting a handout and so forth, a lot of these white people don't know their facts. . . . [cattle] stations have worked Aborigines . . . worked and worked and worked them for five bob a week pocket money. When wages were about £7 the natives got £1 a week. The rest went into a government sponge or the mission. Now this went on for one hundred to one hundred and fifty years. *What happened to all this money?* (Gilbert 1977:49, emphasis added)

Even today, Australia deals with the Indigenous People from a very defensive social, political and economic position. In Queensland, for example,

> When the people of Aurukun and Mornington Island rejected a proposed State Government takeover, and voted to remain under the administration of the Uniting Church, the Government introduced the Local Governments (Aboriginal Lands) Act of 1978.
>
> Under this Act, the reserves were turned into local government shires, thus effectively removing the Uniting Church administration. Not unnaturally, both these communities now fear the large-scale intrusion of bauxite mining companies. (P. Wilson 1982: 81–82; Lippmann 1991: 63–64)

Now, some fourteen years after these events, a high-level Queensland Government Task Force Report shows that:

> while $1.2 million was spent on a court and watch-house complex, Aurukun had no women's shelter, wharf, or youth centre. Attempts to establish viable commercial fishing, arts and crafts, and market-gardening industries are foundering because they lack sufficient capital investment. (G. Roberts 1992: 33; cf. Pilkington 1994:25)

Norma Chevathun, an Aboriginal resident of Aurukun, states:

> We wanted land rights all along and all the Government gave us was a canteen [usually white businesses which sell alcohol to Aboriginal people and keep the profits for themselves] . (G. Roberts 1992: 33)

If, as far back as the 1950s, Australian Government officials were making public statements, boasting about how much money is spent on Aboriginals, then why do the problems continue? Does this not suggest gross mismanagement? Do not the kinds of actions mentioned above betray seriously misguided priorities? The Australian Federal Government is not listening—Aboriginal People are not getting land rights (or self-

---

Islander Commission (ATSIC).

determination); communities are not getting an effective voice over their own affairs; and, money and other resources are being wasted. If Aboriginal People are to make any gains—toward self-determination or even basic human rights—myth and mismanagement must cease.

Failures to Sign (and Act Upon) International Instruments

Australian Government racism is evident in its failures to sign (and act upon) international instruments. The Australian Government seems to have established a three-level system in relation to its ratification of international instruments—signed, unsigned, and "pseudo-signed." The first category, signed, seems to be the instruments which are most popular and, apparently, least threatening—politically, economically, socially, and so on—to Australia. This includes the United Nations Universal Declaration of Human Rights (1948), the *International Convention on the Elimination of All Forms of Racial Discrimination* (1965), the *International Covenant on Civil and Political Rights* (1966), the *Slavery Convention of 1926,* Convention 111 of the International Labor Organization (ILO), and various other (more general) instruments against genocide (1948), against discrimination on the basis of race (1963) and sex (1979), and for the Rights of Children (UN 1992:2–3; EARC/Q 1993:H1; Pattel-Gray 1991a:159; Downe and Rollason 1988:2). In July 1991—and considerably later than most other nations around the globe—Australia signed the First Optional Protocol to the *International Covenant on Civil and Political Rights* (1966) (Whitlam 1992:22–25).

It is interesting to note that this first category has a subdivision: signed and ignored. In case after case, Australian governments have ratified international instruments only to ignore their full implementation or "the spirit of the law." In 1988, for example, the New York Times noted that a report from a working group of the United Nations Subcommission on the Prevention of Discrimination and the Protection of Minorities, which reports to the United Nations Human Rights Commission,

> urges Australia to improve conditions for its aborigines, saying that most of the country's original residents remain poor, unemployed and in ill health [and] . . . accused Australia of failing to uphold certain basic United Nations rights standards for [A]borigines and [I]slanders. (New York Times 1988:15)

So, even signing an international instrument does not necessarily mean that Australian governments will act.

The second category, unsigned, seems to be the instruments which are the most threatening to Australia. These include the ILO Convention

107: *Indigenous and Tribal Populations Convention 1957,* and ILO Convention 169: *Convention Concerning Indigenous and Tribal Peoples in Independent Countries, 1989* (United Nations 1992:2–3). Many, many other countries have signed these Conventions, but Australia has not felt it necessary to sign them (cf. Fernández-Calienes 1993/94:19–21; idem., 1994:3). Australia seems to see itself above the legal, ethical and moral obligations which have moved so many other nations to sign these kinds of treaties.

The two categories discussed so far seem quite straightforward. Yet, interestingly, for Australia there seems to be a third category—"pseudo-signed." This includes international instruments which Australia has "altered" before it signed. It is well-known, for example, that Australia became a party to the *International Convention on the Elimination of All Forms of Racial Discrimination* (1965). It is not well-known, however, that "the Australian Parliament excised the clauses of the Act covering Article 4(a)" (Whitlam 1992:24), which reads:

> State Parties . . . Shall declare an offence punishable by law all dissemination of ideas based on racial superiority or hatred, incitement to racial discrimination, as well as all acts of violence or incitement to such acts against any race or group of persons of another colour or ethnic origin, and also the provision of any assistance to racist activities, including the financing thereof. (UN 1988:59)

This "removal" of such important racial vilification provisions is appalling. What possible reasons could the Australian Parliament have for specifically removing this clause? Former Australian Prime Minister, Gough Whitlam, notes that:

> The Australian Parliament has approved many international instruments but in no other instance has it expressly precluded the Australian Government from implementing a portion of the instrument. (1992:23)

This kind of "pseudo-signing" of legally binding instruments is a continuing embarrassment to Australia's image in the international community. Australia is failing to sign some very important global treaties, and it is being false and hypocritical when it "pseudo-signs" others.

Exclusions from National and International Arenas

Australian Government racism is evident in its exclusion of Aboriginal People from national and international arenas, especially those which deal with relevant issues. In the national arena, for example, Sen. Susan Ryan indicates that as recently as 1985 "only 7.3 per cent of the entire Aboriginal workforce [was] employed by the Commonwealth" (P. Wilson

1985:85). Indeed, the "one billion dollars on specific programmes" which then-Prime Minister Hawke spoke about includes a significant amount for employees of the Aboriginal and Torres Strait Islander Commission; yet this, the highest-level indigenous body in the country, employs only 36.9% Aboriginal and Torres Strait Islander people at all, and only 16% in the 25 highest positions (i.e., Chief Executive Officer, Deputy Chief Executive Officer, Senior Executive Band 2 and Senior Executive Band 1) (ATSIC 1991a:136). In other words, while a "significant amount" of money is allocated for Aboriginal People, a great proportion of it is really being spent on non-Aboriginal civil servants and administrators (cf. SMH 27 August 1994:11; SMH 31 August 1994:18; KM September 1994:3)— implying that Aboriginal People "need help" and "cannot handle" their own affairs. Apparently, the Australian Government has an ideal image it wishes to project to the world which clearly omits the Indigenous People.

In the international arena, in 1992 the United Nations Conference on Environment and Development (UNCED) held the so-called "Earth Summit" (CoA-DFAT September 1991:3). According to the Secretary-General of UNCED, possible outcomes of the meeting included:
1) An *Earth Charter* containing the principles to guide nations in their quest for ecologically sustainable development.
2) *Agenda 21,* a resumé of the current global environment, an action plan for solving problems, and an analysis of available and desirable tools and resources to implement the plan.
3) New legal instruments on climate change and biodiversity to be ready for adoption.
4) Proposals on the international legal and institutional structures required to achieve sustainable development, and the funding and technology transfer mechanisms needed to enable developing countries to achieve the goals set" (CoA-DFAT June 1991:1–2).

> The Earth Summit in Brasilia expects some 6000 participants including at least 100 Heads of State, government, NGO and media representatives, while estimates for the parallel NGO Citizens Conference in Rio de Janeiro are 3500—*the largest United Nations and earth summit ever held.* (Schmider [1991]:[8], emphasis added)

Yet, amazingly,
* An extreme minority of Aboriginal and Islander people were part of the Australian Delegation;
* very few Aboriginal and Islander persons were invited to participate officially in any of the Preparatory Committee meetings (Prepcoms);

* the Aboriginal and Torres Strait Islander Commission (ATSIC) "is not directly represented on this IDC" [the Interdepartmental Committee on International Environmental Issues set up by Cabinet in 1989 to develop policy in this area];[19]
* extremely few Aboriginal NGOs (Non-Governmental Organizations) were informed about, consulted with, or prepared for the Conference (Schmider [1991], at 3.2[a-c]); and,
* extremely few Aboriginal and Islander people even knew that the meeting was taking place or what the meeting signifies for them, their land and their future.

As a result, there was minimal official input from the Indigenous People of Australia to the possible *Earth Charter*, to *Agenda 21*, to legal instruments on climate change and biodiversity, or to proposed international legal and institutional structures. In short, the Aboriginal People of Australia were virtually excluded from *the* most important international gathering in recent memory.

Biased and Xenophobic Immigration Policies

Australian Government racism has been evident for years in its biased immigration policies—favouring white Europeans (especially British) and prejudiced against people of colour and of non-English speaking backgrounds. It is clear that the White Australia Policy had a decidedly negative impact upon immigration policies (S. Encel 1971:36).

> Federation in 1901 saw . . . Australia as a white man's country—white usually meaning English-speaking and certainly not extending beyond north-west Europe. While the *Protection* policy systematically excluded Aborigines from emerging Australian society, the White Australia Policy effectively excluded "foreign" non-whites from coming here. Britain was the vital source for "men", markets and money. In turn, Australia supported Britain in its imperial wars, in the Sudan, South Africa, and World War I. (Chambers and Pettman 1986:14, emphasis added).[20]

---

[19] Schmider 1991, at 3.2(a): ATSIC's "interests are expected by be covered by the Department of Employment, Education and Training" *although* "responsibility for UNCED preparations in Australia is shared by the Departments of the Arts, Sport, the Environment, Tourism and Territories . . . and Foreign Affairs and Trade." In plain English: ATSIC (whose own integrity and adequacy to represent all Aboriginal and Islander people has long been in serious question) is not represented directly in any part of the official UNCED processes.

[20] "Before 1945 almost all of Australia's migrants were British": McConnochie et al. 1989:175; and S. Encel 1971:36.

Australian Government racism also is evident in its protectionist
immigration policies, past and present (and very possibly future). The
policies are based on racist notions fed by alarmism and xenophobia. It
seems that when one group of immigrants begins to get too numerous,[21]
too dependent (welfare, housing, etc.), too employed, or too politically
threatening, the government steps in to "adjust the figures." In the 1800s
the brunt of this racism and exclusion was carried by Aboriginals,
Chinese, Indians, Pacific Islanders, Afghans and others. In the 1900s it
has been southern Europeans, southeast Asians, Central and South
Americans and Middle Easterners (HREOC 1991:48–54; and,
McConnochie et al. 1989:67–81). But always, it seems, it is somebody.

> Under the new regulations, the onus of proof of refugee status will fall on
> the people making the claim. The old system allowed claimants to refuse to
> give information . . . . (SMH 13 February 1992:1)
> . . . they will be required to furnish what documentary evidence they can to
> back up their case. (SMH 14 February 1992:10)
> . . . the [Federal] Minister for Immigration, Mr Hand . . . also foreshadowed
> a cut to next year's immigration target of 118,000. (SMH 13 February 1992:1)

The Opposition Leader, Dr. Hewson, called for a cut of up to 50% in
next year's immigration quota.[22]

"Changing the onus" may be a way to save Australian taxpayers'
money, but is morally indefensible in the case of some political refugees
and boat people, who may not be able to produce or retrieve documents
of any kind. An ever-so-slight change in administrative procedure could
mean quite legal (yet quite immoral) *refoulement* for some asylum seekers,
and could mean the difference between life and death. One again, we see
Australia closing its eyes to the world (especially oppressed peoples) and
coming up with protectionist policies.

There is now, as there has been in the past, significant protest from
numerous sectors of the community. Yet, the Australian Government
listens to some, but not to others. For example, see the following two
comments.

The State-Commonwealth Consultative Committee on Immigration
Matters declares:

---

[21] In the ten years from 1850 to 1860, the population increased from 405,356 to
1,145,586; in the 39 years from 1945 to 1984, the population doubled from 7,500,000
to 15,000,000. Source: Chambers and Pettman 1986:14.

[22] Dr. Hewson, interviewed on 2UE-AM Radio, and reported on ABC-TV News,
Sydney, 17 February 1992.

Cuts to the immigration intake have serious costs which could inhibit national economic recovery. . . . erratic fluctuations in the immigration program are undesirable from the planning perspective. (S. Kirk 1992:5)

Teik Hock Lim, a social worker from Malaysia now living in Australia, puts it this way:

This row about migrants coming into the country, going on the dole and overloading the system is a nonsense. Under our immigration policy, those who sponsor migrants over here have to pay a bond an support them so the Government gets back any money it spends on them. (S. Kirk 28 January 1992:4)

Yet, in spite of dissenting voices, the Australian Government seems intent on ignoring obvious global trends.

Three and a half billion people, three quarters of all humanity, live in the developing countries. By the year 2000, the proportion will probably have risen to four fifths.

The North cannot hope to remain insulated from social and political upheavals in the South; the upheaval will spill over, inexorably, in various ways. This is evident, for instance, from the steady flow of refugees from countries of the South to . . . enter countries in the North—legally or illegally."[23]

In the words of Dr. Peter Wilenski, retiring Australian Ambassador to the United Nations (and Head of the Australian Department of Foreign Affairs and Trade),

the world's borders are now too porous to "permit egocentric isolationism". (McCarthy 1992:10)

These global trends have a direct impact on Australia. Research conducted by Dr. Charles Price, "one of Australia's leading demographers" (Jenkins 1992:7), indicates that:

two out of every three immigrants [to Australia] are now from Asia or the Middle East. (Jenkins 1992:7)

Recently, the Australian Council of Trade Unions reported that

Massive and illegal population movements in Asia are posing the biggest threat yet to Australia's control over its own immigration program. (Millett 23 January 1992:1)

Yet, tellingly, there is another trend.

---

[23] South Commission 1990:1, 212. Indeed: "A total of 400,000 refugees have arrived in Australia since World War II"; McConnochie et al. 1989:174.

Australia has superseded England, Canada and the US as the most popular
destination for these mainly English-speaking, middle-class, *white South Africans*
. . . . (A. Stewart 1988:40, emphasis added)

Politicians Contribute to Racism

Non-Aboriginal Australian history is filled with countless stories of
politicians rising to, and remaining in, power based on ideologies (and
therefore subsequent policies) of racism and exclusion. In fact, it seems
that Australian politicians are not even held accountable by anyone for
blatantly racist statements. Over the past century, Australian politicians
have made the most shocking and amazing statements imaginable—and
seem to have done so with impunity.

From 1901, the extraordinary statement of The Hon. Edmund Barton,
first Prime Minister of Australia:

I do not think that the doctrine of the equality of man was ever really intended
to include racial equality. (*Commonwealth Parliamentary Debates,* cited in S. Encel
1971:33, and Palfreeman 1971:137)

From 1938, the statement of Sir Paul Hasluck (future Governor-
General of Australia) as a journalist on a West Australian newspaper:

. . . the European concept of an ideal location for a group of Aboriginal urban
dwellers [is] as far enough out of town to be out of sight but close enough to
enable the white people to exploit their labour. (F. Stevens 1981:27)

From 1971, the statement of the Hon. Arthur Calwell, first Federal
Minister for Immigration and former Federal Leader of the Australian
Labour Party:

Racialism and nationalism are, in my thinking, synonymous words. (S. Encel
1971:39)

From a 1981 Parliamentary debate (13 May) on unleaded petrol, the
statement of the Hon. Wal Murray, Deputy Premier of New South Wales:

The Government should conduct tests with Aborigines as the control group.
Then the variations (in lead content) would be apparent. (cited in NSWALC
1989)

From a 1983 article in the *Sydney Morning Herald,* in relation to
Aboriginal People at Boomi (in his own electorate), another statement of
the Hon. Wal Murray:

They (the Aborigines) have no right to be there and as far as I am concerned
the solution is for them to go back where they came from. (cited in NSWALC
1989)

These kinds of statements are unbelievable in this day, especially from so-called "guardians of the public trust."

The year 1988 seems to have brought out the worst in Australian politicians. Beginning "from the top" is a quote from former Australian Prime Minister Malcolm Fraser:

> I don't enjoy those Australians who want to go around feeling guilty. When the English came from England they behaved *brutally. That's all right; they were Englishmen. Not me; I'm Australian. We should not feel guilty for our sins of 200 years ago.* (Mydans 25 January 1988:2; cf. New York Times 31 January 1988:3, emphasis added)

To this were added statements by the Hon. John Howard, then-Leader of the Opposition in Federal Parliament:

> I do not accept the doctrine of hereditary guilt. I acknowledge that, in the past, wrongs were done to Aborigines. *But they weren't done by me.* They weren't done by my parents. They weren't done by my generation. (Barnett 1988:159, emphasis added)

And

> . . . Asian immigration should be slowed down in the interests of national cohesion. (HREOC 1991:174).[24]

Here is another statement made at a gun rally in Queanbeyan by Ian Armstrong (who would be elected Leader of the N.S.W. National Party five years later):

> We've got to get rid of crime, drugs, hoons and *coons.* (Coultan 1993:1, emphasis added)

In January 1993—and during the first few days of the United Nations "International Year for the World's Indigenous People"—Tim Fischer, the Leader of the Federal National Party and Shadow Deputy Prime Minister, made the following remarks:

> I am not going to apologise for the 200 years of white progress in this country. Indeed I will take on and fight the guilt industry all the way. . . . Certainly I do not belong to that guilt industry which says we whites must apologise for being here for 200 years, for developing the road, rail, airport infrastructure, for providing heaps of taxpayers' money [for land councils]. . . . I am as Australian as any Aborigine. (Chamberlin 13 January 1993:1)

---

[24] This and other statements at the time raised a storm of protests from many sectors of society: e.g. *Adelaide Advertiser* 1988; Barnett 1988:159.

To his credit, the Prime Minister, Paul Keating, immediately interrupted a restful vacation period to condemn this outrageous statement as an "incitement to fear and resentment" (Chamberlin 14 January 1993:12).

Yet, even this rebuke did not stop Fischer, who five months later worsened his statement by adding:

> At no stage did Aboriginal civilisation develop substantial buildings, roadways or even a *wheeled cart* as part of their different priorities and approach. (Coultan and Seccombe 1993:1)

The "wheeled cart" comment caused a national uproar. Sadly, however, Mr. Fischer was not alone in his understanding of Australian history and politics. Within days of Fischer's January 1993 comments, John Howard—showing an amazing lack of growth since the 1988 statement—declared:

> There is a *guilt industry* surrounding Aboriginal issues. It is strong, intolerant and, if allowed to go on, likely to do great harm to relations between Aborigines and other Australians.
>
> . . . Most Australians accept that as a nation we have a special obligation to enhance the *welfare* and lift the *hopes* of Australia's indigenous people who, despite the expenditure of millions in their special *cause,* remain as a group the most deprived.
>
> The great majority of Australians would find the notion of a *treaty,* or something amounting to the same thing under another name, between Aborigines and other Australians as *quite repugnant.* (Howard 1993:47; emphasis added)

Also during 1993, Richard Court, Premier of Western Australia, threatened "to hold a State referendum on the Mabo decision" (Lagan 12 July 1993:3). This drew the Federal Government to move toward citing him for breaches of the *Racial Discrimination Act 1975,* with the Federal Minister for Aboriginal and Torres Strait Islander Affairs, Robert Tickner, writing to the Human Rights and Equal Opportunity Commission "alerting" it that such a referendum was "being blatantly discriminatory against Aborigines and a breach of Australia's international obligations" (Lagan 12 July 1993:3).

From 1994, Marshall Perron, the Chief Minister of the Northern Territory, ran an election campaign based on racial issues:

> . . . warning of the ALP's [Australian Labor Party's] "Aboriginal agenda" and a "legal apartheid" with separate laws for blacks and whites. (Alcorn 4 June 1994:13)

Amazingly, this tactic worked. A seventh consecutive win by the Country Liberal Party means that "the Parliament will be almost entirely divided along racial lines," with the Australian Labor Party "representing rural seats dominated by Aboriginal voters, meaning a stronger black-white divide in Territory politics than ever before." In 1983, the Country-Liberal Party already had a similar victory, having "won nineteen seats after running a campaign based on opposition to the Federal Government's hand over of Ayers Rock [Uluru] to the Aboriginal traditional owners" (Alcorn 6 June 1994:5).

So, for many Australian politicians, racism works. It is a useful tool in running and winning political campaigns. What is perhaps more amazing is that, at times, even admitting the validity of certain specific *charges* of racism can be used as political tools. On 10 December 1992—Human Rights Day—at the Australian Opening of the United Nations "International Year for the World's Indigenous People," Prime Minister Paul Keating made the so-called "Redfern Statement," which read in part:

> . . . we cannot give indigenous Australians up without giving up many of our own most deeply held values, much of our own identity—and our own humanity.
>
> Nowhere in the world, I would venture, is the message more stark than it is in Australia. We simply cannot sweep injustice aside. . . . the starting point might be to recognise that the problem starts with us non-Aboriginal Australians.
>
> It begins, I think, with that act of recognition.
>
> Recognition that it was we who did the dispossessing.
>
> We took the traditional lands and smashed the traditional way of life.
>
> We brought the diseases. The alcohol.
>
> We committed the murders.
>
> We took the children from their mothers.
>
> We practised discrimination and exclusion.
>
> It was our ignorance and our prejudice.
>
> And our failure to imagine these things being done to us.
>
> . . . we failed to make the most basic human response and enter into their hearts and minds.
>
> . . . we failed to see that what we were doing degraded all of us.
>
> If we needed a reminder of this, we received it this year [1992].

The Report of the Royal Commission into Aboriginal Deaths in Custody showed with devastating clarity that the past lives on in inequality, racism and injustice. In the prejudice and ignorance of non-Aboriginal Australians, and in the demoralisation and desperation, the fractured identity, of so many Aborigines and Torres Strait Islanders. (Keating 1992:5–6)

This brief public statement caused immense controversy. For the first time in Australian history, a Prime Minister made an open, honest and direct statement about the atrocious treatment of the Indigenous People at the hands of (white) non-Aboriginal Australians. He admitted—very much in public—certain specific elements of white Australian racism— dispossession, diseases, alcohol, murders, the taking of Aboriginal children from their mothers, discrimination and exclusion, ignorance and prejudice. White Australia was horrified. Their highest elected official, *their Prime Minister,* admitted acts of racism! The statement was picked up by the media and splashed across the country, indeed around the world. Opposition parties, conservatives, reactionaries and racists had a field-day attacking the "incompetent" and "ill-informed" and "unrepresentative" Prime Minister. They used his public stand toward justice for the Indigenous People of Australia against him, and tried to score political points against him. That a single statement of overwhelmingly-documented fact made by a head of government cause such a public outcry is certainly evidence enough not only that racism continues in Australian society, but that it is a prerequisite for political success in the eyes of some Australians.

Only a few months after the Prime Minister's Redfern Statement, in September of 1993, the Governor-General of Australia, the Hon. Bill Hayden made the following remarks:

> I do not believe that the present can carry the burdens of guilt for the past. . . .
> The sins of the fathers are theirs to answer before history. But where the
> legacies of the past descend to this generation, where there is continuing
> injustice, discrimination, prejudice and social alienation, then it does become
> our responsibility to act, to ensure that we bequeath a fairer inheritance to the
> future. (Meade 1993:8)

Even this statement reveals a calloused disregard for the atrocities inflicted upon, and within living memory of, very many Aboriginal People. It does admit that sins were committed, but quickly skips past restitution, restoration or compensation into the nebulous land of "reconciliation." It is peace without *justice*—and it simply is not acceptable.

Thus, we can see that over the years, the words of many politicians are basically the same. Whether or not they intend it, many politicians still have racism on their agendas.

Business Community Contributes to Racism

The Australian business community contributes to racism in its contempt for Aboriginal People, culture and rights, its continuing violations of Aboriginal sacred sites, its anaemic support of Aboriginal employment and its near phobia of immigrant employment and its collusion with governments in environmental racism.

Contempt for Aboriginal People, Culture and Rights

The Australian business community contributes to racism in its contempt for Aboriginal People, culture and rights. In some sectors there is very little tolerance—much less understanding—of anything other than a white, Western, capitalist identity and culture. One of the most notorious examples comes from the mining sector.

> The leading industrialist Mr Hugh Morgan . . . managing director of Western Mining Corporation told the annual conference of the Victorian branch of the RSL [Returned Services League] that Aboriginal culture had been *doomed* from the start because it was *not as strong* as European culture.

> [Morgan said] "Guilt industry people have great difficulty in accepting, or recognising, that Aboriginal culture was *so much less powerful* than the culture of the Europeans, that there was *never any possibility of its survival.*" (Chamberlin 1 July 1993:1, 2, emphasis added)

Such a pessimistic—not to mention blatantly racist and offensive—view is considerably more common than you might think.

Even such basic rights as the freedom of self-expression are looked down upon. For example, Mr. Morgan also has attacked use of the Aboriginal flag, as well as Aboriginal claims to sovereignty (1993:1–3; Easterbrook 1993:16; Tickner 1993:8).

Such disregard for Aboriginal culture is not restricted, however, to an individual. The Australian corporate world often wreaks havoc upon Aboriginal communities. Another example from the mining sector illustrates the point. In the late 1970s, Australian Government opened the question of mining uranium. Many Aboriginal People stood against this move (cf. DAA 1979:21). Yet, in spite of the opposition, the Ranger Uranium Mine began operations in the Northern Territory. In February and March of 1989, Ranger "*released radio-actively contaminated water* into the Djokmarra billabong next to [a] creek" used by Aboriginal People (Pattel-Gray 1991a:24; cf. Bonner 1990:12–13). Aboriginal concerns for safety and health seem unimportant in the business world's pursuit of the almighty dollar.

Aboriginal People even suffer contempt from overseas businesses with some kind of connection to Australia. In June 1993, "Mr Rob Davies, a *London-based* mining analyst with the investment banking house Lehman Brothers International" stated the following (Beale 1993:7, emphasis added).

> If this [Mabo] decision stands, Australia could go back to being a stone age culture of 200,000 people living on witchetty grubs. (SMH 15 June 1993:16)

Now, it is fair to presume that a mining analyst for a multinational corporation has some modicum of education. Yet, here we have an opinion that is singular in its ignorance, as well as its provocation. Indeed, this outrageous statement sparked a storm of controversy, with one major Australian newspaper indicating that:

> It would be hard to find, in so few words, more abundant *error* and *insult* than in what fell from Mr Rob Davies. (SMH 15 June 1993:16, emphasis added)

Yet, sadly, Davies' concise statement sums up what a great many of Australia's business leaders believe—or would like to believe in order to "remove" the "obstacles" to full economic "development" (exploitation).

There is little to no understanding of a non-Western worldview. In the words of a long-time Aboriginal activist:

> In "white" Australia the free enterprise system with its attendant values, attitudes and myths prevails. Any person expressing doubt in the fundamental tenets of the system is dismissed or marginalised. (Foley 1993:15)

One need only consider the continuing social, political and especially economic disadvantage of Aboriginal People in Australia to see the undeniable truth of this statement.

Even at the level of small business, Australia is filled with racism. Aboriginal People across Australia face being ignored (in favour of whites) in supermarket check out lines (OT: D. Yunupingu 1991); followed by store detectives for no reason (OT: J. Pattel 1993); having their wages withheld without permission (OT: J. Pattel 1994); being refused outright by taxi-drivers (AJN 1992:1); not being served at restaurants or bars (OT: B. Tilmouth 1991); and the list goes on and on. Whether it be from a multinational corporation or from the corner store owner, racist contempt for Aboriginal People is a reality in Australia today.

Continuing Violations of Aboriginal Lands and Sacred Sites

The Australian business community contributes to racism in that it continually seeks profit from inappropriate and offensive—indeed often illegal—access to Aboriginal land. For a key example, for years it has been trying to mine uranium at Guratba (Coronation Hill, in the Kakadu National Park) (Hextall 1991:34, 32), and for years the Aboriginal People of that land (the Jawoyn) have asserted their rights that this is their land, it is sacred and disturbing it in any way will most certainly create a great many serious crises (LRN 1991:5; DPMC-RAC 1990:109 [¶6.47–48], 110 [¶6.54], 133 [¶8.20], 134 [¶8.21]). The Federal Resource Assessment Commission pointed out the significant negative impact on the Jawoyn people (DPMC-RAC 1990:137 [¶8.32]) and eventually a recommendation was made that mining be banned. But this recommendation went against the will of a very strong mining and business lobby, numerous companies of which have instigated legal challenges against the Commonwealth Government (Hextall 11 February 1992:24).

Aboriginal People see the business community's insistence on mining as racist disregard for Aboriginal traditional religious beliefs (LRN April 1991:5). The primary interest of the Jawoyn people is not in the strategic minerals or in the royalties they could make, but rather in something altogether different—keeping the integrity of their traditional Spirituality and culture. Fortunately, two successive Prime Ministers have stood strongly against these business ventures. Bob Hawke supported the ban, and more recently Paul Keating accused the mining industry of "self-flagellation" (Chamberlin 28 February 1992:5),[25] and continued the no-mining policy for the foreseeable future. Two Australian Prime Ministers now have agreed with the expressed wishes of vast numbers of Aboriginal People giving due respect to Aboriginal cultural beliefs going back for tens of thousands of years, yet these simple actions have infuriated and alienated Australian mining and business sectors. These and other actions—namely the mining industry's 1980s campaign against Aboriginal Land Rights (cf. Libby 1989)—promote continuing violations of Aboriginal lands and sacred sites.

---

[25] The Prime Minister "rejected claims that projects were being stopped by unreasonable environmental and Aboriginal concerns, using the approval of the Marandoo iron ore mine in Western Australia, valued at $500 million, as an example"; Chamberlin 28 February 1992:5.

Anaemic Support of Aboriginal Employment

The Australian business community contributes to racism in that much of its support of Aboriginal employment is weak and lacking in substance. Knowledge of Western business principles and practices is essential for Aboriginal People to survive—and succeed—in a society dominated by Western economic theories, structures and practices (cf. Watego 1989:9). Yet many Australian businesses have only minimal or token Aboriginal representation, programing or participation. For example, as recently as 1981, Senator Susan Ryan commented in the Senate—and was reported in *The Age* as having said—that Qantas, Australia's national airline, had ". . . only two Aborigines on its staff of 13,000. [And,] None of the departments in Parliament House employs any Aborigines" (P. Wilson 1985:85).

A more recent study, conducted by the head of the Australian National University's Department of Economics, has indicated that

> the economic plight of Aborigines is *far worse* in every dimension than that of similarly depressed minorities in the United States. . . .
>
> Employment levels for Aboriginal females aged between 25 and 64 were only half those of other women workers in Australia. (Dr. Bob Gregory, reported in Chamberlin 26 February 1992:4)

Indeed, two further studies conducted at the Australian National University (ANU) add to the information. The first study reveals—indirectly (after reworking the data provided)—that the annual income levels for both Aboriginal men and women were significantly lower than those of non-Aboriginal Australians (67% for 1976, and a further drop to 63% for 1986) (Daly 1991:91).

TABLE 3

Real Median Annual Incomes, Aboriginal and Total Population Aged 15 and Over (1980–81 Dollars)

		Aborigines	*Total Population*	*Ab./total %*
1976:	Males	7,013	10,917	64%
	Females	2,790	3,624	77%
	Total	9,803	14,541	67%
1986:	Males	5,103	10,114	50%
	Females	3,824	3,956	97%
	Total	8,927	14,070	63%

(Source: M. L. Treadgold 1988, cited in Daly 1991:91)

The second study, conducted by two senior lecturers in economics from the ANU's Public Policy Programme, has demonstrated that,

> Even to keep unemployment level at the 1986 rate of 35.4 per cent—almost four times the rate of the general population at the time—would mean the creation of 56,000 jobs specifically for the Aboriginal community. (Chamberlin 24 March 1992:8)

This is made even worse by the fact that

> The unemployment rate for Aborigines in 1986 was based upon Census figures and is thought to have blown out even further in the 1991 Census. (Chamberlin 24 March 1992:8)

And, that

> Aboriginal unemployment has quadrupled since 1971. . . . Best estimates now put it at around 40 per cent. (Hartcher 27 March 1992:11)

Such appalling unemployment figures for Aboriginal People (cf. Altman 1991) do not seem to matter to the Australian business community, who thinks nothing of spending literally millions of dollars for employing single individuals. In early 1993, for example, the Westpac Banking Corporation hired a new Managing Director for an annual salary believed to be over A$1 million, with possible benefits and options totalling up to A$7.8 million over the five year period of the contract (Ellis 1993:29). Yet, the Australian business community finds it necessary to consider, reconsider, and often "defer" the employment of Aboriginal individuals and, especially, the establishment of Aboriginal employment, training and recruitment programs (cf. Wootten April 1993:9; Brownley 1981:34–35).

Similarly, the Australian business community contributes to racism in that its interest in immigrant employment centres almost entirely on heated emotional debate over nationalism and intake numbers. Indeed, much of the ongoing "Great Immigration Debate" is centred around "the jobs 'they' will take" (whoever "they" happen to be at the particular political moment: Chinese, Vietnamese, Iranians, etc.). There appears to be virtually no concern for progress in the fullest, truest and most inclusive sense of those concepts. Development, it seems, is only for some (white) people.

Environmental Racism

In many cases, the business community is heavily involved in what has been described as "environmental racism." Dr. Benjamin Chavis defines this as "racial discrimination in environmental policy making" (quoted in W. Brown 1991:32).

Various churches in the United States have pioneered the use of both this term and concept (cf. Cribbs 1993; Commission for Racial Justice 1991; Sindab 1991:42–43; Commission for Racial Justice 1987). As Indigenous People, who have been living in harmony with the land for tens of thousands of years—and with European colonizers for over 200 years—we cannot help to notice that the so-called "Mabo controversy," which has exploded in Australia, has successfully diverted national and international attention away from other, directly-related issues such as environmental racism in Australia. People no longer seem to be concerned that national and multinational corporations are mining *uranium* on traditional Aboriginal lands. In the Northern Territory, for example, these mining operations continually release *radio-actively contaminated water* into the eco-systems where Aboriginal People live; they continue without the support of the Northern Territory Government, and against the expressed wishes of the traditional Aboriginal owners and of the Northern Land Council (Bonner 1990:12–13). It is not too difficult to see that such mining policy and practise is poisoning our land, our water, our food supply—and thus, even our own people.

Also, people seem to have lost interest in the fact that the pastoral, farming and forestry industries all have wreaked havoc upon our lands.

> Australia accounts for about a tenth of all desertified land in the world. . . . Overgrazing has degraded the vegetative cover . . . and expos[ed] the soil to wind and water erosion. . . . About 30% of rainfed croplands are affected by soil erosion due to overcultivation. (Grainger 1990:131)

Deforestation of our watersheds through replacement of vast areas of our native trees with crops such as wheat has increased the salt-level of our soil.

> Saline seepage is a major problem in Australia, increasing the salinity of rivers and reservoirs and causing waterlogging and salinity in lowland agricultural areas. The salinity of the Murray River rose by 84% between 1938 and 1981, while in the country as a whole about 8% of all irrigated lands have been salinized and about four times this area suffers from shallow groundwater tables. (Grainger 1990:93)

This is due directly to "poor irrigation management" (Grainger 1990:131).

Aboriginal land—indeed the Australian continent—is being destroyed by the greed and racism of sectors of the Australian business community.

The Australian business community has a long way to go, to begin to break down the walls of racism that separate us all.

Legal, Police and Prison Systems Contribute to Racism

Racism is evident in Australia in the inequitable legal system, the extremely high rates of imprisonment for Aboriginal People, the high rates of deaths in police and prison custody for Aboriginal People, the frequent and unjustified acts intimidation and violence against Aboriginal and non-English speaking background peoples (e.g., the Redfern raid) and the disgusting and continuing displays of contempt by legal and law enforcement officials.

Who Really Makes (and Enforces) the Laws?

Racism is clearly evident in the foundation, structure, implementation and accessibility of the Australian legal system to non-whites, and especially Aboriginals. In Australia, some people are "more equal" under the law than others—or so it would seem.

> It is clear that the Aborigines are not treated with the respect which they ought to be according to the law and that they are very often subject to the harassment of the police. But the abuses of the law can not just be blamed on the racism of the individual policemen. Rather it ought to be taken as an integral part of the system of "justice" that they administer. Whatever the overt intent of the law, a white man, literate, familiar with his basic rights and usually having access to a lawyer is far better equipped to cope with incursions of the police into his life than an Aborigine who has no knowledge of the law, little education and no money. The law is usually made by the dominant class to maintain an order in which their interests are dominant. Those Australians who have the material and cultural means to deal with the law rarely need to. Their class makes the law and thus rarely comes into conflict with it. The Aborigines fall outside this class almost entirely. The fact that the dominant class in Australia has this position only because of the illegal annexation of the Aborigines' land should always be kept in mind. (WCC 1971b:25)

There is a basic state of injustice in Australia. In the words of Pat O'Shane, the first Aboriginal person to become a Magistrate, "racism is still endemic in the criminal justice system" (Behrendt and Walsh 1991:164).

At the Federal level, the Australian Human Rights and Equal Opportunity Commission (HREOC) was established in December 1986, with "responsibility for four Acts of Parliament and for Australia's compliance with . . . [numerous] . . . international human rights instruments" (HREOC n.d.:1). This means that HREOC is directly responsible for both the Australian Federal *Racial Discrimination Act* 1975, and the *International Convention on the Elimination of All Forms of Racial Discrimination,* 1969. Thus, it is fair to say that HREOC is the official "watchdog" against racism in Australia. Yet, a HREOC investigation into an alleged incidence of racism is often an extremely slow, and energy and resource-consuming, process.

At the State level, various Anti-Discrimination Boards are in existence to enforce the various State Acts, laws and ordinances in this area. These form a second layer of protection against racial and other forms of injustice. Yet, here too investigations are slow and are at a greatly increased level of susceptibility to political whim. Take, for example, the recent move by the West Australian Upper House to

> force the Federally funded Aboriginal Legal Service (ALS) to reveal its
> financial and administrative details to ascertain if an inquiry is warranted.
> (Meade 14 September 1992:6)

This action was immediately condemned—the Federal Minister for Aboriginal Affairs called it a "witch hunt" with "draconian implications"— but it was not the first of its kind. Indeed, Western Australia "has a controversial history of rejecting legislation for Aboriginal people, knocking back a watered-down version of a land rights bill in 1986" (Meade 14 September 1992:6).

So, clearly, Aboriginal People cannot count on the States to be the guardians of justice for them.

Finally, at the local level, cities and towns across Australia continually find themselves without the capacity to enforce equal opportunity laws and anti-discrimination ordinances. They are limited by financial restrictions, personnel shortages, procedural incompetencies, and not least of all, political obstacles. All too often, they face considerable popular resistance. Electoral minorities do not seem to "count" in the struggle for justice.

In summary, racism in the legal system is evident in both existing and proposed legislation. Right now, though there are many laws in Australia "against racism," these laws do not result in substantive progress in the struggle against racism. Indeed,

> evidence to the [National] Inquiry [into Racist Violence in Australia] indicates
> that existing laws are failing to deal with the problems of racist violence and
> intimidation, racist harassment and incitement to racial hostility. (HREOC
> 1991:269)

In Australia, it appears that addressing racism seriously is not part of the political will. It becomes more than proper, then, to raise the question of Australian society, "Who makes (and enforces) the laws, really"?

Extremely High Rates of Imprisonment

Australian racism is clearly evident in the extremely high rates of imprisonment of Aboriginal People. A study by the Australian Institute of Criminology has revealed that imprisonment of Aboriginal People in Australia "is *23 times higher* than that of whites" (cited in Burchill 1987:17; cf. S. Armstrong 1987:17–18).

The same is also true at the State level. Chris Cunneen, Director of Research at the University of Sydney's Institute of Criminology, reports that Aboriginal People represent less than 5% of the population of Western Australia, and yet they make up 74–75% of the numbers in prison. . . . This kind of treatment amounts to cultural genocide (Cunneen, in *Special Treatment* 1991).

New South Wales is another classic example. A few years ago Dr. Stephen Castles, of the Centre for Multicultural Studies at the University of Wollongong, wrote:

> The New South Wales Government should declare that this is an anti-racist state, and that this principle is to be embodied in policy-making in all relevant areas. (Castles 1989)

Yet, the ongoing study by the University of Sydney's Institute of Criminology has found an 80% increase in the number of Aboriginal People imprisoned in New South Wales. In the words of Chris Cunneen,

> The increase in NSW is horrifying. This shatters the illusion that NSW is a more civilised State. It is now a leading "redneck State". (Williams and Chamberlin 1992:3)

While academics may wish New South Wales were an anti-racist state, it clearly is not. Indeed, while many people may wish Australia to be anti-racist, it simply is not.

This is strikingly obvious in the documentation which compares Australia's imprisonment rates in the international community. Examine, as an illustration, Table 4 which gathers information from two recent studies—an address to the 122nd Plenary Scientific Session of the Australian Academy of Forensic Sciences and a study by the University of Sydney's Institute of Criminology.

TABLE 4
Australian and International Imprisonment Rates[26]

*Rates for Australian States**		
Aboriginals in Western Australia	**1,651** per 100,000	
Aboriginals in New South Wales	**1,125**	"
Aboriginals in South Australia	**1,050**	"
Aboriginals in the Northern Territory	**944**	"
Aboriginals in Victoria	**722**	"
Aboriginals in Queensland	**565**	"
Aboriginals in Tasmania	**149**	"
Rates for Entire Nations		
United States	158	"
Thailand	147	"
Singapore	109	"
Canada	95	"
Aotearoa (New Zealand)	88	"
Malaysia	82	"
Germany (West)	81	"
United Kingdom	80	"
Australia (white)	**64**	"
France	52	"
Japan	44	"
The Netherlands	21	"

While the rates themselves are scandalous, the reasons behind the rates are even more shocking.

> ... The major offences for which Aboriginals are serving prison sentences are *property, traffic and minor violent offences*: these account for 80 per cent of sentences. Other evidence suggests that *inability or failure to pay fines* is a major contributor to high Aboriginal imprisonment rates. (DAA 1988:54, emphasis added)

All to often, however, these appalling facts (as well as a great deal of other evidence) regarding imprisonment rates is suppressed or discounted, and most certainly is never linked directly with racism.

---

[26] "Rates for Entire Nations" adapted from Paul Byrne, "Report on Black Deaths in Custody," Australian Academy of Forensic Sciences, 122nd Plenary Scientific Session, November 1987, as cited in Armstrong 1987:17–18; *"Rates for Australian States" adapted from Cunneen 1992:352.

Aboriginal youth are not exempt from this expression of racism. Australian Institute of Criminology figures show that

> the chances of an Aboriginal juvenile going behind bars in Western Australia are *48 times greater* than a non-Aboriginal youth. In Victoria the chances are 37 times greater and in NSW 21 times greater. The national cost for this "over-representation" was $80 million. (Graham 1994:6, emphasis added)

This blight on "Australian justice" is small wonder when you look at the kinds of laws that are in place. The *Juvenile Justice (Serious and Repeat Offenders) Sentencing Act 1992*, recently introduced in Western Australia, is considered "Australia's toughest" legislation against juvenile crime, but has drawn severe criticism[27] because it will affect mostly Aboriginal youth[28] and, importantly, will "breach Australia's obligations to uphold international covenants on human rights."[29] A recent editorial in the *Sydney Morning Herald* stated,

> No amount of ducking and weaving by the WA Government can conceal its intention to oblige those with a vengeful or *racist* view of what should be done with children who repeated commit serious crimes. And only an overwhelming desire for short-term political survival can explain the willingness of the Premier, Dr Carmen Lawrence, to persist with legislation that has been so overwhelmingly condemned by judges and lawyers, church leaders and civil rights and welfare organisations. (SMH 10 February 1992:12)[30]

Yet, to date, the legislation stands.

Though the high imprisonment rates of Australian Aboriginal People are odious in and of themselves, they have more deadly consequences as well.

---

[27] Criticism has come from Aboriginal groups, the Aboriginal Legal Service, the Federal Minister for Aboriginal Affairs, the Federal Attorney General, a former Prime Minister, the Human Rights Commissioner, the NSW Police Commissioner, various church organizations and many others.

[28] Indeed, ". . . about 70 per cent of minors arrested in WA [Western Australia] are Aboriginal"; Chamberlin 11 March 1992:3.

[29] Humphries 6 February 1992:6; Maley 1992:7; Humphries 8 February 1992:6; KM 12 February 1992c:3; Zdenkowski 1992:15; Kirk 11 March 1992:5. Australia's international treaty obligations, which may be violated, include the *United Nations International Covenant on Civil and Political Rights* and the *United Nations Treaty on the Rights of the Child*.

[30] It is more than a little ironic to note that the then-Premier, Dr. Lawrence, is a former Western Australian State Minister for Aboriginal Affairs.

High Rates of Aboriginal Deaths in Custody

A paper presented to the United Nations by the Committee to Defend Black Rights states:

In 1987, "on average, *every eleven days,* one of our Aboriginal people died in custody throughout Australia" (Corbett 1989:2).

From 1980 to 1987, *at least* ninety-nine Aboriginal People died in the custody of the Australian police and prison systems. Finally, in 1987, and after years of public outcry and protest, the Australian Government finally succumbed and formed a *Royal Commission Into Aboriginal Deaths in Custody.* In 1991, this Commission completed its work, finding major irregularities and abuses in police and prison systems all across Australia. The Commission's study ran for three years, cost over $30 million and produced an 11-volume Report containing 339 recommendations (Hewett 1991:1). Yet, incredibly, the Royal Commission had absolutely no power to prosecute anyone (individual or corporate) and cannot now enforce its recommendations since it has been dissolved.

The Hon. Hal Wootten, QC, while Royal Commissioner into Aboriginal Deaths in Custody in NSW, Victoria and Tasmania, stated that in seven of his eighteen reports, he made

a recommendation in general terms that the report be referred to prosecuting or disciplinary authorities to consider whether proceedings should be taken against any person. (Wootten 1991:126–27)

Yet, to date, not one person has been charged with any crime.[31]

A recent study by criminologist Chris Cunneen has found that

There have been dramatic increases in the level of imprisonment of Aboriginal people in New South Wales, Western Australia and Victoria. Over the four year period New South Wales had the greatest increase in Australia with an 80 per cent rise in the number of Aboriginal prisoners. Victoria recorded an increase of 75 per cent. . . . Western Australia recorded an increase of 24 per cent which is particularly alarming given the number of Aboriginal prisoners in that State.

The number of Aboriginal women in prison in all Australian jurisdictions rose . . . 63 per cent . . . during the four year period.

. . . Any government commitment to implementing the recommendations of the Royal Commission into Aboriginal Deaths in Custody will be shallow rhetoric indeed, if the overall thrust of criminal justice policy is based upon

---

[31] Indeed, charges and prosecutions become even more difficult when police records are somehow "destroyed." See for example where it was discovered—completely by accident—that confidential police records relating to two Aboriginal deaths in custody in Queensland had been dumped on a public rubbish tip: J. Walker 1989:2.

locking-up an ever increasing number of Aboriginal people. (Cunneen 1992:352–53, 355).[32]

Perhaps most shocking is the fact that Aboriginal deaths in Australian police and prison custody are continuing, despite the existence and conclusion of the Royal Commission. Since it handed down its *Interim Report* in 1988, for example, an *additional seventy* Aboriginal People have died in custody, according to the National Committee to Defend Black Rights (Corbett 1992: 58). Since it handed down its *Final Report* in 1989, *a further* 55 Aboriginal People have died in custody, according to a study by staff of the University of Sydney Institute of Criminology and the University of New South Wales Aboriginal Law Centre (Cunneen and Behrendt 1994:2; cf. Woods 1993:1–2).[33] Even the Prime Minister of Australia admits that the deaths continue unabated.

> The Royal Commission investigated the deaths of ninety-nine Aboriginal and Torres Strait Islander people in custody.
>
> But at least *thirty more* Aboriginal Torres Strait Islander people have died in custody since the Royal Commission finished its investigations. (Keating 24 June 1992:3, emphasis added; cf. Hartcher 27 March 1992:11)

So, once again, the Australian public—and specifically Aboriginal People—are left with another very expensive set of papers, more deaths, and not much else. In 1992 Amnesty International, took up the issues surrounding Aboriginal deaths in custody when it sent a three-person delegation to Australia to conduct an investigation (Amnesty International 1993: 3–5, 26–27) and further criticised the Australian Government's response in its 1992 annual report on human rights.

> [The Royal Commission] found that there were "glaring deficiencies" in the standard of care afforded to many of the deceased [99 Aboriginal People] which, in many cases, directly contributed to their deaths. Some commissioners recommended that their reports of inquiries into individual deaths should be forwarded to the appropriate authorities to decide whether *criminal proceedings or disciplinary action* should be taken against officials. In the final report one commissioner "strongly suggested" that the reports of all 99 deaths should be carefully studied and that, when appropriate, action should be taken against

---

[32] This report generated heated debate in the media: it was reported on ABC-TV News, Sydney, 17 February 1992; Williams and Chamberlin 18 February 1992:3; Ferrari and Irving 19 February 1992:4; A. Graham [Commissioner of N.S.W. Department of Corrective Services] 20 February 1992:8; KM 26 February 1992:1.

[33] This fact is leading to ever-increasing frustration in the Aboriginal community, with occasional eruptions of violence as even young Aboriginals are dying; cf. SMH 9 November 1993:6.

officials. [Yet] ... no such actions had reportedly been taken. (Amnesty
International 1992:59–60; cf. SMH 11 July 1992:9, emphasis added)

But this was not the only major study in recent times.

Intimidation and Violence against Minorities

In 1988, after significant expressions of community concern (HREOC
1991:xvii, 6; OT: Corbett 1993), the Australian Government Human
Rights and Equal Opportunity Commission finally announced a *National
Inquiry into Racist Violence in Australia*. In 1991, this Inquiry also completed
its work, finding significant problems.

Clearly a major problem brought to the attention of the Inquiry is the problem
of racist violence by police officers ... against Aboriginal people. (HREOC
1991:119–20)

There is a clear problem of police "violence against Aboriginal youth
as part of an *institutionalised* form of racist violence" (Cunneen 1991:213).
At times, these problems come to the surface in ways which shock and
horrify the observer.

On 8 February 1990, for example, "Operation Sue" was initiated in
Redfern. At 4.30 a.m., 135 police (including members of the heavily-
armed "Tactical Response Group") executed a precision raid on the
predominantly Aboriginal Sydney suburb of Redfern, in full riot gear
(sledge-hammers, batons, rifles, handguns, helmets, masks and shields).
For several hours the Aboriginal community—including many women
and children—was terrorized, with no real results. In the aftermath of the
raid, the police defended themselves.

At the time, police defended the raids as the first offensive in a crackdown on
crime and drug abuse in the area. (Office of the New South Wales
Ombudsman 1994:2)

Community outrage initiated a formal investigation by the Federal
Human Rights and Equal Opportunity Commission, which revealed a very
different set of facts.

The crisis in Aboriginal-police relations is illustrated by the so-called Redfern
raid, which constituted *a significant act of racist violence* against the Aboriginal
community. (HREOC 1991:213, 99–104, emphasis added)

Now, many years after the "racist" raid, some of the terrorized
residents (especially the children and the elderly) still bear psychological
scars from the excessive force and violence of this unprovoked attack (cf.
One Australia 1992; S. Harvey 1994:3).

In other areas, the intimidation is more "explosive." In northern New South Wales, there has been numerous incidents of violence, with little police action. In October of 1991, the Ngaku Multi-Purpose Child Care Centre was bombed. In the face of a continuing campaign of vandalism (e.g., ". . . recent graffiti included the words '2 Abos must die'"), police advised Aboriginal People "'to keep quiet' about the problems." Subsequently, two more houses were bombed (KM 12 February 1992:4).

Yet these are not the only examples. Media continuously report cases of such behaviour. Aboriginal women are verbally abused and insulted in public by high-ranking government officials (e.g., Northern Territory Minister for Lands Max Ortmann attacking traditional women in Alice Springs).[34] Aboriginal activists are threatened and attacked and the police do little to nothing (e.g., Queenslander Don Davidson's home and property were fire-bombed for the third time in five weeks and police refuse to provide surveillance in spite of a request by the Federal Minister for Aboriginal Affairs) (cf. SMH 16 March 1992:3; Parker 25 March 1992:3). Aboriginal People are assaulted by drunken policemen (e.g., the incident at Kalkarinji reported by Gary Cartwright, M.P., in the Northern Territory) (MacKinolty 25 March 1992:7). The list goes on and on. This is just in the time span of *one week* and it is only *some* of what took place; many (if not most) cases go unreported in the media.

Further, the Inquiry found that racism also combines with sexism. According to V. Wyles, testifying at the Townsville hearings made statements to that effect.

> . . . evidence by an Aboriginal woman captured the combination of threats of violence towards Aboriginal women when she stated that, while she was in police custody in Townsville, police officers alternated between saying "should we rape her" or "should we hang her?" (HREOC 1991:121)

Contempt by Officials

Australian legal and law enforcement officials continue to show contempt towards non-whites in their actions and attitudes. This is in spite of official policies, documents and other procedures put in place— presumably—to guarantee the contrary result. The New South Wales Police Service, for example, in its *Aboriginal Policy Statement*, declares:

---

[34] Cf., e.g., SMH 17 March 1992:2; MacKinolty 27 March 1992:4; KM 25 March 1992:1; KM 25 March 1992:14. Eventually, the women's Sacred Sites were protected by a twenty-year construction ban: Meade and MacKinolty 18 May 1992:1.

> The NSW Police Service is committed to providing a service to Aboriginal and
> Torres Strait Islander people, which is appropriate to their needs and *free from
> racism* and other forms of discrimination. (NSWPS 1992:1)

On the surface, this appears wonderful; yet the "shine" quickly dulls
upon even just a little scrutiny. Firstly, it is important to note that this
"commitment" is found in the *non-binding* "Preamble" to the official
Statement. Secondly, the two words "racism" and "discrimination" do *not*
appear—at all—in the section entitled "Critical Issues." Does this imply,
then, that racism and discrimination are not critical issues, but rather,
merely, prefatory?

Even beyond the police services, other organizations confirm the
experiences of contempt received by the Aboriginal People in Australia.
The *Royal Commission Into Aboriginal Deaths in Custody* recommended that

> Paramilitary police such as the Tactical Response Group should be kept *out*
> of Aboriginal communities. . . .
> . . . police should refrain from the "use of racist and offensive language or
> the use of derogatory comments in log books and other documents."
> Governments should cease policies that discriminated against Aborigines
> because of their incomes or where they lived. (Hewett 1991:1)

Indeed, continuing police verbal abuse against Aboriginal People is
almost "a given" in Australia (Glover 7 March 1992:2). Consider the
following specific example.

> *Kenneth Quinn, Stipendary Magistrate* in the far-west NSW town of Wilcannia . . .
> in sentencing a local 20-year-old Aborigine for use of unseemly words . . . said,
> "Your race must be (the) most interfering race of people I have heard of. You
> are becoming a pest race in Wilcannia wanting to interfere in (the) job of
> police. There is only one end to pests. Learn this time". (P. Wilson [1982]:85,
> emphasis added)

Indeed, a recent barrage of media reports have provided overwhelming evidence of police racism. In March 1992, a newspaper report
in *The Age* revealed that a South Australian police station displayed a racist
crossword, and that when a complaint was made "a police officer
admitted authorship and $125 was deducted from his pay for a breach of
discipline" (Grattan 1992:5). Later that year, the ABC television
programme *Cop It Sweet* (1992) documented police abuse in Redfern,
creating a national scandal and prompting a formal inquiry by the N.S.W.
Commissioner of Police.[35] On the programme, on-duty police officers

---

[35] Media coverage was extensive: *Australian* 6 March 1992:1; *Australian* 6 March
1992:3; Cornwall, Garcia and Bishop 1992:1–2; Glover 6 March 1992:1–2; Cornwall

were taped referring to Redfern as "Coon County" and its residents as "coons" and "gooks" (*Cop It Sweet* 1992). In addition, the film showed police "repeatedly using obscenities and making derogatory remarks as they went about their business" (Office of the New South Wales Ombudsman 1994:2).

In both cases, numerous specifically-related recommendations of the *Royal Commission Into Aboriginal Deaths in Custody* were ignored and Aboriginal People were imprisoned for their language (cf. Office of the New South Wales Ombudsman 1994:2). A review of the *Summary Offences Act 1988* is underway, yet people continue to be arrested (Bishop 1992:2; Glover 7 March 1992:2).

It seems, however, that national and international opinion does not make an impact upon the Australian legal, police and prison communities, for not more than *eight days* after the screening of *Cop It Sweet*, ABC television aired another report—this time on the so-called "Bourke Outback Trek Incident," which showed portions of a home video of off-duty police officers in "black-face" with ropes tied in "hanging nooses" around their necks, in a sick and vicious parody of the victims of Aboriginal deaths in custody. This action from within the police department created yet another national scandal (SMH 13 March 1992:8; DTM 14 March 1992:18).[36] People all across the country, both Aboriginal and non-Aboriginal, were absolutely horrified. Dolly Eatts, widow of one of the men ridiculed, David Gundy (who had been killed—"mistakenly"— by police in 1989), stated:

> My son can't get over how they can make fun of his father like this. . . . I'm disgusted that they can make fun and expect everyone to sit around and laugh about it. I think it's inhumane. (quoted in Kirk 14 March 1992:7)

Prime Minister Keating declared "the sight of the policemen mocked up as Aborigines with ropes around their necks 'the most disgraceful taunt I have seen'"; the Leader of the Opposition, Dr. Hewson, called the video ". . . a national disgrace"; the Leader of the National Party, Mr. Fischer, declared that the video was ". . . absolutely sickening . . . disgusting and disgraceful" (Chamberlin 14 March 1992:6); "Federal Race

---

6 March 1992:2; Brown and Burton 6 March 1992:2; SMH 6 March 1992:12; Jones and Bilkey 6 March 1992:27; Waller 7 March 1992:1–2; as well as lead stories on both radio (e.g., JJJ- and MMM-National Networks) and television (e.g., ABC, SBS, Seven-, Nine- and Ten-National Networks).

36 Cf., e.g., Morrison and Ferrari 1992:1; Riley 1992:1, 4; Cornwall 13 March 1992:4; Chamberlin 14 March 1992:7; Cornwall 14 March 1992:7; Chamberlin 14 March 1992:1; Wockner and Buckley 14 March 1992:1, 4; Scott 14 March 1992:5.

Relations Commissioner . . . Irene Moss, described the video . . . as 'absolutely appalling'" (Kirk 14 March 1992:7).

Just how far so much "public disgust" will take the Australian community towards action and justice remains to be seen. Over two years after *Cop It Sweet* and the amateur video were aired on television, the Office of the New South Wales Ombudsman released a report which, among others, made the following statements:

> . . . there can be *no doubt* that [police] officer behaviour is *often racist* at a variety of levels. . . . It is of particular concern that one of the reasons police do not accept allegations of racism is that they simply do not have any real understanding of the dimensions of the term. . . . Regrettably stereotyping or negative labelling is part of a learnt police culture. (Office of the New South Wales Ombudsman 1994:46, emphasis added).

> . . . the Police Service acknowledged regrettable and unfortunate *incidents continued to occur.* (Morris 1994:6)

Despite a severe lambasting in both public and official circles the "police culture" had not progressed, and the "public disgust" had not produced a change for the better. One could interpret, then, that Australian society has a very high tolerance level for racist contempt.

There is a great lack of interest in moving towards action—especially if there is any kind of "cost" involved. At the State Government level, N.S.W. racial vilification laws have been attacked for failing to provide adequate protection (García 1992b:7). Parallel legislation in the ACT, Western Australia and South Australia similarly have been criticised for various weaknesses and limitations (Ethnic Affairs Commission of N.S.W. 1992:16–19). More generally, at a Commonwealth Government level the Federal Minister for Aboriginal Affairs, Robert Tickner, has attacked State Governments across Australia,

> for failing to provide additional funding for a crucial sector of recommendations out of the Royal Commission into Aboriginal Deaths in Custody . . . despite about half of the 339 recommendations being directed at the States. (Chamberlin 28 March 1992:24)

At a popular level, a series of polls conducted by Irving Saulwick and Associates for the *Sydney Morning Herald*—and taken after the various recent highly-publicised incidents of overt racism—showed little change. One poll showed that while 66% of respondents agreed that "Aborigines come in conflict with the law because they have been badly treated for so long," only 25% agreed that "the law treats Aborigines more harshly than non-Aborigines" (Muller 20 March 1992:7). Another poll showed that

". . . a substantial minority—four out of 10—believe we [Australians] don't care . . . about how Aborigines are treated in this country" (Muller 21 March 1992:6). Interestingly, even New South Wales Police Commissioner Tony Lauer criticised the survey, calling the questions "over-simplistic" (Cornwall 19 March 1992:1, 4). Yet another poll showed that while "65% of respondents say they support in principle the idea of a treaty . . . 64% are against the proposition that a treaty should provide cash compensation or reparation to Aborigines" (Muller 24 March 1992:8). It seems that "public disgust" does not change "public opinion," much less move it towards critical self-analysis and positive action towards justice.

The unjust legal system, the high rates of imprisonment and deaths in police and prison custody for Aboriginal People, and the frequent acts of intimidation and violence against Aboriginal and non-English speaking background peoples and the disgusting and continuous displays of contempt by officials are undeniable. The evidence is clear—in many ways Australian legal, police and prison systems contribute to racism.

Health and Medical Systems Contribute to Racism

The Australian health and medical systems contribute to racism in several ways, including their serious lack of provision of water and sanitation to Aboriginal communities, their grossly inadequate services, their severely under-resourced services, and their continuing inaction and complete failure to implement the National Aboriginal Health Strategy.

No Clean Water

Many Aboriginal communities across Australia face the daily crisis of a serious lack of provision of water and sanitation. Aboriginal People have been protesting these inhuman conditions for years. They have lobbied politicians, town and city councils and even lodged formal complaints with government bodies. Australian governments have responded by ignoring them, or by "putting this on their agendas" for some nebulous "future consideration," or by commissioning studies of one kind or another. The response, however, has *not* been to make a significant and positive impact upon the problem.

A classic example of this is the so-called Toomelah Report, an investigation launched by the Australian Federal Human Rights and Equal Opportunity Commission. It found, among other things, that

> The community has *for decades lived without an adequate and certain water supply.*
> . . . (HREOC 1988:61)

Commissioners came and went and, years later, the community still faces a very uncertain water supply.

In May 1994, the Federal Race Discrimination Commissioner released the results of yet another study, this time "a report on the provision of water and sanitation to remote Aboriginal and Torres Strait Islander communities" (Chamberlin 31 May 1994:13; cf. HREOC-Federal Race Discrimination Commissioner 1994). This report, tabled in Parliament by the Attorney-General, again revealed a shocking pattern of failure.

> For example, there are 19,000 Aborigines served by water supply schemes which have *insufficient capacity* to meet the reasonable water demands of their communities. . . . Then, there are 21,000 Aborigines living in communities . . . which do not have a reticulated water supply. (Chamberlin 31 May 1994:13)

The release of this report only makes public, once again, what Aboriginal People have known—and cried out about—for years. The crisis exists mostly—if not exclusively—in *Aboriginal* communities, for non-Aboriginal (white) communities would never tolerate this kind of failure in "basic services." The lack of clean drinking water and sanitation facilities for Aboriginal People is just one part of the appalling reality of racism in the Australian health and medical systems.

Inadequate Services

Australian racism is visible in the grossly inadequate health and medical services offer to Aboriginal People. Services may be "offered," but that does not mean that they are "delivered." Of primary concern is the fact that very often services simply are not "available" to Aboriginal People because they live too far away from the clinics and hospitals; or the roads between them and the services are poor or non-existent; or the hours of operations are limited; or there are not enough trained or qualified practitioners; or any number of other reasons.

A recent Federal Department of Health document confirms the problem.

> It is clear . . . that the benefits of Medicare are not reaching Aboriginal and Torres Strait Islander [P]eople, particularly those living in remote and rural Australia where often there are no hospitals and few doctors. (Meade 24 June 1994:7)

Again, this situation is not the case for non-Aboriginal Australians, who enjoy not only very high quality of service but also very effective delivery of service. The inadequacy of the services to Aboriginal communities is shocking (cf. Alcorn 11 April 1994a:46–47, 49–51; Alcorn 11 April 1994b:48). This is made crystal-clear in the case of Toomelah.

> The Toomelah community of five hundred Aboriginal people endures *appalling* living conditions which amount to a denial to them of the most basic rights *taken for granted by most other groups in society*, and by other Australian communities of similar size. (HREOC 1988:61, emphasis added)

The fact that the inadequacies continue even after comprehensive studies into the causes, and after significant public outcry, is appalling. The health and medical community must bear some of the responsibility for their extremely inadequate services to Aboriginal People.

Severely Under-Resourced Services

Australian racism is also seen in the severely under-resourced health and medical services for Aboriginal People. Communities face severe shortages of trained and qualified personnel, constant budget and administrative fluctuations—at times subject to political whim (cf. KM 20 April 1994:1), and scarcity of products and specific medicines and sophisticated—and in some cases even basic—medical technologies.

In 1994, former Federal Minister for Health, Sen. Graham Richardson, proposed to implement a one billion dollar increase to Aboriginal health. Political debate—fighting, actually—slashed this figure first to $800 million, then to $400 million, and finally to a mere $40 million (cf. Meade 26 April 1994:5; KM 4 May 1994:1). In real terms, the numbers are even lower. The President of the Australian Medical Association, Dr. Brendan Nelson, indicates that

> his post-Budget analysis showed the additional funding amounted to just $17 million a year. (Meade 24 June 1994:7)

Such underfunding is appalling, in the face of the amount of money spent on health and medical services for non-Aboriginal communities. Aboriginal People face restrictions at all levels—personnel, financial and material—whereas non-Aboriginal People do not. This is a reality of constant concern for service providers around the country, and confirms the severe under-resourcing of services.

Continuing Inaction

The horrific health status of the Aboriginal People is not a new situation. Indeed, non-Aboriginal people have known about these deplorable situations from the very beginning of "contact" (cf. Reynolds

1989, esp. chap. 2). Racist denial will have some Australians claiming, "I did not know." The fact, however, is that Australian society has long been "receiving" very well-documented studies and reports not only condemning the deplorable conditions, but also outlining possible measures to be taken to remedy them. The list of examples is overwhelming—from last centuries' damning public inquiries such as the 1849 *Select Committee on Aborigines and Protectorate* (cf. Cannon 1993:255), to "historic" (and often notorious) legislative measures such as the Queensland *Act to make Provision for the better Protection and Care of the Aboriginal Half-Caste Inhabitants of the Colony 1897*, to the severe criticism of Queensland's *Aborigines Act 1971–1979* and its *Community Services (Aborigines) Act 1984* by the Federal Human Rights and Equal Opportunity Commission as violating human rights (cf. HREOC 1985:21–22), to the many publications on the topic (cf. Thomson and Merrifield 1989), to the more recently well-publicized—and controversial—visit by then-Federal Minister for Health Sen. Graham Richardson to the Northern Territory. Australian society "knew," and did not act.

The churches are not exempt, for they also knew all too well about the situation. Throughout history, there are numerous reports by clergy and missionaries protesting degrading conditions imposed by whites upon Aboriginals (cf. Reynolds 1987b:90–92). More recently, the evidence is even more clear. The world ecclesial community, for example, has informed about these grave situations during briefings and media conferences, as well as through internal studies and reports, through the World Council of Churches (WCC) World Conference on Mission and Evangelism in Melbourne in 1980 (cf. WCC 1980:326–28), the WCC Central Committee in Geneva in 1990 (Pattel-Gray 1990), the WCC 7th Assembly in Canberra in 1991 (*Cry for Justice* 1992; OT: Gilbert 1991), the International Team Visit to Aboriginal Communities (cf. WCC 1991b), the International Pastoral Visit to Australia (cf. WCC 1993), and, most recently, the International Round Table Visit to Central Australia (cf. *Insights* July 1994:5).

Here, again, the case of the Aboriginal community at Toomelah is helpful. In 1988, the Hon. Justice Marcus Einfeld, then-President of the Human Rights and Equal Opportunity Commission, made the following statement.

> The white community has profited at the expense of Aborigines and Islanders, and has preferred itself to them, for two hundred years. . . . Successive white generations have both *deliberately* and by careless neglect—and to their own advantage—deprived successive black generations, or permitted

them to be deprived, of everything human beings have ever had or wanted—
land and home, dignity, decency and privacy, culture and language, a proud
heritage for their children, equality of opportunity with others, education,
health and employment, even life itself.

By contrast, the Aboriginal and Islander population has not inflicted any of
these sufferings on the white population. It has been a quite ruthless one-way
street—strewn with blood, violence and victims. (HRA 1988:1, emphasis added)

Both the government and the church have known all along about the
problems, and they are unable to claim ignorance of these issues. The fact
of the continued existence of these crises for Aboriginal People is a
testament to continuing inaction by the Australian health and medical
systems. Perhaps this is stated most clearly by the President of the
Australian Medical Association, Dr. Brendan Nelson, who stated in a
nationwide television interview that he is "ashamed" of the medical
profession for allowing this state of affairs to continue (1994).

Complete Failure to Implement the National Aboriginal Health Strategy

Just as the Australian health and medical systems have known about
the critical situations for Aboriginal People for a very long time, so also
have they known what actions to take to address them for many years.

In December 1987, Federal State and Territory Ministers for
Aboriginal Affairs and Health formed the National Aboriginal Health
Strategy Working Party (NAHSWP 1989:xix). This group developed a
massive document (over 300 pages), providing explicit details in such
areas as, "The Current State of Aboriginal Health," "Commonwealth/
State Responsibilities," "Health Systems Infrastructure," "Training and
Education Issues," "Women's Business," and "Aboriginal Health
Research." Importantly, the group made concrete recommendations
throughout the text. The resulting National Aboriginal Health Strategy
became not just "another study," but rather a "blueprint for action."

Today, some seven years later, the National Aboriginal Health Strategy
has yet to be implemented. The blueprint for action sits on shelves
around the country, and Aboriginal People continue to die.

The serious weaknesses—some might say planned deficiencies—in the
Australian health and medical systems reveal a profound pattern of
racism against Aboriginal People. They stand as a blatant betrayal of the
Hippocratic oath and the medical-ethical standards of the professions
involved.

Academic World Contributes to Racism

The Australian academic world contributes to racism by distorting facts, ignoring "inconvenient" research, exercising Machiavellian control over what is deemed "history" and legitimizing racism.

Distorting the Facts

Australian academics distort facts about Aboriginal People, cultures and traditions. As shocking as it may seem, many academics believe—and teach—information about Aboriginal People that is unproven theory, wild supposition, or simply falsehood. The people who are supposed to be the most trustworthy in terms of "pure research" and the pursuit of truth are the ones who do not get the facts straight. Two of the clearest examples are that: 1) the population of Aboriginal People was increasing, and 2) a great number of traditional Australian Aboriginal societies were egalitarian, and *not* patriarchal as many academics claim (OT: G. Yunupingu 1991).[37]

Firstly, there was the idea that Aboriginal People were dying at a very high rate. The so-called "Doomed Race Theory" (cf. Loos 1982:24, 161) was a complete fabrication and distortion of the facts. Distorted facts led to distorted actions, as whites began to "soothe the dying pillow" of this "dying race" (Rowley 1972a:203). This myth conveniently facilitated white European land acquisition (read theft), since there "were no Aboriginals left." It also, however, conveniently overlooked the facts that Aboriginal numbers were increasing. Simpson indicates that while the population of "full-blood" [*sic*] Aboriginal People was on the decrease—due to "punitive expeditions," mass poisonings, white destruction of Aboriginal food sources, and so on—that of "part-blood" [*sic*] Aboriginal People was actually on the *increase* (1951:182f).[38]

Secondly, Aboriginal patriarchy is a distortion. In fact,

> Among some tribes, the (mythical) women are even considered the inventors of the rituals and the original owners of the sacred objects.
> . . . Even more intriguing are the traditions that at the beginning the ritual objects were discovered and owned by women. (Eliade 1973:121, 123)

Yet, the patriarchal invasion that came to this country still continues today. This goes to show that the invaders could not accept the egalitarian

---

[37] This has been confirmed by a number of other traditional Aboriginal leaders—both male and female—from various parts of Australia.

[38] Both these terms are extremely offensive to most Aboriginal People; they are considered racist and classist.

system they encountered. Because women did not have a role within European society, the newcomers deliberately and *completely repressed* the women's role in the society which they invaded. They believed this, and their scholars set out to prove it. They have not been able to do this because the truth does not support their theories and, somehow, facts are distorted anyway, leaving contemporary Australian society with all manner of lies, myths, and misunderstandings about Aboriginal People.

It is as if uncovering the truth does not matter because "politically correct decisions" have already been made by those in power in the academic world. Lorna Lippmann writes,

> *Prejudices* are more than simply misconceptions, since when confronted with contradictory facts the prejudiced person is still not prepared to alter his opinion. (OCCR 1979:49, emphasis added)

Dozens of historians, anthropologists and Christian authors have written doctoral dissertations, published books and gained all manner of academic and international honours for their work stating and elaborating upon ideas that are contrary to the facts about Aboriginal People. They claim most, if not all, of our societies are patriarchal, basing this on interviews and field research that was conducted by men, with men, and with male interpreters and translators. What little contradictory evidence males have admitted above is simply discounted along the lines of, "Yes that's true, but it's not really important." The writings of renowned historian of religion Mircea Eliade, for example, in reference to the traditions of two different groups of Aboriginal People, embarrassingly demonstrate sexist contradictions by both acknowledging and then rejecting stories of Aboriginal matriarchy (Eliade 1973:123).

Considerable and significant research by and about women does not seem to have mattered much in the academic world, and certainly has not made as much of an impact upon our society as the patriarchal theories (cf. Gale 1978; Bell 1983). In spite of this, Aboriginal People will continue to make, and now record, our own history, countering old views and thus keeping the integrity of the facts.

Ignoring the Evidence of Over 60,000 Years

Aboriginal Dreaming stories tell our people that we have been on the Australian continent since the beginning of time. The academic world does not accept this as true, however, because it must rely on "scientific data" rather than "oral tradition." Yet, interestingly, it ignores its own scientific data. Gordon Allport puts this as:

Prejudgements become prejudices only if they are not reversible when exposed
to new knowledge. (OCCR 1979:49)

A classic example is the complete disregard for information about how
long Aboriginal People have been on the Australian continent. Recent
discoveries by world-renowned scientist Dr. Rhys Jones, of the Australian
National University, published in the highly regarded scientific journal
Nature, can *confirm* Aboriginal presence in Australia to over 60,000 years
(LRN 1990:11; cf. Roberts, Jones and Smith 1990:153–60). Other scholars
such as Dr. Neale Draper, State Archaeologist of South Australia, indicate
the time figure is "for over 100,000 years" (J. Roberts 1981:1; cf. Armitage
1992:5). One study even uncovers evidence indicating the figure is more
like 140,000 years (O'Neill 1992:5). Whatever figures are used, we are
clearly one of the oldest living cultures in the world (cf. *One People, Sing
Freedom* 1988). Yet, many scholars insist on using very low estimates.
Scientific data is said to be the most important factor in interpreting
"evidence," but it is as though there were different "types" of scientific
data—some which will become "valid" and others to be ignored.
"Scientists" would of course claim their academic integrity by distancing
themselves from blatantly political issues. Yet, somehow, data *indicating*
the presence of Indigenous People to the Australian continent for over
140,000 years, and *proving* it for over 60,000 years—and thereby directly
contradicting and undermining the theory of *terra nullius* which
rationalised genocide and dispossession—is ignored. Such politically
explosive information is deemed not worthy of attention.

Exercising Control Over "History," but with "Skeletons" in the Closet

From the very foundations of the colonialist enterprise, non-Aboriginal
people have been exercising control over what is taught in schools,
written in books and magazines and, therefore, what is passed down as
"history." Knowledge and information have been controlled to serve the
people in power and oppress all others.

In the late 1700s academics developed the legal fiction of *terra nullius*
(detailed above). During the same period, and into the 1800s, the world
academic community developed concepts of "scientific racism." They
practised such fictitious "sciences" as "phrenology"—"beliefs that skills
and traits of character were located in specific areas of the brain and that
the configuration of the skull reflected the shape of the brain
underneath." They held to such theories as "Social Darwinism"—where
Aboriginal People were seen as the bottom rung in the hierarchized

Great Chain of Being, and as the missing-link between animals and humans. Renowned Australian scholar Baldwin Spencer stated that the Tasmanians were

> living representatives of palaeolithic man, lower in the scale of culture than any human beings now upon earth. (1901:8; cf. Reynolds 1989:107–8, 114)

As late as 1921, the Natural Museum of History in London published a guidebook describing Aboriginal People as "the 'Black Fellow' . . . perhaps, better regarded as *low-grade Caucasians*" (British Museum 1921:17).

Academics around the world scrambled to become part of this "exciting new field of study." Social Darwinism, however, was in fact a pseudo-scientific theory which sought to justify horrific actions against indigenous populations on the part of "scientists," anthropologists, linguists, politicians, doctors, pastoralists, church people and others. And, Australia was involved—*directly*. According to S. L. Larnach, former Curator of the Shellshear Museum, Department of Anatomy, University of Sydney:

> perhaps the most important work hitherto done was carried out by Hrdlicka in 1925 when he measured almost a thousand Australian crania located in institutions in Adelaide, Melbourne and Sydney. (1978:10)

And, how did the "crania" get into these institutions?

> British and Australian scientists ran one of the biggest *grave-robbing* networks ever organised. Studies by an Australian academic researching in Oxford indicate the graves of between 5000 and 10,000 Australian Aborigines were desecrated, their bodies dismembered or parts stolen to support a scientific trade.
>
> Worse, it appears that Aborigines were *murdered* to obtain specimens for science. Recently-discovered documents, including a diary found in an attic in Britain, confirm Aborigines were killed for display. Bodily parts from these murders may be in a museum in Hamburg, others from less specific massacres in London institutions. (Monaghan 1991:31, emphasis added)

Such proof of murders and massacres should have been reason enough to call in the police. In Australia, however, calling the police is precisely how these "specimens for science" were obtained in the first place.

> NSW missionary Lancélot Threlkeld described an incident in the 1840s: "A large number [of Aboriginal People] were driven into a swamp and *mounted police* rode round and round and shot them all indiscriminately until they were all destroyed, men, women and children . . . but 45 heads were collected and

boiled down for the sake of 10 skulls! My informant, a magistrate, saw the skulls
packed for exportation . . . in a case at Bathurst ready for shipment to . . .
England." (Monaghan 1991:34, emphasis added)

Most "civilized" societies would have been outraged, were they not
involved. Germany and Great Britain, for example, could not very well
protest against such abominable actions when they were "commissioning"
them.

But, what did Australian society think about this? Most Australians
probably did not know—just as most Germans "did not know" about the
holocaust taking place in the fields around their own backyards during
World War II.

It is clear, though, that at least the media knew and understood what
was happening.

A Sydney newspaper of the time described the shipment of Aboriginal skulls as
the colony's new "export industry". (Monaghan 1991:34)

Indeed, such horrific actions continued well into the twentieth
century, with the general public and the international community
completely ignorant of Australia's death-trade.

The last [Aboriginal] body was logged into the Royal College of Surgeons
museum as recently as *1951*. (Monaghan 1991:38, emphasis added)

Today, academic institutions and museums in Australia and around
the world are ignoring their complicity in genocide, and are actively
engaged in trying to keep these collections together (cf. Mydans 26
January 1988:2). They are disregarding the demands of Aboriginal People
and organizations that the remains of these Aboriginal People be
returned to Australia for proper burial (Monaghan 1991:38; OT:
Weatherall 1991, 1992). They seem oblivious to the fact that their
behaviour is extremely offensive to Aboriginal People and culture, and
that it is the height of dehumanization when the remains of Aboriginal
People are treated as scientific specimens or historical evidence to be
dissected, studied and displayed to the fee-paying public. It is clear that
the academic world has "skeletons in its closet," and it has a great deal for
which to answer.[39]

---

[39] For an example of a recent claim of scientific racism in the political arena, see
SMH 8 April 1994:2).

Legitimizing Racism

Academics are proud to claim "open debate" as a hallmark of their profession. In the course of their careers, many are bound to make controversial statements and take unpopular stands. Sometimes, however, such statements and stands become excuses for racism. As a case in point, in 1984 Professor Geoffrey Blainey made a public speech claiming that

> the Australian Government's immigration policy was allowing in too many "Asians", and that this policy threatened to destroy the tolerance which had developed in Australia's post war society. (McConnochie et al. 1989:221; cf. Singer 1985)

These comments did, indeed, spark enthusiastic debate; indeed, perhaps too "enthusiastic." The expression and subsequent defence of such a position by an academic seemed to give it some kind of moral legitimacy. It was as if racism became vogue.

> The press coverage of the speech and the various reactions to it triggered the "great immigration debate" . . . in the newspapers, talkback radio and political forums, which lasted for several months, with echoes and consequences which are still with us.
> Blainey did not make immigration, or Asian immigration, a public issue; rather, he articulated and accelerated concerns which were already growing.
> . . . the subsequent debate . . . helped *legitimise the expression of racism*, and highlighted racial distinctions and stereotypes. In this way, many "closet" racists, who had been discouraged by government and popular rejection of explicit racist ideology, "came out", and those who had maintained their opposition to non-Europeans or non-Anglo Australians, now had a field day. (McConnochie et al. 1989:221)

"Open debate" became a public circus, and even fellow academics scorned Blainey's approach.

> Debate of the key aspects of immigration policy should continue. Policy issues such as multiculturalism and the size and composition of migrant intake are not sacred cows; nor is the Hawke government beyond reproach in these matters. However, when contributions to such debate are laden with racist, xenophobic nationalism and publicly amplified by an eager media, they should be viewed with alarm, and challenged on every front. (Collins 1985:55)

In more general terms, Australian academics continue to teach the lies of *terra nullius* and British sovereignty; erroneous and undocumented beliefs about indigenous and non-western traditions and cultures; outdated and unsustainable theories of race, migration and human development; racist and reactionary concepts of the relationships between immigration, employment, wealth, national security and the common good; protectionist policies of commerce and trade; and more. All of these work together—sometimes purposefully and sometimes accidentally—to keep public understanding of Aboriginal People and cultures confused. In many ways, the academic world continues now, as it always has, a tool of the powerful to oppress the weak and exclude all that threatens the *status quo.*

Yet, in spite of all these negative factors which distort, ignore, control and warp facts, there is hope. The academic world has the potential to become a deathbed of racism and a cradle of justice.

Educational System Contributes to Racism

The Australian academic world lays the foundation upon which is built the Australian educational system. Taking information from researchers and scholars, educators read, write curricula and teach. Thus, flawed research and scholarship produces flawed educational theories and practices; this in turn both perpetuates and reinforces racism. The Australian educational system contributes to racism in many ways—by using flawed textbooks, perpetuating lies, reinforcing stereotypes, allowing racist role models, omitting facts, omitting people (or keeping Aboriginals out), and failing to self-examine.

Using Flawed Textbooks

It is clear that there are many problems with the academic world distorting facts, controlling research and selectively interpreting data, legitimating racism, and more. A directly related problem is that such academic errors and transgressions have a negative and corrosive impact on Australia's educational resources. Documentation based on flawed research is itself flawed. As with most Western countries, the Australian educational publishing industry is well-developed and active. In many cases, however, outdated documentary resources propagate racist views. Thus, Australian educators are likely to be using flawed textbooks and other resources. Indeed, one noted authority has written that

> the *majority* of Australian books still perpetuate *racism* and inaccuracies. (Lippmann 1980:65, emphasis added)

They portray Aboriginal People as a kind of native oddity to be studied along with all the other creatures of the continent. We are objectified. Alan Doobov writes:

Many social studies books do, in fact give a brief summary of Aboriginal culture. This is commonly found in the first chapter, immediately following the section on native flora and fauna. In keeping with this approach, the description concentrates largely on the physical appearance of the Aborigine, on what he eats and how he gets his food, rather like a zoological treatise on the feeding and mating habits of the polar bear. . . . Throughout the description of Aboriginal culture, emphasis is placed on technological aspects—tools, weapons and houses, with frequent unfavourable comparisons with the technology of the white man. . . . There is no serious attempt made usually to discuss Aboriginal religion, art, literature or social organisation. This contrasts sharply with the detailed consideration given to these matters when they relate to the white man's civilisation. . . . It is notable that much of the way of life of the Aborigine is described in a way which children are likely to find repugnant—eating witchetty grubs, wearing no clothes and covering themselves with mud as protection from mosquitoes. (OCCR 1979:44)

Such descriptions degrade our People and our Spirituality. They deny critically important truths about the complex and profound relationships between Aboriginal People and the land.

One of the greatest areas of weakness in the presentation of Aboriginal material in textbooks is indifference to the spiritual link between people and land.

. . . The extent to which a history book correctly portrays the close spiritual link between the Aborigines and their land is a fair test of whether the author is concerned primarily with relating history, or with rationalising the dispossession of the Aborigines.

Because of the nature of the relationship between Aboriginal clans and the land they occupied, the taking of their land from them, both in itself, and because of the violence with which it was done, is the root cause of the destruction of Aboriginal society.

The injustice of that taking of land lies in its assault on the spirituality of a people. (OCCR 1979:24)

Just as our spiritual understandings of land are violated, so also are many other elements of our lives (cf. Lippmann 1980:62–63). Racist books and resources deny our valuable contributions in many other areas. Flawed texts can come in different forms, touching upon many different topics.

Prejudiced attitudes may be built up in school not only from the more obvious texts in history and social studies, but also through literature, music, art, sciences—indeed every other discipline to which the schoolchild is exposed. (OCCR 1979:48)

When educators use such defective texts, they affect all of us negatively. They take something away from us as individuals and as a nation. They remove layers of significant human effort and achievement which robs all of us of the richness and diversity of truth. They make us a less informed, less capable people. In the words of Humphrey McQueen,

> Most school textbooks—although there are a couple of better ones in the process of production just now—portray the Aborigines as victims [of the historical process]. The people who suffered at the hands of whites for whom children must feel sorry, and for whom they must try to do better things in the future. The Aborigine active in history is yet to make a popular appearance on the stage. *Prehistorians and anthropologists all know about the active Aborigine but historians as a group don't, so students of history don't.* (OCCR 1979:21, emphasis added)

Indeed, the effects of using racist texts are disastrous and far-reaching. Not only do such resources impede our individual and corporate progress, they also rot the social web that keeps us together. They begin to destroy relationships between people.

> Although random material outside the formal social studies or history curriculum is beyond identification in reading lists, the material used may have a powerful impact in forming, reinforcing or modifying children's attitudes. (OCCR 1979:48)
>
> The trouble with textbooks is that they *sound* right—even when they are wrong.
>
> The traditional biases in Australia schoolbooks have much to answer for, in not only perpetuating racial misunderstanding at the individual level but more particularly for damaging the fabric of race and group relations in our society. They have been effective instruments for locking many minority group people into situations of chronic disadvantage resulting from the downgrading of their culture and a general apathy towards their social situation. At the same time the sense of white Anglo-Saxon superiority has been daily reinforced until it becomes a massive barrier to equality.
>
> . . . In testifying before the Senate Standing Committee on Social Environment in its 1973 enquiry into the social conditions of Aborigines and Torres Strait Islanders, Uri Windt described a study of attitudes conveyed in the three principal commercially available textbooks then in use for primary school social studies. The chief finding was that latent negative connotations were put on Aboriginal culture and lifestyle without making any overtly hostile comments. Rather, a much more subtle form of racism was conveyed through a paternalism degrading Aboriginal culture and militating against the development of a self-image by black children, or any sort of conscious acceptance of Aboriginal culture by white children. (OCCR 1979:6)

Using flawed textbooks deprives us of many different kinds of opportunities for growth, warps our personal and public development and, importantly, diverts our pursuit of truth and justice in education (cf. Windt, et al. 1970).[40] When the Australian educational systems uses racist textbooks, it obliterates any sense of educational integrity that might otherwise be claimed.

Perpetuating Lies

Just as Australian educators sometimes use flawed textbooks, they also are likely to be perpetuating lies passed down through over two centuries of romanticized and revisionist history stemming from white, British hegemony. The word lie denotes a degree of intention. This is the case here as, from the very beginning of colonization, those having power (white, Western Europeans) clearly *intended* to keep those without power out of the picture. The British *intended* to take the Australian continent as their own, (killing and) removing the Indigenous People, their culture and, therefore, their history.

> In the many textbooks he has analysed, Ian Spalding characterises the approach to the teaching of Australian history, in so far as they touch on Aboriginal affairs, as having two broad themes: firstly, the history of the Australian nation is presented as though it dated from 1788. The 40,000 years of Australian prehistory and the concept of a national heritage springing from two roots are conspicuously absent. Secondly, in the modern history of Australia, the events are presented solely through European eyes and through the documents of literate Europeans.
>
> Aborigines play an incidental role if they appear at all, and are commonly portrayed as savages to be civilised and displaced by God's own colonisers, as curiosities of passing interest like the kangaroo or platypus, or collectively as a transitory problem for the hardy pioneers, governors and explorers to deal with. Attention is seldom drawn to the fact that documents such as explorers' accounts and governors' reports express conditions and attitudes of a distant period and need to be viewed in an historical light today. (OCCR 1979:13–14).[41]

The Great Australian Lie began with the governmental lie of Lt. James Cook disobeying very explicit orders from the English crown to negotiate with any Australian natives encountered (Pattel-Gray 1991a:14), and proclaiming the legal lie of *terra nullius* (Pattel-Gray 1991a:15, 35–38),

---

[40] Australia is by no means the only country to use flawed textbooks; cf., e.g., Starr 1929.

[41] Considering our previous arguments this time frame is far too conservative.

resulting in the continuing practical dispossession of Aboriginal People from not only life-giving secret/sacred sites but also life-sustaining economic bases of land. It degenerated with the linguistic lie of "dispersals,"[42] to cover up the many white massacres of Aboriginal People (cf. Elder 1988); it continued with the historical lie of "peaceful settlement," which ignored the vast, incontrovertible and well-documented evidence of active, armed resistance (cf. Reynolds 1981; Rowley 1970; Loos 1982; Reynolds 1987a; Camron 1990);[43] it deteriorated with the political lies of over a century of "Protection" and "Assimilation" Policies;[44] and, it continues today with the academic lies of teaching unproven theories of Aboriginal migration based on flawed models, questionable "evidence" and, often, pure speculation. Indeed, the Great Australian Lie became institutionalized in the concept of Australia as "The Lucky Country."

Fortunately, the Indigenous People of Australia kept our history orally (cf. Rintoul 1993). We *remembered* that much of what we were taught in school was false. Indeed, a great deal of the white, Western destruction of Aboriginal society is *within the living memory* of our people. Lies may be passed down through generations, but so also is the truth. For Aboriginal People, Australia is not The Lucky Country. In Australia, it seems, racism breeds contempt of truth—even in the education system.

Reinforcing Stereotypes

Educators at times reinforce ignorant and often malicious stereotypes of Aboriginal (and immigrant) peoples. As lies are perpetuated, they begin to be institutionalized into actual descriptions, and working "models." For example, when Europeans first landed on Australia they were resisted by the Aboriginal People, thus completely disrupting the British plan of taking over the land and establishing a penal colony (cf. Reynolds 1981). So they created the false concept of *terra nullius* which states not only that the continent was uninhabited, but also that the land was "unworked." This served the dual purpose of both rationalizing

---

[42] Reid writes: "'[D]ispersed' [was] a term commonly used by the Queensland Native Police Force when killing Blacks who resisted white invasion of their lands," Reid 1990:x; cf. Pilger 1989:27. For a concrete example, see the "Letter to the *Queenslander,* 8 May 1880," Reynolds 1989:15.

[43] "Although statistics of the period are unreliable, it has been estimated that more Australians died on the Queensland battlefields than were killed in the wars in Korea and Vietnam"; Pilger 1989:34.

[44] See elsewhere in this text.

dispossession and dehumanizing the indigenous population (cf. Reynolds 1987b). If the beings found on the land were somehow "sub-human" or even lazy, Europeans could (at least in their own minds) "rightfully" take the land (cf. Lippmann 1980:61–62). This sickening series of irrational leaps in thinking helped to establish the destructive and persistent stereotypes of Aboriginals as being too lazy to work the land for their own survival. Such illogical leaps fail to take into account the complex cultural, social, political, linguistic, physiological and other factors involved. They fail to grasp and include the sacredness of certain places, the special relationships of tribes and individuals to motherland and fatherland, the geographic specificity of dietary requirements, and much more. Many stereotypes like this remain unsubstantiated and persist to this day. They are reinforced, both explicitly and implicitly, by the education system.

> Many of the racial stereotypes established themselves in the earliest days of culture contact and have varied little in the 200 years since that time. In so far as the Aborigines have featured at all in the Australian school curriculum, it has traditionally been according to this stereotype of a primitive Stone Age race whose fate it was to be expropriated, expelled, "civilized" or at best protected— as much from their own racial inadequacy as from exploitation by the European settlers. Thus throughout white history in Australia, the *school has been a prime agency for the transmission of a stereotype* at once cruel and invalid. The textbook writers have reinforced this stereotype in each generation. (OCCR 1979:2, emphasis added)

Racist names are still used all across Australia—and therefore taught in very many Australian schools (see table below).

TABLE 5		
Examples of Racist Names *Currently* Used in Australian Geography		
Name	*Location*	*State*
Black Gin Creek	Bruce Highway	Queensland
(between Ingham and Townsville)		
Blackfellow Creek	Edmonton	Queensland
Little Gin Creek	Bruce Highway	Queensland
(between Ingham and Townsville)		
Nigger Creek[45]	near Herberton	Queensland
Darwin	—	Northern Territory
Townsville	—	Queensland

To take just one specific example, some school children will know that the Queensland city of Townsville is named for Captain Robert Towns. What they—and probably most Australians—are not taught is that Captain Towns is the founder of the form of Australian slavery known as "blackbirding."

> Importation of the islanders, who were known as Kanakas, began in 1863, when Captain Robert Towns brought sixty-seven labourers to Moreton Bay to establish a cotton plantation on the Logan River. (Yarwood 1971:150)

Thus, instead of school being the place where people go to learn what is accurate and fair, it is often where they get half-truths and preconceptions. It becomes a place of uninformed habituation and indoctrination. Thus, the problem of reinforced stereotypes continues.

Allowing Racist Role Models

All of the above factors combine to create two forms of racist role models—those Australian educators teach about and those they become. As Australian educators use flawed textbooks, perpetuate lies and reinforce stereotypes, they also *teach about* racist role models. Great Australian Soldiers are praised for their courage, but not for their honesty in admitting that they were often out-manœuvred, out-strategized, and basically "out-soldiered," by generations of armed Aboriginal resistance fighters. Great Australian Explorers are often praised for their bravery, but not for their truthfulness in revealing they were "led" by Aboriginal guides. Great Australian clergymen are praised for their charity and

---

[45] Cf. Evans, Saunders and Cronin 1975:33 and n.23.

humanitarianism, but not for their integrity in confessing that they often physically beat and starved Aboriginal People in order to "save" them from "hell," and took Aboriginal babies away from their mothers in order to "civilize" them. Murderers become "founders of the nation," incompetent boy scouts become folk heroes, and genocidal missionaries become saints—and are taught to young people as such!

> School materials can subtly undergird prejudice. Teachers using prejudicial material may not themselves be aware how far they are influenced by racial prejudice. (OCCR 1979:49)

The Australian educational system does not teach critical thinking in this regard. Australian students (particularly schoolchildren) are not taught to re-read history, to uncover layers of story, to do proper historiography. (Just ask any of today's thousands of Tasmanian Aboriginal People about their supposed "extinction." Or, indeed, ask virtually any Aboriginal person who they were taught "discovered" Australia.)

As educators teach about racist role models, they *become* racist role models themselves. Some find it much too difficult to do proper research, or re-write curricula once errors are discovered. Others take the easy way out and avoid "the issue," developing an attitude and practice of total carelessness about our People and our culture. Both approaches propagate all kinds of warped versions of reality, not the least of which is what teachers themselves represent. If educators do not care about teaching truth (or as close to complete truth as is possible), why should students be worried about learning it?

Omitting Facts

Go into a school anywhere in Australia today and, at some level, you are likely to see educators omitting facts about Aboriginal and immigrant peoples.

> Racial discrimination . . . usually remains in European Australian minds, right through Australia's education systems. At primary school, we have textbooks constantly referring to Aborigines as being dirty, Blacks, nomadic, etc. When Wentworth crossed the Blue Mountains, these same books state that they (the great White explorers) were accompanied by Blacks. It doesn't clarify the fact that the BLACKS showed them the way (surely if these White explorers were great, then the Aboriginal guides must have been greater, for didn't they cross the mountains first?). Towards Secondary level, we find that the racist attitude of White Australians becomes somewhat subdued! Prejudices more veiled!

Discrimination rather subtle! Nevertheless, the book-bias remains.
(McGuinness 1971:150)

Across Australia, school textbooks provide a strong and constant
misleading influence, showing only part of the story, omitting details or
perspectives which could otherwise plant the seed of truth, give even basic
credibility to the vast positive contributions made by the indigenous
Aboriginal People. It seems that, in Australia, history is indeed told by the
victors.

> One of the main reasons why historians and school textbooks have tended
> to dismiss Aborigines from "Australian" history has been the conviction that
> they have had no impact on national development in any sphere—economic,
> cultural, political, intellectual or whatever. There is mounting evidence that
> this assessment is not justified. The role of the Aborigines in assisting white
> exploration, the establishment and maintenance of the northern cattle
> industry, even Aboriginal techniques of land management, opened up the way
> for the pastoral industry. As more detailed regional studies are made, further
> evidence will doubtless come to light of the role of Aborigines in the shaping
> and development of Australia. (OCCR 1979:29)

> Not only are the Aborigines ignored as a matter of policy, but when clashes
> have to be reported, they are related in a way which glorifies the settler and
> vilifies the Aborigine. Thus the student reads of the "treacherous murder by
> the blacks of isolated settlers" followed by a "punitive expedition in which a
> hundred natives were executed."

> Perhaps more important than this one-sided presentation of the facts are
> the events which are simply omitted. We do not read anywhere of the poisoned
> waterholes or poisoned flour. We are not told of the starvation of those tribes
> whose land had been taken. No mention is made of the native police,
> organised and trained to destroy their own people*. Events which cannot be
> ignored, such as the extermination of the entire** Aboriginal population of
> Tasmania, are glossed over as just one of those things, unfortunate, but not
> really anyone's fault. None of the history books consider it worthwhile to quote
> from an 1826 edition of the Tasmanian newspaper:

> "The government must remove the natives—if not, they will be hunted
> down like wild beasts and destroyed."†

> Misleading or inaccurate statements about Aborigines abound in the
> schoolbooks, especially when dealing with more recent history. The aim is
> usually to present the situation in a more favourable light than is justified by
> reality. (OCCR 1979:12).[46]

---

[46] *Rowley 1970; **"Entire" extermination is inaccurate, as any of today's
thousands of Tasmanian Aboriginals will tell you (in no uncertain terms!); †*Colonial
Times,* 1 December 1826, cited in OCCR 1979.

If children are not given the facts—all of the facts, without prejudice—by their own schools, who can they trust? How are they supposed to "understand" history, society, life? How are they supposed to grow in virtue? How can they consider that they truly have been educated?

Omitting People—Keeping Aboriginals Out

Even beyond omitting facts, the Australian educational system has contributed to racism by omitting people; that is, by purposefully keeping Aboriginal People out. From first contact, the Indigenous People of Australia were deemed by the invading colonists to be "inferior," and therefore "incapable" of learning. We were thought to be unsuitable for education. Whites believed it possible to, at best, "domesticate" Aboriginals (cf. Cummings 1990:10, 20). Such beliefs were reinforced by teachers and other educators. In many places, exclusion was the practice. Noted author Kevin Gilbert recalls:

> When I went to school, I remember that the teachers used to make the black kids go out and clean up the shelter shed because they felt we wouldn't learn anything anyway. (Gilbert 1977:47)

Beyond being the practice, in some places exclusion was even the law. European colonists made it illegal for Aboriginal People to get an education. An Aboriginal man from Queensland, Eric Kerr, recalls school in the 1940s.

> I remember when I went to school . . . my brothers and sister, the older ones, weren't allowed to go to school. That was the law. They didn't want the Aborigines to get up so they passed a law. No Aborigines were allowed to go to university. (Gilbert 1977:48)

In more recent times, overt exclusion has become "illegal," at least theoretically.[47] Yet exclusion continues in many other, covert ways. While the descendants of the colonists now let it be possible for Aboriginal People to go to school, they do not make it entirely easy or pleasant. Take, for example, how Aboriginal People are excluded from "advancement" in school. A young Aboriginal woman from Western Australia, Gloria Brennan—later to become President of the Aboriginal Medical Service, Perth—recalls school in the 1960s.

---

[47] This is due to the adoption of anti-discrimination legislation and, in some states, of special policies. In New South Wales, for example, see the *Aboriginal Education Policy* (NSWDOEDSP 1982) and the *Ethnic Affairs Policy Statement of the Ethnic Affairs Commission of NSW* (1986).

The teachers'd pick on us, we'd stick up for ourselves and then go home and tell our father and he'd go round and bawl them out for being racist bastards. One of the reasons we left Menzies was school again. I'd just topped the school there. There was a citizenship award prize. It was a small school. The teacher took all of them from grade one to grade six and I'd be teaching grades one to three really while the teacher took the higher classes. Because I came top and as a citizen and helping inside the school, my father reckoned I was more entitled to the prize than the white boy who got it. This little kid went up to my father and said that he didn't feel that he deserved the book and he didn't know why he'd got it. Then my father approached the teacher who was raving on about the politics of the town and how he couldn't really give it to me. He had to give it to this kid who was the son of a station owner. Then he asked why my father was kicking the system because there was no hope for me anyway. My father said, "That girl is going to university." The teacher said, "No hope, no hope. If you must, spend your money on a boy. She's just going to end up with seven kids anyway." My father was really angry. In fact they starved, starved to send me to high school. They refused to take a government scholarship. Always too proud to take a handout. (Gilbert 1977:80)

Thus, though some Aboriginal People do brave all manner of obstacles and harassment, and actually make it into school, not all stay. Documentation shows that the Australian education system is failing to encourage Aboriginal People to stay in school, and is failing to help them graduate (cf. Pattel-Gray 1991a:129–31). In short, in Australia today, the vast majority of Aboriginal People are excluded from the education system.

Failing to "Self-Examine"

Clearly, the Australian educational system has some problems and is failing to address them. Some educators consciously deny certain critically important truths about people and land. In some cases, it is clear that "education" is being used as a weapon. The Australian Catholic Commission for Justice and Peace put it this way:

History as learned by most Australians is the history of Europeans, and especially of the British, and of their descendants in Australia. It is the history of the dominant races and nations, written by them, and for them. (OCCR 1979:9)

Surely we cannot expect our children single-handedly to monitor the content of the curriculum presented to them for historical accuracy and objectivity. It is our responsibility as adults to ensure this. Educators and educational administrators are failing to "self-examine" the content, presentation, and approach of their curricula (Keirl 1992:24).

All of us—teachers more importantly—must deal with these issues, because the problems are not going away.

> Nevertheless justice demands that the concerns that move the Aboriginal· people so deeply—and which are perpetuated by the very racism reflected in schoolbooks—should not continue to be ignored in Australian classrooms. The approach to their presentation, the stances of the authors, the means of involving Aboriginal people in the process—these questions are yet to be tackled. But the basic principle that Aboriginal understandings of justice and human dignity form a proper study for all young Australians seems beyond debate. (OCCR 1979:31)

Aboriginal Action and Change

But, action on the part of Aboriginal People is correcting the imbalance.

> Bryan Havenhand [a recognized Aboriginal leader] speaks of "*utter falsities* of Aboriginal history, culture and black/white relations perpetuated in the classroom." He points out that it was only in 1969 that some teachers, academics and students became consciously aware of this. However this consciousness did not spring from any acute sensitivity by whites: "Rather it was the Aborigines who woke up white Australia. It was the growing militancy of Aborigines who were no longer willing to accept the scraps from affluent Australians. It was black people who started saying that it was white, and not black Australia that was the problem. It was the black movement which made white conscious of their own conditioning". (OCCR 1979:20, emphasis added)

There are many examples of how Aboriginal People themselves are taking control of their own and their childrens' lives and changing the educational system. Through valiant community and individual efforts, Aboriginal People have finally gained access to primary, secondary, vocational, and even tertiary education. Some are even succeeding, with the rare Aboriginal graduate in education, law or medicine. At least there is hope.

> One day an historian will write a fully integrated history, in which the account of black/white relationships in this country will be shown to reflect and to have helped shape the Australia of today which true history seeks to explain. Until then, Aborigines will remain as much on the fringe of our history as they do on the fringe of our present society. (Hill and Barlow 1978:n.292)[48]

---

[48] Some of the best examples of such "integrated" histories are found in the writings of Associate Professor Henry Reynolds, of James Cook University.

In spite of a dismal record to date, the Australian educational system has the potential to nurture recent initiatives and fully encourage young minds and lives towards true egalitarian and just learning. It can lead the way in racism awareness for generations to come.

Media Contribute to Racism

The Australian media contribute to racism. Even the former Australian Federal Race Discrimination Commissioner, Irene Moss, admits this. In her own words,

> The Australian media are guilty of racist stereotyping and contributing to racial tensions. (Powell 1992:11)

The Australian media contribute to racism in their one-sided reporting, their offensive language, their inflammatory rhetoric, their irresponsible supervision, and their blatant excuses for racism (cf. Grant-Taylor 1993:5).

One-Sided Reporting

Aboriginal People are continually portrayed by the media in negative terms. Race Discrimination Commissioner Moss continues:

> . . . the [Australian] media tended not to print positive stories about minorities. Headlines such as War Zone (referring to Redfern), Black Terror and Black Crime Wave were socially irresponsible. (Hill and Barlow 1978)

If the general public has only negative images of Aboriginal People, how can it ever hope to know the complex realities of daily life for Aboriginal People? How can its understanding of the Indigenous People ever transcend the skin-deep colour politics of Australia?

Offensive Language

A major newspaper once ran a story with the title, "How the People of the Top End Will Commemorate their *Blackest* Day." One might expect this kind of language to have been used in the time of James Cook (late 1700s), or perhaps the time before federation (middle and late 1800s), but the appalling fact is that it ran in one of the nation's major papers, the *Sydney Morning Herald,* in 1992 (SMH 25 January 1992:20)! In 1994— almost two years later, and after running numerous articles on the United Nations International Year for the World's Indigenous People—the same newspaper ran an article with this opening statement.

Thalidomide—the drug that represents one of the *blackest* marks in the history of medicine—is about to be redeemed . . .. (Ewing 1994:4, emphasis added)

In fact, these are not isolated incidents of racist and offensive language. There are many such examples being published every day in Australia. What is worse, this kind of thing is not isolated to certain parts of the country. In Western Australia, Perth's only daily newspaper has been described in the following terms.

. . . over the years its reporting on Aboriginal affairs has been at best inconsistent and, at worst, has confirmed racist stereotypes. (Brady 1993:13)

Nor is this racism limited to certain types of media. Indeed, offensive language much worse than this has been quite common on Australian radio. A recent study revealed that a popular radio program and its broadcasting station (i.e., 6PR) are

. . . inciting racial hostility towards Aboriginal citizens in Western Australia.
. . . promot[ing] the most bigoted ideas about Aboriginal cultural heritage to the public.
. . . reinforc[ing] stereotypes of Aboriginal people that underpin racist and discriminatory treatment of them, in some cases with deadly consequences.
. . . arguabl[y] . . . manufacturing "public opinion" out of a tiny section of a non-representative audience. (Mickler 1992:[iii])

Inflammatory Rhetoric

It does not seem to be enough to be simply "offensive"; some need to "walk the second mile" and be outright inflammatory! For example, one of the largest-circulation daily papers in Australia, the *Sunday Telegraph,* recently ran this editorial:

Migrant Fodder for the Dole Queue
. . . The focus of the [migration] debate should not necessarily be on quantity, but rather of the quality of migrants. Migrants with high levels of job skills are the migrants Australia needs. The Government should look at reducing the quota if it cannot ensure that it will be filled by highly-skilled, employable migrants. Given the prevailing economic climate, unskilled migrants are little more than cannon fodder for the dole queue. (Miller 1992:48)

What kind of behaviour can we expect, if this is the kind of "informed opinion" millions of people are receiving from the media? Is it that newspapers are playing on racial tension and hatred? Could it be that newspapers are manipulating the emotions of people, in order to gain profit?

Irresponsible Supervision

In 1989, intensive investigations were launched into the program standards and broadcast practices of two major radio stations, in relation to racism. One station, 2GB, was investigated "following allegations in the Senate yesterday about links between an announcer, Brian Wilshire, and the extreme right-wing League of Rights" (SMH 1989:2). The other station, 2KY, was investigated by the Australian Broadcast Tribunal due to irresponsible supervision of their personnel and programs resulting in major public complaints of racism. It was reprimanded "for allowing racist remarks by a talkback host Ron Casey to go to air" (*Australian* 1989:2) and then ordered to broadcast and publish the reprimand. It is disturbing that irresponsible supervision of racism causes such humiliating inquiries and punitive measures in this "lucky country." Yet, private research and reports indicate these are not isolated incidents; indeed, similar media racism continues in other states (cf. Mickler 1992). Turn on some radio station somewhere in Australia, and racist views continue to be propagated.

Excusing Racism

A generally prestigious national magazine, *The Bulletin,* recently published an article containing this statement by a self-titled "social researcher":

> Our multi-racialism is established beyond doubt. But now, we are trying to cope with a new concept: multiculturalism. . . . Needless to say, we are having a great deal of short-term difficulty with the proposal that we should redefine our cultural identity, and *outbreaks of racism* and nostalgic yearnings for the cultural simplicities of earlier periods in our history *are perfectly understandable.* (Mackay 1991:36, emphasis added)

Such blatant and calloused discounting of racism is what fans the flames of its existence and destructive power. Firstly, "outbreaks" of racism are not acceptable—full stop. Secondly, equating "outbreaks of racism" with "nostalgic yearnings" is offensive in the extreme and reveals a blinding ignorance of both culture and history, especially in a country where "earlier periods in *our* history" are filled with countless massacres of Aboriginal People and genocidal destruction of their culture. Thirdly, the fact that such a derogatory opinion is published in a national magazine, and specifically in an article reviewing "the Australian character," gives it an implicit endorsement and shows the general public that it is worthy not only of serious consideration, but also of acceptance. This action is inflammatory and racist, in and of itself.

Importantly, these are but very few examples of the daily bombardment of subtle and not-so-subtle negative stereotypes we receive from television, radio and print media. To be "Australian" is to give up outdated vestiges of "the old country" and become white European (read British) in our thoughts, words and actions. The media reinforce this in what they define as news, what they tell us is important and what they suggest we think, read, buy and want. The media keep up a façade of self-regulation, but when criticized claim all manner of rights and freedoms— rights and freedoms which they do not allow to minority peoples or dissenting opinions.

It is clear that the Australian mass media are in need of vast reform. Ray Martin, a noted television personality and member of the federal Council for Aboriginal Reconciliation, stated in a recent interview,

> All journalists have an obligation to tell what they know about racism and about the achievements of Aborigines and of people of non-English speaking background. (*Ethnos* 1992:9)

Racism in the Australian media (or any media for that matter) is simply not acceptable. Someday, perhaps, the Australian media could provide unmatched leadership in racism awareness and education.

Society Contributes to Racism

Australian society itself contributes to racism. As far back as 1841, Sir George Grey, Colonial Governor, wrote:

> If we enquire into the causes which tend to retain them [Aboriginal People] in their present depressed condition, we shall find that the chief one is— "prejudice". (Reynolds 1989:144)

In the time since these words were written, the situation has not changed much. Many Aboriginal leaders still consider Australian society to be racist (e.g., Lagan October 1993:3A). This is evident in the great chasm between Australian self-image and reality, the presence and activities of right-wing and explicitly racist groups and, perhaps most clearly, in the 1993 High Court Native Title (Mabo) decision.

Self-Image vs. Reality

Racism is deeply embedded in the Australian psyche (cf. Immigration Reform Group 1962:116; Encel 1971:30; ACC 1981:8; *Special Treatment* 1991; See 1991:13; Devine 1992:17–18; Lagan October 1993:3A).

Australia's self-perceived identity confirms this quite clearly. In the words of renowned Australian historian, Professor Manning Clark:

> We are all inheritors of the Australian Dream and that has at least two manifestations. One is that in Australia blood will never stain the wattle. The absence of civil wars and revolutions has been one of our boasts. That was relatively easy so long as there was one dominant group in Australia, *so long as violence against the Aborigines did not count.* (Clark 1988:10–11)

> ... when Aborigines were massacred during the colonisation of Queensland, the acts were simply described as "frontier expansion"; when the people of Mapoon were forcibly evicted from their homes, the act was described as "resettlement"; when Aboriginal lands are taken for mineral exploitation, the process is simply called "development". (P. Wilson 1985:96)

Even fifty years ago, overseas visitors could see the "blind spot." Noted clergyman E. Stanley Jones once commented:

> I thought before I came to your shores that the Aboriginal was just dying off; I did not know that he was *being killed off.*
> ... You have taken away his means of subsistence, the land, without compensation. . . . Justice between the white man and the Aboriginal has been unequal. . . . You have infected the natives with the white man's diseases, mostly venereal, which have decimated them. . . . The lie that has been at the basis of all this has been that the Aboriginal is so low that he is unfit to survive.
> ... I have heard it said on several platforms since my arrival that no blood has been shed in the conquest of this land, and swords have never been crossed here. A casualty list of 240,000 and yet no blood shed? Each nation has its blind spot, and this is Australia's blind spot. (E. S. Jones 1943:5–6)

One scholar has described "four aspects of racialism which have been particularly important in Australian social development":

> (i)   Fear of the "Asian hordes" or the "yellow peril."
> (ii) Discrimination against, and repressive treatment of Aborigines. . . .
> (iii) Suspicion of separate ethno-cultural identity among immigrant groups.
> (iv) Solidarity with the white racialist regimes of Southern Africa. (Encel 1971:30)[49]

---

[49] Support for South Africa was seen in support for the British during colonial wars; liberal immigration policies; trade, cultural and sporting exchanges; etc. While in more recent times the connection with South Africa has been less evident it seems that this has only been a passing moralistic phase in that, before the 1994 elections, Australia already had begun to gear-up its formal and informal relations to South Africa against the expressed wishes of many groups there, notably the South African Council of Churches.

The facts indicate, very strongly, that even the Australian people consider themselves racist. The *National Times* "Survival of White Australia" Survey revealed:

> In 1981, 49 per cent agreed that Australians were racist in their attitudes. (Sipka 1984:11)[50]

A simple exercise will illustrate Australian racism. A 1991 article in *The Bulletin* described the ten best and worst elements of the Australian character (B. Jones 1991:27–29). Among the best elements were:

1. Generosity. There is a tradition of personal kindness. . . . We are generous donors to charity. . . . We wish the government gave far more in overseas aid and would pay more tax to fund it.

5. Professional excellence. Our medical services are among the best in the world . . .

6. Egalitarianism. . . . Australia appears to be a classless society because . . . there is a high degree of homogeneity in social behaviour . . .

9. Loyalty. We are loyal to our mates, our political party, our football team, our family, our locality . . .

10. Tolerance. . . . has helped to make multi-racial migration a success . . .

Among the worst elements were:

1. Passivity. We ignore challenges, or leave them to somebody else to take up. Lack of challenge leads to a lack of response . . .

4. Ambivalence about excellence/egalitarianism. . . . We have a long tradition of cutting down tall poppies . . .

5. Uncertainty about our own identity. . . . We won't address these issues until we work out who we are.

6. Inability to empathise with other cultures. We may once have benefited from isolation and the tyranny of distance, but not any more. A certain autism running through Australian society makes it very difficult for us to understand how it feels to be an Aborigine, a Japanese, a Brazilian or an Indian, and to attempt to come to terms with them on their ground.

Interestingly, both the best and worst elements reveal racism, arrogance and self-delusion in the Australian character.

In relation to the "best" elements:

1. Generosity: If Australians are so *generous,* why do many, many Aboriginal People still live in "third world" conditions in this paragon of

---

[50] This does not even include additional data, documenting racism against migrants, refugees, or other groups. For example, a Queensland study concentrating on Asians found, ". . . that almost 50 per cent of Australians believe their fellow-citizens are racist"; Secord 1993:1.

"first world" progress?[51] Indeed, why are significant numbers of Aboriginal People "denied access to clean drinking water" (OT: Gilbert 1991; HREOC 1988:61; cf. Parker 8 April 1992:7; HREOC 1994)?

5. Professional Excellence: If indeed "our medical services are among the best in the world," then why do Aboriginal People suffer some of the highest rates in the world of infant mortality, malnutrition, hepatitis B, diabetes, trachoma (i.e., *curable* blindness), hearing loss, tuberculosis, parasitic infestations, leprosy, etc. If indeed our professions are so excellent, why do statistical studies (and Aboriginal life testimonies) prove continually that we have been excluded from housing, safety, education, employment, law and justice, positive media, politics, development and free religious expression?[52]

6. Egalitarianism: Why do Aboriginal People in Australian police and prison custody suffer *the highest rates in the world* of imprisonment and death (cf. Cunneen 1991:204–18; Cunneen 1992:351–55; Pattel-Gray 1991a:132–35)?

9. Loyalty: The Australian Pocket Oxford Dictionary states that "loyal" comes from the Latin word *legalis,* or legal, and defines "loyal" as "faithful (to); true to . . . ; devoted to . . ." How can Australians be "loyal" to anyone or anything if the entire continent was stolen and is today held on the now demythologized *legal fiction* of *terra nullius,* the continuous occupation of the land is based on force, the government stands devoid of integrity—having promised a treaty time and again—and the popular culture and educational systems propagate lies, injustice and racism?

10. Tolerance: Why did the recent *National Inquiry into Racist Violence in Australia* conducted by the Human Rights and Equal Opportunity Commission find that Aboriginal and Torres Strait Islander people and people of non-English speaking backgrounds suffer high levels of racist violence, intimidation and harassment (HREOC 1991:387–89)?

In relation to the "worst" elements,

---

[51] Even Australian trade unions are not immune to the charge of racism: The Australian Workers' Union "refused to admit Aborigines to membership . . . until 1969"; Encel 1971:36.

[52] These are amply documented by the Australian Government in their Department of Aboriginal Affairs *Annual Reports,* and now their Aboriginal and Torres Strait Islander Commission *Annual Reports.* Of course, there are notable exceptions, such as the tremendous work of Dr. Fred Hollows, who spent much of his life curing infectious eye diseases amongst Aboriginal People. If we had a few more professionals like him, perhaps we would not suffer such high rates of illness.

1. Passivity: What are we doing to combat passivity, or are we too passive to do anything about it?

4. Ambivalence about excellence/egalitarianism: What is wrong with a tall poppy or two, especially if they are Aboriginal or of a non-English speaking background? Could we not report *complete* implementation of *any* of the 67 recommendations of the *Report of the National Inquiry into Racist Violence in Australia,* or is our "excellence" only related to how the "majority" (white) population is treated?

5. Uncertainty about our own identity: Why are we not admitting our past and present faults, addressing the tough issues and learning from the many rich traditions and cultures all around us in the Aboriginal People, immigrants and refugees?

6. Inability to empathise with other cultures: Why do we insist on propagating this myth of multi-culturalism if we are not willing to fully embrace it's implications?

This simple exercise shows the vast separation between the Australian self-image and the Australian reality. Australian society is racist, and it only can change when it faces this fact, and changes both its heart and its actions.

Right-Wing and Racist Groups

Beyond this basic difference between perception and reality, there is the very real presence in Australia today of far right-wing and explicitly racist groups. These vary tremendously, and include the Ku Klux Klan (cf. Lyons 1992:12–13, 15–17, 19); the League of Rights, Citizens Electoral Councils of Australia Group, LaRouche movement, Australian Nationalists Movement (Henderson 1994:70–74, 77–78, 81); and, the Church of the Creator (Henry 1994:73–74, 77–78). While specific numbers of participants vary—and while Australians may not admit it as fact—it is clear that these groups reflect racist tendencies in Australia.

Case Study: Native Title (Mabo) Judgement and Act

Australian society is full of examples of racism. Perhaps one of the clearest and most comprehensive is the recent social backlash against Aboriginal Native Title. This one example provides instances of racism from all sectors of Australian society—from government, to politicians, to the legal and educational systems, to the media and more. The non-Aboriginal (mostly white) backlash against Aboriginal Native Title bears further analysis as a case study in Australian racism.

Background

From the beginning of the European invasion of Australia in the late 1700s, Aboriginal People have been fighting for our land. At first, this was through direct, active resistance.[53] During the nineteenth and early twentieth centuries, Aboriginal resistance was expressed less directly—but no less actively. During the reign of the White Australia and Assimilation Policies, resistance often took the form of non-cooperation and passive resistance (e.g., in the missions and reserves), basic community organizing (e.g., the 1938 Day of Mourning), and strikes (e.g., the 1946 Pilbara pastoral strike), and others. More recently, Aboriginal resistance has taken the form of national and international actions for land rights. Many of these have challenged the legal and legislative bases of *terra nullius*.

Just four examples show Aboriginal resolve in this regard. First, in 1884, in Queensland, the Kalkadoons came to prominence in colonial Australia not because they were massacred, but because they fought a pitched *battle* against white Europeans at what is today remembered as Battle Mountain (LRN March 1988; cf. Loos 1982:58; F. Stevens 1981:109). Contrary to the white myth of "passive acceptance of their fate," a massive force of about 600 Kalkadoons fought to the last man (cf. R. Armstrong 1980:145). They gained notoriety in white eyes for their fierce resistance, but have been remembered by Aboriginal People throughout history as "heroic" (LRN March 1988).

Second, on 26 January 1938, Aboriginal People in New South Wales took the unheard-of step and published a strong manifesto entitled *Aborigines Claim Citizen Rights,* held an Aboriginal Conference and Day of Mourning and Protest in Sydney; they followed this up with a delegation which presented a ten point plan for Aboriginal equality to the Prime Minister (cf. Parbury 1986:107–12). Though they did not gain much positive action, the events generated significant public and media interest.

Third, on 1 May 1946, some 800 Aboriginal People took the unprecedented step of walking off a white station on strike in the northwestern Pilbara region of Western Australia (cf. McLeod 1984). The Aboriginal Pastoral Workers Strike lasted until August 1949, and made it abundantly clear that the pastoral industry indeed was dependent upon Aboriginal Peoples' labour.

---

[53] See previous references to Pemulwuy and other Aboriginal resistance leaders, as well as to the so-called "frontier wars"; cf., e.g., Reynolds 1982; et al.

Fourth, in 1972, Aboriginal People established the "Aboriginal Tent Embassy" in Canberra. This became a focal point for Aboriginal protests against denial of rights and abysmal "living" conditions and political inaction in Aboriginal affairs by both federal and state governments. This original Tent Embassy was taken down—violently—in full view of the national press, which created an international furore (cf. Parbury 1986:133). Twenty years later, in January 1992, Aboriginal People took over the old Parliament House in Canberra to commemorate the establishment of the first "Aboriginal Tent Embassy" (Austin 1992:3; J. Wilson 1992:1, 5).[54] A "Declaration of Aboriginal Sovereignty" was presented to the Federal Minister for Aboriginal Affairs, and a few hours later all protesters were thrown out by federal police and four Aboriginals were arrested, laying the groundwork for subsequent appeals to the Australian High Court and the International Court of Justice in the Hague (Chamberlin 29 January 1992:3).

These are just four of the many instances that show the solid mettle of the Aboriginal pursuit of justice. These, and many other cases like them, laid the groundwork for the land rights struggles that were to come.

Land Rights Struggles

In the last four decades, the Aboriginal struggle for justice has become much more focused on land rights. In that time, Aboriginal People have taken bold actions against governments and in the courts of white Australian law. Not surprisingly, until 1992, *all* of these actions were unsuccessful—in law.

In 1963, the people of Yirrkala, on the Gove Peninsula in North East Arnhem Land, Northern Territory, sent a bark petition to the Federal Parliament.

The Humble Petition of the undersigned Aboriginal people of Yirrkala . . . [shows that we] pray that no arrangements be entered into with any company which will destroy the livelihood and independence of the Yirrkala people. (Reynolds 1989:85–86)

Though the petition was highly publicized, it nevertheless was ignored, and a church-backed multinational corporation began massive bauxite mining operations that ripped-up the traditional lands of the Yolngu People. Importantly, the case drew significant attention to Arnhem Land (cf. Williams 1987). Yet, unbelievably, things got worse.

---

[54] See also television, radio and print reports (e.g., ABC) for coverage of both events.

> In 1971, the Northern Territory Supreme Court determined that they had no
> legal rights to their traditional land. (Reynolds 1989:86)

The year before (1970), the Aborigines Advancement League had sent
a petition to the Secretary-General of the United Nations.

> This is an urgent plea of several hundred thousand so-called "Aborigines" of
> Australia that the United Nations use its legal and moral powers for the
> vindication of our rights to the lands which we have traditionally occupied.
> (Reynolds 1989:86–87)

This plea too went unheeded.

As direct appeal was failing, Aboriginal People began to try their hand
in the High Court of Australia. For their efforts, they have gained nothing
but frustration. For example, in 1971 the Yolngu People took their
concerns to the High Court in the landmark case, *Milirrpum v. Nabalco,*
but were denied justice (cf. *Milirrpum v. Nabalco Pty. Ltd.* (1971) 17 F.L.R.
141). In 1978, Aboriginal People from the southern part of the country
returned to the High Court in *Coe v. Commonwealth,* but again were
defeated in (Western) law (cf. *Coe v. Commonwealth* (1978) 18 A.L.R. 592,
and *Coe v. Commonwealth* (1978) 24 A.L.R. 118). In 1982, in *Koowarta v.
Bjelke-Petersen,* Aboriginal People made a historic gain in law that was only
limited in its impact (cf. Hanks and Keon-Cohen 1984:61–64), and did
not yield title for the traditional owners (cf. Brennan 1992a:1–2). Indeed,
until 1992, every major case had seen substantive defeat for the
Indigenous People of Australia.

The 1992 High Court Native Title (Mabo) Case

All this changed, however, when in June 1992, the Aboriginal People
finally won a case in this area of law. Ten years earlier, five Indigenous
People from the Murray Islands in the Torres Strait, off the northern tip
of Australia, set in motion what has become one of the single most
significant legal challenges to the Australian nation-state. These plaintiffs

> brought an action against the [Australian] State of Queensland for declarations
> that the [indigenous] Meriam people were entitled to the Islands as owners,
> possessors, occupiers or as persons entitled to use and enjoy the Islands; . . .
> and that the State of Queensland was *not* entitled to extinguish the title of the
> Meriam people. ([1992] 175 C.L.R. 1 at 2)

In a landmark decision, *Mabo v. Queensland* ([1992] 175 C.L.R. 1)—
notably not unanimous—, the High Court of Australia declared:

the Meriam people are entitled *as against the whole world* to possession, occupation, use and enjoyment of the lands of the Murray Islands. ([1992] 175 C.L.R. 1 at 2)

Further, the judgement by Justice Brennan stated,

The common law of this country would perpetuate injustice if it were to continue to embrace the enlarged notion of terra nullius . . .. ([1992] 175 C.L.R. 1 at 57–58)

In other words, *terra nullius* was dead. After ten years of legal wrangling, during which time even one of the plaintiffs in the case died, the High Court decided to end the myth: British *claims* to sovereignty did not extinguish *native title* to the land (Chamberlin 1 February 1992:21).[55]

The Redfern Statement

In December of 1992, Prime Minister Paul Keating made a historic speech at the Australian launch of the United Nations "International Year for the World's Indigenous People" (Keating 1993). In this speech, he raised a storm of controversy by accepting "white guilt" in the *dispossession* and *murder* of Aboriginal People, and by making unprecedented statements of support for Aboriginal People's rights (Keating 1992).

In a "post-Mabo" Australia, this kind of daring speech by an Australian Prime Minister shocked non-Aboriginal society in ways never before seen.

The Public Reaction: Racism!

The High Court decision on Native Title, discarding the myth of *terra nullius,* as well as the acknowledgement by the Prime Minister of white injustices, drew immediate and strong reactions from the Australian public—including shocking displays of racism.[56] People from all walks of life seemed unable to restrain themselves, and poured out vicious statements of hatred, fear and misconception (cf. M. Dodson 1993:13–16). This could have been expected from those with direct economic interests in specific areas of land (e.g., mining companies, pastoralists and farmers), but the surprise was that it came from all sectors of Australian society—from "the person on the street" to newspaper editorials, to public figures, even to former Prime Ministers!

---

[55] This decision could alter radically the land rights struggle in Australia; cf. FAIRA 1992. Indeed, the full impact of this legal milestone upon the rest of Australian society will take some time to be determined; cf. *Age* 1992:10; Forman 1992:48–49; T. Treadgold 1992:46–51.

[56] The documentation is widely available in the media, and is far too substantive even to attempt to list here.

Fear-mongering, omissions and distortions of fact were the order of the day. Australians made wildly inaccurate charges that Aboriginal People were trying to "get my backyard" (cf. Nettheim 1994:1), working to the economic detriment to the nation (cf. Hugh Morgan quoted in Sproull 1994:17; Hextall 1993:43),[57] and setting up "reverse racism." Certain groups went as far as producing or sponsoring extremely offensive print, radio and television advertisements, venting extraordinary prejudice.

Needless to say, these actions crushed the immediate hopes for justice for Aboriginal People across the country. If such basic moves toward justice for the Aboriginal People as a court decision and a politicians' speech can spark such public fury surrounding such a fundamental issue as Native Title, then it is clear that Australians have not come to terms with either their dispossession of the Indigenous People or their racism that prolongs "the lies."

Public Stands on Native Title

The Native Title debate has people taking very public stands in the issues involved. With quite bizarre similarity, groups as far apart as religious and social leaders and mining executives have signed their names to very public documents, published far and wide across Australia. On the one hand, efforts such as "Native Title and Australia's Future" (part of a very expensive series of full-page advertisements in the nation's major newspapers) pulls together the heads of such corporations as CRA, MIM Holdings, Shell Australia and (the ever-present) Western Mining to "express concern" (AMIC 1993:16).

On the other hand, efforts such as "A Call for Reconciliation" draws together everyone from the Anglican Archbishop of Perth to the Director of the Baptist Peace Fellowship to the Western Australian Senator for the Greens, in an effort to "demonstrate commitment."

> . . . we call on the Christian community in Australia to respect Aboriginal culture and spirituality. We also express our solidarity with Aboriginals and

---

[57] It is interesting to note that less than one month earlier, Paul Reardon, senior international resource analyst for Moody's Investors Service, had stated that, ". . . native title has *not* affected the credit quality of *any* of the Australian companies we offer ratings on"—which include BHP, CRA and *Western Mining Corp.*; M. Stevens 1994:17, emphasis added. It is even more fascinating to know that two months earlier, the Australian Mining Industry Council, a major voice in the mining sector, released the results of its annual survey indicating that, "Expenditure on mining, smelting and refining assets is expected to *increase by 14 per cent* next year to *$3.1 billion,*" Hextall 1993:43, emphasis added.

Islanders in their quest for justice, self-determination and land rights, which should not be understood as land "granted" gratuitously but as land restored belatedly! (Carnley, et al. 1993:3)

Fortunately, some of the positive efforts are yielding fruit. The Australian churches are a prime example.

Church Actions on Native Title

The Christian Churches in Australia have come together on the issue of Native Title as never before. (cf. Matthews 1993:2)

One source of hope in the Native Title debate has been the supportive actions taken by the churches. In impressive displays of ecumenical cooperation, the churches have come together to stand in solidarity with the Aboriginal People. They have made public statements, lobbied politicians and legislators, organized conferences and study groups, published study materials and more.

The Native Title Act 1993 and the Future

The Native Title (Mabo) decision became part of Australian law as the *Native Title Act 1993* came into force on 1 January 1994. The Act recognizes Native Title rights. Determinations of Native Title will be made by the National Native Title Tribunal and the Federal Court of Australia.

The Significance of Native Title

For Aboriginal and Torres Strait Islander People, native title may provide less security and fewer rights than a statutory title—such as the inalienable freehold title available to traditional owners under the provisions of the Aboriginal Land Rights (Northern Territory) Act 1976. Nevertheless, the confirmation of native title has great symbolic importance for Australia's [I]ndigenous [P]eople: it is a title not granted or given by the Crown; it preceded colonisation; and has survived the assertion of sovereignty by foreigners. (ATSIC 1994:7)

The Act is a first step toward addressing the injustices of over two-hundred years of European colonization and subjugation of the Indigenous Peoples of this land. However, Aboriginal People still struggle for more than just words on paper. We require the enactment of visible justice in our country, where Aboriginal People have a pride of place and heritage that not only can be shared but also respected.

Further action needed toward the cementing of a just reconciliation is the current issue of debate. The Native Title Act will establish a "National Aboriginal and Torres Strait Islander Land Fund," for the purpose of enabling dispossessed Indigenous People who will not benefit from the Act to acquire land. In addition, the Australian Federal Government is finalizing plans for a major "Social Justice Package" (cf. M. Dodson November 1993:13; M. Dodson December 1993), which will provide resources to redress needs in such basic human rights areas as water, housing, medical care and education.

The Native Title judgement and Act, as two elements of a case study in Australian racism, reveal some very disturbing realities for contemporary society, yet ones with the very real possibility of transcending "abstract words" (cf. M. Dodson 1993:35). Some Australians have stood against the racism expressed by all sectors of the Australian society on the occasion of the Native Title decision. Some have shown that solid leadership for justice for Aboriginal People offers hope to the nation. In short, the Native Title judgement and Act could be catalysts for recognition of the rights of Australia's Indigenous Peoples to both land and social justice.

Summary

Clearly Australian society has some questions for which it must answer—to itself and to all of the people which comprise it, as well as to the global community. It has some very grave problems to address and, in view of the life-and-death situation of many of its people, not much time to do it.

In summary, Australian society is saturated with racism, from the government, to the politicians, to the business community, to the legal, police and prison systems, to the academic world and education systems, to the media.

Yet, this is not the only place where Australian racism is evident. Racism also is found in the Australian church.

CHAPTER 3
RACISM IN THE AUSTRALIAN CHURCH

The Rev. Dr. George D. Kelsey, Professor of Religion and Philosophy at Morehouse College, once stated that

> racism is a phenomenon of modern *Christian* civilization. By and large, the people who have been the racists of the modern world have also been Christians or the heirs of Christian civilization. (1965:10)

A decade and a half later, the Hon. Don Dunstan, former Premier of South Australia, said:

> the churches should stop simply making pious noises about racism and *do* something effective about it. (1980:5, emphasis added)

Both the noted theologian and the noted politician were right, and both statements apply—*directly*—to Australia. For over two centuries in Australia, European "Christians or the heirs of Christian civilization" have contributed to racism against the indigenous Aboriginal People. From the very beginning of contact, the outsiders brought this "phenomenon of modern *Christian* civilization" and planted it firmly on Australian soil. They nurtured it, gave it plenty of opportunity to grow, rationalized it, defended it, and even passed it on to their children. Over time—and in the face of considerable pressure, both internal and external—the Australian church eventually began "making pious noises about racism."[1] Yet, today, racism is alive and well in the Australian church. The fact that racism still is not only present in the Australian church, but also vigorously denied by it, is a sign that the churches have failed to "*do* something effective about it." Worse, it is a sign that they are not even in touch with the pervasive and corrosive effect racism has on harmonious and just social relations. Perhaps worst of all, it is a sign that the Australian church is not willing to deal with its own sin of racism. This chapter traces the history and current situation of the abominable reality of racism in the Australian church.

---

[1] For the sake of simplicity, this chapter will use the term "Australian church" as including individual Australian Christians and Australian church-related organizations.

Background:
The Australian Church Contributed to Racism

Jesus Christ stood for equality of, and justice for, all peoples. One would logically assume, then, that Christian people would believe and stand for the same things. Yet, in the name of Christianity, white Euro-Australians have committed all manner of horrors upon Aboriginal People. Their beliefs in a loving, living God must have somehow "fallen" off the ships as they travelled the oceans on their journeys to the Great South Land.

In the words of Alice Briggs:

> as far as Christianity is concerned, well our people's way of life was based on Christianity. They knew Christ *long before* white people ever come to Australia. (Gilbert 1977:53–54, emphasis added)

Throughout the New Testament, Jesus condemned the Pharisees and the law-keepers because continually they were twisting the laws to suit themselves. Their actions had nothing to do with what God was teaching them. Jesus spoke clearly about partiality, condemning any kind of preference for the rich over the poor (Jas. 2). In the story of Lazarus and the rich man (Lk. 16:19–31), the message is clear—the faithful servant receives fruits for his service and the unfaithful servant is punished. While we see that God and Christ fought for the liberation of the poor and oppressed, we also see clearly that the Australian Christians and their churches fought for the rich and the powerful.

In the words of noted Aboriginal theologian, the late Rev. Charles Harris:

> Christianity practised in this country is definitely *not* New Testament Christianity. . . . The massacres and the genocides that took place in the name of Christianity and God are part of the colonisation in this country. (Harris 26 February 1992:19, emphasis added)

The Australian church contributed to racism through its roots, heresies, theological imperialism, hypocrisy, collusion with the Government, and its tacit and often active support of racist institutions, individuals, theology and teachings, and violence.

Australian Racism's Roots in European Society and Church

The Australian colony and church were founded upon the principles and practices of the European society and church of the late eighteenth century. Thus, it is not too difficult to discern that Australian racism has its roots in the racism of the European church and society. It is important, then, to trace those roots.

With the European Reformation came tremendous advances in human knowledge. A first pivotal fact is that Western scientific theory developed the idea that

> the material world is composed of lifeless material bodies acted upon by immaterial forces. . . . nature, which had been experienced in previous eras as an organismic and direct unity, is abstracted and made remote. . . . This, then, has become the elementary belief of Western man [sic]. (Kovel 1970:109–10)

This basic abstraction was then applied to the world, creating immense material wealth for the West and transforming

> an intermediate stage of scientific understanding into a philosophical truth, and beyond that, into the substance of Western man's [sic] belief about the basic structure of the world. (Kovel 1970:111)

A second pivotal fact is that Western economic theory "made the world a market" (Kovel 1970:112). Here the idea of "property" was deeply imbued—"things" could be "owned," "work" could be "owned," "capital" could be "created." A third pivotal fact is that the Western religious belief (the Church) lost its power to bind together and shape society, due to its corruption and greed (Kovel 1970:123). The Reformation found a new moral restraint: Luther came up with "direct access to God" (Kovel 1970:124), and Calvin with "the spirit having to *prove* itself to God" (Kovel 1970:127). All these factors combined in an ever-increasing cycle of abstraction and rationalization.

> Through the expedient of abstraction, most forcefully expressed in Calvinist theology, a God-symbol arose to justify individual suffering by turning it to economic use in the complusions of work without pleasure and gain without joy. (Kovel 1970:137)

Europeans believed that work not only created wealth, but also made them virtuous. So, European life—Catholic as well as Protestant—began to focus upon, and be driven by, a "work ethic" and the geometric expansion of the market. This brought the age of exploration and the dawn of the colonial era. The lands encountered became sources of raw materials or markets, and the Peoples (often black) became "property," to be *used* in the creation of wealth. Indigenous and black Peoples became black bodies, which became less-than-human commodities to be owned, exploited, traded or destroyed at whim. The enslavement of black Peoples became "a given" of European "civilization."[2] European society and church not only accepted this state of affairs, but also blessed and expanded it.

This "psycho-historical matrix" (Kovel 1970:139–75), was the very root of European society and church. This is the *Weltanschauung* that was transported to the Australian colony and church, and transposed—often by force—on to the Aboriginal Peoples of Australia.[3]

For example, European missionaries believed and enforced upon Aboriginal People that the expression of an individual's Christianity was evident through their practical and profitable labours.

> The Aborigines were expected to express their Christian commitment in the manner in which they undertook their duties. Work lay at the core of the missionary scheme of things. . . . The concept of regular work for rations (or [meagre] pay), integral to capitalism, was also taught to them, a notion of exchange very different from the traditional rights and obligations of Aboriginal society. (cf. Attwood 1989:23)

It is not difficult to see that these racist roots would take hold in Europe's "Australian experiment," and would lead to further distortions and aberrations—especially in relation to the church (cf. Attwood 1989:1).

Australian Church Racism Was Heretical

The English word "heresy" comes from the Greek *hairesis,* meaning "choice." The Australian Pocket Oxford Dictionary defines heresy as

> Opinion contrary to doctrine of Christian Church or to accepted doctrine on any subject. (Turner 1984:327)

If we take the "doctrine of the Christian church" to be based upon that which Jesus taught the disciples and the early believers, then, in essence, the Christianity practised in Australia was heretical right from the start because of its roots in European social and ecclesial racism. Australian history shows the church establishing a consistent pattern of "choice against" the indigenous Australian race known as the Aboriginal People. Australian church racism was heretical because it violated not only many of the direct teachings of Christ—for example, in relation to "loving your

---

2 For a fuller discussion of slavery, see W. L. Rose 1982, and S. M. Elkins 1959; in comparison, for more on the enslavement of Peoples in the Americas, see Bartolomé de las Casas 1966.

3 For a discussion of related, contemporary "development ideology," see, Coombs, McCann, Ross and Williams 1989:3–5.

neighbour" (cf. Matt. 22:34–40), and to having faith, hope and love (cf. I Cor. 13)—but also many of the doctrines of the Christian Church (creation, incarnation, resurrection, etc.), and "accepted doctrines" (e.g., truth and justice) (cf. Adler 1974:9).

In a more explicitly theological vein, heresy also has been defined as

> any activity or teaching that contradicts the liberating truth of Jesus Christ. . . . the refusal to speak the truth or to live the truth in the light of the One who is the Truth. (Cone 1975:36)

Here, again, Australian history provides more than enough evidence to substantiate claims of heresy against the Australian church because of its more than two centuries of racism against and subjugation of the Indigenous Peoples it encountered. The Australian church, in its activities and teachings, continually contradicted the liberating truth of Jesus Christ. It refused to speak the truth in the face of dispossession, massacres, cultural genocide, physical and mental tortures of many kinds, and more. It refused to live the truth in the light of the One who is the Truth; that is it chose to live, not in truth, but rather in the lie of racism against the Aboriginal People.

The heresy of racism pervaded the Australian church—from its theology, right throughout its Christology, to its exegesis and hermeneutics, ecclesiology, missiology, discourse and praxis. Each of these areas is addressed below.

Theology

Noted theologian S. C. Guthrie defines theology as "the quest for the ultimate truth about God, about ourselves and about the world we live in" (1968:11).

Taking this definition as an illustrative starting point, we clearly see that the Australian church believed, propagated and implemented a theology that was heretical, as it did not search for the ultimate truth but rather stopped short in the netherworld of racism, genocide and oppression against Australian Aboriginal People. The Australian church's theology did not seek for the ultimate truth: 1) "about God"—especially as God was found amongst the Aboriginal People and our unique cultural, ceremonial, linguistic, artistic and other traditional expressions; 2) "about ourselves"—for it did not question the quasi-theological rationalizations Europeans used for the wanton massacres and other abuses of Aboriginal People; or, 3) "about the world we live in"—since, from the very beginning of contact, it had vested interests in the religio-political drama being played out in the colonial enterprise. Australian church theology always has been caught in the trap of justifying the ferocious colonization machinery that protected and defended its very existence in the colony, through its similarly—but certainly not admittedly—ferocious missionization policies and practices.

As a case in point, it is common knowledge (and, indeed, well-documented) that the Anglican church had a very close relationship to the political structure of the colonies—to the point that it was recognized as the "establishment" church, and that it "defended its territory" against intruders, such as the Wesleyans (cf. Brook and Kohen 1991:108–9).[4] For years, the Anglicans had a virtual monopoly over what might be called the "religious rights" to the colonies. How could it criticize or question atrocities against Aboriginal People, when it was part of the colonial system that committed them—however indirectly? How could it "seek truth," when it seems to have been more politically expedient for the church to set up territorial and denominational perimeters and "spheres of influence"? How could it stand with integrity, when it was establishing racial boundaries, and laying the foundations of individual and institutional racism in Australia?

A theology resulting in racism is directly contrary to the doctrines established by Christ himself. Such theology was heretical—a "choice" against several doctrines of the Christian Church. This can be seen in any number of areas.

Guthrie indicates that "the task of theology" is, "to understand the truth about God, [hu]man[ity] and the world as it is made known, believed and experience in (1) Jesus Christ, (2) the Bible, (3) the church" (1968:20).

Again, taking this framework, we clearly see that the Australian church's theology had no real interest in pursuing any of these areas, but rather was tangled up in its own cultural imperialism and racism. The experience of Aboriginal People, as well as the abundant historical evidence, confirms this.

Christology

In many ways, Jesus Christ was a stranger to the Europeans who claimed to be bringing "Christianity" to Australia.

---

4 For more on Protestantism and politics, see, e.g., Bollen 1972.

The understanding of Jesus of Nazareth has been strongly influenced by the image of the Western man [sic]. Accordingly, in artistic depictions of Jesus and in assumptions about his personality and behaviour much has been read into the New Testament that was derived from European and American culture. He became the white Jesus, alien and unrecognizable for the peoples in Africa, Asia and elsewhere. (WCC 1975:5)

The European so-called "Christians" did not bring The Christ, the Anointed One; they did not share a liberating Christ with the Aboriginal People of Australia. Rather, they brought a "christ" that saved and liberated only the white colonists but not the black Indigenous Peoples, who were considered to be non-human or, at best, "a relic of the childhood of the race preserved by Australia's isolation" (Reynolds 1989:114). Australian theology brought a christ that dispossessed, enslaved and killed; a christ full of hatred and fear; a christ of racism.

Australian theology did not teach or share with Aboriginal People about a Christ that was "about his creative, reconciling, renewing work" (Guthrie 1968:21), for it was too busy seeking to justify the "dividing walls of hostility" (cf. Ephes. 2:14) that quickly were being constructed—walls such as *terra nullius,* slavery and segregation. The "law of Christ" (Gal. 5:2), as the principle or norm of love for one another, was being broken continuously. The colonist christians did not bring the Christ of the Bible and, thus, The Story certainly was not The Good News.

Biblical Exegesis and Hermeneutics

The Australian Church practised racist heretical biblical exegesis and hermeneutics. Aboriginal Peoples' experiences of the transcendent were expected to be limited to white Western understandings. Indeed, their expressions of God, church, faith and life were forced into being limited to Euro-Australian ones (cf. Attwood 1989:1). Most European "Christians" actually came to prosper from the "new" land, but the presence of Indigenous Peoples restricted this process. Thus, Aboriginal People were taught falsehoods and heresies in order to rationalize the "takeover" of their land. The Australian church played right into this plan, with its racist heretical biblical exegesis and hermeneutics. From the very first missions to the later, more organized denominations, the Australian church "read out" the meaning of the actual text of the Bible in a way that distorted much more than just the words (cf. Reynolds 1989:5; Barrett 1966:196). The Biblical injunction found in Genesis 1:28 provides an excellent example.

God blessed them, and God said to them, "Be fruitful and *multiply,* and fill the earth and *subdue* it; and have *dominion* over the fish of the sea and over the birds of the air and over every living thing that moves upon the earth." (emphasis added)

Heretical European exegesis and hermeneutics turned this passage into a mandate for the "conquest" (colonization) of the land and the "dominion" (subjugation) of the "natives" (cf. C. Harris 1992:19; C. Harris 1996; Bolton 1992:11; Carne 1980). Reinforced by European racism and pretentions to "superiority," they supported the denigration of the black-skinned Indigenous Peoples. A passage that originally was intended to have humanity propagate the earth was twisted into one "justifying" theft, enslavement, imprisonment and more.

The Australian church had the benefit of literally thousands of years of analytical study of the Biblical text, complemented more recently by the development of critical tools (tools which would subsequently be refined into textual, historical, grammatical, literary, form, tradition and redaction criticism; Hayes and Holladay 1983:14–23). And, what did the Australian church do with all of this learning? It warped it to serve its own selfish desires.

Another outstanding example is found in the Australian churches' teaching of the heretical (so-called) "Curse of Ham" (OT: G. Paulson 1993; cf. Evans, Saunders and Cronin 1975:11–12)! One of the most notorious examples of Western theological deceit across Australia, this "church teaching" of the Hamitic curse supposedly condemned all "black-skinned peoples" to eternal inferiority, based on a very specific kind of interpretation of the story in Genesis 9:18–27.[5]

The Australian church made sure it told Aboriginal People about the supposedly negative biblical verses that cursed black people. It forgot to mention, however, that this so-called curse originates exclusively from one specific type of hermeneutics.

Further, it consistently and continuously omitted from its exegesis the numerous positive instances of black people—and people of colour—in the Biblical text (cf. Felder 1989; Felder 1991; Copher 1993).

The church established by Jesus taught and practised love and inclusiveness in the community of all people (John 3:16). The Australian church, however, taught—either directly, or by implication—that the

---

5 Sadly, some missionaries were quite efficient and a few older Aboriginals still believe they are condemned by God to be "less than whites"; cf. J. Harris 1990:658, n. 169.

people in the Bible were white, and that to be white was a good thing because it was to be "like God." Thus, until very recently, Aboriginal People never heard of the black identity of many biblical figures, such as Hagar, in Genesis 16 and 21 (Waters 1991:187–205); Moses' wife, in Numbers 12 (Felder 1989:42); Tirhaka, king of the Ethiopians and Pharaoh of all Egypt, in Isaiah 37:9 and II Kings 19:9 (Felder 1989:43; cf. Snowden 1970); the Queen of Sheba, in I Kings 10 (Felder 1989:32–36); Symeon, in Acts 13:1 (Felder 1989:47); and various others. Quite the contrary, black people in the Bible were portrayed by the Australian church to be either white or "colourless," or simply were avoided (OTs: Garrawurra 1992; G. Paulson 1992; I. Paulson 1992; C. Grant 1992; Harris 1992; D. Broome 1992). This kind of selective exegesis of the Bible kept Aboriginal People from having possible and positive role models (cf. Trompf 1987:7–9). It deprived them of the full and complete Biblical text, which showed blacks not only as full members of the community of believers, but also as wealthy people, leaders and rulers. It betrayed the church doctrine of "love your neighbour" because "some of the neighbours" were black. In short, its exegesis was racist—and heretical.

Ecclesiology

The Australian church was founded upon racist ecclesiology, which led to heresy. The church that was established in Australia included within its sphere of influence all people in the colony, but specifically excluded the Aboriginal People. Based upon this racist ecclesiological interpretation, one could ask what were the church's intentions and goals for the Indigenous People, because nowhere in Australian church history has the church ever stated that its intention was to raise up and develop independent black churches that could participate on equal grounds with other white churches. In fact, what we did see was the white church's clear intention—visible through practice—to subjugate the black Christians, to the point that all black churches come under the authority and control of the mainline white churches. Even now, over two hundred years later, there is not an authentic, independent black church in Australia.

This could be because many of the colonists did not consider the Indigenous People of the continent to be human beings. As far back as 1688, British navigator William Dampier wrote:

The Inhabitants of this Country ar [*sic*] the miserablest People in the World . . . setting aside their Humane Shape, they *differ but little from Brutes.* (quoted in Reynolds 1989:97, emphasis added)

Over a century and a half later, public opinion had not changed much. In 1845, the Assistant-Protector of the Aborigines at Port Phillip, James Dredge, wrote,

In almost every reference to the moral condition of the Aborigines of Australia which has obtained publicity, they are represented as a race of beings either *entirely destitute of rational mind,* and thus ranging only *at the head of the order of inferior animals;* or, if allowed to be men [*sic*] at all, are described as possessing such *diminished mental capabilities,* and exhibit such a humiliating specimen of the degradation of which human nature is susceptible, as to indicate their position at the *very lowest point in the scale of rationality.* (quoted in Reynolds 1989:114, emphasis added)

Even well into this century, popular opinion about the Aboriginal People was atrocious. The church, it seems, was no exception; note following two examples. In 1915, a Presbyterian Minister, the Reverend J. R. B. Love, made this remark:

It would be foolish to argue that all men are equal. The blackfellow is *inferior* and must necessarily remain so. (Evans, Saunders and Cronin 1975:19, emphasis added)

In 1934, a Presbyterian Padre of the Australian Inland Mission made the following remarkable statement.

. . . the niggers . . . [t]hey've *never been any good and never will be.* The best they've a right to expect is *a decent funeral.* (Duguid 1972:96–97, emphasis added)

Aboriginals were not considered people by any means—certainly not in any European understanding of the word. How else could "explorers" rightfully claim "discovery" and "sovereignty," without claiming *terra nullius?* This geopolitical tactic had a direct and negative impact upon the basis and foundation of the Australian church. Aboriginal People were, therefore, specifically *excluded* from every aspect of the church—its communal life, its corporate worship, its social interaction and so on. Aboriginal People were not welcomed into the *family* of Christ or the *koinōnia.*

The churches had difficulties in defining their own autonomous ecclesiology, considering they so often blurred their function with the functions and policies of the government. They did not protest, for example, against many racist government proclamations and policies. In fact, quite the contrary, the Australian church already had begun practising quite a different ecclesiology—it had already taken on the role of "Enforcer" of such racist policies by going along with Government "Protection" policies, for a start.

Another major area in which the church revealed a racist and therefore heretical ecclesiology was in its involvement in the "Protection" of Aboriginal People, which included their segregation and the institutionalization of their children. From the 1800s, clergymen and missionaries (along with certain government officials) were appointed "Protectors" of entire Aboriginal communities (cf. Rae-Ellis 1988). Church records document wide applications of this practice. Most, if not all, denominations participated, including the Anglican, Roman Catholic, Lutheran, Congregational-Methodist-Presbyterian (now Uniting) Churches. Protection is not about equality, or justice, or truth, but rather isolation, regimentation and cultural genocide. Protection policies are understood to have been part of the political tactics of segregation and Australian-style apartheid. How can the church claim to have been "protecting" Aboriginal People by taking them from their land and away from their mothers and fathers and families (cf. Attwood 1989:18; Pilkington 1994:25; Blaskett 1983)? How are you "protected" if your oral traditions or cultures or languages are destroyed?

Thus, the church, by losing its identity and acting as an agent of the state and by becoming involved in "Protection" of Aboriginal People, sold its soul. It betrayed the community of believers—its ecclesiology betrayed an engrained racism leading to a heretical theology.

In addition to being found in the three areas of Christology, exegesis and ecclesiology, theological heresy was present in racist Australian missiology, polemics and praxis.

Missiology

The Australian church engaged in racist missiology, which led to heresy. Europeans saw that they were fulfilling the Great Commission by colonizing *Terra Australis del Espiritu Santo* (as Australia was then known), and thus spreading Christianity to "the ends of the earth" (cf. Attwood 1989:82).

> The history of contact between Aboriginal and Western cultures is full of racism, classism, sexism and other forms of colonial, expansionist oppression— with the Aboriginal people bearing the brunt of the violence (cf. Pattel-Gray 1991a; Gilbert 1977; Rowley 1970; as well as, Reynolds 1981; Reynolds 1987a;

Reynolds 1987b; Reynolds 1989). The church was very much a part of this assault, drawing its personnel from the same society, and its theology from the same lines of thought and analysis, as the European invaders who stole the continent by force of arms and legal hocus-pocus. The church preached the language of love, yet enforced "mission policies" based upon hate, fear, violence, division and denominationalism. Church and State worked together, and the results of this two-pronged onslaught have been nothing short of genocidal (cf. WCC 1991). (Pattel-Gray and Trompf 1993:170)

The church either could not, or would not, separate their evangelism from Westernism. Indeed, the church syncretized their Christianity with Western values and adopted a theology that validated this practice.

The pious British establishment saw religion as an integral part of the colonial (convict) endeavour. In 1792, the Secretary of State for the Home Department appointed the Rev. Samuel Marsden as Assistant Chaplain to the convict colony of New South Wales, and in time, Marsden even became known as "the agent and founder of missionary enterprise in the South Pacific" (Yarwood 1977:18–19).

British clergymen and missionaries encountered the (black) Indigenous People of Australia, as had British soldiers and jailers before them. They expressed a variety of opinions about the people themselves, but agreed that it was their duty to "save" them. In 1820, (the Rev.) William Walker, of the Wesleyan Methodists, was appointed the first missionary "to the black natives of New South Wales" (Brook and Kohen 1991:104; Wright and Clancy 1993:8, 11–12). Thus, the British (and later European) Christian mission to the Aboriginal People was born.

A true missiology seeks faithfully to respond to the call of Christ, to fulfil the Great Commission. It takes the Gospel message in love to other places, and naturally encounters other peoples, cultures, traditions and languages. It seeks to understand the people and to share a divine gift.

When the Australian church missionized other areas of the Pacific (such as Papua New Guinea, Aotearoa and Fiji), it had an empowering missiology. It focused on education—secular, religious and theological. It established and developed schools—primary, secondary, tertiary and even theological. It centred in on leadership—social, political, religious. And then, most of its expatriate agents left. It helped to empower the people and then it went home. In short, it left behind a self-sufficient theological infrastructure.

The missiology that was inflicted upon Australia, however, was not this (cf. Malone 1991:1). Clergymen [*sic*] and colonists who came to Australia were rigidly influenced by their own particular understandings and expressions of white, Western theology (cf. Lindsay and Miles 1989:18–19). Their encounter with a non-white, non-Western spirituality was simply more than they could fathom.

As far back as 1848, observers noted the failure of "Christianization." Port Phillip Superintendent C. J. La Trobe wrote that

> ". . . the Wesleyan missionaries have faithfully labored in vain" . . . [and] could not show even one example of success. (quoted in Cannon 1993:197)

Contemporary scholars agree. Brook and Kohen write that

> The selection of an inexperienced missionary to supervise the "Christianization and civilization" of the Aborigines of New South Wales contributed to the ultimate failure of the mission. (1991:266)

Loos writes that

> All attempts by missionaries had produced negligible results. Settlers did not understand the reasons but they did see the failure. (1982:24)

Missionaries did not understand. Worse, they did not seek to understand. In the words of Prof. Colin Bourke, of the University of South Australia:

> [The missionaries] were after the minds and souls of Aboriginal people, which invariably led to the destruction of Aboriginal culture. (quoted in *Aboriginal Studies* 1993)

From the very beginning, colonial response to Aboriginal religious traditions were filled with fear, misunderstanding, distortion, and calumny. Colonial religious workers, as well as an overwhelming majority of colonists, firmly believed that Aboriginal People had never heard of God. They thought we were pagans and considered our ceremonies to be pagan rituals. They firmly believed that only their own beliefs would save us from eternal damnation in the fires of hell—and, amazingly, they did not hesitate to use force to smooth the beginning of this process of "salvation."[6] Helped by white, colonial expressions of religion, misconceptions became myths. Many colonists, "fed" by the clergy of the day, believed our expressions of traditional Aboriginal Spirituality to be absolutely without worth, unhuman, indeed demonic.

------

[6] For example, the Rev. Samuel Marsden, hailed as something of a legendary missionary hero in some circles, was also known as "the flogging chaplain"; cf. Prentis 1988:71.

Myths can be dealt with, but the problem was that they did not remain static. Myths became excuses. Falsities and lies became the foundation-stone of "The Australian Church." A thoroughly flawed racist European missiology became a thoroughly flawed racist Australian polemic.

Discourse and Praxis

The Australian church engaged in heretical discourse and praxis, which resulted in racism against Aboriginal People. The church actually believed that it was practising the fruits of the Spirit:

> love, joy, peace, patience, kindness, generosity, faithfulness, gentleness, and self-control. (Gal. 5:22–23)

Yet, in reality, the church was engaged in a concerted self-deception. It really did not want to hear about the "difficulties" of the colonial process—much less about its victims. While Aboriginal People were being dispossessed, murdered, raped, abducted and enslaved, the churches sat silent or indifferent. Aboriginal beliefs, indeed Aboriginal People themselves, summarily were discounted. Yet, even early colonists saw the falsehood. For example, in 1826 one person wrote that:

> Civilization has been the scourge of the Natives; Disease, Crime, Misery and Death, have hitherto been the sure attendants of our intercourse with them. Wherever we trace the steps of white population we discover the introduction of evil, the diminution of numbers, the marks of disease, the pressure of want, the physical and moral ruin of this people. . . . Should such a state of things be realized what will future generations think of *our boasted Christianity,* of our lauded Philanthropy, when our posterity read in the early page of Australia's history the misery and ruin which marked our adoption of this land;—when they find recorded that our proprietorship of the soil has been purchased at such a *costly sacrifice of human happiness and life.* (quoted in Reynolds 1989:2–3, emphasis added)

Logically, heretical Australian church discourse led to heretical Australian church praxis. The "christianity" it practised in Australia betrayed a praxis of hate (and not love), greed (and not justice), lust (for the land, for the women, etc.), exclusion (and not Christian community), and much more.

Thus, much of what the Australian church held to be divine truth was distorted beyond recognition. From its very inception, British evangelism was in fact totally flawed. British colonization of Australia brought a Christianity in which: love became lust; Gospel became greed; charity became chastisement; doctrine became defensiveness; and explanation became extermination. In short, in the Aboriginal People's experience of Australian Christianity, "the Christ" became "the crucifier."

Theological heresy came across the waters and became theological imperialism, which is what unfaithful servants are on about—establishing humanity's kingdom, rather than the kingdom of God.

> The violation of the rights of the poor is not something that "just happens." It is a permanent, ongoing process. (L. Boff 1989:43)

Thus, the Australian church's theology not only was heretical, but also wreaked havoc for the next two centuries.

Theological Imperialism

From the very beginning of the white invasion of Australia, the Aboriginal People tried to enter into dialogue with Christianity through its representatives, the missionaries. It seems, however, that neither the new faith of Christianity, nor its representatives, could handle the strength of our traditional beliefs. Our own religion was not recognized or accepted as a religion in its own right (cf. Trompf 1990:4–6). From the time of its arrival, Western Christianity rejected our faith systems and practices (cf. OT: G. Paulson 1993). It was arrogant, pedantic and brought attitudes of superiority. Because of this, colonizing Christians felt they knew what was best for us and as a result treated us horrifically. Theological heresy became theological imperialism, which in turn became heretical practice and blasphemy.

Theologian, Dr. James Cone writes,

> Any theology . . . that fails to accept the finitude of its categories, speaking instead as if it knows the whole truth and nothing but the truth, is guilty of blasphemy, that is, an ideological distortion of divine reality. (1975:96)

The positive relationship between faith and deeds (Jas. 2:14–16) did not match up with their actions. White Europeans never came to *share* Christianity; they came to *impose* Christianity.

Robert Cantilla, Adviser on Aboriginal Culture with the Victorian Department of Education and Special Services, remembers:

> When [the mission station of] Yuendemu was first built, our people didn't like it because Christianity came and brainwashed them. They'd say if you don't believe in God you go to hell. And through that, our people, our culture was dying slowly because Christianity was pumped into them all the time. (quoted in Gilbert 1977:213)

The Christianity that came here was an immoral and unethical cover-up for the genocidal greed of the racist European colonial powers that invaded us. It rationalized murder, theft and all manner of inhuman oppression against the Aboriginal People, using the weapons of technology (such as firearms) and of language (such as the legal jargon of the mythical *terra nullius,* as well as the questionably conceived and applied theological language of "salvation" and "mission."

> ... no full effort was made by the missionaries to learn the Aboriginal language. There were so many tribes, and the number of languages was also so great that the missionaries often thought that the best way to teach the natives about the Lord Jesus Christ was to teach them English first and then give them the Gospel story in that language. Even today, because the population of the tribes is so small, some people consider that it is not necessary to learn the languages. (National Missionary Council of Australia 1944:5)

The pristine faith of the true believer in a liberating and empowering Christ was buried under layer after layer of lies, self-deception and projection. The Christianity that came here put us down as pagan and Satanic—or, at best, less than human. Yet, to this day, it claims to have come "with the best of intentions" to *save* us.

> The whip was frequently used to reinforce the message of the Gospel;

and

> ... Kimberley Missions were described as being administered by "fear and repression.. (F. Stevens 1981:51, n. 73; cf. *Western Australian Parliamentary Debates* 1939:2138, 12152; Pickford 1962)

What they came to save Aboriginal People *from* is not clear—even to this day.

But, Aboriginal People are living with the Creator, in our daily lives and relationships to each other and to the land. We always have lived with the Creator and we always will. We continue to strive towards acceptance and communication.

Hypocrisy

The church and Christians preached about the full equality of all people, but words did not match behaviour. It seems that "equality" meant, "You must believe as I do." See, for example, the detailed journal record (in 1860) of South Australian missionary George Taplin's argument with the brother of an Aboriginal man recently converted to Christianity.

[Taplin:] [The brother] . . . had been with others persecuting [Waukeri] and compelling him to comply with their customs and I expostulated with him, at the same time telling him that I should help Waukeri to break their customs.

[Brother:] He replied, "What for you do that? You know God tells us to do these things."

[Taplin:] "O," I said, "Where in the Bible does God tell you to do them, for there is only one God, Jehovah, and only one Bible."

[Brother:] "Well," he answered, "how do you know that Bible (is) Jehovah's book? Did he give it to you? Did he tell you it? Did not white fellow make it?"

[Taplin:] "No, Jehovah gave it to my fathers long time ago."

[Brother:] "Well, our God tell my father these customs long time ago, so we must do them."

[Taplin:] "Yes, but your God is a devil, he is not Jehovah. Jehovah only tells people to do things to make them live. White fellow do these things and they increase and get to be many in number, but your God only tells blackfellow to do things to make them do, because he wants to kill them. Where all Adelaide blackfellows? Dead, because he did what [his God] tell him. And you know that this blackfellow only a few now, to what they were a long time ago. So we know what your God is a devil."

[Brother:] "No, No," he answered, "we must do what he tells us."

[Taplin:] I replied "You do not believe what I say."

[Brother:] "No," he said, "we don't."

[Taplin:] "Well then Jehovah tells me to tell you that if you will not believe, you will go to hell when you die."

With this the conversation closed. (Reynolds 1989:165–66)

And, on a more personal level, the education of clergy children, again words did not seems to match actions. In 1954, the Western Australian Parliamentary Debates recorded that:

a *minister* of the Church of England withdrew his children from a West Australian public school and enrolled them at the Catholic school in protest against admission of children from the Aboriginal reserve to the State education system. (F. Stevens 1981:29, n. 106)

These two examples, almost one hundred years apart, seem to indicate that the missionary endeavour made little impact on the missionaries themselves. The church needed to face its own hypocrisy, and hear and practise its own preaching on equality and justice.

Hypocrisy in the Extreme

One of the worst—and yet relatively unknown—examples of the church's amazing ability propagate self-justifying lies is the story of the Rev. Samuel Marsden. This clergyman is considered by the church, as well as by many Australians today, to be a hero, a "pioneer missionary" who "gave his life" in the service of God and for the people of Australia. But the truth is quite different. Marsen's aspirations in relation to the church were strictly limited to white Europeans—and, perhaps, to Aotearoan Maoris—but certainly not Australia's Indigenous People.

During the course of his life and ministry, the Rev. Marsden engaged in a variety of practices. Today, some people would believe his actions virtuous, but others would consider them classist, genocidal and self-serving. The ship which carried the missionary and his wife also carried "their" convict girl servant (Yarwood 1977:23). So, before he even began his new ministry "in the field," the Rev. Marsden endorsed the concept and practice of domestic service by a servant "class"—thereby setting a precedent for classism in the colony's church structures. After arriving in Australia, in the 1790s, the Rev. Marsden expanded this idea by "taking in" an Aboriginal boy named Tristan ("taking in" being considered cultural genocide today) (Yarwood 1977:52). He believed in, and acted upon, policies of strict order and discipline (gaining him a reputation as the "flogging chaplain"; Prentis 1988:71). Later on, he pursued major agricultural enterprises (which destroyed vast areas of natural vegetation, as well as Aboriginal access to their own food, water and culturally significant sites) (Yarwood 1977:88). He developed an interest in "the other" "pastoral" area, becoming an award-winning sheep breeder, and pioneering the Australian sheep industry (and its legacy of deforestation, land erosion, and "natives removal") (Yarwood 1977:75, 88–89).

Yet, it did not end there. Marsden also had a long-standing (and consuming) interest in the "welfare" of the Indigenous People of other lands, particularly Maoris and other Polynesian Peoples of the South Pacific (cf. Brook and Kohen 1991:63). For decades, he encouraged them to leave their lands and travel to Australia (ignoring the dangers to their health from strange foods, climates and cultures); he opened institutions for them (his biographer uses the term "hostages"); and, he provided for their exclusive rights to education (pointedly "excluding" Australian Aboriginal People from his Parramatta seminary) (Yarwood 1977:216).

Together, all these facts point to a life of hypocrisy, greed, and callous disregard for the rights and needs of the Indigenous People of Australia. Even his biographer indicates that Marsden ignored the claims of the Aboriginal People (Yarwood 1977:16).

When Marsden died, his will instructed that "his stock was to be sold, and the proceeds, with his other liquid assets, were to be shared equally by his heirs." Now, one might expect a clergyman, who for many years earned 10s per day, to be poor, and for the inheritance to be, rather, "spiritual." After all, his First Fleet predecessor, the Rev. Richard Johnson, returned to England "a poor preacher" (Lindsay and Miles 1989:6).

But, the appalling truth is that, at the time of his death, the Rev. Samuel Marsden, "pioneer missionary," *owned* 29 farms, 11,724 acres of land, 9,236 sheep, 1,100 cattle, and 18 horses, and benefited from the services of no less than fourteen convict shepherds (Yarwood 1977:278–79). Indeed, when the humble pastor's inheritance was sold, the estate was,

> sworn . . . to have a value of £30,000, which in terms of present-day currency made Marsden a comfortable *millionaire.* (Yarwood 1977:279, emphasis added)

This is the result of the life's work of an English *clergyman* in Australia? It can be stated truthfully that Aboriginal People did not benefit from this inheritance, spiritually, materially or otherwise. The land purchased *for* Aboriginal People was not purchased *from* Aboriginal People; this money derived from *their* land did not go to them; the institutions set up for Aboriginal People excluded their very presence; the education provided for Aboriginal People actually enslaved them into subservience; and, the gospel preached at Aboriginal People did not liberate them. This representative of the church, revered by many white Australians today, was not truly concerned for Aboriginal People.

It is easy to criticize the Rev. Marsden with the luxury of hindsight. Yet, his own words provide a profound insight to this man's psyche and theology.

> The Aborigines are the most degraded of the human race . . . the time is not yet arrived for them to receive the great blessing of civilisation and the knowledge of Christianity. (cf. quoted in J. Elder 1932:231–32)

And

> there never would be any good done until there was a riddance of these natives. (quoted in Brook and Kohen 1991:266)

It is difficult to express the immense significance of the Rev. Samuel Marsden's example in the subsequent treatment of and approach to Australian Aboriginal People. As the Senior Chaplain of New South Wales, he set an example, directly and implicitly, that would be followed by generations of subsequent clergymen, missionaries, Christians, government officials, and other colonists. His actions towards the Indigenous

People of Australia can be summarized as perfunctory and ineffective—
bordering on contemptuous. Thus, it can be stated that the ministry of
the Rev. Samuel Marsden towards Aboriginal People was extreme
hypocrisy, and that for the church to believe otherwise is hypocrisy in the
extreme.

Collusion with the Government

Beginning in the early 1800s, the Australian churches and governments actively worked together in the area of practice and policies with
regard to Aboriginals. In many places, these became almost indistinguish-
able. In South Australia, for example,

> Colonial Office policy became almost *identical* with missionary policy because of
> the powerful links between the office and missionaries. (Reid 1990:1, emphasis
> added)

In fact, three of the leading figures of the Colonial Office (James
Stephen, permanent Under-Secretary; Charles Grant, later Lord Glenelg,
Secretary of State for the Colonies; and, Sir George Grey, Parliamentary
Under-Secretary) were also leading figures of the Church Missionary
Society (Reid 1990:1–2). Very often, this kind of close connection went
far beyond people, and into actual policy decisions and actions.

One of the best-known examples of such collusion was the joint
creation of numerous mission stations and reserves into which
Aboriginals were "placed" (with or without their consent) (cf. CoA-MT
1958b:6). Located all across the entire continent, these missions and
reserves mostly were run by the churches on behalf of the governments;
they formed a central part of the government policies of the day. The
Australian Colonial—and later Federal—Government even allocated
prime Crown lands and considerable resources (including direct financial
aid) to the missions for their purposes (CoA-MT 1958b:8; cf. Gale and
Brockman 1975:29). They saw this as their prime work to be done.

> Practically all 19th century missionaries saw their task as not only the
> conversion of their flock but also their "civilization." In practical terms that
> meant imposing all aspects of Western culture and at the same time
> suppressing Aboriginal customs and ceremonies. They were proud of their
> moral tyranny and wrote extensively of their triumph over "savagery" and
> "heathenism." Marriage and funeral rites were often the sharpest point of
> conflict. (Reynolds 1989:160)

The church and the government shared a vision of how the
Indigenous People of Australia should be treated, and they took action to

implement this vision. They worked in collusion with each other to deal with the so-called "Aboriginal problem" (cf. CoA-MT 1960:23).

> In most mission areas the techniques of administration used were little different to the coercion of the government settlements. (Stevens 1981:20)

In some cases, the church actively encouraged this unholy alliance. It vigorously advocated for cooperation with the government. Some see this as the churches simply being co-opted into pursuing the government's agenda. After all, the churches did receive more than just praise for their allegedly "unstinting, selfless and humanitarian" efforts; the churches received *land* and *money* for their "services" to the state. It is not well-known, but it certainly is well-documented, that the government provided churches with both land (cf. Reid 1990:135) and money (cf. Brook and Kohen 1991:57, 225–26), according to their "body-count"—that is, the specific numbers of Aboriginal People in the particular missions.

In contemporary times, the collusion between government and church intensified when valuable minerals were found on Aboriginal missions and reserves. All across the country, churches were pressured into "moving the natives"—supposedly for the sake of the nation. There are many cases of the churches selling-out the Aboriginal People for money. And big money it was. The Presbyterian betrayal of Weipa, for example, began with the Mission making a claim for compensation of about three-quarters of a million dollars (F. Stevens 1971:141). Yet, even this negotiation was bungled. The Queensland Department of Native Affairs accepted a much lower offer from the mining giant Comalco.

> For $300,000, plus five cents per ton [of bauxite] royalty, to be paid into Consolidated Revenue, an area of 1,485,000 acres was excised from a native reserve of 1,600,000 acres. (F. Stevens 1971:142)

After some protest, 150 acres were set aside for the Aboriginal People. Though this area eventually was increased to 2,500 acres, "no form of tenure was extended to the Aboriginal people involved" (F. Stevens 1971:142). To put into perspective a royalty payment of five cents per ton, the value of the ore at the time was $6.00 per ton; and, it has been estimated that the multinational mining company was assured "of a return of somewhere in the region of 60% of two and one-half *billion dollars*" (F. Stevens 1971:143, emphasis added). Thus, in the end, the church colluded with the government and was directly responsible for the dispossession of the Aboriginal People, and the relocation of Weipa.

Institutionalizing Racism

The Australian church has been racist through its own institutions, its own members and representatives and its inaction on racist violence. In the history of this country, it is not difficult to find many, many examples.

Racist Institutions

By joining forces in the establishment of missions and stations, church and government began institutionalizing racism. In 1814, for example, the "Black Native Institution of New South Wales" was established at Parramatta (cf. Brook and Kohen 1991). The idea was conceived by the church and implemented by the government; the proposal came from William Shelley, a former London Missionary Society missionary, and the law came from Colonel Lachlan Macquarie, Governor of N.S.W. (Brook and Kohen 1991:54–55). This joint effort has been described alternatively as "an experiment" towards civilizing the Indigenous People, and as "the first serious attempt to gradually assimilate Aborigines" into white European society (Brook and Kohen 1991:ix, 54).

The church and the government claimed to be sharing of their own culture by offering religious instruction, general education, knowledge of domestic arts and other forms of social encouragement. They were trying to "improve" the "condition of the Natives," variously described as "wretched" and "destitute" (Brook and Kohen 1991:60). Some scholars go so far as stating that white society felt a kind of guilt and began to "make reparations" by establishing the Institution.

> Here we see at least some Europeans beginning to recognise that it is *their activities* in clearing the land which has resulted in the impoverished state of the Aborigines. The Native Institution was one of the first attempts to pay restitution for the loss of their traditional means of sustenance. (Brook and Kohen 1991:67, emphasis added)

Thus, it is clear that many (white) people believed this was a good idea. Yet, some of the Rules and Regulations for this Institution reveal very disturbing facts.

> *Fourthly*, That the main Object of the Institution shall be the *Civilization* of the Aborigines of both Sexes.
>
> . . .
>
> *Sixthly*, That this Institution shall be an Asylum for the Native Children of both Sexes; but no Child shall be admitted under for [*sic*], or exceeding *Seven Years of Age*.
>
> . . .

Fourteenthly, That *no Child* after having been admitted into the Institution, *shall be permitted to leave it, or be taken away by any Person whatever, (whatever Parents or other relatives)* until such time as the Boys shall have attained the age of *sixteen* years, and the Girls *fourteen* years, at which ages they shall be respectively discharged. (Brook and Kohen 1991:61–62, emphasis added)

In other words, what the Christian gentlemen and colonial officials of the day were doing—all in the name of Christian charity and "paying restitution"—was essentially kidnapping Aboriginal children from their families, holding them prisoner for seven to ten years of their early lives, deculturalizing and brainwashing them into the "more civilized" ways of the whites, making them completely dependent, and then enslaving them back into the domestic service of white society. This behaviour amounts to cultural genocide and, shockingly, the church openly supported it.

It is clear that church and state worked together in the Native Institution at Parramatta. The rules for this Institution were generally suggested by missionary Shelley, formally declared by Governor Macquarie, and practically implemented by Lieutenant-Governor Molle, the Rev. William Cowper and the Rev. Henry Fulton, among others; the institution was funded by the New South Wales Government; and, the plan was endorsed by the Rev. Samuel Marsden and the Church Missionary Society (Brook and Kohen 1991:55–63).

Indeed, the Native Institution at Parramatta was more than just a school for Aboriginal children; it was an "experimental station," a small working model which would be replicated across the rest of Australia. Church and state were collaborating in a much broader pattern which would be repeated again and again in the colony—"initial friendly contacts, followed by open hostility, and ending with the establishment of some form of mission or institution" (Brook and Kohen 1991:x). Church and state were setting up a mechanism by which white society could exploit Aboriginal People for the rest of their lives; they had begun to institutionalize racism.

Practices which supported this racist strategy included the prohibition of any and all expressions of the indigenous cultures. Aboriginal Sacred Ceremonies and language were forbidden, thought by whites to be satanic or heathen (e.g., OTs: C. Harris 1988; G. Paulson 1993; I. Paulson 1993). Speaking any Aboriginal languages or dialects was thought to be regression into cultural and social inferiority, and promptly attacked. Indeed, any expression whatsoever of traditional Aboriginality was strongly discouraged, often with violent force.

Another clear example of church and government working in collusion towards institutionalizing racism is the "removal" of Aboriginal children and young children from their families. It is well-documented that huge numbers of Aboriginal babies were taken, by force, from their mothers and families, removed from their communities, and placed into the many missions—with government blessing and, often, help (cf. Cummings 1990; Edwards and Read 1989). The practice of taking away Aboriginal babies eventually became law.

A further example of church and government working together is the institutionalization of "Protection Laws" all across Australia. This process began with white missionaries (or other clergymen) or white government officials being appointed "Protectors" of Aboriginal People. These were clergymen, policemen, or other "interested citizens," who were named "in the best interests of the Aboriginals," to defend them against the atrocities of other white colonists.[7] Protection Laws came into force throughout the country, giving select white people *absolute*—and unquestionable—control over the lives of Aboriginal People, who could no longer speak for themselves regarding physical presence, marriage, personal affairs, and many other areas.

On 28 August 1844, for example, the *Protection of Aboriginal Children Act* was passed in New South Wales. The Chief Protector of Aborigines became legal guardian of Aboriginal children (in "white" categories, "half-castes" and "full-bloods") and many children were taken from their families and placed in missions or stations. The process continued unabated for years, until it became common practice. To continue the previous example, in 1883 the Aboriginal Protection Board (N.S.W.) was formed and literally thousands of Aboriginal children were separated from their families—by "official government policy." Thus, from the "Black Native Institution of New South Wales" of Parramatta, to the missions and reserves, to the various state "Protection Laws," we see a clear line of development of both church and government institutions as racist institutions.

Racist Individuals

The Australian church racism is seen through individual persons—be they church members, officials, representatives, etc. Further, through successive generations of church leadership, we see some of the worst

---

[7] It is more than a little worthy of mention that, in some cases, the worst atrocities were committed by the Protectors themselves!

elements of racism coming to the surface of Australian ecclesiastical life. Some people were quite obviously racist, as evidenced in earlier stories; others betrayed a more veiled kind of racism.

A first—and blatant—example of individual church racism is one of the early Roman Catholic Archbishops of Sydney. In 1845, this churchman gave evidence before the New South Wales Select Committee of the Legislative Council on the Aborigines, and *strongly supported* the gradual *civilization* of Aboriginal People by their strict *segregation* away from whites (Gale and Brockman 1975:56–57). This personal aversive racism paved the way for subsequent institutional dominative racism by the hegemonic socio-political machinery. His own racism lent quite significant social and "moral" weight to an imminent political decision, which would have a very negative impact upon several future generations of Aboriginal People. His views supported the racist views of the day, in spite of his religious obligation to the contrary to strongly support equality and justice.

A second—and possibly the most amazing—example of a racist individual in the church (not to mention of church insensitivity and genocidal practise) is the story of Fr. Francis Xavier Gsell. In 1911 this French priest went to Bathurst Island and established a Roman Catholic mission. He soon discovered the ancient indigenous practice of arranged marriages, which his worldview and personal morality simply could not "allow" to continue. In his own words, Fr. Gsell declares:

> There is a crisis. If I can find some way of winning Martina's freedom, then, perhaps, there will be freedom for other little ones. . . . I pray that God, now, will guide me so that I may find a way. There comes to me an idea. I will *buy* Martina from these men. *But this is not the custom.* . . . Yet I must try. It can cost me nothing to try, and I must not fail. *Now I proceed with great cunning. . . . No line must be seen on the hook that holds the bait.* (Gsell 1955:84–85, emphasis added)

All told, Fr Gsell *bought* one hundred and fifty young Aboriginal girls— in his mind "saving them" from traditional arranged marriages (Gsell 1955:90). Even worse, he did not stop there. Acting with monumental hypocrisy, he proceeded to arrange marriages for these Aboriginal girls *himself*.[8] In more of Gsell's own words on his activities, we read this staggering comment:

---

[8] See, for example, where the very same Martina already mentioned received "permission" from Fr. Gsell to marry "someone of her own choosing"; Gsell 1955:87.

> ... whenever I engaged in this novel form of *black slave traffic,* I saw to it that, for an appropriate consideration, the son-in-law as well as the husband surrendered all rights. (Gsell 1955:89, emphasis added)

Even making historiographical allowances, with admissions such as this questions about the man's mental stability arise—rather quickly. How could someone talk like this, using such powerful words, and be so completely oblivious to the meaning and implications of what he was saying? How could someone take such actions—in the name of God? How could he possibly show *pride* in this "novel" practice?

In one fell swoop, then, this minister of God destroyed hundreds of family connections, deculturalized a whole generation, and erased forever the rich spiritual connection, Dreaming stories, kinship and other cultural traditions of the Indigenous People of the area. In short, this one unarmed priest did more damage than an entire regiment of soldiers could have done with bullets; he single-handedly, and peacefully, decimated the Indigenous People of an entire island.

Perhaps most shocking is the official reaction to this episode of Australian ecclesiastical history. Fr Gsell had the *direct approval* of the Australian Government and, incredibly, the *apostolic blessing* of Pope Pius XII (Gsell 1955:106)![9] In fact, for his efforts, the Roman Catholic Church made him Bishop of Darwin; the Government of France awarded him the decoration of Chevalier of the Legion of Honour; and, King George VI bestowed upon him the Order of the British Empire (Gsell 1955:142, 140).

A third—and perhaps, to some, shocking—example is the legacy of the Rev. Professor A. P. Elkin. Though revered as a pioneer priest-anthropologist, the life and work of this man leave behind a blurred picture of both positive intention and negative result (for background, cf. Markus 1990:144–57). Many people are aware that this Anglican clergyman was passionately interested in the Aboriginal People of Australia. Some know that during the latter part of the 1920s, "as the only Professor of Anthropology in Australia, his views commanded respect" (Markus 1990:145). Others know that in the 1930s, he was made President of the Association for the Protection of Native Races, and that, indeed, he had the ear of government (Markus 1990:155).

Many people are not aware, however, of elements of another side of Elkin. There is a growing body of evidence that the part played by this

---

[9] It is interesting to note that Gsell and Pope Pius XII were old schoolmates; cf. Gsell 1955:165.

white priest-anthropologist with regard to the well-being of the Aboriginal People was indeed questionable. Firstly, there is Elkin's written work, which provides ample documentation of his continuing views that Australian Aboriginals, though human, were clearly inferior to white and yellow races (Markus 1990:146), and showed limited mental capacity (Markus 1990:147). Secondly, there is Elkin's central role in the development and implementation of the notorious Assimilation Policy. Elkin was directly involved, to the point that Rowley described him as "the prime mover in New South Wales for an assimilation policy" (1972:32). Markus describes his role in the following terms.

> By 1935 . . . his growing influence with the government allowed him to assume his preferred role: Elkin liked to work behind the scenes; be favoured private meetings with people of influence over the writing of detailed letters of the addressing of crowded public meetings. *He wanted to be at the centre of power,* to exercise a say not only in the formulation of policy but in appointments to office. (1990:155, emphasis added)

Was it, perhaps, that Elkin was pushing his own views—his own (racist) agenda? One wonders why he would not want anything to be written. Was it modesty, or that he not want "evidence" of the extent of his involvement?

Thirdly, there is Elkin's pivotal role in the start of nuclear testing at Maralinga, in Central Australia. Aboriginal anthropologist Marcia Langton indicates that Elkin was *instrumental* in *convincing* the Australian Government that nuclear testing at Maralinga would *not* be harmful, as there were not enough Aboriginal People there to be injured in any way (*Aboriginal Studies* 1993). Any good researcher—not to mention a scholar of Elkin's standing—would have known that there were many Aboriginal People who lived throughout the area, and who had deep spiritual links to those specific land areas proposed for testing. Indeed, numerous public writings—not to mention many unpublished reports—documented the strong presence of hundreds of Aboriginal People in the area (e.g., FS 1985:25; cf. Mattingley and Hampton 1988:89). Langton further adds that another white anthropologist (Donald Thomson of the University of Melbourne) opposed Elkin's position on this, and was subsequently—and actively—persecuted by Elkin (cf. *Aboriginal Studies* 1993). Though revered by many for his courage in confronting the racism so prevalent in his day, Elkin also had a side which condemned him for the same offences of which he charged others.

Thus, even in these three brief stories, we see that racism in the church was found not just in the institutions, but also in the individuals.

The Violence of Racist Theology and Teachings

In the church, both racist institutions and individuals had a common grounding: both were informed by racist church theology and teachings. The church had so central a role in the public image of Australian piety that its words often became mandates, blindly obeyed by uncritical followers. Church proclamations about "saving the natives" from hell by teaching them the "lessons" of Western civilization were believed and applied—literally. Thus, whites began to missionize the Aboriginal People by Westernizing them. One Aboriginal scholar even indicates that, in many areas of the country, missionaries pointedly were selected to "evangelize" an Aboriginal group or community as a first step in their *pacification* and eventual domination (cf. OT: G. Paulson 1993).

This process of blurring the lines between missionization and Westernization often led to erroneous and quite bizarre interpretations of Scripture. Take, for example, a pastoralist in New South Wales who used the Bible to support his racist rationalization of vengeance murders.

> "He that spareth the rod hateth his child." Every true friend to the Aborigines must desire that they be *made to learn by terror* those lessons which they have refused to acquire under a milder discipline. We are now to oppose strength to strength, that an end may be put to the effusion of human blood. (Gilbert 1988a:10)

Such horrifying and ill-informed exegesis only betrays a more disgusting failure on the part of the Australian church. Racist theology and teachings were being communicated—either directly or indirectly—and sustained by the church, thus lending an element of moral weight to the genocidal behaviour being rationalized by so-called "Christian" interpretations of the Bible by rank and file "Christians" working for their own interests!

The Australian church allowed racist violence to exist and, worse, to continue unabated for decades. For example, the official "Protection" policies and laws had a tremendously negative impact on the lives of generations of Aboriginal People. Yet, they remained in force, sometimes with tacit church acknowledgement and sometimes with active church encouragement.

Aboriginal People remember all-too-well the brutal force of such policies and practices. Even though white policy prohibited mothers from interacting with her own children after the imposed separation coming as a direct result of the "Protection" policies, it did not stop Aboriginal women from risking severe punishment to have just the slightest glance of and interaction with their child(ren). In the words of Vi Stanton:

> This is a very important point. You hear a lot of stories about the tribal people rejecting their children, the half-castes. It's not true. It's incredible what my mother learnt about herself when the tribal people weren't even supposed to come near her. My mother was in the compound, huge wire fence, concentration camp fence and the tribal people, old tribal women would come up to the fence and call the little children over. When the children came over they would hold their little hands through the wire and tell them who they were, who their mothers were, where they'd come from, what their skin was, what their totem and dreaming was. They were caught, belted by the authorities and told not to mix with the dirty blacks, told that they should drive the black people away. There was this constant battle for the children's minds. (Gilbert 1971:11)

Both the church and the government saw this "battle" as the "key to success in their task of 'civilising the natives'" (Reynolds 1989:170). May Smith, recalling life at Yarrabah Mission House, Queensland, stated:

> The boys had a big house with a cement floor. I don't know how they used to sleep on the cement floor. We went there one day to look. I said, "Oh goodness. You're cold eh, at night time?" They had to have two blankets—one for underneath, one for cover. (Thomson 1989:34)

Gloria Brennan remembers that children were kept in dormitories as virtual prisoners, with no privacy, where even their mail was opened (cf. Gilbert 1977:83). They also were forced to "earn their keep" (cf. Rowley 1971a:28). Tom Allen remembers himself and other children working at Yarrabah Mission.

> The boss we had was a white bloke by the name of Thompson. He was a very strict man. After pulling the grass out we would have blisters and cuts all over our hands. We would have to work till about 4.30 in the afternoon and we wouldn't get any pay for working. (Thomson 1989:40).[10]

The church had been instrumental in establishing the "Protection" system for the alleged safety of the Aboriginal People. Yet, in case after case, historical records document that the "Protection" system was an abysmal failure.

---

[10] See also recollections about Aurukun in G. Roberts 15 February 1992:33.

As Professor A. P. Elkin has pointed out, "Protection policies not only failed to ensure the survival of the Aborigines; they also failed to protect them from harsh treatment". (Reynolds 1989:10)

What kind of harsh treatment? Taking another example,

> . . . this man had two boys in his employ, the eldest being thirteen years old, both speaking English. They ran away after having been flogged, were pursued and were driven back with a stock whip a distance of thirty miles. Having arrived at the station the elder boy was stripped, lashed to a fence in a crucifix position and then flogged until he fainted. The second boy was treated in the same manner and after having worn out one lash he began to put on another, when the boy in his agony called out, *"Oh, Master, if you want to kill me cut my throat, but don't cut me to pieces".* (Gribble 1886:44)

Specifically "Christian" efforts were not exempt from such severity. In many missions, Aboriginal People were *forced* to attend church services every Sunday so that they would give *thanks* to the Lord *their* God for all the *blessings* that God had bestowed upon them during that week. Such hypocrisy is unmasked in Aboriginal memories. In the words of the Rev. Dhalanganda Garrawurra, an Aboriginal Elder from Arnhem Land and currently Assistant Principal of Nungalinya Theological College:

> If we didn't come to church our rations were not given to us, so the only way we could get food to eat from the missionaries was to attend church. (OT: R. Garrawurra 1992)

This kind of racist violence took place in numerous missions in Queensland and Western Australia, such as Murrumbidgee, Cootamundra Girls Home, and the Kinchela Boys Home.

> From 1915 to 1939 any station manager or policeman could take Aboriginal children from their parents if he thought this was for their moral or spiritual *welfare.* (OT: Garrawurra 1992; Rowley 1971a:14)

Such treatment constitutes *genocide*—even today, a large percentage of these children have never seen their parents again,[11] "because government policy was designed to break up Aboriginal families" (Parbury 1986:89), and to remove them from their lands and therefore

---

11 This constitutes *genocide,* as defined in the internationally recognized United Nations *Convention on the Prevention and Punishment of the Crime of Genocide (1948),* and violates Articles 1, 2, 3, 4, 5, and 6 of the Convention: ". . . genocide means any of the following acts committed with intent to destroy, in whole or in part, a national, ethnical, racial or religious group, as such: . . . (e) Forcibly transferring children of the group to another group," UN 1988:143–144.

control and destroy them (UN 1988).[12] An eighty-four year old Aboriginal Elder from Townsville, Queensland, recently stated:

> I left the mission when I was 18. I went back to my family to find them and I was lost because I could no longer speak my native tongue, did not know the cultural laws and no longer was a part of them. The mission destroyed every connection I could possibly have with my people. I was alone, angry and bitter. (OT: Iles 1989)

Incredibly (or perhaps not), this policy was in effect until *1969*, and its practice continues right up to this very day (cf. *Special Treatment* 1991).

Many times, it is conveniently forgotten that Aboriginal People needed protection from the protectors—including, and especially, the church. Indeed,

> Missions, in their own way, accomplished almost as much harm to Aboriginal culture and society as the more cruel methods of many frontier settlers. (Gale and Brockman 1975:29)

With racist, theologically-based (and ecclesiologically-endorsed) violence such as this, it is no wonder Elizabeth Pearce describes Aboriginal People in Arnhem Land this way:

> Most of them have an inferiority complex towards white people and towards missionaries in particular. (Gilbert 1977:15)

With this kind of "treatment" from both the church and the government, who would not be made to feel inferior?

It is amazing that the violence of such racist theology and teachings had any positive effect upon Aboriginal People at all. In the words of Betty Pierce, an Aboriginal participant at the World Council of Churches 7th Assembly in Canberra:

> It *staggers* me to think that Aboriginal People would even consider Christianity. (*Cry for Justice* [Video] 1991)

Perhaps most sickening is the fact that in many ways, the Australian church laid the groundwork for the Australian government's oppression. That is, the government can truthfully claim that in establishing its

---

[12] Other paragraphs under the definition of *genocide* are: "(b) Causing serious bodily or *mental* harm to members of the group; . . . (c) Deliberately inflicting on the group *conditions of life* calculated to bring about its physical destruction in whole or in part"; emphasis added. The fact is that direct commitment of, as well as indirect conspiracy to and complicity in, genocide are punishable in international law (see Article 3 of the Covenant).

policies of segregation and then assimilation, it was simply following the lead of the churches (cf. Gale and Brockman 1975:30; Brook and Kohen 1991:54–55). Racist institutions, individuals and theologies set in motion an ecclesiastical racism that endures to this day.

Practice: The Australian Church *Still* Contributes to Racism

In the early 1970s, Charles Spivey made the following comments to a national conference on education.

> What is the issue in Australia? It is not about racism around the world, but *white racism here.*

> . . . And where is the Church? Churches are supposed to reconcile folks, we have to love one another. . . . The problem as I see it is to get them to lift their feet off the black folks' neck and let them live and have a chance. And that doesn't mean fifty years from now. (ACC 1971:17–18)

Australian church racism existed in the past. It is eminently obvious, however, that Australian church racism continues today. A number of contemporary realities show this to be true. Among them are: the lack of land rights; the distorted memory that continues to be the foundation for teaching and action; the critical shortage of leaders among people of indigenous (and non-English speaking) backgrounds; the ambivalence of the church's statements of support; the church's failure to stand united against racism in this country; and, the church's absolute rejection that it still has a very serious racism problem.[13]

In the early 1980s the Hon. Don Dunstan, a contemporary politician, made the following statement.

> I believe that it is not enough for us simply to do what many of our churches have so far done on this issue—to pass a resolution and make a public statement. . . . I believe that the aborigines in this country today have just as much right to say to the churches in this country, "Look, stand up and fight with us in the way that you were induced to fight internationally for the rights of the people in Africa because that is what Christianity demands of you." Well, in saying that to the churches, and they are saying that to the churches, I go along with them entirely. If that means at times I do things which some people in Australia might consider going beyond the bounds of the sort of thing that a Premier would have done in the past, if ultimately it leads us to standing up

---

[13] Many, many Aboriginal People believe this, though they do not always express it publicly. One exception is noted Aboriginal author and poet Kevin Gilbert who has made very direct statements that there is a great deal of racism in the church today; cf. Gilbert 1988a:13.

there and actually resisting and saying "You will not come further, we will not submit, you cannot do this to these people", then I'm going to be prepared to do it, and I hope that there are going to be a great many Christians in this country who will do so too. (Rollason 1981:13)

Such prophetic words, such progressive thinking—now, if only the church could catch up! If only it could take the lead! If only the Australian church could take its place at the side of Christ—on the cutting edge of justice in this land!

Still No Land Rights

Racism in the Australian church continues in that Aboriginal People still enjoy virtually no land rights. The church exhibits this racism in its greed, and in its questionable remorse and actions.

Church Greed

As history would show, the Australian Church (as an institution—e.g., excluding businesses) is the second largest land-owning organization in the country behind the Federal Government. The Anglican, Roman Catholic and Uniting Churches (as well as many others) have vast land-holdings in every state and territory of Australia. They control—literally— billions of dollars worth of real estate. To take just one example, a single unit of one Diocese (Sydney) of the Anglican Church of Australia "had under its management and supervision assets totalling $360 million," including churches, office buildings, industrial parks and a retail complex (Anglican Church of Australia 1991:408).

The Australian church's vast wealth is not accidental. It is not a historical irregularity, which somehow "blessed" the church, or its alleged "good works." Its origins are far more mundane, and derive from one of the most basic human drives: greed.

The British lie of terra nullius rationalized the colonizers' theft of the land. The Australian church then "accepted" grants of land from the Australian Government. In this way, the Australian churches "stole" most—if not all—of their land, because they were "accepting" stolen property from the Government. In fact, to date, Australian churches have not given back these stolen lands—much less paid rent or compensation for them—since they arrived over 200 years ago (cf. J. Brown 1994:2–3).[14] The Catholic Commission for Justice and Peace has stated:

---

[14] As recently as 1970, the Australian Council of Churches "publicly advocated" for

> The challenge presented by the just demands of Aborigines for Land Rights,
> for restitution of and compensation for land, is crucial both for Aborigines and
> for the rest of the Australian community. . . . Silence on the part of the
> Christian community . . . is not neutrality: it is acquiescence in injustice.
> (OCCR 1979:30)

The Australian church is acquiescing in injustice by remaining silent about its own greed. It never questions how it acquired its lands. It never reflects upon how much it had to give up to get the lands—integrity, authenticity, truth, purpose. It never ponders how much could have been gained by not selling it soul. It never even critiques how it used the lands—separation of families, cultural genocide, socio-cultural imperialism. In fact, public scrutiny about the activities and effects of the use of church lands has intensified only recently, and only because of the revelations of horrific treatment of Aboriginal People in church missions and mission stations. As we look toward the future, we find that only rarely does the church even discuss what they might do with some of these properties. The sad fact is that in many instances, land that has remained unused for years in the hands of the church suddenly develops "ministry potential" overnight, often within days of an Aboriginal group seeking to make some use of it (e.g., OT: D. Broome 1992; C. Broome 1992; A. Jackson 1992). History shows—and church balance sheets prove—that greed has been a very powerful motivation for the silence of the church on issues of land rights for Aboriginal People.

Questionable Remorse

It is noteworthy—but of dubious value at best—that some churches have made public apologies to Aboriginal People for the cruel and despicable behaviour of their members (both ordained and lay), and the destructive impact of their organizational structures and decisions. A classic case in point is the Uniting Church in Australia, which in 1990 made a very *public* apology to the Aboriginal People of Mapoon for having removed them from their traditional lands—twice;[15] for having destroyed

---

land rights by lobbying in Canberra for a policy which read in part: "The Council believes that the measures set out below would help speed up the pace of Aboriginal advancement and eventual *assimilation*. . . . *New reserves* should be created after a survey by an appropriate authority to establish Aboriginal needs": F. Engel 1971:182; emphasis added. It is clear that the church does not "help" by pushing for assimilation and new reserves! Fortunately, the church—at least the mainline denominations—has "seen the light" and refrains from such appeals; indeed, it is making considerable progress (cf. Pattel-Gray 1994:3).

[15] By very public, I mean that the reports of the apology intentionally were

their traditions and culture, and made them utterly dependent for their livelihood; and, for then having completely abandoned them in the midst of this destruction. Notably absent in the apology were references to the historical background of the events that had taken place, which would have uncovered the fact that the church had conspired with the Government and with the mining company (Comalco)

> to expel [Aboriginal People] from their home so that the land could be mined" for bauxite. (P. Wilson 1985:38; cf. J. Roberts 1975)

Many years after-the-fact, the Public Defender's Office collected volumes of statements by witnesses, who remember events in the following way.

> In 1963, a much disliked missionary . . . suddenly left the settlement. Then the flying doctor service to the mission was suspended, closely followed by the discontinuation of the supply boat to Mapoon, which led to the closure of the local store. . . . The local school was closed. Then, in the most dramatic event of the Mapoon story, a government boat arrived at the mission on the night of 15 November 1963, carrying both white and native police. The police went from house to house ordering the people to pack their bags and to sleep, under guard, at the mission cottage.
>
> As Rachel Peter recalls, nearly everything on the mission was burnt down, including homes, church, cookhouse, school, workshops, butcher-shop and store.
>
> Rachel saw the Department's carpenters "going to the coconut trees, getting dry coconut branches, putting them under the homes and into the homes and striking a match." The destruction of Mapoon was virtually complete. Armed police, forced transportation and arson were the weapons used to solve the problems of Comalco, the Church and the Government. (P. Wilson 1985:39–40; cf. J. Roberts 1975:8–20)

Yes, the Uniting Church apologized for the actions of its Presbyterian ancestors (*Journey* 1990:16),[16] but it *completely* failed to address the issue of compensation for its past injustices, and for its present and future benefiting from (exploitation of) such injustices. As a result of the actions of the Uniting Church in Australia in 1990, the people of Mapoon became the proud new owners of—you could have guessed it—a few words and a truck (actually, "an *appeal* to provide a vehicle for the necessary trips to Weipa for supplies"—Henderson 1992:8). To this day,

---

"splashed" all over the media.

[16] At that time, the Rev. Dr. John Brown was General Secretary of the Commission for World Mission of the Uniting Church in Australia.

most people still are unaware of this pathetic episode of church history. To this day, Aboriginal People remain hurt and angry with the church for such actions. Rachel Peter puts it this way.

> This is what they do, but the world doesn't know. People don't know how we were treated. They destroyed the homes, burnt them down you know. And I seen all the burning down of the homes, the church. . . . It was destroying our culture, our lives. You know, the land is part of our lives. I said, you know, you destroyed everything from us and we want to return. (OCCR 1979:24)

The Uniting Church seems to have missed the point—completely. Its racism seems to have blinded it to the fact that it takes considerably more than "an apology" to make up for cultural genocide. Perhaps this could have been expected from the mining industries, or even the government; but for the self-proclaimed guardians of the moral good of Australia, the church, to have done this seems almost inconceivable.

> Racial discrimination is not about racist attitudes only, but is also about the oppression—the crushing—of one racial group by another more powerful racial group. It is about one racial group using its power to maintain cultural, economic, political or social power over another, and to denigrate or destroy that group. (Rollason 1981:36)

The Uniting Church *crushed* the people of Mapoon—twice. Then, almost three decades later, it tosses them a few words and moves on. But, the Aboriginal People remember what happened.

> The Mapoon story may well be forgotten by whites, but blacks in all areas remember it well. (P. Wilson 1985:82)

Indeed, Aboriginal People cannot forget the questionable remorse of the church.

Questionable Actions

Aboriginal People also have come to question the actions of the church—especially in the area of the so-called "land returns." While it may be true that some lands are "returned," the true, legal definitions and implications of these moves need to be carefully analysed, as they are misleading—if not illegal and immoral. For example, in Western Australia, there was a

> transfer [of] several parcels of land held by the [Roman] Catholic Church to five Aboriginal communities in the Kimberley region. (KM 8 April 1992:7)

This move was promoted by the Western Australian Government as a significant step forward in the area of self-management and economic development. Indeed, it was hailed in the media. What is not obvious to most people, however, is the fact that

> the land would be held by the Aboriginal Lands Trust with 99-year *leases* to Aboriginal communities . . .. (KM 8 April 1992:7, emphasis added)

The Roman Catholic Church, which already had controlled the land for up to 100 years, still did not give the ownership of the land over directly to the Aboriginal communities. In other words, Aboriginal People only are trustworthy enough to be *lent* our own land.

There are many other cases like this. Thus, even on the rare occasions when it appears that the church has "returned land," the truth of the matter is that it has not. This kind of "church justice" remains a noisy gong and a clanging cymbal (I Cor. 13:1)—insincere, unethical and racist.

Land rights remains a burning issue for very many Aboriginal People, in spite of the church's help—and in many cases *because* of the church's so-called "help."

Crises in Leadership and Theological Education

Racism in the Australian church also is clearly seen in the current crises of leadership development and theological education. Aboriginal People face a critical shortage of their own indigenous leaders, as well as an inadequate theological education system for the few leaders that do exist.

Shortage of Indigenous Leaders

The Western, Christian missions which came to Australia had as their stated purpose "to Christianize the natives" (cf. Brook and Kohen 1991:104; Reynolds 1989:155–81). They were joined in this endeavour by the state; indeed,

> From 1823 it was Government *policy* to convert Aboriginal peoples to Christianity . . .. (Parbury 1988:51)

Why then—after over two centuries of "actively" implementing all manner of action plans supposedly established to reach this goal—are there *no fully qualified* Aboriginal theological professors or Christian educators? Why are there *no Aboriginal People at all* with earned teaching doctorates, such as the Ph.D. or Th.D. degree? Why are there *no* Aboriginal General Secretaries of denominations, or even of Councils of

Churches? Why are there *no* Aboriginal Directors of national church-related organizations? Why did it take until 1975 to ordain the first Roman Catholic priest (former-Fr. Pat Dodson)? Why is there *today* only *one* ordained Aboriginal Baptist minister (the Rev. Graham A. Paulson)— and only *one* Aboriginal Bishop (the Rt. Rev. Arthur Malcolm of the Anglican Church)? Why are there only a handful of Aboriginal clergypersons, and very few fully trained lay leaders?[17]

Indeed, why are the prospects for such leaders emerging in the near future—or, for that matter, the distant future—dismal to non-existent? Furthermore, why do so many of the limited numbers of leaders that are around die so young of stress-related diseases such as heart attacks?

The extent of the injustice becomes clearer with a simple comparison, as all of the above-mentioned shortages exist in light of the fact that there are literally hundreds, if not thousands, of white Europeans who have achieved full theological qualifications or received full theological training; who have been ordained or consecrated; who have been elected and serve as church leaders all across the country, from every denomination.

Clearly, those who "brought" Christianity to the Indigenous People of Australia have failed in "sharing" it with them. Indeed, they have failed to "live" Christianity here—and as a result, the Aboriginal People still face a severe leadership crisis.

Inadequate Theological Education

Closely related to this crisis is that of a woefully inadequate theological education system. Until very recently, theological education in Australia was an exclusively non-Aboriginal undertaking. While there are examples of Aboriginal People being handpicked for religious training in the past (e.g., Pattel-Gray and Trompf 1993:172–73), these cases are rare. It was not until the 1970s that Nungalinya Theological College was established in the Northern Territory for the training of traditional Aboriginal People. Even so, it is only relatively recently that it began offering certificates and diplomas in theology. This has been complemented by a few additional centers and programs here and there (e.g., Wontulp-Bi-Buya in Queensland, and Bimbadeen in New South Wales).

---

17 This is part of a generalized trend, documented as far back as 1975, when "the Aboriginal Consultative Group [ACG] recognized four areas of need with respect to the education of Aboriginal People: administration and decision makers; professionals; children; and, the excluded," ACG 1975: 27.

The fact remains, however, that the institutions and programs that do exist are paradigms of "second-class citizenship." That is, while they may appear to be continuing the great European tradition of providing classical theological education for the Indigenous People of Australia, the truth is that they are not even academically accredited. In themselves, the "certificates" and "diplomas" in theology earned by Aboriginal People from these institutions are not recognized by Australian universities. This means that they are virtually *worthless* towards graduate study for advanced degrees (such as Master of Theology, Doctor of Theology, or Doctor of Philosophy). No wonder there is a leadership crisis today.

Aboriginal People are being given "Sunday School" training, and being kept in positions of theological and ecclesiological dependency. Australian church hierarchies and structures are keeping the "power of knowledge" to themselves. They are actively excluding the Indigenous People from truly empowering knowledge and understanding. Aboriginal People are not being equipped to deal with non-Aboriginal ecclesiastical structures, committees, decision-making processes or polity intricacies (which "happen" to control the resources of the church). They are not being given exegetical or hermeneutical tools (e.g., higher Biblical criticism). They are not being taught the Biblical languages (e.g., Aramaic, Hebrew, Ugaritic, Greek). They are not being educated in the skills of critical thinking. In short, the theological education of Aboriginal People is inadequate (at least)—if not morally and ethically negligent. The responsibility for this injustice lies squarely on the shoulders of the Australian church.

Here, again, all of this is in light of the fact that hundreds, if not thousands, of white Europeans are receiving full theological educations; they are earning higher theological degrees; and, they are gaining theological qualifications that will enable them to minister or teach anywhere in the world.

Once more, it is clear that those who "taught" Christianity to the Indigenous People of Australia have failed to "share" it with them. They have failed to "live" Christianity here and, as a result, the Aboriginal People face a deep crisis in theological education.

The double crises of inadequate leadership development and theological education for Aboriginal People confirm the Australian church's racism.

Distorted Memory

Australian church racism is seen in its distorted memory of its own history and mission effort on this land. The church has a disturbing knack of omitting major elements of its own past. Take, for example, the experience of Elizabeth Pearce, an Aboriginal woman from Arnhem Land.

> It sounds so fantastically marvellous when Dr Keith Cole writes all those stories about the missionaries and the workers on those missions. He wrote a book about a Mr Perriman but he forgot to mention that he was the man who introduced the *stocks* on Groote Eylandt. Any girl causing trouble was put into these stocks and leg-irons. Nothing is ever said about that and I had to force it out of my mother even. The girls were allowed no contact with the tribal people on Groote Eylandt. This also wasn't allowed at Roper River but because many of them were mothers of these children of course they used to sneak in to see their kids and so on. (Gilbert 1971:7–8, emphasis added; cf. Cole 1973a)

It seems church people, or at least church historians, writers and teachers, have selective amnesia. Such "memory lapses" have a hugely negative impact on the church in its contemporary setting. They continue the lies and cover-ups of history; they violate the integrity of the church; and, perhaps most importantly, they block the movement of the church toward true justice and reconciliation. How can we walk together when the church does not adequately address its own repressive past, which continues to have a very malignant impact on Aboriginal People today?

The church is just as guilty as others of distorting memory through prolonging stereotypes. Take, for example, a Roman Catholic missionary to the Aboriginal People people of the Kimberleys, who are described in the following terms:

> . . . after 7 years of active work in Africa, I was sent by my Superiors into a new Mission Field in Australia. . . . Fearfully, I undertook the new task. . . . but once I arrived at the Beagle Bay Mission, I realized that they were just ordinary people like us with faults and imperfections. If they were still in the Stone Age, or an *earlier stage of development,* it did not make them different from other humans, only *simpler* and *less demanding,* in one word, *children.* (Walter 1982:7, emphasis added)

Perhaps more shocking is the self-congratulatory rationalization of such racist views and writings by the *current* Bishop of Broome in his introduction to the book. This contemporary church official legitimates racism with a shocking amount of praise heaped on the efforts of such early "pioneers of salvation" (Walter 1982:6).

There are many, many more examples that could be mentioned, but the fact remains that such "distorted memory" on the part of the church undermines its mission.

Continual Self-Justification

Australian ecclesial racism is seen in the continual self-justification on the part of the churches. On occasion, they do admit that racism exists in Australia. At times they even admit it exists in the church. But never, it seems, are they willing to look at the destructive effects of this presence on the lives of Aboriginal People, their children, or their children's children. Take, for example, the following statement:

> In the years 1850 to 1880 revival swept through the white churches of Australia. They grew in number and strength and social concern was awakened. People became very aware of the evils around them and tried to do something about them. One of the results was a renewed effort to pass on the gospel to the people *whose land they had taken over.* (Lindsay and Miles 1989:7, emphasis added)

If this had been written in 1850—or 1950 for that matter—it *might* be understandable. But that such a statement is made in 1989 is shocking—on a number of levels.

On a historical level, the statement reveals profound theological flaws betraying the Gospel's very message. How could these so-called "Christians" claim to "pass on the Gospel"—the very message of God—to the Indigenous People, without any mention whatsoever of justice for them? How could they "preach the Good News" without returning the land they stole, or pay for it, or even pay compensation for it? On a contemporary level, the statement also shows theological flaws. This may only be a passing reference, but how can contemporary writers skim right over this without so much as one word of condemnation? How—and on what grounds—can they seek to justify it? What kind of "Christianity" is this?

Such insensitivity and theological error are shocking, though not uncommon. The Australian church shows its racism when it continually engages in this kind of self-justification.

Ambivalence in Statements

Racism in the Australian church is evident in the great ambivalence in statements that are made in support for Aboriginal People or concerns.

Some statements are made with great fanfare, only to be subsequently withdrawn, denied, or worse—discounted. For example, in 1991 the World Council of Churches (WCC) held its 7th Assembly in Canberra. At that meeting, the Assembly (and, implicitly, over 300 member churches from around the world) agreed to support the claims of the Aboriginal and Islander People for land, land rights and sovereignty. Amazingly, less than two months later the General Secretary of the Australian Council of Churches, the Rev. David M. Gill, stated that the World Council of Churches'

> identity problem distorted the assembly's output. Take what happened with the *seriously flawed* statement on Aboriginal People and Torres Strait Islanders. . . . Australian delegate Michael Horsburgh traces the statement's shortcomings to the defective process:
>
> "The blame for the presentation of such unsatisfactory material belongs entirely with the (Assembly's) Public Issues Committee. . . . The Committee was unable to draw an appropriate distinction between a statement made by Aboriginal people on their own behalf and a statement made by a world body such as the Assembly. Not making this distinction, they failed to attend to the accuracy and meaning of the statement, preferring solidarity with the oppressed to content. They abandoned policy to *emotion*."
>
> Michael Horsburgh is right. . . . (1991:7.1b.3)

Perhaps not surprisingly, then, other ecumenical "leaders" from around the world "repeated" the example. Less than eight months later, the Archbishop of York gave a public address in which he stated:

> Elsewhere the [WCC] Assembly said: "We recognize that indigenous peoples of Australia were independent, self-governing peoples long before Europeans invaded their land, and that they have a rights to regain such control over their land under their own rule."
>
> Some resolution! But of course *nobody meant it* in any straightforward sense. They meant to express sympathy and solidarity, but what they actually said was *absurd*. (Habgood 1991:16)

This kind of disingenuous and ambivalent support from church leaders never can lead to authentic self-determination for Indigenous People in Australia—or anywhere else for that matter. If the church is not serious in its commitments with Indigenous Peoples, it must be willing to stand and pay the price, up-front, and in the light of public scrutiny—and not in the dimly-lit alleys of "we-take-it-back-right-after-the-meeting-when-the-world-is-not-looking-anymore." The church must recognize that the word of God reaches out to all, especially through popular movements.

Here prophecy is no longer just the word of one prophet, rather it is also spread in the popular movements and in the writings which encourage persecuted people in their faith, resistant against the oppressive power. (Mesters 1990:95, translated from the Spanish)

Ambivalent statements of support from the church and its leaders reveal their racism, and make a mockery of the Christ they claim to serve.

Failures to Stand

The Australian church's racism is evident in its abysmal failure to stand united against racism in this country. Recognizing the existence of racism *in general* is the easy part, and so, many churches decry this "evil" in the widest possible terms. Some churches even go the next step and recognize the existence of racism *in the church* itself. The Uniting Church in Australia, for example, admits that

> *racism* is still respectable in parts of our society, and in some parts of our church. There are still myths and stories and attitudes that deny a full place in society to Aboriginal people and to many people from Asia. (UCA 1989:4)

But, churches decry racism on very general terms in their policy statements and declarations, and it is very rare to see churches or even individual church people *take a stand*—especially when and where it counts. A very simple example highlights this fact. In early 1991 two major, national-level, multi-million dollar studies were released: the *Report of the Royal Commission into Aboriginal Deaths in Custody,* and the *Report of the National Inquiry into Racist Violence in Australia.* The publication of these reports caused a tremendous stir in the media, with many sectors of Australian society stating how shocked they were at the findings. And, what did the churches say or do in response to either these reports? Virtually nothing. The church's silence is deafening—its lack of action is shocking.

> . . . nonengagement will be tantamount to *accepting* the situation and thereby implicitly *espousing* the cause of the privileged. (L. Boff 1989:128, emphasis added)

By keeping quiet, the Australian churches are accepting the situation of racism against Aboriginal People, and implicitly espousing the cause of the privileged white majority. The churches are reinforcing their own racism, as well as that of society in general. They are endorsing inequality and injustice.

Never before in the life of the Australian ecumenical movement has there ever been such a strong stance and visible support for obtaining justice for the Aboriginal People as what was seen during the debate surrounding Australian High Court's Native Title decision and subsequent Native Title legislation. The Heads of Churches moved in to lock arms with Aboriginal leaders, both church and secular, to ensure the safe passage of the Native Title Bill.

Yet, the responses of Australian Christians at the parish level centered on resolution and reconciliation, rather than focusing on their own racism underlying and endorsing the offensive actions on the parts of government and business. Where there seems to be a desire for active repentance and justice within the national ecumenical movement, there is, nevertheless, much more work to be done at the level of the local congregation, before Australian churches on the whole are seen to be taking a stand for (or with) Aboriginal People.

"Exemptions"?

Australian church racism arguably is most condemnable when the churches proclaim themselves "exempt" from certain specific statutes of civil law, namely the codes involving racial discrimination (as well as equal opportunity legislation) (ACC 1993). The churches have long maintained that they are somehow "different" than any other institution or organization in Australia, including government, business, education, and other private sectors (cf. Matheson 1993:11). This belief has led them to exclude themselves—in no uncertain terms—from the provisions of law which enforce non-discrimination on the basis of race, sex, etc. If a case arises in which the churches are accused of racism, or racist practices, they simply hide behind the curtain of "exemption" and walk away free.

On the one hand, the churches claim to be the paragons of virtue, upholding none other than God's own moral integrity. Yet, on the other hand, the churches consider themselves to be above and beyond mere human laws on racism and sexism. This shocking state of affairs raises very profound questions about the churchs' morality and integrity. How can the churches possibly *exempt* themselves from upholding the cause of justice?

Worse yet, the churches are not worried about this blatant discrepancy. The Australian church today is—and is seeking to remain—exclusively "judge," and never "defendant," by claiming exemption from charges of racism.

Ignoring the Problem

Racism in the Australian church is perhaps most evident in that the church absolutely ignores (and denies) that it still has a very serious racism problem. For decades, the churches have been receiving reports regarding the horrific situation of the Aboriginal People of Australia. Yet, the problems continue—unabated; in some cases, they worsen with the passing of time. The Australian churches do not have the political will— much less the moral will—to see, and effectively address, the multilayered issues and the root causes of racism.

Yet, other churches around the world can see the Australian church's racism. Some of the Statements from the Fifth Assembly of the World Council of Churches in Nairobi describe this well.

> To our shame, Christian churches around the world are all too often infected by racism, overt and covert.
> . . . many argue that they are free of racism as if its reality could be undone by ignoring it;
> . . . in leadership privileges and in programmatic priorities churches tend too easily to indulge in racism without even recognising it. (van der Bent 1986:54)

Racism in the church is a betrayal of Christianity, of the very principles and ethics which the church claims to stand for, and cannot be ignored. Christ stood for equality and justice. For Christians to ignore such obvious injustice is a betrayal not just of their claims of faith in Christ, but also of Christ himself.

The Australian church cannot wash the blood off its hands, for there are literally thousands of Aboriginal People who, today, bear the physical and emotion scars of Australian church abuse and violence. The horrors of children who were stolen away from their parents by the church; or of adults who were forcibly removed from their land by the church; or of others who were starved and beaten by missionaries for the most trivial (white-defined) "offences"; or the savage emptiness of destroyed languages and culture—all these things are *within living memory* for many, many Aboriginal People. The church cannot simply discount all this pain and grief by ignoring the fact of racism. Racism exists in Australia. Indeed, racism is *growing* in Australia, due to many factors—social, economic, political and religious. For the Australian church to deny even the possibility of its own racism surely is reflective of a slavery to sin.

Slaves to the Sin of Racism

In Romans 6:15–23, the Apostle Paul talks of "the two slaveries."

What then? Should we sin because we are not under law but under grace? By no means! Do you not know that if you present yourselves to anyone as obedient slaves, you are slaves of the one whom you obey, either of sin, which leads to death, or of obedience, which leads to righteousness? But thanks be to God that you, having once been slaves of sin, have become obedient from the heart to the form of teaching to which you were entrusted, and that you having been set free from sin, have become slaves of righteousness."

Sinners are slaves to sin. Having become "obedient from the heart," however, people have the possibility of becoming "slaves of righteousness" and no longer obeying their former master.

Using this simple biblical illustration, it is clear that the Australian church is a slave to the sin of racism, because it continues to serve the master called "Racism." The Australian church does not struggle to its *maximum* capacity for land rights; it distorts its memory; it allows the crises of leadership and theological education to continue; it makes ambivalent statements; it fails to stand for justice on Christ's integrity; it claims exemptions; it ignores the problem of racism. In short, by obeying the master of sin which enslaves Australian Aboriginal People today— exegetically, hermeneutically, theologically, Christologically, missiologically, ecclesiologically, polemically and practically—the Australian church stands condemned of the sin of racism.

An Aboriginal Womanist Critique
of Australian Church Feminism

Another major area of racism in the Australian church is found in Australian church feminism. This study presents an opportunity for critique of this movement.

Over the years Aboriginal women have come to see several flaws in the feminist movement, as well as severe limitations in the way it relates to Aboriginal women. When Aboriginal church women speak to me about feminist theology they say it is not about them, but rather about white women wanting to rule. This chapter will endeavour to uncover the negative impact of feminism upon Aboriginal women of Australia, and how it hinders the Aboriginal womanist movement, which is based on our law, culture and identity by highlighting a few flawed assumptions and methodologies, reviewing some of the historical and contemporary differences as well as highlighting some Aboriginal women's literary contributions.

Within the global Black[18] Womanist movement it has became obvious that feminism is not without serious limitations, even though the feminist movement has made an important impact upon the church and broader society. Black women from around the world perceive that

> Feminist theology is inadequate for two reasons: it is White and racist. (Grant 1989:195)

Their reasoning for this is that the black women's experience is totally different from that of the white women. As Grant clearly states,

> Feminist theologians are white in terms of their race and in terms of the nature of the sources they use for the development of their theological perspectives. Although there are sharp differences among feminist theologians, . . . they are all of the same race and the influence of their race has led them to similar sources for the definition of their perspectives on the faith. Of course, chief among the sources is women's experience. However, what is often unmentioned is that feminist theologians' sources for womens' experience refer almost exclusively to White womens' experience. White womens' experience and Black womens' experience are not the same. Indeed all experiences are unique to some degree. But in this case the differences is so radical that it may be said that White women and Black women are in completely different realms. (Grant 1989:195)

In Australia, Aboriginal women and feminism are in very different realms.

Flawed Assumptions

Many of the assumptions made by feminist theologians are flawed. These include beliefs in the commonality between white women and Aboriginal women in such areas as social origins, epistemology and experience.

Social Origins

One flawed assumption is that both black and white women come from the same hegemonic society. Aboriginal women do not think of themselves as being white, or integrated to the point of being colourless or cultureless—if anything, we take great offence when these assumption

---

[18] The use of the term "black" in the Australian context of this section refers to Australian Aboriginal People.

are made on our behalf. When we take a closer look at this white dominant, hegemonic society we need to view the truth of this situation. Aboriginal women in this society find themselves at the bottom of the social ladder, mostly unemployed or restricted to menial jobs, uneducated, poor and excluded from the broader community. In this hegemonic society there is little or no work for Aboriginal women (for background, cf. Daly 1991:91–100). Nine times out of ten when an Aboriginal woman has managed to gain an education and has gained even a small level of success, and subsequently tries to advance her career to a position of leadership within this Australian society, she will come up against a brick wall, as a white woman will always be given priority over her, since, "Everyone knows" that "white is best." An Aboriginal, the mistaken assumption goes, can only offer leadership to other Aboriginals, and certainly not to the white society. This assumption also certainly is made by white women when it comes to theology and leadership in the church.

When we look at the social, gender and race structure within this Australian society we find a hierarchical social order which places white men at the top and Aboriginal women at the bottom.

DIAGRAM 3
Australian Social Hierarchy
(Pattel-Gray 1995:66)

Highest

    white men
       white women

           migrant men (European)
             migrant women (European)

               migrant men (of colour)
                 migrant women (of colour)

                    refugee men (European)
                      refugee women (European)

                         refugee men (of colour)
                           refugee women (of colour)

                           Aboriginal men
                            Aboriginal women

                               Lowest

If the Australian social order is an indication of Aboriginal women's status in this society, then it is no wonder that both "racism" and "classism" are major issues for black women today. For feminist theologians to speak of an inclusive women's movement and exclude classism and racism as a part of their critique, is to speak only of a white middle-class women's movement—because its very nature excludes Aboriginal women from participation.

Epistemology

Another flawed assumption of feminists is that black and white women's epistemologies are the same.

In fact, nothing could be further from the truth. The grounds of knowledge for Aboriginal People are centred on *dharrpal dhalatj* ("sacred knowledge") and on *rom* ("cultural law"), both of which date back to the beginning of time (OT: M. Yunupingu; D. Yunupingu and D. Yunupingu

1996:94–98).[19] Aboriginal People have passed these down from generation to generation for hundreds of thousands of years.

The vast gaps are obvious—at least to some white Australians. Dr. Andrew Dutney, Professor of Systematic Theology at Parkin-Wesley Theological College in South Australia, writes that his teaching experiences confirm a great epistemological difference between white and Aboriginal students, stemming from racism passed on by white missionaries (1996:259).

To state, imply or assume that Aboriginal and non-Aboriginal epistemology are the same is to deny our religion, Cosmogony and identity. Our Cosmogony is vastly different from that of both the Genesis and "evolution" positions of non-Aboriginals. Our values, religious practices, languages, culture, experience and history—to name but a few—are unique. We begin at a different point than Western epistemology.

Experience/History

Perhaps the most flawed of the assumptions is that the experiences and histories of white women and black women in Australia are the same, or somehow comparable.

> Slavery and segregation have created such a gulf between these women, that White feminists' common assumption that all women are in the same situation with respect to sexism is difficult to understand when history so clearly tells us a different story. (Grant 1989:195–96)

This is true for Aboriginal women in Australia, when we experience this same assumption being made by white women—that because they speak of eliminating sexism from within the white patriarchal institutions, that all women will be liberated. This is not the case, as black women have to struggle with the tri-dimensional oppression under which they suffer: racism, sexism and classism (cf. Cannon 1989:16–17; Gill 1983:88; WCC 1992a; WCC 1992b). When we take a look at our common history in Australia, we see various differences between the white womens' experiences and the black womens' experiences.

---

19 It is important to note that the concepts and term *dharrpal djalatj* and *rom* are from the Gumatj language, used in North East Arnhem Land. Aboriginal People from different parts of Australia refer to these concepts by different names.

Slavery and Servitude from 1788

Upon the 1788 invasion of the Europeans, Aboriginal women, along with their men and children, were classified and considered to be the lowest species of Humanity—indeed barely human and more like animals. Therefore, we were to be hunted down and shot on sight. We were also considered to be intellectually, socially, politically and culturally inferior, and to be discarded as waste within this our own land.

Our homelands were taken, as were the lives of our men, women and children. Aboriginal women have suffered under great sexual harassment since 1788. There were no laws to protect Aboriginal women from such harassment; and even if there had been—as there are today—no one really would have cared.

> So strong was the idea that all women in penal colony Australia were whores that women who were not convicts became its victims too. Aboriginal women carried a double burden. As women, they were seen as sexual objects and fair game for white men; as members of a subject people they were also victims of the whole range of indignities bestowed by a brutal invading colonialism which considered itself to be the master race. (Summers 1994:322)

Aboriginal women suffered much horrendous treatment from the white invading society. They suffered such physical violence as being beaten, or worse, having their water holes, sugar and flour poisoned, or even being shot down like dogs (cf. Elder 1988; Loos 1982:57–58, 61). It is well-documented that white men committed atrocities against Aboriginal women, such as repeated assaults, pack rapes and enslavement (cf. Reynolds 1981:70–72; Reynolds 1987a:73–74). If the Aboriginal woman were unlucky enough to survive such savage attacks—when the men had finished with her, or rather when she had "served their purpose"—the men then shoved spears into her vagina until she died (cf. Roberts 1981:19). These women ranged in age from grandmothers to young girls.

Aboriginal women were kidnapped by white men and taken as slaves, and sexually and physically abused and, sometimes, during these continual beatings, died as a result. This did not cause the white men or women any reason for concern because neither cared what happened to the Aboriginal women. White men would just go and get another to take the place of the one that died.

The indignities suffered by Aboriginal women was a reflection of the immorality of the white society.

Ready access to black women was one of the attractions of outback life and there is abundant evidence that women were forcibly abducted in all parts of Australia from the early years of settlement until the 1930s and 1940s. There were casual episodes when women, seen by chance in the bush, were run down and raped in brief, brutal encounters. On other occasions parties of stockmen went out on "gin hunts" deliberately seeking women for sex. The Normanton Protector of Aborigines explained in 1904 that it was a common practice for Europeans ... to round up "small mobs of wild natives" and despoil their women. To prevent escape women were kept under lock and key, chained, tied up, terrorised. An experienced station manager explained that after they had been taken by force the women were "even kept in irons until they are too terrified to make any attempt to return to their own tribe". (Reynolds 1987a:73–74)

Victorian moralizing led white women to close their eyes to the gross violations of the human rights of Aboriginal women. They considered the Aboriginal women to be inferior to them. In order to give themselves status in their white communities, white women felt it necessary to subjugate black women to a life of immorality and vilification. By closing their eyes to the actions of their men, white women condoned immoral and degrading practices.

The Australian ideology of white supremacy was to be maintained for many decades. The brutal force and flexing of white "superiority" on the backs of Aboriginal women and girls was to be felt for a long time to come. The white people of Australia believed themselves to be civilized— and therefore superior to the Aboriginal race. Yet, when you consider the ways they dehumanized Aboriginal People through their barbaric trade of selling and buying Aboriginal children, you have to wonder who really was civilized.

Aboriginal children were kidnapped in all parts of Australia. Boys as young as five and six were taken to be "bred up to stock work"; girls only a little older were abducted to work as servants and to double as sexual partners. The trade in children probably began in the first half of the nineteenth century and developed rapidly during the settlement of north Australia between 1860 and 1920. ... two [White] Europeans had stolen two boys, locked them in a hut and then taken them to the gold diggings to sell. He [a squatter] feared the practice would continue "because it pays so well". (Reynolds 1987a:74)

These atrocities were well-known and well-documented, in various forms, in official reports. No one could plead ignorance about the goings-on and enslavement and trade of Aboriginal youth. In addition, they filled a gap in the servant class, which made life easier not only for the white men but also for the white women of this "new" land. It is no surprise, then, that no actions toward justice were taken as the police were just as guilty. For example:

> ... In his annual report for 1871 he [the Police Commissioner] explained that many Aboriginal attacks took place "on account of settlers carrying off gins [young Aboriginal girls] and small boys to be made servants." The police magistrate at Normanton had no hesitation in telling his superiors in Brisbane in 1874 that the stealing of women and children was "a matter of frequent occurrence here." Twenty years later a retired northern JP wrote to the Queenslander arguing that kidnapping was "done every day both in the interior and on the coast, and one of the greatest offenders are the police". (Reynolds 1987a:74)

We even find that white women were not excluded from this lucrative industry, as they participated in the full knowledge of how these children were obtained—even to the point of receiving their "chattel" (slaves) through inheritance. In his *Report of the Northern Protector of Aborigines for 1902,* the Normanton Protector of Aboriginals wrote the following:

> A large number of individuals had an idea that they can trade an aboriginal as they would a horse or bullock. Some of these people are good church-goers. One lady informed me an aboriginal had been left to her by will. (quoted in Reynolds 1989:143)

During this time white people not only kidnapped Aboriginal children and engaged in the lucrative slave trade, they also continued the progression toward physical and cultural genocide of the Aboriginal People. This can be considered as the next stage of the export industry of Aboriginal skulls that had begun at the very foundation of the colony (cf. Monaghan 1991).

Brutality

White people believed themselves superior to Aboriginals. In order to maintain their presumed authority as masters and mistresses over the Aboriginals, they deemed it necessary to continually administer physical violence upon them, including beatings, floggings and whippings. Records reveal some of the thoughts of the era.

> When the settlers wanted the land they used guns; when the needed cheap labour they put them down and picked up their whips, brandishing them just as freely and with a little interference from the law. "The only and best way to keep the blacks from annoying you" ... in the 1850s "is to pitch into some of them with a whip and let them know you are the master [or mistress] and not them." Outback settlers "did not look upon the flogging of a black girl or the ill

treatment of a black boy as anything wrong", . . . "people out here make as light
of knocking down a blackfellow with a slip-rail or flogging him [or her] with a
stock-whip as though it was having a drink." . . . "a native had a hide, and not
an ordinary skin like a human being." Whips used for official flogging only
"wiped the dust off a native." . . . "Flogging is all very well in its way, . . . but a
nigger can take a power of it to convince him". (Reynolds 1987a:70–71)

This kind of flogging was considered by whites as "keeping the
Aboriginal 'down' or 'in their place.'" Befriending them was seen as
giving the black an air of equality with the white, and so floggings were
administered to make sure blacks never forgot that they were (supposed
to be) inferior. Jean Devanny (the novelist) shares a conversation with
one of her hostesses,

"You've got to keep them down . . . otherwise they become as cheeky as they
are stupid". She found that the belief that blacks were ruined if whites actually
talked to them was "subscribed to by almost the entire white population".
(Reynolds 1987a:70)

In one way, you could say we have shared in our history, but only in the
role of the oppressor and the oppressed. As we continue to move through
our history we will continue to parallel the difference between white
women's and black women's experiences.

From Segregation to "So-Called" Protection

From 1849 on, segregation became the acceptable social norm, as no
white people wanted Aboriginal People near their towns or communities
because they were considered by whites to be filthy, dirty beasts (cf.
Threlkeld/MLS). At white people's insistence, the government moved to
implement a policy of segregation. Aboriginal People were literally
herded out of white settlements and towns on to, and kept in, compounds
called reserves and missions, in massive numbers and restrained there
indefinitely. This was said to have happened in order to protect
Aboriginal People from the brutal heritage of the frontier. But for
Aboriginal People it just meant a continuing practice of "cultural
genocide" upon their tradition, culture and race. This legislation may
have been—at the time—justified as an instrument for the protection of
Aboriginal People, but it literally denied them their basic human rights.
The Protection legislation defined "Aboriginals" and rendered them a
special, and in effect, subject class of Australia, without rights or
entitlements under "normal" Australian law. Under this legislation,

Aboriginal People were firmly restricted in their rights of residence, mobility, association and ownership.

> This period of protection differs markedly from those of the earlier nineteenth century. They [the government, missionaries, philanthropic societies and other "do-gooders"] sought to protect the rights and entitlements of the Aboriginal people, to apply the law to them equally as British subjects, to train them for "civilisation" and equip them to participate. It was almost "assimilationist" in intent, but the twentieth century protection was distinctly segregationist, physically and legally: it controlled Aboriginal lives, work, education, and children, deprived them of their citizen status, and gave them minimal opportunity for equal participation. (Daylight and Johnstone 1986:102; cf. Rowley 1971)

During that time Government and churches worked together creating mission stations and reserves in which to place Aboriginal People. Aboriginal babies and young children were ripped from their mothers arms and placed into these many institutions. The Chief Protector of Aborigines became legal guardian of Aboriginal children. This was done so as to "re-educate" the Aboriginal children to learn the "superior" white people's way—not to mention to remove them from their lands and therefore control and destroy them (cf. Parbury 1986:89). Whites taught Aboriginals such things as how to be good servants, to never question whites and to be always obedient and submissive. This was reinforced through their white, Westernized Gospel. They could not accept Aboriginals as they were, created as equals by God.

> The missionaries and other philanthropic Europeans believed that the Aboriginal children were the key to success in their task of "civilizing the natives." If only they could be removed from tribal influences at a tender age they could be brought up in the ways of the White man. Such was their enthusiasm for this task that "parsons" gained an evil reputation among Aborigines as people who stole children. On reserves and missions where it was possible to impose white authority children were taken from their parents and raised in single-sex dormitories. Such institutions still existed in the 1960s and 1970s. The view was that because the task was so difficult extremely rigid training was necessary to overcome the "wildness" in the children. (Reynolds 1989:170)

In looking at the experiences of Aboriginal women and white women, the difference would have to be how Aboriginal women suffered under great oppression and how white women did not suffer such oppressive control within this society. They were not told where they could live, whether they could raise their own children, who they could marry or if and where they could work. White women where not subjects under special legislations, and were not controlled by the "protection" of the government.

Assimilation

Assimilation refers to the next stage of cultural genocide. It meant Aboriginal status would be "raised" and "by rights" would entitle them to "full participation" within the white society in their own land. This, of course, meant that they could become "like" whites, taking their values, law and tradition, and being happy with being "second class citizens."[20]

> The cost of protection for Aboriginals had been the loss of virtually all their basic human rights; the cost of assimilation was to be the loss of their Aboriginal identity: they were now to disappear culturally rather than literally. (Daylight and Johnstone 1986:105)

The basis of the Assimilation policy was that Aboriginal culture and lifestyle were worthless and that Aboriginal People should have the same values as all Australians. For this reason assimilation is now regarded as cultural genocide (cf. United Nations 1988:143–44). This practice was certainly the worst manifestation of this policy, whereby officialdom bequeathed unto itself the rights to say that those children born of "mixed" Aboriginal decent would be better off if they were brought up as "second class whites." On the one hand it was a wonderful way of ridding unscrupulous whites of the embarrassing end results of their promiscuity; on the other hand though, it backfired absolutely, as in most cases the children still suffered discrimination, perhaps more, because they could now be labelled "mongrels," having brown skin rather than black.

Little wonder that, when it was open to individuals to decide where their identification lay, almost invariably they chose to identify with the Aboriginal side of their heritage, rather than the white. But for those who were one of the lost generation, who found that their fathers were clergymen, politicians, police, station owners, and other "pillars of white society," the scars are deep indeed.

One of the saddest issues relating to Aboriginal People is the taking of Aboriginal babies and children from their mothers and communities. Many never found their mother again. Those few who did find their mothers sadly discovered that they had nothing in common, other than

---

[20] This fact is all the more ironic when we acknowledge that Aboriginal People were not even counted in the Census until 1967!

the fact that they were established as mother and son or daughter. In the implementation of the inhuman Assimilation Policy, there are even reports of "children being dragged from their mother's breast." For example, an Aborigines Department inspector in the north-west of Western Australia wrote in 1908:

> ... it is the duty of the State that they be given a chance to lead a better life than their mothers. I would not hesitate for one moment to separate any half-caste (sic) from its aboriginal mother, no matter how frantic her momentary grief might be at the time. They soon forget their off-spring. (WCC 1991:88)

Aboriginal women's experience of white women during this time was classified as a part of the white oppressor system, and often the women were more ruthless than white men.

> Many Black women experienced White women as the white supremacist group who most directly exercised power over them, often in a manner far more brutal and dehumanizing than that of racist White men. (Even) today, despite predominant rule by White supremacist patriarchs, Black women often work in a situation where the immediate supervisor, boss, or authority figure is a White woman. (Hooks 1984:49, cited in Grant 1989:198)

Margaret Tucker tells of her own experience as a child, and how she had been taken and put into Cootamundra Domestic Training Home for Aboriginal Girls, then farmed out to serve in a white family. Margaret gives explicit details regarding her treatment at the hands of this white mistress. During Margaret's time in this white home she was continually abused and beaten by her white mistress. She tells the story herself.

> One morning I was washing up outside ... I did not do something properly. She [the mistress] was in a bad mood and I copped it as the saying is. She boxed my ears as she held me by the hair. She slapped my face as I cried, "Don't, you are hurting me." She was like a mad person. She didn't stop until her husband came to the door and begged her to stop because she was upsetting herself. (Tucker 1977:119–20)

Margaret also found herself being humiliated, the victim of her mistress's torment. With great pain Margaret recalls the story.

> ... I was made to suffer more indignities. I don't know why she would get cross with me when I least expected it. She would take a great delight in making me strip, and then she would turn the hose on me in front of the men working on a building next door ... I just wanted to die, nothing mattered any more. (Tucker 1977:124)

This was to be a young Aboriginal girl's life, and not only was she to be subjected to physical and mental abuse, she was also denied any compassion and friendship that would ever come her way. Margaret's "miserable days turned into weeks—months—years" (Tucker 1977:114).

> Winters and summers came and went. I was always scantily dressed in a thin blouse and skirt and underneath a hessian sugar-bag singlet that Mrs Smith made; I had no other underclothing and my legs and feet were bare. In winter the cold was unbearable. I would wait for the first streak of sun and would stand in that spot or move when the sun shifted. The sun was my friend when it was not covered by clouds. On frosty mornings I would sit in the shed, and cover myself with a bag. One of my duties was to get up early . . . and get Mr and Mrs Smith a cup a tea. I would snatch a cup of tea for myself. Then they would get up. The boss had to go to work. I would not be allowed inside all day. The early morning cup of tea was stopped after a while, because I put too much milk in my own tea. . . . That meant they didn't have enough milk for breakfast. Tea went off my diet. I suppose I was an expense. (Tucker 1977:114–15)

Even these horror stories are only but a few of the memories of one woman. The suffering of Aboriginal girls is not an isolated case as there are thousands of Aboriginal women today who have had the same experience, and have also taken it upon themselves to write it down. Some of these works are described below.

Aboriginal Women Tell Their Stories

As an Aboriginal woman, I feel that we are very fortunate that our women elders have taken it upon themselves to record some of the horrific atrocities which they suffered under the appalling legislation and social practices imposed upon them by the white Australian society. These stories bring about the pain within ourselves that we have tried to forget. Yet, somehow, with enormous courage, these women found the strength that was necessary to document their lives. For white women who want to learn more about the lives of Aboriginal women and Australia's unspoken history, I would suggest that they read some of this literature, as it uncovers the racism and white supremacist ideology that still is to be found today, as we approach the 21st century.

Biographies, autobiographies, and narratives reveal many of the stories of how black women experienced white Australia. These stories share the pain and agonies suffered by Aboriginal women. In Margaret Tucker's autobiography, *If Everyone Cared* (1977), we feel the pain of a young girl torn from her family and then subjected to a life of servitude and abuse.

Shirley Smith's autobiography, *Mum Shirl* (1981), records the many struggles of her life as a powerfully outspoken woman on justice for her people, and as a well-known leader of the Aboriginal community. Labumore's (Elsie Roughsey) *An Aboriginal Mother Tells of the Old and the New* (1984), exposes the racist impact of government policies during her life on Mornington Island. Ida West's *Pride Against Prejudice* (1984), speaks about the social life and customs of her people on Flinder's Island and the Aborigines of Tasmania.

Ruby Langford's *Don't Take Your Love to Town* (1988), takes us on a journey, and shares with us her own struggles in raising her family in a world in which racism divided white and black people in Australia. Coral Edwards and Peter Read's edited work, *The Lost Children* (1989), speaks of the stories and struggles of Aboriginal women and men who were kidnapped and institutionalized, the horrific treatment and, through the Aboriginal organization Link-Up, finding their way home. Barbara Cummings' *Take This Child . . .* (1990) is a well-documented book on the forced institutionalization of Aboriginal children within the Northern Territory, the government policies active during this time, and the practices which were used to fulfil the letter of the law of the policies. Through the personal stories of the anthology, *The Wailing* (1993), we are exposed to the treatment of Aboriginals and to their social conditions.

It is important to highlight the substantial contribution made to the literature by all Aboriginal women. It is impossible, however, in this limited chapter, to identify all Aboriginal women—so, I just mention a few. There can be no denying that Aboriginal women have made a significant impact in exposing the racism, sexism and classism which they suffered—and continue to suffer in this present day.

Feminist Theological Assumptions

For the past 206 years, in the different timespans of government policies, it becomes quite obvious that Aboriginal women's role within Australia was one of inferior being, slave, servant, prisoner and beast of the frontier. The role of the Aboriginal woman is reflected very clearly in the telling of their stories. The history of white-black women in Australia is one of the domination of white women and the subordination under which black women existed. This was (and is) a reflection of the attitude within the broader Australian society.

Three dimensions of this situation are important for our topic: 1) Physical brutality toward Blacks was continued, and even extended to violence outside of the work context. 2) The immediate relationship between White women and Black women did not change; White women were still the oppressors and Black women were still the oppressed. 3) As a part of this continued relationship, Black women were still treated as property. These dynamics between White and Black women represent some of the negative dimensions of Black women's experience.

What is apparent in this context is how Black women's experience involves a convergence of racism, sexism, and classism. Within the limited arena of domestic labour, the sexist assumption that women's place is (only) in the home is reconfirmed, as well as the classist practice of paying those who do "menial" jobs little or nothing, and the assumption that such work is more appropriately done by those of the servant class. These patterns are compounded by the racist assumption that White women need protection from actual work and therefore should function in a supervisory capacity. (Grant 1989:198)

This needs to be a painful reminder to feminist theologians—that to speak of an inclusive theology is to make sure the different experiences of Aboriginal women and white women are identified, and to challenge the dominant role white women played in the oppression of black women, so justice can be seen as being done within their own struggle. It seems to black women, that white women think they do not have to deal with the reality of their oppression towards Aboriginal women, and that white women's only focus is about "disempowering" white men who are their oppressors. The fact remains that white women need to be reminded that they too are black women's oppressors, along with their white men.

Thus when theologians speak about women's experience as the source for doing feminist theology, it is necessary to specify which women's experience is being referred to, for the above discussion demonstrates that the experience of White women and Black women have been far from the same. (Grant 1989:198–99)

One of the areas feminist theologians do not look at is the contributions Aboriginal women can make—for instance, Aboriginal women's religious tradition and Dreamings, and the role of the Aboriginal women within their own society. It is quite sad to see not only what little knowledge white women have about Aboriginal women, but also that they do not even see this knowledge as having importance within their theological framework—especially when some white women scholars clearly state the relevance.

Until recently the majority of writers on Aboriginal culture have been males, who have taken for granted the dominant position of men in Western society and therefore have not noticed that Aboriginal women, on the whole, enjoyed a greater degree of economic independence then did their own women. (Gale 1978:1)

It is important to note that at some point white women just might be able to learn from Aboriginal women that they have never taken away from their men the role which they play within the community. We have managed to complement each other's strengths because the concern is for the survival of the whole community and not just for the individual. Aboriginal culture could not have survived without the interrelated workings of the men's and women's roles, that are clearly defined within an Aboriginal community. Aboriginal men also know and have acknowledged that the survival of our people has been through the major contribution and strength of the Aboriginal women. Aboriginal women are not on about denigrating or disempowering their men, as they respect the partnership enjoyed with their men. The role of the family within a community is of top priority for both women and men. This we see is an indication of the status enjoyed by Aboriginal women, that white women have yet to obtain.

Flawed Methodology: Conspicuous by Our Absence

Aboriginal women have long been active in the Australian church—despite the destructive effects of Western Christian missions and church practices (cf. Gondarra 1989:10–11). Yet, we have been excluded from both participation and leadership in our own churches. Our voices have not been heard, and we are pushed to the periphery, or "forgotten" altogether. What is even more painful is that Australian church feminism excludes us.

There is significant historical documentation to prove it. Even a cursory review of the literature shows that Aboriginal women—indeed Aboriginal People—simply have not been dealt with (until very recently). Numerous studies, papers and reports show that Aboriginal women are conspicuous by our absence.

We are not part of the agenda of meetings; we are not the authors of the conference documents; we are not even mentioned in the contents of the reports. In the area of ecumenism, for example, the Commission on the Status of Women of the Australian Council of Churches (New South Wales State Council) produced a report in 1974 on the Enquiry into the

Status of Women in the Church. Aboriginal women were virtually invisible. There was no mention of the significantly disadvantaged and disempowered position of Aboriginal women in both the Australian church and society. In the area of church history, to give another example, *Women, Faith and Fetes: Essays in the History of Women and the Church in Australia* was published in 1977; again, Aboriginal women were nowhere to be found. It is as if we did not exist.

We also find, in the international arena, that women of colour felt it necessary to construct their own committee to address their own issues, as they felt unable and—to some extent—excluded from the World Council of Churches Women's Program.

In 1986, the international Women Under Racism and Casteism Consultation gathered in Geneva, and called for very specific improvements to the living conditions of the women in Australia, including ". . . immediate attention and action concerning the cultural and physical genocide being practised through alienation and forced removal of Aboriginal peoples from the land" (WCC 1986:85–89). Yet Australian women have not taken up the challenge.

Splitting the Movement

Two Australian feminists, for example, present the idea that there are "two different and conflicting systems of meaning" (White and Tulip 1991:1). The first, they say, is patriarchal. Drawing on Elizabeth Schüssler Fiorenza (1983:29), they write that

> Power is organised hierarchically, according to sex, race and class, so the people at the top tend to be rich white men, and the people at the bottom poor black women.

This appears to be the beginning of a solid, all-encompassing argument against sexism, racism and classism. The authors then present the next system, the feminist view.

> The second way of seeing reality emphasises mutuality between people rather than structures of dominance, and has emerged at many times and places throughout history to challenge the patriarchal system, though so far with only limited success. Broadly one could say that the ideological battle in relation to both race and class has at least been taken into the general discourse in the sense that although dreadful poverty and racial oppression still continue, they are widely recognised as destructive and inhuman. But sexual oppression is not yet widely condemned: in fact it is still justified and even promoted in our male-dominated society. (White and Tulip 1991:1–2)

What began as a (well-deserved) attack on the oppression of patriarchy disintegrates into a flawed and divisive—and, dare we say, utopian—"defense" of feminism. Though feminism does have its merits, it is not well served by their line of argument, as there are numerous problems with this kind of statement. Many people—from any number of gender, racial and socio-economic loci—could easily refute their assumptions. Firstly, the "one" they refer to is not a value-neutral point of origin, as "one" could also say that "the ideological battle in relation to both race and class" has not been "taken into the general discourse." The past history and current experiences of—quite literally—millions of black peoples corroborate this. In Australia, specifically, this is confirmed by over two centuries of racist oppression, and especially by the continuing "justification and even promotion" of racism in our white-dominated society evident today.[21] Secondly, the use of the phrase and concept ". . . at least . . ." in this argument reveals tremendous contempt for any position other than one that keeps sexism as the primary, if not exclusive, focus of any and all discourses. It splits sexism away from racism and classism, implying that somehow it has—or should have—far greater importance.

Australian Feminist Theology as Racist

In Australia the racist ideology that is found in the dominant white society is absorbed into the lives and works of theologians and their writings. To assume that they are not affected by this racism means that, somehow, they have separated themselves from society in general. From our experiences, we find that: 1) they have not separated themselves from the society; and, 2) racism finds itself, consciously or unconsciously, permeating their theological assumptions. White women, as a part of that society, are affected the same way.

> It would be inaccurate to assert that because feminist theology is White, it is also racist. To be White does not necessarily mean to be racist, though the behavior of Whites makes the distinction difficult. Nevertheless, my claim that feminist theology is racist is best supported by a definition of racism.
> Racism, according to Joel Kovel ". . . is the tendency of a society to degrade and do violence to people on the basis of race, and by whatever mediations

---

[21] Former Australian Prime Minister Gough Whitlam notes that Australia *still* has not enacted the racial vilification provisions, Section 4(a), of the International Convention on the Elimination of All Forms of Racial Discrimination, 1994:forthcoming; cf. UN 1988:59.

may exist for this purpose" [1984:x]. These mediations are manifested in different forms, and are carried on through various media: the psychology, sociology, history, economics and symbolism of the dominant (White) group. Racism is the domination of a people which is justified by the dominant group on the basis of racial distinctions. It is not only individual acts but a collective, institutionalized activity. (Grant 1989:199)

For feminists to say they are non-racist is to say they are not a part of the broader society which does maintain racist values, which nurtures and develops these attitudes and passes them on to their children and so the cycle of racism continues. If they are not part of this society, then where are they?

For racism to flourish with the vigour it enjoys in America [and Australia], there must be an extensive climate of acceptance and participation by large numbers of people who constitute its power base. It is the consensus of private persons that gives racism its derivative power. . . . The power of racism is the power conceded by those respectable citizens who by their actions or inaction communicate the consensus which directs [and] empowers the overt bigot to act on their behalf. (Lincoln 1984:11–12, cited in Grant 1989:199)

White women, as a part of this society, gain substantial privileges and benefits. They have status over other—black—women. They have not previously suffered, and do not presently suffer, the same racial oppression which is continually thrust upon Aboriginal women. For white women and their praxis to exclude black women, black women's theological reflections and black women's experience is to ignore their own racism.

Of course, not all white women are racist. Some have, consciously, begun to critique their role in the oppression of black women. Only when white women begin such journeys do they realize the benefits and privileges they have taken at the expense and dehumanization of black women—the only criterion being that they are white women.

For white women to say that their theology, and their society, is non-racist is to deny how they have benefitted from the institutionalized racism found in every aspect of our society.

If racism is not the basis upon which oppression is applied, then basically white society is blaming the victim for their own oppression because they are not racist. I cannot conceive that Aboriginal People choose to be at the "bottom" of society.

Perhaps the easiest way to proceed is to provide examples.

Australian Feminism as Racist—In History

The women's movement in Australia is perhaps best described, historically, by the women's suffrage movement of the late 1800s and early 1900s. It can be said that Australian women were relentless in their pursuit of "their rights" to vote in "their country." It is well-documented that they were supported by numerous social institutions, which were directly involved in the active political effort that was the suffrage movement. Oldfield (1992) indicates that those making major contributions included British intellectual society (p. 10), the British educational movement (p. 11), churches (p. 15), the Woman's Christian Temperance Union of the United States (p. 15) and others. An idea of the comprehensive nature of the campaign can be gleaned from the following passage.

> In every colony, beginning in the 1880s, campaigns for female suffrage were fought. Each colony had its suffrage society, or societies, and all issued a great variety of propaganda leaflets. Debates and public meetings were organised and the speakers, male and female, were not only in demand in capital cities, but travelled extensively, usually by rail, addressing meetings in the open air or in halls owned by town councils, by the School of Arts movement, and by churches and temperance organizations. Branches of suffrage societies were active in many country towns. The suffragists who were letter-writers kept the debate alive in city and county newspapers. Deputations waited on Parliaments, petitions were presented, and there was intense lobbying of candidates before elections and of members of Parliament before suffrage bills were presented in the Lower or Upper Houses of the states. (Oldfield 1992:14)

This massive social effort led to women being enfranchised in South Australia in 1894, and in Western Australia in 1899. Indeed, Australian women made history when, in 1902, "all Australian women" were given the Commonwealth vote (Oldfield 1992:15).

Yet, in the midst of this unparalleled social advancement, there was a deep, integrity-consuming secret.

> The proud boast that Australia was the second nation in the world to federally enfranchise its women ignores the fact that *black women and their men in two states had to wait until 1962* to gain access to the ballot-box. (Oldfield 1992:65, emphasis added)

A wait of sixty years (for Aboriginals in Queensland and Western Australia) was not the only corrosive element of this equation, for it is clear that discrimination also played a major part.

> There was no reaction from the [white Australian] women about the special
> exclusion of Aboriginal women who did not have votes in their own state, just
> as there had been no concern shown during the campaigns for the voting
> rights, or plight, of Aboriginal women in any colony. As far as we know, there
> was not one Aboriginal woman in any of the suffrage societies, and it is unlikely
> that they would have been welcome. (Oldfield 1992:65)

It is clear that the Australian suffrage movement was racist and omitted
Aboriginal People. Indeed, Aboriginal women were excluded directly and
specifically.

> The Secretary of the Woman's Equal franchise Association of Queensland told
> its annual meeting in 1896 that "we are always prepared to accept the hand of
> all white women in membership, irrespective of wealth or standing". (Oldfield
> 1992:65, 119)

Aboriginal women were present in the society but were not considered
to be part of the society. To make matters worse, the specific exclusion of
Aboriginal women by white Australian women was not limited to the area
of voting rights.

> Insulated in their urban areas, most suffragists knew little about, or preferred
> to turn their eyes away from, the cruelties and sexual degradation being visited
> upon black women by white men in the period. (Oldfield 1992:65; cf. Summers
> 1994:322)

Thus, while the white women in Australia enjoyed the support, not
only of the church, but also of various other domestic and international
social institutions, the Aboriginal women did not even have the support of
the non-Aboriginal women of their own land.[22] It is obvious that the white
women did not view the liberation of black women as a part of their own
movement for liberation. The women's suffrage movement in Australia,
in reality, referred to the white women's suffrage movement in Australia.

Australian Feminism as Racist—Today

> Even if some individual feminists are not racists, the movement has been so
> structured, and therefore takes on a racist character. In a racist society, the
> oppressor assumes the power of definition and control while the oppressed is
> objectified and perceived as a thing. (Kovel 1984:x, cited in Grant 1989:199–
> 200)

---

[22] In this regard it is relevant to note that "Aboriginal women have yet to be elected
to parliamentary seats, despite their active role in community politics"; Sawer and
Simms 1993:157.

A prime example of racism co-opting Australian feminists and the Australian feminist movement is found in the widespread white support for the so-called "Thursdays in Black" campaign. Initiated by the World Council of Churches, the effort was described, in one of its original flyers, as a call for

> women and men to wear black on Thursdays as a protest against rape and violence—the by-products of all war and conflict. (TIB 1993)

Australian women picked up the idea, and have promoted it with a vengeance. A paper avalanche of flyers, notes and articles has streamed across the country, calling for Australians to join the efforts (cf. Partamian 1993:13; Insights 1993a:3, 1993b:12). The effort has garnered significant support among numerous (white) women and women's groups.

Yet, white Australian women did not stop to think what such a campaign meant to the Aboriginal women of the land. Aboriginal women—and men—are outraged that such a racist concept was not only accepted, uncritically, but also that it was promoted without consultation with the very people it was meant to support. Aboriginal People have suffered over two centuries of terror and genocide. Aboriginal women, especially, have suffered rape and violence. For Australian women— especially Australian feminists—to endorse this campaign shows not only that they already have "taken on a racist character" (Grant 1989:200), but also that they, and their movement are tremendously immature, insensitive which dehumanizes Aboriginal women.

We were not asked what we thought of the campaign. We—clearly— are against any kind of oppression; but we—obviously—prefer another colour (such as purple). Aboriginal People—indeed, people of colour— do not support any kind of efforts that link the colour black to rape, violence or death.

Yet, this is not the sum total of the problems of this campaign. It has been plagued by gross and deeply offensive errors. For example, numerous publications have promoted that the Argentinian *Madres de Plaza de Mayo* wear black on Thursdays (e.g., Rebera 1993a). Yet, the National Newsletter of the *Madres de Plaza de Mayo* states that at the recent World Conference on Human Rights held in Vienna:

> ... the Mothers of Plaza de Mayo had meetings with numerous other entities. For example, the Mothers of Political and Disappeared Prisoners of South Korea, Turkey, Bosnia and other places. The Koreans emphasized that since

1986 they too used the white handkerchief following the example of the Argentinian Mothers of Plaza de Mayo. (1993:22, trans. from Spanish)

In Argentina, the *Madres* wear white. They have been wearing white for almost two decades. In Argentina, Korea and many other parts of the world, the colour of protest against oppression (including rape and violence) is white, not black. Around the world, people know that to use the colour of any race of oppressed peoples in this way is outrageously offensive. Indeed, the Australian Solidarity Group for the *Madres de Plaza de Mayo* is outraged, that:

1) the colour black has been used, repeatedly, in promotional and other material, despite the fact that they find it offensive, as they have provided unquestionable support for Aboriginal People and their rights;

2) the original Australian flyer incorrectly places the *Plaza de Mayo* in Brazil, rather than in Argentina where the mothers still mourn the "disappearances" of over 30,000 people (TIB 1993) (though this problem was corrected);

3) the name of their organization has been used in an endorsement in Australia, without their consultation or permission; and,

4) they were excluded from the effort, when they could have provided it with not only significant support, but also with indispensable integrity (e.g., OT: J. Ramírez 1993–94; G. Ramírez 1993–94).

When Aboriginal women made an approach to some of the Women's committees that launched and supported this campaign, we found ourselves being ignored or attacked because of our critique of "Thursday in Black." We found that our positive suggestions towards addressing this issue was totally dismissed; further, when interviewed by white women in the church about how Aboriginal women viewed "Thursday in Black," and the comments were not what they wanted to hear, we found that the stories never got published, as the white women have control what is said and who says it. Aboriginal women who are being co-opted need to be mindful that they do not get caught up in the feminist agenda that excludes, or does not embrace, racism or classism as a part of its focus.

No Self-Criticism

Australian feminists' greatest weakness may be their failure to self-analyse and critique. They continue to benefit at the expense of Aboriginal women by universalizing their values and imposing them on us. "With the best of intentions," Australian feminists continue to define the agendas of all women.

. . . white women have defined the movement and presumed to do so not only for themselves but also for non-White women. They have misnamed themselves by calling themselves feminists when in fact they are White feminists, and by appealing to women's experience when in fact they appeal almost exclusively to their own experience. To misname themselves as "feminists" who appeal to "women's experience" is to do what oppressors always do; it is to define the rules and then solicit others to play the game. It is to presume a commonality with oppressed women that oppressed women themselves do not share. If White women's analysis were adequate, they would be more precise in naming their own movement and would not presume to name or define the experience of others. They have simply accepted and participated in the racism of the larger American [and Australian] society when they have done so. This partially accounts for the negative response which Black women have had with respect to feminism. (Grant 1989:200)

Hypocrisy is found in the feminist movement to the point that this privileged group defines and determines the particular feminist interests as representing the common interest of all women. Somehow these feminists spend a great deal of time and energy proving that their views reflect universal values, that encompass all women within Australia. If this is so, then feminists need to consider how much they distort reality in order to maintain their interests.

It is quite obvious that there is a need for Australian feminists to address and confront their own racism and classism, and the status that they enjoy because they are white and how, because of their colour, privilege is obtained and maintained within this society. Aboriginal women have yet to obtain such status and privilege in Australia, as they still struggle for clean drinking water, education, health and housing, which are considered as one's basic human rights. We have yet to hear a strong voice from feminism towards the call for justice, addressing the basic human rights of their "so-called" Aboriginal sisters in Australia.

White Australian women, especially feminists, seem to have fallen into the trap of definition and control—a trap from which it does not appear there is any escape for them. They are co-opted by their own racism as well as the racism permeating the society they support. They continue to objectify us—to all our detriment.

Conclusion

Aboriginal women's freedom is limited by the racism of Australian feminism. Our origins are different and our histories are incomparable. Our experiences of Australian church feminism, in the past and in the present, confirm pervasive racism. We do not need women who are trapped by their own complicity, and continue to benefit from our suffering and exclusion. In short, we do not need to be liberated by our oppressors. Rather, Aboriginal women of Australia welcome women who are willing to listen, and learn—to open their hearts. Then, perhaps, we will walk forward as *tiddas* (sisters).

Having reviewed racism in the Australian social and church contexts, we now move to the next chapter, which will look at the legacy of Australian racism.

CHAPTER 4
THE LEGACY OF RACISM

The Sin of Racism

Racism is perpetrated in every nook and cranny of Australian society. It saturates the entire social structure of the country. Indeed, Australian racism is like a festering sore that has been left untreated.

Australia has become infected. Over the period of time since European contact, the lies and massacres and oppression have obstructed the circulation of the blood of truth, and the infection has become necrotic, and turned into gangrene. This has required the amputation of certain vital parts of the whole. In Australia, racism already has caused the amputation of the limbs of integrity and justice. As it stands today, the prognosis for the patient Australia still is terminal.

This illustration is an example of what happens when racism in a society is left untreated: racism eventually becomes a chronic disease that plagues the entire society. No one is immune to it. This is the situation found in white Australia. It no longer can stand the legs of integrity or justice, because these have been amputated by the gangrene of racism. If the problem is not addressed immediately, it eventually will kill the patient.

In fact, there are signs that point to the death of the Australian conscience. As mentioned in the previous chapters, there have been numerous national and international reports condemning racism and racist violence in Australia (e.g., HREOC 1991; WCC 1991). Yet, to date, no profound changes have taken place in Australian society. No just settlement between black and white has been attempted seriously. Aboriginal People still face severe poverty, denial of education, and economic and political injustices. Aboriginal deaths in police and prison custody have continued—and in some cases increased. And—perhaps most damning—Australian society continues to dehumanize Aboriginal People.

Naming the Problem

The reasons for this continuing dehumanization are quite simple. White society does not want to identify that it has a problem—much less name it as *Racism*. Instead, it buries the issue—it makes "racism" the unmentionable word in Australia. Yet, Euro-Australians would have you believe that racism in Australia is a non-issue, or simply does not exist. The sad fact is that for white-skinned people in Australia, racism *is* a non-issue, since they are the majority that dominate this society and are never on the receiving end. They are the perpetrators of racism and, as history clearly shows us, the Aboriginal People have been on the receiving end of the dehumanizing and racist attack by the invading white Europeans since their arrival. The subjugation of the Indigenous People is rarely told by the white people—let alone found in the documentation of Australian history. There is no denying that the resulting dehumanized situation of Aboriginal People is due to white racism. Our rights as Indigenous People have been violated and ignored, and our human rights as a People continually are denied.

Tracing the Problem

Reviewing government and church policies and practices, and the impact they have had upon Aboriginal People, would lead you to wonder what this racism and domination have done to Aboriginal People.

> Racism is clearly more than simple prejudice or bigotry. Everyone is prejudiced, but not everyone is racist. To be prejudiced means to have opinions without knowing the facts and to hold on to those opinions, even after contrary facts are known. To be racially prejudiced means to have distorted opinions about people of other races. Racism goes beyond prejudice. It is backed up by *power*. Racism is the power to enforce one's prejudices. More simply stated, racism is prejudice plus power. (Barndt 1991:28, emphasis added; cf. Kelsey 1965:46)

From the time of invasion, the Euro-Australians have waged an untold war against the Indigenous People of this land called Australia (cf. Arthur 1971). We have been brutally massacred at the hands of the invading British (or so-called "peaceful settlers," as the Euro-Australians would have us believe). Euro-Australians considered themselves to be the masters of this land and, therefore, they ruled according to this self-perceived "superior" ideology. This racial prejudice became racism, and was reinforced through the ideology of white colonial society. This racism was so powerful that it dominated and controlled Aboriginal People.

According to Euro-Australians, Aboriginals were inferior because of their black skin, lack of technology and allegedly "pagan" religious practices (cf. Reynolds 1989:11–17, 155–81). We were considered as nothing more than beasts of the wilderness, and game for Euro-Australians to hunt and slaughter when ever they felt the need for a little excitement (cf. Rowley 1972). Euro-Australians never considered that Aboriginal People had any form of humanity—let alone any feelings, consciences, morals or souls. Their racist assumptions led them to believe that they were commissioned by God to take this land—and even blessed by God at Federation in 1901 (cf. Kirby 1993).

They lied about this land being empty, so they could do whatever they liked to the Aboriginal People—especially since the Aboriginal People "did not exist," according to the lie of *terra nullius*. This, of course, was a rationalization so as not to have to recognize the original inhabitants and owners of this land, so no treaty ever had to be signed, officially formalized or enforced by the invading whites.

The Psychology of Racism

Kevin Gilbert wrote:

> It is my thesis that Aboriginal Australia underwent a rape of the soul so profound that the blight continues in the minds of most blacks today. It is this psychological blight, more than anything else, that causes the conditions that we see on reserves and missions. And it is repeated down the generations. (1977:3)

The psychological legacy of racism is, simultaneously, the most complex to explain, yet the most necessary to illuminate. Human development proceeds through various stages that have been studied, analysed and debated for many years. Psychological research has led to numerous ideas being posited, as well as to several basic theories being generally accepted. These are most helpful in understanding racism and, on the Australian scene, in comprehending Australian racism against Aboriginal People. They are central to our being able to grasp the legacy.

Uncontrolled Sexual and Aggressive Drives

Part of white Australian racism is related to uncontrolled sexual and aggressive drives. According to Freudian theory, if we can be excused for exploring how far it pertains to the Australian situation, humans are driven by sex and aggression. These drives are frustrated by the impositions of life and channelled into certain basic conflicts which, in turn, generate fantasies that are directed toward particular symbolic organizations (cf. Kovel 1970:256–58).

As we analyse the psychological legacy of Australian racism, it is interesting to note that Australian history reveals an amazingly Freudian development. In both general society and in the church, Australians seem to have been driven by an overwhelming and uncontrolled preoccupation with both sex and aggression in relation to the Aboriginal People.

Historical records well-document that from the very beginning of European-Aboriginal contact, whites sexually enslaved the indigenous men, women and children of Australia. Whites acted upon their aversive racism and separated themselves from the blacks. They built up missions and reserves, and eventually allowed the creation of fringe camps. They enforced all kinds of practices, policies and even laws to keep blacks "in their place" (i.e., away from whites). Yet, throughout, whites were forcing sexual contact with Aboriginals. In what appears to be exceedingly irrational behaviour, whites curbed their aversion at whim in order to satisfy their sexual drives. White men, and women, viewed Aboriginals as sexual objects, not as people. Whites from all walks of life—"settlers," politicians, government officials, farmers, business-owners, and yes, even clergy—forced themselves upon Aboriginal women, as well as upon Aboriginal men and children.

Further, documentation also exists to show that whites sexually mutilated blacks during the violent European colonization process. There are countless stories of white atrocities against blacks—rape, genitalia being cut off, spears being inserted into bodies, etc. (cf. Parbury 1986); rarely, however, does one find incidents of similar white actions upon other whites. The European colonization process brought much horrific treatment to all the people of Australia, but it seems that the horrors were quite uneven, with blacks bearing the brunt of the violence—often sexual violence.

Whites seemed unable—or unwilling—to control their sexual and aggressive drives in relation to Aboriginal People. In very many cases, white aggression was not channelled into fantasy, but rather acted upon—directly—leading to the physical genocide of hundreds of thousands of Aboriginal People. In other cases, white aggression has been channelled into conflicts, generating aggressive fantasies that continue the genocidal process within the psychological realm.

Unresolved Oedipal Complex

Another part of white Australian racism is directly related to an unresolved Oedipal complex. History records that white power and dominance were connected to white sexual behaviour.

Male

In many Aboriginal societies, the men were hunters and the women were gatherers. When the European *Weltanschauung* invaded upon this scene, it enforced a radical change, imposing its own patriarchal version of reality. Early colonial history records many instances of whites literally (physically) emasculating Aboriginal men. Later on, with the advent of the missions and reserves, whites symbolically emasculated black men.

The Aboriginal men that whites could not kill, they confined, or isolated, or "addictified," or marginalized. They removed them from the nucleus of the family structure. They removed them from their traditional roles of defender, provider, partner. They took them away from any kind of decision-making process, be it societal, political, economic or religious. Aboriginal men were given absolutely no place in white society, and were overpowered by the violent force of white technology—humiliating and marginalizing them from their own. Whites totally destroyed the role and function of the Aboriginal male in both societies.

In an effort to deal with the continuing psychological dilemma, white Australian males act upon the racist fantasy.

> [The] white male simultaneously resolves both sides of the conflict by keeping the black man submissive, and by castrating him when submission fails. In both these situations—in the one symbolically, in the other directly—he is castrating the father, as he once wished to do, and also identifying with the father by castrating the son, as he once feared for himself. All that he has to do to maintain this delectable situation is to structure his society so that he directly dominates black men. (Kovel 1970:71–72)

White racism gave whites the power to enforce their prejudices. Whites structured their society so that they could dominate Aboriginal men. Westernization and missionization worked together in a parasitic symbiosis to deny Aboriginal males their traditional roles in society. Their authority was undermined and subverted at every turn. Aboriginal males were denied their freedom; they were not allowed to gather or hunt or fish; they were prohibited from practising their male ceremonies and other "men's business." They were forced to take the role that women would have traditionally maintained (cf. Attwood 1989:60–80). As if this was not enough, white society vilified the Aboriginal male, developing the myth of black violence. The black man became—at least in white minds—"the black rapist of white females," a myth that was wildly exaggerated (Evans, Saunders and Cronin 1975:71; cf. Kovel 1970; Keneally 1972). White sexual fantasy was projected on to Aboriginal People, both male and female. White racism combined with white sexism and not only castrated the Aboriginal male, but also "sexualized" the Aboriginal female.

Female

Whites were obsessed with Aboriginal women. They developed all manner of fantasy regarding black female sexuality (cf. Reynolds 1987a:73–74); worse, they acted upon their fantasies. Black women were objectified to the point of suffering systematic attacks upon their persons and identities (cf. Evans, Saunders and Cronin 1975:102–17). For example, common colonial practices included white farmers, stockmen, miners and fishermen simply "taking" Aboriginal women by force. Later colonial policies included whites arranging marriages between Aboriginal women and white male convicts. Black women, it seems, had no control over their own bodies or destinies. They were physically and sexually exploited by the whites who were "civilizing" them, or "employing" them, or "protecting" them. Yet, at the same time, some Aboriginal women were entrusted with washing and cooking for white families, and even at times caring for white children. This severe ambivalence revealed significant psycho-social problems in the white culture of racism.

Guilt

Another important part of the ordering of racist white society was the concrete and conscious concealment of guilt.

> What had been directly acted upon in those simpler days of domination becomes the fantasy of today. (Kovel 1970:59)

Guilt was hidden, often through the creation of fantasy. White Australian history provides a prime example. From the very first point of contact between whites and blacks, white Australian society "remembers" a "peaceful" "settlement" of an "empty land." Captain Cook was ordered to take possession of the land *with the consent of the natives* (cf. Hocking 1988:vii-viii; Reynolds 1987b:51–52). When he arrived in what is now northern Queensland, Aboriginals threw spears at him and he eventually retreated, fearing for his life (cf. Loos 1982). Yet, white historical revisionism deposits "historical" facts and memories that never have existed. It omits references to the numerous armed resistance campaigns by the Aboriginals (e.g., Loos 1982). It downplays the immense violence of the frontier wars (e.g., Reynolds 1982; Reynolds 1987a). It even creates a myth of terra nullius, rationalizing any possible guilt over dispossession. It even develops a special "language" to deal with guilt: genocide was called "dispersal" (cf. Rowley 1972:42, 161–63, 169, 186, 193); murder was called "self-defence" (cf. Prentis 1975:65); enslavement and socio-cultural obliteration of tradition was called "deliverance" (cf. Gsell 1955:inside back cover); family break-ups were called "shield[ing] from . . . familial cultural influences" (cf. Dewar 1992:25); child kidnapping was called "adoption" (cf. Edwards and Read 1992:xviii-xxv); and the list goes on and on.

Yet, no matter how hard they tried to conceal their guilt, no matter how much they tried to distance themselves from it, whites simply could not escape it. Kovel writes: "Guilt is indeed the specific oedipal emotion" (1970:74).

Even today, a great many white Australians immediately—and in no uncertain terms—reject any and all "guilt" associated with alleged wrongs done by previous generations of white Australians. In fact, whites often defend themselves against charges of racism by distancing themselves from previous atrocities (cf. *New York Times*, 31 January 1988:sec.4:3) and referring to the so-called "*guilt* industry" (cf. Howard 1993:47; D. Barnett 1988:159; Chamberlin 13 January 1993:1). It seems—to them—that by quickly dismissing such charges as subversive plots originated by some nebulous, unknown guilt industry, they are somehow exhonourated from any and all culpability. The most amazing thing is that *they* bring up the guilt; Aboriginals do not, as they tend to be dealing with other elements of the arguments.

Here, again, whites seem unable—or unwilling—to resolve the Oedipal complex by running from, or wallowing in, the guilt, rather than by developing a healthy superego.

A Flawed Superego

A part of human psychological maturity consists in the development of a superego—to balance and supervise both the id and the ego. This facilitates the control of fantasy and the sublimation of aggressive and other drives. White Australian racism seems to focus on either the id or the ego, with no rational superego response to the continuing deprivation and dehumanization of the Aboriginal People of this land.

In fact, whites actively encouraged specific behaviour in blacks to perpetuate the racist oppression. For example, whites conceived and empowered the formation of the Native Police, a unit of the white police that often was used in hunting parties to track down certain Aboriginal people who whites considered needed to be apprehended (cf. Rosser 1990). Whites actively encouraged Aboriginal men to join the Native Police, and thus to "contribute" to this "newly-established civilization." The truth, however, is that the Native Police was one of the most ruthless and violent tools of white, colonial Australia.

The Native Police became one of the mechanisms for the release of white, racist aggression against the indigenous black peoples of Australia (cf. Reid 1990:113–27). Neither the individual nor the collective white superego had to expend massive amounts of energy in restraining itself. It did not need to control the id; indeed, it did not *want* to control the id. One of the often publicly stated goals of the early white self-titled "settlers" was to "remove" all Indigenous People from the land so that they could take over the continent, establish colonies and farms, and create "a new nation" (cf. Loos 1982:22). One of the easiest ways to free yourself from the psychological pressure of having to control members of your own society who are committing murder and rape and other brutalities against the Aboriginals in the cities and along the so-called "frontiers" is to create a substitute to do it for you. Whites formed the Native Police; they originated it, financed it, and controlled it. Further, they rewarded it for continuing the patterns of massacre and murder that had preceeded it. The psychological mechanism that allowed the Native Police not only to exist, but to flourish, and indeed to reward internalized racism in its membership, reveals a deeply disturbed reality—a flawed superego.

A Non-Autonomous Ego

White Australians have not created an autonomous ego. Indeed, white Australians are psychologically dependent upon Aboriginal People. They need a target, a scapegoat. Their identity is reliant on their continual oppression of the Indigenous People, and the subsequent "facts" of their "inferiority," to uphold their own "superiority." For example, during the heated debates surrounding Native Title, whites who were confronted with the possibility of having to recognize Aboriginal sovereign rights to the land, or to recognize injustice, or to pay compensation, continually saw these as a direct threat to their personal and corporate identities. They resorted to slander and a justification of our alleged inferiority.

One public figure even based this charge of inferiority upon the fact that we did not "invent the wheeled cart," and therefore could not do anything with the land were it to be returned to us (cf. Coultan and Seccombe 1993:1). He claimed that Aboriginals never contributed to the development or the economic progress of this country. This denigration of Aboriginal People led to his grandstanding about the West, as it did "civilize the natives," and make roads, and otherwise develop the Australian nation.

Such an argument says more about the speaker than it does about Aboriginal People. Not only does it highlight whites' racism and supposed "superiority," but also does it clearly show that their identity is tied directly to "proving" the "inferiority" of Aboriginal People. They "need" us.

Indeed, throughout post-contact Australian history, whites in many ways have depended upon Aboriginals for their very survival. Aboriginal People provided intimate knowledge of the plants and herbs (nutritional and medicinal value), of the animals (edible vs. non-edible), of the physical features of the land (location of water, rivers, mountains, etc.), and much more. Indeed, even the detailed study by Reynolds (1990) is not nearly enough to describe the numerous and significant Aboriginal contributions to white Australia.

Yet, white Australians refuse to admit this evidence. They claim to have tamed the land without anyone's help. They reject the fact that there is an immense part of the history of Australia that is tied to Aboriginal participation and initiative. They forget that Blaxland, Wentworth and Lawson were *led* across the Blue Mountains by an Aboriginal guide, or that Bourke and Wills died because they would not accept assistance from Aboriginal People. They omit numerous other examples of Aboriginal personal and cultural worth. It is just too threatening.

> . . . autonomy has not been gained: the organism is crippled from within and scarcely able to adapt outwardly. (Kovel 1970:282)

The history of Australian racism precludes simple acceptance of Aboriginal social, economic, political and other contributions in many different areas—farming, pearling, fishing, mining, and more. Australian psychological development only allows the existence of an Aboriginal as a foil, an antithesis, an antihero or antiheroine. Even after two centuries, they continue to attempt to define our identity and our role on our own land.

The Racism of the "Normal"

The Oxford Dictionary defines "normal" as "conforming to a standard, usual, regular, ordinary, sane" (Turner 1984:462).

Taking this definition, white Australians will never consider Aboriginal People to be "normal," as the latter cannot possibly conform to a European standard (cf. Barndt 1991:60). A European worldview—with its attendant values, ethics, mores, religious beliefs—cannot ever be presumed to be "the standard" for any other group of People outside of itself. To believe otherwise is to fall into the traps of nineteenth century cultural and colonial imperialism.

Aboriginal People have our own cosmogony, values, tradition, languages, etc. We have our own "standards." Only we can define what is "normal" for ourselves. It is the height of racism to presume that one race can define what is to be considered "standard" for all other races. For any other race to do just that is to show their own ethnocentrism. It reveals their arrogance in assuming that they have the authority to set definitions for everyone else, and to force conformity to their definitions upon everyone else.

The Workings of Racism

The racist ideology found in the Euro-Australian context explicitly postulates the "superiority" of Europeans—who define themselves as "white." This ideology also assumes the inherent and biological inferiority of the black-skinned, Indigenous Peoples of Australia, and is reflected in a certain set of practices.

> . . . the idea of racism is still useful and analytically powerful . . . when racism is analyzed as culturally acceptable beliefs that defend social advantages that are based on race. Racism is not simply bigotry or prejudice; and it should not be confused with ethnic hostilities. Although specific expressions of racism clearly change . . . , sociologically speaking the analytic features of the concept stay the same. Regardless of its historically specific manifestations, racism today remains essentially what it has always been: a defence of racial privilege. (Wellman 1993:3–4)

Basically this is the case for Euro-Australians and the Indigenous Peoples of Australia. In describing the relationship between whites and blacks in Australia, it clearly is seen that the whites have all the privileges and advantages and the blacks are disadvantaged and at the bottom. This relationship reflects the social structure rooted in Australia, which is organized in such a way that maintains the racial advantage of the Euro-Australians. This structure supports the Euro-Australians' ideology, which is based on their alleged position of superiority in the so-called racial hierarchy.

When we add these two items together, we get a very powerful mixture. This is the case of Australian history: Euro-Australians have vigorously resisted any view of Aboriginals other than the one that maintained their distorted racial prejudices.

> Racist belief is based on fantasy rather than fact . . . the essential belief of the racist is indifferent to its truth value. (Kovel 1970:46)

Exploitation

Euro-Australians have obtained great wealth and privilege through their biases, and through their inhumanity towards Aboriginal People. Why would they question the very systems that brought them these "rewards"?

Racism develops when the dominant group seeks justification to enforce its own prejudice as acceptable societal behaviour. The social structure of Australia easily (and often) reveals the racial prejudice of the dominant white race against the Aboriginal People being *perpetuated* in every aspect of *their* lives, as well as *perpetrated* on every aspect of *our* lives. This domination of white Australia over the Indigenous Peoples becomes quite frightening and dangerous when expressed in terms of power, for they literally dominated and controlled every aspect of the Aboriginals' lives. This power not only was limited to a white individual over an Aboriginal individual, but also was found in the collective Australian power and was seen and expressed through laws, political and economic systems, educational, cultural, religious and all other social systems and institutions. This collective power continues to seek justification for its subjugation and dehumanization of the Indigenous People, in maintaining the benefits and privileges it has gained for itself. In response to the claims of "special treatment" of Aboriginal People, noted Aboriginal author, Kevin Gilbert, writes:

> . . . many say: "Aboriginals get too much." There is much ado about "tax-payer" money and this from a society that has murdered us, the rightful owners, placed us in exile and then used the mineral and natural resources of our estates to grow and wax fat like maggots upon the carcass of the stolen

inheritance, an inheritance which is and remains rightfully Aboriginal inheritance. (1988a:6)

These privileges are seen when, at an international level, Australia is seen as a so-called "First World" country (with all benefits and advantages gained only by the whites), while the indigenous suffer "Fourth World" poverty (with no advantages and certainly no privileges), simply because they are black-skinned (cf. Tinker 1992:12). If the Aboriginal People lived in a Third World country, we could receive international aid; but, because we live in a so-called First World nation, we cannot get it. Thus, Aboriginal People use the term Fourth World, because we find ourselves in a situation of having to accept our poverty, and to be totally at the mercy of the racist, hegemonic society.

> Racism (prejudice plus power) develops when personal opinion and individual bigotry are codified and enforced as societal behavior. Racism structures a society so that the prejudices of one racial group are taught, perpetuated, and enforced to the benefit of the dominant group. Racism harnesses the energies and loyalties of the dominant group for that group's purposes. Racism provides better service and facilities for the dominant group through that group's institutions. Racism decrees more severe restrictions and control over its victims than it does over the dominant group. (Barndt 1991:29)

The white control of Aboriginal People is clearly identified in the black-white relationship in our history, and also in the current situation. Aboriginal People literally have been enslaved by the whites of Australia, through the government policies of segregation/protection and assimilation/integration, with the aiding and abetting of the Churches, which assisted the enforcement of these racist policies. This literally determined *where* Aboriginals could live, *whom* they could marry and *if* they could raise their own children. This meant that the Aboriginals were vulnerable, and subject to the whim of the racist white society. But also, we must note in consideration of today's complex situation:

> Racism can be expressed with an iron fist or with a velvet glove. At its coarsest and most unsophisticated, racism uses violence to enforce explicit laws to subjugate and control. . . . Racism also assumes sophisticated forms that depend less on brute force than on psychological methods that dissipate resistance. In such forms, racism may in fact create the illusion that it does not exist and therefore be far more difficult to detect and eliminate. Yet its power to oppress is no less than that that of open and blatant racism. Iron fist or velvet glove, the results are the same. (Barndt 1991:31)

Genocide

The genocidal practices that took place in Australia, starting with the white invasion of 1788, led to the destruction of many of the Aboriginal societies throughout Australia. The futile massacres, and other genocidal practices, by the white people led to thousands upon thousands of Aboriginal People being slaughtered. This is the "proud history" of white Australia. Today these genocidal practices come in more sophisticated forms, such as cultural genocide through the assimilation process, and the continuing "special treatment" that white Australia claims we still receive. Racism in Australia certainly has moved from an iron fist to a velvet glove; yet, the impact and outcome remain the same.

In whatever ways racism is expressed, the end results never change. For example, the evil force of blatant racism was very visible during the first one hundred and fifty years of European colonization of Australia. Australian law was so explicitly structured, and dictated to the subjugated Aboriginal People with such force (cf. Nettheim 1981), as to control where Aboriginal People could live, whether or not they could get an education (and if so, to what level), where they could work, if they were to receive a salary, and who would control and administer their earnings.

> This system was open to abuse by the administrators, and open they stole a lot of money from the Black people. Many of the indigenous people of this land worked all their lives for rations—which were a bit of tea, a bit of sugar, some flour and blankets. They never saw the wages which supposed to be kept in trust for them. Now, after forty years, some still are asking what happened to that money. Nobody seems to know. My old granddad was whipped like an animal one day, because he dared to question the police sergeant (the administrator of his account) about his money. . . . The police sergeant didn't think he should answer to an old Black man. So he whipped granddad. (Pattel 1994:84)

Most times the Aboriginal People would never even see any of their wages. If at any time an Aboriginal bucked at this control and domination of their lives, they would be considered as "a trouble maker" and sent to one of the many Aboriginal punishment prisons (such as Palm Island; cf. Rosser 1978).

Dependency

Today, Aboriginal People no longer have explicit legal restrictions as to where they can live, or limitations on what level of education they can obtain, or controls over their employment. Yet, they are still living in poverty, still largely unemployed and still uneducated. Racism is seen to have become more sophisticated within the Australian systems. Of course, the whites who control these systems emphatically deny that racism exists. In fact, Australia spends billions of dollars a year in order to maintain the illusion that racism does not exist today. The racist's greatest ability is to create the illusions to delude the victims and the perpetrators into a false reality.

> It deludes the victims into believing that their rulers have only their best interest at heart. It deludes the dominant group into being that it is not racist, that it is treating its victims well, and that there is no need to change. This power to create illusions is devastating, for it provides justification to the dominant group for its actions. (Barndt 1991:32)

While Australian society continues to maintain this illusion that it is not racist, the constructive energy directed towards addressing this will focus only on improving white attitudes and actions. This is seen in the recent Federal Government move of establishing the Council for Aboriginal Reconciliation, which will fail to address the critical problems of racism and its power that are so deeply embedded in this society. Institutions will be left untouched. One of the reasons why white people are so fooled by such illusions is because they do not consider that they themselves are participating in directly enforcing their own prejudices and racism. They fail to see that *they* are exercising this power that continues to victimize the Aboriginal People. Whether they participate in this expression of power directly or indirectly, they still certainly benefit from it—even when it is administered by other white people on their behalf.

A State of Illusion

The political and economic institutions of power have created many illusions in relation to black-white reality. These include the illusions of the British invaders: that the land was empty; that we were animals; that the protection and segregation policies were made and enforce "with the best of intentions"; and, that the assimilation and integration policies would make Aboriginal People become so-called equals with white Australia. Once again, however, these policies meant the destruction of the Aboriginal families, which also was the rationalization for the kidnapping of Aboriginal children from their Aboriginal families and their placement into mission and reserves. This led to the criticism by the

Aboriginal People of the churches and governments committing cultural genocide.

> Christianity in this country has been responsible for creating division, animosity, jealousy etc. in Aboriginal and Islander communit[ies] through its division, and diversity of doctrine, denominationalism, and the false spirituality that it brings. (C. Harris February 1992:19)

The conditioning of the Aboriginal People's minds has been so successful in some cases that Aboriginal People have come to believe that their enemy is the radical Aboriginal who fights for their rights. White people say that they make things bad for other blacks because they dare to challenge the white rule as being oppressive and racist. Many of our people are happy to accept this interpretation by whites, and then to criticize their own people for not being prepared to accept their subjugation—to even consider that things possibly could be different for the blacks. This conditioning is so successful that we find that blacks end up fighting blacks. We get lost in the endless bickering and backstabbing that leads to fragmentation within the black struggle. This often is found amongst oppressed people, and is a perfect expression of their oppression. The people get so lost in the infighting that they forget who is their real enemy. White people continually use this as a weapon to move the focus off themselves as the oppressors and dominant rulers and, for some reason, we black people fall for this each and every time. The enemy is not your own people; it is the oppressive white society (cf. Foley 1993:15).

As long as the white society can so easily throw a spanner into the political movement of the Aboriginal People, and as long as the Aboriginal People accept the velvet glove of oppression by the white people, then the black struggle will continue to fight against itself and waste all its creative energy.

> If our people cannot change how it is amongst themselves, then the Aboriginal people will never climb back out of hell. Each Aboriginal has to uphold the rules of right living because if we don't do those things then our Aboriginality will die out "till there is nothing left . . . like the coals of a long-dead campfire". (Grandfather Koori, quoted in Gilbert 1977:305)

Without this change, the struggle never will be won. The main objective, to be achieved by the black people, is to be clear as to who their oppressors are, what the oppressor has done and still is doing to keep them subjugated. Then, and only then, can we become a strong and united People against this oppressive system, and struggle towards full liberation for all our people.

Liberation never will come to the Aboriginal People if we depend upon the so-called reconciliation process, because this is only about changing white attitudes towards Aboriginal People. It is not about the dismantling of the oppressive systems and institutions that are structured on white racism. It is not about changing the balance of power. It is about making the white people think better of Aboriginal People—if this can ever be possible—and acting accordingly. The process that the government and the churches have now endorsed is about dealing with the symptoms of racism not its sources.

White Australians as Racist

When defining racism as prejudice plus power and in light of the historical information just covered in this work, we could well ask, "Who has all the power"? The answer is equally obvious: the Euro-Australians—as they certainly never have let the Aboriginal People forget this. Through their oppressive control and the administration of this control, Aboriginal People literally have been enslaved by the white society. Clearly at the mercy of the white society's will—and whether their will was based on racial hatred or paternalism—the result was always the same: the denigration of the Aboriginal People. We, Aboriginal People, often wonder if the whites would have responded in the way they wished us to respond, if their lives literally were dominated and controlled by an outside influence. We wonder if their cries of injustice would have been any different than those of the Aboriginal People.

Solving the Wrong Problem

Now that we have identified that white Australians have all the power and, as we have seen in our history, how they have administered this power, it is obvious to state that Euro-Australians are racist. In reviewing the actions of Governments and Churches for the past several decades, whites have identified the problem as the "Aboriginal problem." Even today, they still refer to Aboriginal justice as the "Aboriginal problem." It has become clear that the situation in which Aboriginal People now find themselves is due to the racism of white Australians—and not out of the choosing of the Aboriginal People. This being the case, then, have we not been trying to solve or change the wrong problem?

The racial problems that are found in Australia are not the problems of the Aboriginal People, but rather the symptoms of the sickness of the white majority. The racial problems are caused by, and founded within, the white society—yet their effects are felt within the Aboriginal society. The white Australian majority "owns" the poverty in which the Aboriginal People find themselves, as they control, maintain and condone these impoverished communities. What happens there is determined by the institutions and agencies of the white majority of Australia. All the Government, Church and other institutionalized programs in Australia— aimed at changing the poverty and racist reality to which Aboriginal find themselves being confined—ultimately will be useless if those institutions and structures that created the conditions in the first place (and still control them) are not dismantled.

This is very difficult for the dominant white society to handle, as all their privileges have been gained from the racist basis upon which their institutions and structures where founded—this, in order to maintain the benefits and lifestyles to which they have become accustomed. Their desires to change such systems are not very beneficial to themselves, as their comforts depend upon those institutions and structures staying in their present form.

White Australia has failed to see that the "Fourth World" conditions of the Aboriginal People come as a direct result of the white majority pursuit of "having it all" (cf. Rowley 1972). It is not very surprising to the Aboriginal People, then, that all the white efforts to solve the so-called "Aboriginal problem" have caused much frustration for the white rule, and very little—if any—success for the white majority. This is because the white rulers have tried—without success—to limit the effects of racism *without* cutting off the flow of its benefits to themselves. So, the white rulers have kept trying to change the victims of racism—in this case the Aboriginal People—without realizing (some would say without accepting) that they are the ones who need to change. The white society firmly believes that its problems are caused by the Aboriginals themselves, rather than by its own white institutions. The white rulers then assume that the "cure" for their sickness begins with the Aboriginals, and that the so-called "cures" need to be administered by the very institutions that created the sickness in the first place.

Wrong Methods

In recent months we have seen the Australian Federal Government trying to double—and even triple—its efforts to bring about change in the horrific social conditions suffered by Aboriginal People. They have done this by increasing programs for better health, education, employment and other social improvements. These may bring about some slight statistical improvements, but what they inevitably will do is produce a greater contradiction within Australian society. On the one hand, the white rule creates and perpetuates the "Fourth World" conditions of the Aboriginal People; then, on the other hand, it tries to address these conditions by throwing money at them. So, what becomes obvious to the oppressed, is the sickness is an integral part of the white society, and not of the Aboriginal People. Yet, the abysmal social conditions of the Aboriginal People in Australia (actually the symptoms of the sickness of white society) continue to go unchallenged, because the white people are trying to change the wrong people.

To oppressed people it becomes obvious that the racial problem that exists in Australia is white racism. The only way we ever will change this situation is to deal with the issue head-on. This means changing the systems and institutions of Australia that continue to dominate, control and exploit the Aboriginal People for the benefit of the white majority. To change only white attitudes is not enough; and, to continue offering only benevolence or charity to ease white conscience is not enough. There is only one way to address this situation that is found in Australia, and that is to reduce the power that enforces white prejudice. Only then can significant progress be made in dismantling white racism.

This is a critical point for the white society as they continue to administer the social programs defined for, and aimed at, the Aboriginal People. Whites must come to terms with the continual failure of their so-called "Aboriginal programs"—there is not one success story to be told. When will the government and churches finally realize that the problem facing Aboriginal People for the past two centuries—and even today—is the racism of the white society? When will they become pro-active in *addressing* and *naming* the oppression as racism? It has become too easy for the white Australians (including the government and churches) to blame the Aboriginal People for their plight (cf. Champion 1994:3). Government officials and church leaders often make statements to the effect that, "We have given Aboriginals everything, and still they complain. What more do they want?"

Yet, if they stopped long enough to listen to the Aboriginal People, they would know what we want—that is, freedom from all white oppression. But this requires the whites to address their own racism; it demands them to change their institutions, which are based on this racism.

It is no longer acceptable for the white society to continue blaming Aboriginal People for their enslavement and poverty. The reality that needs to be faced by the white society is that their structures and institutions have led to the dehumanization of the Aboriginal People. This will not be readily solved by whites' occasional charity or handouts. No longer are the Aboriginal People satisfied with the crumbs that might fall from the whites' table. We demand what is rightfully ours—that being the land and all resources that may be found under the land; self-determination; self-government; and, the basic human right which all whites enjoy, the right to control our own lives. Until this fact is accepted by the white society, then so-called "solutions" to the "Aboriginal problems" will not amount to anything except condescension and further oppression. White society is unable (or unwilling) to see that the conditions of the Aboriginal People are a direct result of the white majority's greed.

Confronting the Truth

The liberation of the Aboriginal People from white dominance is not only an issue of how much money we can put into addressing this problem, but also a question of how white people can become liberated from their own sin of racism. White Australians need to ask themselves, "How do we become free from our racism?" and "As Christians, how do we achieve a closer relationship with God?" Answers only can be found through whites' just relationship with the Aboriginal People. The time has come for white Australians to be honest with themselves—about their history; about the contributions that each and every one of them have made towards the direct and indirect oppression of the Aboriginal People; about the wealth, privilege and power they have gained through their oppression; and much more. It is no longer acceptable for white Australians to continue ignoring their injustice to and oppression of the Aboriginal People, while presenting to the outside world the pious "front" of their great generosity toward other (non-Australian Aboriginal) oppressed peoples. The world is now catching-on to their game, and global knowledge about the racial oppression of the Aboriginal People is now damaging Australians' so-called credibility.

While whites remain (consciously or unconsciously) ignorant of what the real problem is—namely, themselves, and their own racism—nothing will change for the Aboriginal People. One has to wonder how long the Aboriginal People can continue suffering under this genocidal oppression before it is too late. Will it only take a decade, or maybe another hundred years, before white society finally sees the Aboriginal People totally exterminated? Perhaps then, white Australians honestly could say that they no longer have "an Aboriginal problem."

So, it is important for Aboriginals and non-Aboriginals to continue identifying the problem as racism, or "white racism," since the tendency for most white Australians is to evade the issue altogether. Such a response no longer is acceptable, as our history in this so-called "great nation" clearly demonstrates the lengths to which white Australians will go in order to avoid the issue of racism. We have seen, read or heard of many different national and international reports that name the problem for the lack of positive white-black relationships as due to racism. We know that these reports have been highlighted in the media, and admissions have been made. Still, the dominant white Australians have trouble admitting that racism exists, and that they are the perpetrators of this racism. All too often, admissions are dismissed quickly or are swept under the carpet by the general public, and the root cause—racism—is forgotten.

Reports on Racism and Deaths in Custody

An example of the brevity of public memory about racism is found in the many reports and inquiries regarding racism itself and regarding Aboriginal Deaths in Custody (cf. CAR 1993:15). The Royal Commission into Aboriginal Deaths in Custody, the Human Rights Commission's National Inquiry into Racist Violence, the television documentary *Cop It Sweet,* various other televised reports such as the Bourke Outback Trek Incident—all showed the racism suffered by Aboriginal People. The outrage expressed by the Euro-Australians over these reports could be likened to a family scandal that had been made public. Australians were shocked that their racism against Aboriginal People made the prime time news, and gained such *public* attention. They were angry at the attention that this issue was given by media. The unmentionable realities had become a national scandal. They quickly went into denial, and tried to justify the unscrupulous actions by placing the blame squarely on the shoulders of a few "isolated incidents" or "random acts" of individuals. Once public, these scandals were quickly "buried in plain sight." That is, inquiries were set up, systems were assessed, procedures were checked and, often, recommendations made; yet, the major issues remained unaddressed, the root causes forgotten as quickly as possible. White racism was never identified by name.

Even now, racism is not on the national agenda, and is not spoken about as a national problem. It is considered to be counterproductive to the improvement of relationships between black and white Australia. So, Australians continue to highlight "other" issues and skirt around the edges, rather than deal directly with what is the problem—namely white racism.

If better relationship between Aboriginal and non-Aboriginal people in Australia is the ultimate goal, then we cannot avoid going to the crux of the matter. Speaking "nicely" to one another will not address racism. There must be the courage to confront racism head-on.

Individual Racism

It is important to state that no individual ever is born a racist. So, we must try to understand how and when whites become racist. In fact what happens over a period of time, beginning with early development (cf. Kovel 1970:47), is that the process of socialization begins and, inevitably, by the time you are an adult you have been conditioned to accept all societal behavior as "normal."

> The culture that nurtures us in childhood is nurtured by our leadership in adulthood. (Peck 1990:285)

Applying this to Australia, we see that the white culture that nurtures racism in its children is nurtured by its own racist leadership in adulthood. Thus, it should come as no surprise that racism is not only perpetuated in Australian society, but also built into the very system of growth, education and development of the individual Australian. Thus the racist biases are taught through their families and peers.

Church and society also have played a major role in the nurturing of racism. By giving sanction to racism, the church reinforces it. Just as in the Australian education system children are taught to be racist from a very young age, so also in the Australian church (and church school) system are children taught to hold racist beliefs from their youth. A prime example is the teaching of the so-called Hamitic curse myth, which continues to this day in Sunday Schools—and from pulpits—across Australia (cf. J. Harris 1990:29–30).

These are the seeds of theological imperialism, based on cultural imperialism, that contribute to the status quo. Euro-Australians actively participate in the system that gives them power and privilege—the only prerequisite for their participation is their white skin. Because of racial classification structured into Australian society, rights are determined by race. White Australian society has taken great pains to guarantee the success of this socialization process. Consciously or unconsciously, white Australians struggle to maintain and justify their biases. Thus, for a white Australian person to say that they are not racist is for them to be ignorant to the racist indoctrination that they have received since early childhood—through the self-deluding mechanisms of white history, government, religion, education, media and is found in every aspect of society. It is to deny the racist socialization process of Australian life. The nexus between personal racial prejudices and the systems of power are transformed when an individual actively participate in the system that gives privilege and power on the bases of racial identity. By cooperating in this system your racist socialization becomes complete.

So the Legacy Lives On

Australia is generally in such a state of denial with regard to its own racism, that it has orchestrated many illusions, which it inevitably tries to hide behind, in order to conceal racism from anyone on the outside "looking in." It deludes itself into believing that it was not complicit in the dispossession, genocide and the dehumanized state of the Aboriginal People today. Just as so many of the Germans denied their genocide of millions of Jews, Australia also could be seen as hiding behind its refusal to take notice of their participation in such horrors.

> Before and during World War II, the National Socialists (or Nazis) had carried out the extermination of more than six million Jews. After the facts of this holocaust became known, the majority of Germans insisted that they didn't know it was happening. In response to these denials the entire world asked incredulously, "How can it be that you did not know?" (Barndt 1991:56–57)

So, Australia can be likened to the proverbial three monkeys: see no evil, hear no evil, speak no evil. Australia does not see, hear or speak of the evil, and is completely "in-sensitive" to the flagrant racism being perpetrated upon Aboriginal People because it has its hands over its eyes, ears and mouth. It prefers to wallow in its own self-delusion—with all its attendant material, economic and political gains—than deal with the realities of the life and death that are raging around it. It is pure escapism.

Privileges and Rewards

White Australians have come to take for granted those privileges and rewards which fall continually into their laps, from the day they are born until the day they die. They have been so conditioned by their society to consider these as "normal" that they are blinded by the fact that only those persons with white skin ever benefit within this society. They deny that because of their white skin they benefit. They are deluded by the concept that "they have worked" for this or that, and "if you do not work you do not benefit." This is not the case, however, for Australian society has been structured so that if you are not white-skinned you do not benefit from the system. Whites in society never has had any reason to look at themselves, because they do not want to feel what it is like not to be white-skinned. Thus, they cannot understand that there are very solid reasons to change such structures, since they do not live in "Fourth World" poverty, or suffer racist abuse, or racist attacks. They have access to good education, and good jobs, and all the benefits of higher salaries. They certainly have better living conditions and better health care, as well as many other rewards, purely on the grounds of the white colour of their skin. White Australians never have considered that because of their white skin, they have gained all manner of privileges—such as the ease with which they can cash a cheque, or walk through a department store without being under suspicion by the store detectives, or know that their colour can never used against them when applying for jobs, or renting houses, or when relating to police, or to public authorities, or even to hairdressers when in a salon. Whites consider that Australian history only began in 1788. They elevate "their contributions to history" higher than any possible contribution made by Aboriginal People—if ever these are identified at all. They portray themselves in particular ways in the media, as compared to Aboriginal People. The list goes on and on. White Australia has no idea of the hardships suffered by those who are not white-skinned.

White Australians believe the myth that is based on the concept that if you become like them, you just *may* get some of their benefits. They believe that they are *owed* certain benefits because of their whiteness and superiority. They perceive it is their right to adequate health, complete education, full employment, fair wages. Yet, statistics clearly prove that these same "rights" are denied to the Aboriginal People.

White Australians' misconception is that only white people are hard workers, as they are the one that forged this country and made it the Great Nation it is today. Their believe that they have "built this country," from the ground up with their sweat, blood and brains. They believe that Aboriginals have done nothing to contribute to this society. Thus, we have national "leaders" making absolutely outrageous statements in public, indicating, for example, that it is not worth it to provide fresh tap-water to Aboriginal People because they only will destroy the pump houses and filtration tanks (cf. Chamberlin 28 April 1994:3; cf. Chamberlin 31 May 1994:13).

White Australians have become so insulated by their deceptions of being "The Lucky Country," that they either are unable or unwilling to come to terms with the truth of the reality. Due to their social conditioning, they are not aware that because of their white skin, certain advantages and benefits come their way. To some degree they participate in their own deceptions, believing that they have earned these privileges. They hold to the illusion that Australia not only is a wealthy country, but also is wealthy enough to be quite charitable to other nations around the world by giving away millions of dollars as foreign aid. They create even greater deprivation for Aboriginal People, by denying that so-called Third and Fourth World conditions can be found in their own backyard.

Their own non-willingness to face facts perpetuates the poverty and oppression of the indigenous people in this country. White Australia really understands itself to be "The Lucky Country." White Australians firmly believe that no one goes without here; that they don't have "those conditions" here; that they are very humane—indeed, that they are great humanitarians and philanthropists, always ready to come to the aid of the underdog; and, that everyone gets "A Fair Go." They believe that they already have given huge amounts of money to Aboriginals, in the way of charity, but that Aboriginals are quite unfair by still demanding more.

White Australians know that the values passed on within this society are based on white control and the assumption of white superiority. This is maintained through their distortion of white achievements over and against the failures of the Aboriginals. It is twisted and untruthful, as shown in the recording and documenting of the history of this country. It is maintained through certain sectors of Australian society—such as government, church, business and industry. The situation is compounded by the continual denial of the inherent rights of the Aboriginal People, in order never to question the powers that be.

White power, white control, and white superiority are presented to us as natural, the way things are and the way things ought to be. (Barndt 1991:60)

So thorough is the socialization process in Australia that white people do not even realize they are participating in it. They do not grasp that making racists out of them is a relatively simple task. From early childhood the process begins and—consciously or unconsciously—a racist mentality begins to be created. Whites are taught to have pride in their identity, and to fear, hate, or to be suspicious of the Aboriginal People. They are taught to act in a paternalistic way—and even to openly pity the Aboriginal People. So subtle is this process that it becomes so deeply embedded into the white psyche that the very core of their being is permeated with these racist assumptions and values.

Malice and Slander

Over the past two hundred and six years, white Australia basically has sunk to the dehumanizing level of name-calling, and the creation of lies in describing their perception of the inhumanity of the Aboriginal People. Racist calumny was reinforced right throughout the white society, and this form of malicious slander has been handed down from one generation to another. It was found in all aspects of this society—the church, education, laws, policies, structures and attitudes.

Because of the demographics associated with European expansion, and even well before we became a minority, most Europeans had little or no contact with Aborigines. This meant that their attitude towards us has been determined and moulded through the influence of other peoples' creations. These images were used to justify certain action against us and they continue to have an important influence on present day attitudes. (Behrendt 1994)

Some of the denigrating terms and lies perpetrated and perpetuated by white Australia about Aboriginal People, are that we are inferior, dirty, violent, lazy, drunken, untrustworthy, savage, pagan murderers. These lies for the most part would be accepted as the fundamental truth and such perceptions would be passed on through either jokes, songs on radio programs and projected within movies or television. This is used to justify the alleged superiority of their whiteness and their subjugation of the black race. For a black child to grow up in Australia is for him or her to be subjected to the tormenting of the white bigot. The ignorance of the white people comes as no surprise to the Aboriginal People, as white society is so structured as to keep and maintain their ignorance. This is reflected in their own ignorance about their Australian history. This racist ignorance is then portrayed within Australian life.

It is commonplace in Australian life to hear the white racist bigot denigration of the Aboriginal race because no one thinks anything about it, and because whites participate in this denigration. It is usually the common view held by the dominant white society. Racism within the life and practice of white society is so ingrained into their psyche that they no longer can distinguish between fantasy and reality. To be a racist has become so much a part of white life in Australia that it is considered "normal"—part of the norm—because the indoctrination has been so subtle, and yet so successful, that racism is now a daily part of western society.

> To this day, such racist indoctrination influences our daily language and cultural symbols. To us, the color black symbolizes evil, sin, death; white stands for purity, virtue, and joy. (Barndt 1991:61)

The Impact of Racism

When we review racism in Australian history, we see that the racist legacy still lives on in Australian society today. We see the legacy of this racism in the faces of the Aboriginal People and in their communities. The racist oppression to which they have been subjected for over two hundred years has now become internalized. The goal of this chapter is to identify and analyse those negative Euro-Australian traits—brought here with the invading Europeans—as well as their impact upon the Indigenous Peoples of Australia. We will see how we have internalized these racist practices and this oppression into our own psyche, and how we justify our own oppression of our People.

> At the core of racism is an ideology of white superiority, which presupposes the inferiority of others; its success is contingent upon the imposition of this idea as a normative value. Racism distorts the views and perception of the oppressor as well as the oppressed. Oppressed people are stripped of amenities that announce to the world that their existence is a consequence of divine intent, not an accident of history. On the other hand, the benefactors of racism are embellished with the notion that, because they are white, it is their destiny to be the inheritors, guarantors, and controllers of the resources that shape and direct history. The values that affirm white humanity also affirm the subjugation and denial of humanity to others. (O. Turner 1991:21)

This certainly has been the attitude of white Australians for two hundred and six years. The way that the whites interacted with the

Aboriginal People reflects this very racist attitude and treatment. This is not isolated within any given area of European society, but rather is found in all areas, including: the church, government, media, police, academia, education and many others.

Internalized Oppression

When a race of people are subjected to racial hatred and name-calling, and to the denial of their very humanity for well over two centuries, it is inevitable that they suffer some form of lasting negative effect. Indeed, this racist oppression takes it toll and becomes internalized. Aboriginal People have found themselves literally enslaved by the invading British, through their racist laws, legislation and policies imposed on the indigenous people of this land to control their very lives. Therefore, it is no surprise to consider that when a people have suffered this domination and racism so long, that they invariably internalize some of this oppression—even though they have struggled against white racist ideology that is found in Australian society. Aboriginal People have found themselves at the mercy of the whim of the white society, and forced into accommodating this whim for the last two centuries.

Racist Doctrine

It is well documented that during the first half of the century the Aboriginal People were dispossessed of their land and a genocidal process began in Australia (cf. Reynolds 1982; Reynolds 1987b). But, when it comes to the missionization process of the Aboriginal People, Euro-Australian Christians and churches deny that their imprisonment of the Aboriginal People was anything more than their being "well-intentioned" in order to "save" the Aboriginals from "destruction"; and, their patriotic obedience of government instructions. Of course, this is partly true, but what is not known is that during the nineteenth and twentieth centuries the Aboriginal People encountered a second onslaught, led by the missionary agents of European civilization, whose desires were to change the Aboriginal psyche.

This led to missionaries committing cultural genocide, as their intention was to remake the Indigenous People into their own image (cf. Attwood 1989; Pattel-Gray 1991a). This pious attitude—so often found in the missionary during this time—reflected their racist theology, their Biblical interpretation of their alleged superiority, and their brazen arrogance to assume that they had a right to "civilize" the Aboriginal

People. It reflected their desires not only to control, but also to dominate the Indigenous People (cf. Attwood 1989, Pattel-Gray 1991a). This social Darwinist ideology, expressed through European theology, led the missionaries to believe that such control and domination only could be completed through a continuing and total subjugation of the Aboriginal People. This, in turn, led to the destruction of Aboriginal culture and traditions (as they knew them) and to their replacement by European values and traditions. The missionaries truly believed that the "saving" of the Aboriginals meant the total destruction of their traditions, beliefs and practices.

> The severing of black fingers for use as pipe rammers; the staking of decapitated black heads on gate-posts and the chopping up of helpless black men, women and children with cutlasses were acts which sank even lower than the "lowest depths of barbarism" and one wonders if the Sons [*sic*] of England had the necessary qualifications to *"Christianise"* and *"educate"* the Aborigines of Australia! (Rosser 1990:13)

Missionaries, though not necessarily involved in such practices themselves, nevertheless did not do enough to stop them. The missionaries firmly believed that civilization and Christianity went hand and hand, that the two could not be separated. So, the process began, and missionaries sought land that was neither close to Europeans settlements or towns (giving life to their latent aversive racism), nor to traditional lands to which the Aboriginal People related (giving life to their dominative racism) (cf. Kovel 1970). They sought an environment that was totally isolated from all that could interfere with their plans, so that the Aboriginal People would become totally dependant upon them for all their physical needs (cf. Attwood 1989; Pattel-Gray 1991a).

Today, as many Aboriginals recall their confinement to the many mission and reserves starting from their early childhood and lasting several decades until they reached adulthood, they express enormous pain and heartache. They remember stories of being taken from their families and communities, only to be imprisoned under the illusion of being "protected for your own good"; having no worth as an Aboriginal, except for being the servant class for the elite European masters and mistresses; having their worth expressed as nothing more than chattel, to be bought or sold at any given time by the European slave owners (cf. Tucker 1977; Rintoul 1993). There was never any thought given to what the Aboriginals might desire for themselves, or to whether they wished to be treated as a chattel, as it was perceived by the Europeans that

Aboriginals did not know "what was best for themselves." They were believed, certainly, to not "possess the capacity" to make decisions for themselves. Therefore, the Europeans considered that it was their right to take actions on their behalf. This led to the total domination of the Aboriginal psyche, and to the destruction of Aboriginal self-worth and rights.

The control that was exercised over Aboriginal People by the missionaries literally denigrated any worth that could be found belonging to the Aboriginal tradition or identity. It led to strict control, and denied traditional languages being exercised by the Aboriginal "inmates" or personal interaction with Aboriginal families and society. Just as the European colonists were reshaping the environment for their capitalist purposes, so also the missionaries were compelled to change and reshape their environment. This was not just limited to the landscape but also included the Aboriginal People into this endeavour to transform these into what they perceived as their "Christian duty" and to have them reflect what they considered to be a "Christian environment."

The abuse inflicted upon the Aboriginal People by the white invaders was not only limited to physical, but also included intellectual abuse. The re-enforcing of their white superiority was supported by the whites (literally) pounding into the blacks that they were inferior. This took place in all areas of Europeans society. The "new order" could not take place without the blacks knowing their "place"—which often led to the whites exercising brute force upon the Aboriginal People by "teaching the blacks a lesson" (cf. Reynolds 1987a:32–42). Several generations of Aboriginal People speak of this practice inflicted upon them, through the many reserves and missions, or through prison settlements. The aim of the European "Protectors" or "Guardians" of the Aboriginal People was not to judge their behaviour as sinful, but rather as shameful.

This view permeated all areas of Aboriginal life, including their identity, culture, traditions, practices and religion (OT: Iles 1989, Gilbert 1990–93, C. Harris 1987–93; cf. Attwood 1989). This was pounded into their psyches day after day, starting when they were infants and continuing right throughout their lives until adulthood. It is no wonder many Aboriginals were ashamed of who they were, and also of their own people, because the white oppressor worked hard at striping them of any racial pride they had and replacing it with feelings and emotions of inferiority and shame. The negative indoctrination took place over several decades, and was visible in all aspects of life in the interacting of the whites and the Aboriginal People—through education, Christianity, laws, social attitudes of European society. Aboriginals were led to believe through European practice and teaching that they were the most abominable creature on this earth, and certainly had no worth to any industrial or European society; they were considered to be the beast of burden to everyone (cf. Rowley 1972). This psychological indoctrination had an enormous impact on the Aboriginal People's own behaviour and attitudes towards the white people, and is still seen in many Aboriginals today—although many are now freeing themselves and their people, and an upsurge of racial pride is now becoming visible today in our society. But, their is still along way to go.

The Aboriginals were made to feel inferior, and they expressed this as a lack of self-esteem. As identified earlier in this chapter, the white socialization process towards their own people—and now when we find the white socialization towards Aboriginal People—cannot be seen as accidental but rather as intentional. When comparing these two levels of indoctrination process, one cannot help but consider the intent behind it. This socialization process was a necessary means if white people were to maintain power and control over every aspect of this land. The subjugation of the people was a necessary prerequisite to the theft of the land. The dominant collective power of today, of course, would deny that this socialization process has been the most critical factor in their taking possession of this land and all that is in it. So when the government and church take a humanitarian stand, looking beyond their shores at other poor and oppressed peoples, and make such pious and derogatory statements in regards to the poverty of these people, we cannot help but see the irony behind it when we know their lack of concern for the rights of the Indigenous People of the country in which they live.

But this in itself is difficult when Aboriginal People find themselves at the bottom of the society and absorbed into this structure even to the point of being trampled. How does a marginalized race of People struggle against racism in a dominant white society? We find ourselves being forced to accommodate to oppressive structures, and unconsciously taking in oppressive values (cf. O. Turner 1991:21).

The Aboriginal People have found that within our struggle to survive, there have been many of us unable to keep our strength and courage to continue. There are those individuals that Aboriginal People consider to be "coconuts," who sold their people out for material benefits. There are others who have taken to alcohol in order to forget about their dehumanization by whites, and yet, they still struggle to survive.

One of the many consequences of internalized oppression is a transference of responsibility for one's oppression. The oppressed are blamed for their own oppression as part of the ideology of racism, diverting attention from its real source. This internalized oppression inhibits our ability to perceive the contradictions in personal and social reality. How we see ourselves informs how we exercize volition and respond to the way we are treated. The distinction between what we do to oppress ourselves and what others do to oppress us is blurred. It becomes easy to blame all of our woes on racism and we are further inhibited. Internalized oppression complements paternalism: racism regulates the relationships between oppressors and oppressed and the interrelationships of the oppressed themselves, and oppressed people are forced by habit, circumstance, and conditioning to depend upon oppressors for guidance, direction, and affirmation. Even when the material and other resources necessary to solve some of our basic problems are within our grasp, dependency still remains. Dependency may have its rewards, but the attendant liabilities are astronomical by comparison. (O. Turner 1991:21–22)

Today, within Aboriginal society, we find a blurring of what are symptoms of oppression and the sources of oppression. Through the controls of white domination and oppression, inflicted upon the Aboriginal People for so long, Euro-Australians literally have dominated and enslaved the Indigenous People through colonization and missionization to the point that they had total control over our lives.

Liberation and Freedom

The move forward for ourselves is to be liberated from all forms of oppression. This can only be done when we take control over our own lives and begin to be fully self-determining and self-empowered.

It is better to walk on your own with a limp than to be carried in style. It is not the physical limp that is the problem, it is a frame of mind that disposes one to be dependent rather than independent. The essence of oppression is mental, not physical. The essence of liberation is likewise mental, not physical. Mental liberation is a prerequisite for changing one's social reality in a way that results in freedom. (O. Turner 1991:22)

While Aboriginal People continue to base their liberation wholly and solely on the generosity of whites' minor policy changes and the hope of whites' attitudinal change, we will be confined to our continual bondage and oppression. As we have seen throughout our history, the move from Protection to Assimilation Policies did not in any way offer us freedom from racist oppression, because those Policies were being predefined and structured outside of our race. While Aboriginal People continue to talk about the significant gains that have been made by our own political movements, we need to do more psychological analysis as to whether or not these gains have been minor or major achievements, because oppression comes in many beautifully wrapped gifts, but these in no way signify liberation or freedom.

We need to expose the continuing fallacies of the Assimilation Agenda that lie behind current and future government proposals. We need to ensure that we move toward true self-determination from an Aboriginal perspective. We need to analyse more closely the connection between racism and power to ensure that we do not continue to internalize our oppression, as we strive toward the goals that are desperately needed in the genuine fulfilment and empowerment of self-determination.

In reviewing the racist legacy in Australia, we now have to consider seriously the implications of the government-initiated Council for Aboriginal Reconciliation, because the reconciliation process could be yet another smoke-screen to hide Australia's abysmal record of continual denial of human rights to the Indigenous People.

CHAPTER 5

RECONCILIATION: A FACSIMILE OF JUSTICE

Nothing suits the resolution of an inner conflict so much as the presence of an outer facsimile of it, distant enough to spare the self direct guilt, yet close enough to allow a symbolic correspondence. (Kovel 1970:203)

A Euro-Australian Dream, An Aboriginal Nightmare

Today, within the government and church institutions in Australia, the buzz word that is going around is "reconciliation." One has to wonder what is meant by this when, after two hundred and six years of subjugation, Aboriginal People still are suffering under a racist and oppressive, dominant white society. In the Australian reconciliation movement gaining in popularity today, Aboriginal People are facing "justice by facsimile"—distant enough to spare whites' direct guilt, yet close enough to allow a symbolic correspondence (Kovel 1970:203). If we look at current Euro-Australians' attitudes towards the Indigenous People, we can see clearly that the future looks grim not only for Aboriginal People but also for non-Aboriginal people, as liberation is impossible not only for the oppressed, but also for the oppressor.

> . . . there are strong moral grounds for ending the domination of black people by the white people. Tinkering with a system which by its very nature has reduced Aborigines to beggars in their own land, cannot provide the best solution. Providing remedies for discrimination and over-representation in prisons; better housing, employment and welfare facilities; even providing mechanisms through which Aborigines may claim small lots of land, cannot overcome the despair and dependence which comes from alienation in a white nation. (APG 1993a:3)

Aboriginal People speak out about the injustices which they suffer, and expose the racism of the past and of the present, and defend themselves against the continuing brutalities inflicted upon them by this white society. Yet, it never fails to amaze Aboriginal People that so-called Christians then ask, "What about the Biblical doctrine of reconciliation? What about Christian forgiveness and turning the other cheek?" It should not surprise the white people who ask such questions when Aboriginal People get up and walk away. How does reconciliation begin when

219

repentance, conversion and justice are not the preconditions for reconciliation?

> Those who believe that, despite all the evidence, we can all be reconciled to live harmoniously under one nation, believe in tooth fairies and fantasy. Australia is a racist country. The reaction from too many Australians to token efforts to provide practical human rights for Aborigines is just one indicator of the futility of the dream. (APG 1993a:4)

How can white people talk about reconciliation when it was they who raised (and raise) the dividing walls of hostility, racism and hatred through the theft of Aboriginal land, genocide, slavery, segregation and the denial of human rights to the Indigenous People of this land? They now want to know if the Indigenous People of this land are ready to forgive and forget, but they never once address the source of this oppression, or change the balance of power. White Australia wants to know if the Aboriginal People have any hard feelings towards them, though they kidnapped our children and committed cultural genocide upon much of our race. They want to know if we love them, even though we are still oppressed and brutalized by them each and every day of our lives. What can Aboriginal People say to white people when they speak of reconciliation and yet continue to oppress us, and then surprisingly get upset when they are rejected by Aboriginal People?

For white people reconciliation does not mean that a price has to be paid, or that the injustices need to be addressed. They do not feel that there is a cost involved, or that they need to change their privileged status. When Aboriginal People speak to the church and society about the "truth," they are usually met with an attack of angry denial by the white people—leaving Aboriginal People with many questions about what is the Biblical doctrine of reconciliation.

> The Christian view of reconciliation has nothing to do with black people being nice to white people as if the gospel demands that we ignore their insults and their humiliating presence. It does not mean discussing with whites what it means to be black or going to white gatherings and displaying what whites call an understanding attitude—remaining cool and calm amid racists and bigots. To understand the biblical view of reconciliation, we must see it in relation to the struggle of freedom in an oppressed society. (Cone 1975:226–27)

Trick or Treaty?

What does reconciliation mean for Aboriginal People in Australia— especially when we reflect upon numerous publicly available facts and figures? First, as used by the Australian Government today as a kind of policy, the word and concept of "reconciliation" originally emerged out of the *Final Report of the Royal Commission into Aboriginal Deaths in Custody* in 1991 (RCADC 1991). Second, the only "justice" achieved for Aboriginal People was a "list" of 339 Recommendations, which are yet to be implemented a full three years after their release. Third, Aboriginal People are feeling violated and extremely frustrated by the slow process of justice in this country. In one tragic example, an Aboriginal mother felt so betrayed by the absence of justice for the death of her son that she committed suicide (KM 20 May 1992:1, 3). Fourth, other Aboriginal families, whose loved ones also have died in Australian police and prison custody, still are terrorized by the police and white racists in communities where they live. Indeed, for the past several years, some have been forced to move from town to town, fearing for their safety and, in some cases, for their very lives. Fifth—and never ceasing to amaze Aboriginal People—is that there was *not one,* single criminal charge made against any of the white police and prison wardens in *any* of the 99 Aboriginal deaths that were investigated by the Royal Commission. The Aboriginal People are expected to swallow that all 99 persons either committed suicide or died of natural causes, that none were murdered. Sixth—and perhaps most sickening—is the fact that Aboriginal deaths in custody are continuing. Since the cut-off date for the Aboriginal deaths investigated by the Royal Commission (i.e., 31 May 1989), *another 43 Aboriginal People* have died in Australian police and prison custody (Howlett and McDonald 1994:13).

> . . . this represents an average of 10.5 deaths of indigenous people per annum, the *same annual average* as was observed during the period covered by the Royal Commission. (Howlett and McDonald 1994:13, emphasis added)

In light of this shocking evidence, it is no small wonder that Aboriginal People remain profoundly sceptical of what "reconciliation" means within this Australian context.

In 1994, three years after the conclusion of the so-called Royal Commission into Aboriginal Deaths in Custody, current statistics show that Aboriginal deaths have continued (D. Graham 1994:6; Chamberlin 28 June 1994:13); that the imprisonment rate of Aboriginal People has *increased* (A. Harvey 1994: 1, 6; M. Brown 1994:6); that racist violence and attitudes have *amplified* within Australian society (SMH 16 April 1994:8); that the poverty of the Aboriginal People has *escalated* (cf. Dwyer 1977:41, and Tickner 1992); and, that the continuing disadvantage of the

Aboriginal People—reflected in poor housing, health, education, employment, and the continuing racist oppression by the white dominant society—has *intensified* (Signy 1994:6). But still this white Australian society has the audacity to want to speak about reconciliation between Aboriginals and non-Aboriginals when the social, political, economic conditions of the Aboriginal People have not been rectified, let alone addressed.

Federal Government Provision for Reconciliation

> The Council for Reconciliation admits that it can only hope to change attitudes. Attitude change is always an escapable target. The real problem is that Aboriginal needs are totally dominated by white people's needs, forcing Aborigines to rely on their masters for the basic necessities of life. (APG 1992a:20)

If changing white attitudes is the government's solution to Aboriginal People's state of poverty and injustice, then no wonder Aboriginal People continue to hold the so-called "reconciliation process" in question. One of the major criticisms made by Aboriginal People about the reconciliation process is that the whole idea is so ambiguous that not even the Council for Aboriginal Reconciliation itself is able to say what its objectives are—apart from "changing white attitudes."

> Dogging the government's new approach is the criticism that the whole process is so vague as to be meaningless and that it will simply result in a waste of tax payers' funds. This only further exposes Aborigines to the racist but oft-stated view that we are over-privileged. Instead of Aborigines standing to gain from the process, we may well find ourselves resented even more by whites, through no fault of our own. (APG 1992a:20)

The white racist attitudes that have existed in Australia for the past several decades are that Aboriginal People get "special treatment," and that they get too much money given to them and all they do is waste it. If these are still the current attitudes, then why would the situation change "all of a sudden"? This form of racism is to be found in all levels of Australian society—from poor whites, to middle and upper-class whites, right through to the politicians that represent them.

Even today, white attitudes include beliefs that Aboriginals are stone-age people (cf. SMH 15 June 1993:16), and lazy, dirty animals. Why would this change, when white society has been established on the belief in theories of Darwinism and Social Darwinism; when it holds that it is the superior race and the Aboriginal the inferior; when it still considers us to be the lowest link in the Great Chain of Being (cf. Spencer 1874)?

How does one go about changing these kinds of attitudes without attacking the source of the problem? Challenging the symptoms—as they are defined by the current Reconciliation process—does not bring about change. It could be said that the whole reconciliation process is just about making the whites feel good about themselves, and about making it seem like they are doing something when they are not. They become hollow moralists, vehemently avoiding "self-denial" and flagrantly indulging in "self-aggrandizement" (R. Niebuhr 1932:47).

> Failure to recognize the stubborn resistance of group egoism to all moral and inclusive social objectives inevitably involves them [moralists] in unrealistic and confused political thought. (R. Niebuhr 1932:xx)

If the reconciliation process is not about bringing positive change to the political, social and economic status of the Aboriginal People then there cannot be reconciliation—not without justice.

> The only way for a people who have become demoralised and are denied the opportunity to stand with pride and dignity as a people is to completely remove the causes of the problem; and, when that has been agreed, to allow us to develop as we see fit, not as individuals but as a people. It is high time we seriously questioned policies aimed at lessening the pain while prolonging the agony. (APG 1993a:3)

When reading the educational materials produced by the Council for Aboriginal Reconciliation, it is unclear as to what will be the outcome of the ten-year process already underway. No one knows if there will be some sort of social policy document (or documents) put in place, or if Australian governments will or will not implement them if they are developed. We already have seen, repeatedly over the past two hundred and six years, the continual failure of Australian governments to devise effective solutions in addressing the dehumanizing and oppressive position of the Aboriginal People. Perhaps the perfect example is the list of 339 Recommendations that came out the *Final Report of the Royal Commission into Aboriginal Death in Custody*. How much more money will be spent on costly administration overheads, large salaries for the white bureaucrats and massive expenses on consultations and glossy educational materials before the simple logic of the solution becomes obvious to them?

They need to spend these millions of dollars on changing the root causes of the abominable social conditions and the source of oppression, instead of talking and reporting about them—over and over again (cf. HREOC 1988; HREOC 1991; Tickner 1992; Keating 1992). Aboriginal People feel that the Council for Aboriginal Reconciliation should be addressing the critical issue, already identified by Aboriginal People: the denial of a full humanity for Aboriginal People. This is the source of the problem and not the symptom. The Council for Aboriginal Reconciliation is avoiding the problem when it focuses on changing white attitudes. Aboriginal People feel that whites will never change their racist attitudes, and that the reconciliation process is a waste of time.

> The Reconciliation Council was set up to alter these attitudes but the deeply ingrained attitudes have not been seen to have changed one bit. The reason for the Council's vain efforts to date is because of the insurmountable problem: attitudes against Aborigines are caused by the entrenched belief that white domination should prevail. The Council's approach is to address the symptoms of that attitude, not the source of it. It is of little note that the public be encouraged to speak better of Aborigines when the system leaves untouched the dispossession, control and domination of Aborigines. (APG 1993a:4)

White, Western institutions have been—and are—so ordered as to keep Aboriginal People down, and therefore out. They are born from racist attitudes, nurtured to support the oppression and maintained to continue the exploitation. In turn, these institutions reinforce the initial racist attitudes. It is a circle of inequality, injustice and oppression (cf. R. Niebuhr 1932:231).

> The violation of the rights of the poor is not something that "just happens." It is a permanent ongoing process. (L. Boff 1989:43)

For justice and equity to be brought about, more than just change in general *attitudes* will be required from the white society. White Australians must address the source of the oppression, not just the symptoms. The Council for Aboriginal Reconciliation is not addressing the sources of Aboriginal dehumanization. It is not combating the ideologies behind Australian racism against Aboriginal People. It does not challenge the injustices of the social, political, economic or even religious powers. It, therefore, ignores the real problems.

In the Report of the Royal Commission into Aboriginal Deaths in Custody, Commissioner Elliot Johnston QC states under the heading "Reducing the number of Aboriginal people in custody—the fundamental question—empowerment and self-determination," that

... running through all the proposals that are made for the elimination of [Aboriginal] disadvantages is the proposition that Aboriginal people have for two hundred years been dominated to an extraordinary degree by the non-aboriginal society and that the disadvantage is the product of that domination. The thrust of this report is that the elimination of disadvantage requires and end of domination and an empowerment of Aboriginal people; that control of their lives, of their communities must be returned to Aboriginal hands. (APG 1993a:7)

If this white domination is so obvious, even within some of the government ranks, then why is it not being challenged? In Australia there never have been a People so dominated and controlled as we, nor have there been People who have endured what Aboriginal People have had to endure from white Australians. Australian history shows us that, for some reason, white Australia has found it necessary to control all areas of Aboriginal life, to the point that they were in charge of where Aboriginals would live, who we would marry, whether or not our children were "under the Act," and more.

Did white Australia feel a sense of power, knowing that the Aboriginal People were nothing more than chattel to be bought and sold, and mated with the appropriate partner only when they deemed it? Aboriginal People were at the mercy of the white people's whim. Aboriginal People often wonder how the white Australians would have responded if they were subjected to such oppressive control for over two centuries. The white outcry would have been heard throughout the world, and no doubt the United Nations, the International Court of Justice and others would be here investigating the situation right now. Yet, white Australians always seem amazed when they hear Aboriginal People speaking out about their domination, and they deny that Aboriginal People get a raw deal. Their continual repudiation of Aboriginal People becoming self-determining and self-managing still is happening to this day, to the point now that the Government has co-opted the meaning of both "self-determination" and "self-management" (M. Dodson 1993:42). They have defined these, weakening them to the point of meaninglessness.

It is very difficult to reconcile the approach of the Royal Commission with the statements made by Labor Party Ministers controlling Aboriginal Affairs, especially where protocol is washed way to reveal the real meaning of the Government's version of self-determination. Pam Ditton, in a frank assessment, said:

"Self-management . . . is merely a political term used within Australia, without a precise, internationally accepted meaning. Therefore, if it wishes, a government could use 'self-management' as a smokescreen to 'sell' programs to Aboriginal communities that they would otherwise find unacceptable". (APG 1993a:8)

Obviously, governments have failed to be honest in their use of these words, and have lulled the Aboriginal People into a false security. Over time, however, the Aboriginal People have come to realize that governments do not mean for us to be self-determining or self-managing. We see that this is nothing but a smoke-screen in order for them to justify themselves to the broader society. So, when Aboriginal People criticize governments for not allowing us to be self-determining and self-managing, and for their programs not addressing our communities' needs, then they are accused by the broader white society of "getting too much." They jump on the bandwagon and make such claims as, "Are we not all Australians? Then why do the Aboriginals get more than us? Should not the Aboriginals get the same as the rest of we Australians?"

This would be acceptable if it were true, but even though Aboriginals are the Indigenous Peoples of this land, we still do not enjoy the same level of human rights as the broader white Australian society with their privileged status.

The most serious consequence of broad acceptance of the *"Aborigines are Australians"* view is that Aboriginal right to land, and control over ourselves must take on a new dimension. No longer could we assert our inherent right as the only legitimate owners as a basis for our demands. Instead we would have to rely on any such rights to be **granted** by the Government rather than **returned**. Hence, the Government would be final arbiter on the matter, effectively limiting Aboriginal access to international forums or world standards which will continue to be developed and applied to other indigenous people. That being the case, it would be pretty reasonable to expect that we would get far less than our counterparts in other parts of the world. (APG 1993a:8)

As we see, Australian governments still are not recognizing the rights of the Aboriginal People and this places them outside of the claim that "we are all Australians." The original owners of this country and our inherent and distinct rights on this basis have been denied within this country. This should be one of, if not, the most critical points that the Council for Aboriginal Reconciliation should be addressing; they should not be placing their whole focus on changing white attitudes.

The Constitutional Centenary Conference in 1991 stated as one of its three points on Aboriginal issues that:

... the process of Reconciliation should, among other things, seek to identify what rights the Aboriginal and Torres Strait Islander people have, and should have, **as the indigenous people of Australia**, and how best to secure those rights, including through constitutional changes. (APG 1993a:23)

Instead, the Council for Aboriginal Reconciliation considers that it has the right answers by identifying that, through its process, the injustices against Aboriginal People will be addressed and, therefore, the process needs to focus on changing white attitudes.

The Council of Reconciliation adopts the view that we are "Aboriginal Australians." Under its charter, it believes that everything is headed in the right direction and that Aborigines can achieve equality so long as we overcome the prejudiced attitudes. For that reason, its emphasis is to change attitudes in Australia. (APG 1993b:36)

Aboriginal People still do not see how this is possible, or why all this energy should be given to changing white attitudes—especially when we are the ones who are dying and being brutalized every day, and are at the bottom socially, politically and economically. Why do the Aboriginal People have to wait until the year 2001 to see *if* their rights will be recognized? What happens if all we get is white people being nice to us, and still no change in our social, political and economic realities? What then? Are we to accept that "We are now reconciled"?

What Does the Church Say About Reconciliation?

Imagine the surprise of the Aboriginal People when the Australian churches so quickly jumped on the band wagon to support the government's move to implement the reconciliation process within this country.

Or, should the Aboriginal People be so surprised when the churches come out to affirm the government for its initiative to reconcile black and white in this country? Not only is it continually visible within Australian history that the churches always are lagging behind the government, and never leading the government, but also is it clear to the Aboriginal People that the Australian churches are waddling behind the government. The churches seem to lack vision and initiative in addressing the issues identified by the Aboriginal People.

One of the Aboriginal church organizations that never made a statement of support for the Australian government's reconciliation process is the Aboriginal & Islander Commission of the (then) Australian

Council of Churches—even though it is identified, erroneously, by the Federal Minister for Aboriginal Affairs in a report as having given its support (Tickner 1991b). The Aboriginal & Islander Commission has been somewhat suspicious of the reconciliation process—and with good reason if the government's history is any example to go on. This ecumenical Commission felt unable to give any support because the outcome of the process is so unclear, and because the Commission wonders if the process will change much—or even any—of the oppression suffered by the Aboriginal People under this imperialistic dominant society. Aboriginal church people say that it would be easy to feel good about this process, but if they stop and think about it, they have to wonder if there is any hidden intent behind it. When all is said and done, and the process is completed, what would have changed for the Aboriginal People? If not enough changes have been made, then what? Does this mean we have to accept "our lot" and be satisfied by the few crumbs given to us by the white people?

> ... There can be no justice in our world without a transfer of economic resources to undergird the redistribution of political power and to make cultural self-determination meaningful. (Adler 1974:15)

Or, are the white people ready to change all institutional structures and "share the pie" equally? We do not think so, as the white government already is indicating to us that they have set the agenda, they control the agenda, they control the guidelines of this agenda and they have final say as to what they will and will not accept at the end of the day. How can Aboriginal People get excited by the reconciliation process when the government determined what the process would be, and how the process would go, and what the process would achieve?

Once again we see the dominant white society controlling the agenda and setting the guidelines, and then soliciting Aboriginal People to "play the game." How does reconciliation take place when Aboriginal People have had no input into either the guidelines or the outcome? How does it take place, especially in light of the fact that in the so-called "bipartisan agreement" that initiated this whole process it was made clear by the then opposition leader, Dr. John Hewson, that he would not support a process that spoke of justice or treaty or a just and proper settlement outcome for Aboriginal People (OT: Hewson 1991)? So what do we have if we do not achieve justice? Aboriginal People seriously wonder.

When we reflect on the God-given principles found in the Old Testament, and then in the New Testament, we only can ask why is it that

Christians and their churches have not been able to identify and address the issues of justice as a precondition for reconciliation.

The 1966 World Conference on Church and society brought such issues to the floor.

> Not charity, but a radical change in structures, was proclaimed as the answer to the problems . . . that reconciliation cannot be "mere sentimental harmonizing of conflicting groups" but calls for nothing less than solidarity with the oppressed and the determination to break down unjust structures of white domination. Only this can lead to an authentic human community. "For Christians to stand aloof from this struggle is to be disobedient to the call of God in History." (Adler 1974:6)

Why were the churches not at the forefront in the quest for justice for Aboriginal People? Why is it that the church is always coming up the rear? Is it because they themselves have not addressed their complicity in the dehumanization of the Aboriginal People, and now want to ignore the seriousness and implications of their rule, but say all is forgiven and forgotten? This agony can never be forgotten by the Aboriginal People as the atrocities are still within living memory for most Aboriginal People, and they are not considered to be something that happened over two hundred year ago. Aboriginal People do not want to hear hollow apologies from the government and churches. We want instead to see serious change take place, change that addresses the balance of power and not the sweet gestures and posturing by the government and churches—for which they are known.

1988, the *March for Justice, Freedom and Hope* and "Covenanting"

In 1988 (the so-called bicentennial year), the Australian Council of Churches called for churches not to be involved with the bicentennial celebrations (cf. ACC Archives 1987). Of course this fell on deaf ears, as many—if not most—of the churches in Australia participated in the celebration of the two hundred years of lies, dispossession and denial of Aboriginal People's human rights. Even the *March for Justice, Freedom and Hope*—initiated and organized by the Rev. Charles Harris as the President of the Uniting Aboriginal and Islander Christian Congress (UAICC) of the Uniting Church in Australia (UCA)—was ignored by the so-called Aboriginal and white "Christians." The vast majority of Aboriginal members of the UAICC withdrew their support because the majority of UCA Christians said, "It is wrong to march in protest against the Bicentennial of 'Our' Country." But the Rev. Harris stood strong against his own members, and rallied the Aboriginal secular organizations and communities to support and march with him. Out of hundreds of UAICC members, only five persons actually participated in the March—although, it is most interesting to note that, now, the entire UAICC accepts credit for the overwhelming success and achievement of the March. Out of the enthusiasm and commitment gathered around the *March for Justice, Freedom and Hope,* the Rev. Harris envisioned a "Covenanting Process." His dream was to harness the white and general Aboriginal support achieved through the March, toward a Covenant agreement between white and Aboriginal People—what might, in secular society, be conceived of as a treaty agreement. This Covenanting process was launched later that year.

Since the serious illness and subsequent death of the Rev. Charles Harris, the UAICC and the Covenanting process have lost their vision. As it stands today, Covenanting lacks truth and integrity. There still is a tendency for white people to want to play down the destructive role of the church in Australian history. Now, we find that the great passion, energy and conviction injected into the Covenanting process by the Rev. Charles Harris have been transformed into a sedative. The church is attempting to numb the pain and hurt felt by the Aboriginal People by giving us a sugar-coated tranquillizer. The way the churches describe Australian church history pacifies the viciousness and the destructive intent of their presumed "superiority" and their colonization of our land; indeed, it continues the rationalization of their horrific actions and policies. In fact, even some of the educational materials created by the white staff in the UCA are incredibly paternalistic towards the Aboriginal People, using V-E-R-Y S-I-M-P-L-E L-A-N-G-U-A-G-E. We Aboriginal People find these kinds of documents to be quite "illiterate," and very insulting, to say the least. They slow any kind of true Covenanting process.

The fact is that the process already is slow enough. In 1988, at its 5th National Assembly, the Uniting Church in Australia received a timetable for the Covenanting process (cf. UCA 1991:113). In 1991, at it's 6th National Assembly, the UCA amended the previous timetable because it "did not provide sufficient time for the process to be developed" (cf. UCA 1991:113). In 1994, at it's 7th National Assembly, the Uniting Church still is stumbling around with the process. It proposed and executed a "Covenant Statement" ("Apology") read by the President of the Uniting Church Assembly. The texts of this document reinforces some of the most racist ideologies and oppressive myths that Aboriginal People have been fighting against for over two centuries (UCA 1994:151E–151F; cf.

Covenanting June 1994:6–10). Some Aboriginal People find these documents offensive and disempowering.

Once again we see the church floundering in its deception, its cowardice of facing the truth. This statement is seen by Aboriginal People as self-flagellation by the white church. One of the points made in the text reveals the arrogant assumption that white Christians have in regards to sharing our grief. How dare white people assume that they could be in touch with the enormity of the grief that Aboriginal People have endured over 206 years. No people in Australia have suffered the tragedy that we have endured in our struggle for survival.

Posturing About Their Aboriginal Enclaves

Whereas the Uniting, Anglican and Catholic Churches have made similar attempts to address their relationship with Aboriginal People, we see no genuine progress for Aboriginal People, but instead the uncritical support of the Government's reconciliation process. The churches speak of their liberalism by parading their Aboriginal enclaves within their denominations. The Australian churches may appear to be giving Aboriginal churches self-determination by giving them some money, as they think this is addressing the problem, but they fail in their efforts by failing to address the sources of Aboriginal oppression as identified by their own Aboriginal bodies—namely, the racist structures and the dominating oppression of the white churches. The small amount of money they will give is a drop in the bucket, compared to the vast amount they already have exploited and reaped off the backs of Aboriginal People in this country.

If the Australian churches were serious about Reconciliation or Covenanting, they would have to take seriously their own institutionalized racism, and name that racism, and change that racism.

Freedom From Oppression

The ultimate freedom for Aboriginal People is to be free from all white oppression—especially when we consider God's covenant of the land of promise. We relate this to being liberated from the oppression of white people. For the Australian churches to take seriously the liberation of the Aboriginal People they must change their oppressive ways of having to have total control and domination over Aboriginal People. Liberation and freedom can only happen when the dominant white church relinquishes its power over the oppressed Aboriginal People.

Why is it that the dominant church feels unable to share even some of its power with the Aboriginal People? Why do they feel it necessary to have total control over all aspects of our church life? Is this because they themselves lack the wisdom and maturity that is given by God, which enables them not to have such insecurity that stops them from living unselfish and egalitarian relationships with the Aboriginal People? If we are all God's children, then what do we fear, that does not enable us to have this egalitarian relationship? Is it because the dominant church thinks of itself as the superior being and the possessor of the "true" knowledge? Do they actually believe that they are the ones who possess "true" enlightenment, and this truth cannot be found in or through the Aboriginal People? Liberation, when defined through this ideology of "white supremacy," only can limit God's definitions of freedom and liberation, and cannot be expressed as supererogation on behalf of the white church.

Liberation as a Precondition to Reconciliation

This work is presented as an analysis of the racism in the social, political and ecclesiological life within Australian society. It becomes very clear from this analysis, then, that the oppression of the Aboriginal People has continued far too long, and that radical changes need to be made in order to address the needs identified in this work. If we continue to draw on the Bible for our objectives, we see that changes must take place, justice must become reality.

> In the Bible the objective reality of reconciliation is connected with divine liberation. This means that human fellowship with God is made possible through his activity in history, setting people free from economic, social, and political bondage. God's act of reconciliation is not mystical communion with the divine; nor is it a pietistic state of inwardness bestowed upon the believer. God's reconciliation is a new relationship with *people* created by his concrete involvement in the political affairs of the world, taking sides with the weak and the helpless. (Cone 1975:229)

The Biblical doctrine of reconciliation is certainly the way to start, but there are several stages to be gone through before we can ever achieve reconciliation. For instance, the Biblical doctrine of—as well as the divine mandate for—reconciliation, firstly, calls for repentance—and this calls for individual and corporate regret, contrition for individual and corporate action or inaction; secondly, God calls for conversion—and this means individual and corporate changes to beliefs and opinion; and thirdly, God calls for justice, which is individual and corporate justness, fairness, fair treatment and due appreciation.

> If we take seriously the objective reality of divine liberation as a precondition for reconciliation, then it becomes clear that God's salvation is intended for the poor and the helpless, and it is identical with their liberation from oppression. That is why salvation is defined in political terms in the Old Testament and why the prophets take their stand on the side of the poor within the community of Israel. (Cone 1975:230)

If this is what God calls for, then why is not the church also calling for the same principles? Why has not the church identified that in order to achieve reconciliation in this country we need firstly to repent, and then convert, and then establish justice amongst God's people?

Let us not simply ask questions but let us also look at the historical accounts of God's reconciliation with the poor and oppressed to God's self. In the Old Testament, God heard the cries of oppression and slavery of God's people in Egypt, and their call for liberation from their oppression. In Deuteronomy, Israel reflects on its covenant with God.

> My father was a homeless Aramean who went down to Egypt with a small company and lived there until they became a great, powerful and numerous nation. But the Egyptians ill-treated us, humiliated us and imposed cruel slavery upon us. Then we cried to the Lord the God of our fathers for help, and he listened to us and saw our humiliation, our hardship and distress; and so the Lord brought us out of Egypt with a strong hand and outstretched arm, with terrifying deeds, and with signs and portents. (26:5b–9, NEB).[1]

The release of the Israelites was not a purely spiritual liberation, God's liberation meant freedom from bondage of political, social and economic servitude, because God's power is not limited only to partial liberation. Instead, God's liberation is holistic to the liberation of the full humanity from all forms of oppression.

> Israel is Yahweh's people, and he is their God because, and only because, he has delivered them from the bondage of political slavery. . . . There could have been no covenant at Sinai without the Exodus from Egypt, no reconciliation without liberation. Liberation is what God does to effect reconciliation, and without the former the latter is impossible. To be liberated is to be delivered from the state of unfreedom to freedom; it is to have the chains struck off the body and mind so that the creature of God can be who he [or she] is.

---

[1] It is acknowledged that some (Palestinian) theologians would never use this part of the Bible; cf. Gottwald 1980.

> Reconciliation is that bestowal of freedom and life with God which takes place on the basis of God's liberating deeds. Liberation and reconciliation are tied together and have meaning only through God's initiative. They tell us that [hu]man[ity] cannot be [hu]man[ity], and God refuses to be God unless the creature of God is delivered from that which is enslaving and dehumanizing. (Cone 1975:229–30)

If this is so and God is found to be on the side of the weak and helpless, then God most certainly must be on the side of the Aboriginal People because they are the weak and helpless here in Australia. Why is it that the churches in Australia have not been more active in the liberation of the Aboriginal People if they themselves are the children of God, when God was clearly so active in the Old Testament liberating oppressed people from political bondage?

> As we have demonstrated, throughout the biblical story, God takes his stand with the weak and against the strong. Thus fellowship with God is made possible by his righteous activity in the world to set right the conditions for reconciliation. His setting right the conditions for divine-human fellowship is liberation, without which fellowship would be impossible. To speak of reconciliation apart from God's liberating activity is to ignore the divine basis of the divine-human fellowship. (Cone 1975:230)

If God's salvation is intended for the poor and helpless, then this is identical to liberation from oppression. Why is it, then, that Christians never ask why racism still is tolerated? Why do they accept Aboriginal People being so disadvantaged economically, socially and politically, and that they and their children suffer with high rates of infant mortality, malnutrition, diabetes, trachoma, hepatitis B, tuberculosis, and more, at much higher levels than whites (cf. Tickner 1992:8–15; DAA 1990:32–42; Choo 1990)? And, why is it that Aboriginal People still are at the bottom of the ladder of every social indicator of prosperity in this country (cf. M. Dodson 1993:9)? What is considered the human right for all people still is denied to Aboriginal People. Why is it that Aboriginal People are the most imprisoned people in the world? Why is it that Aboriginal People still are dying in Australian police and prison custody (cf. Howlett and McDonald 1994:13)?

It seems Australia's failure is a failure to find within itself the compassion and love that is needed to stand and struggle for justice for the Aboriginal People of this land. How much longer do Australians need to be convinced of their oppression of the Aboriginal People before something is done about it? How many more conferences, talkfests, reports and deaths do they need to convince them that Aboriginal People are "the conscience of their souls"?

As long as white Australians continue to ignore the social, political, economic and other poverty of the Aboriginal People—which they have created—, they cannot expect not to be criticized by the international community (both religious and secular) for their endless genocide of the Aboriginal People. Their doing nothing *concrete* to change the balance of power identifies them as accomplices in the act of genocide.

Christ the Reconciler and Liberator

When we look into the New Testament we still find the close relationship between liberation and reconciliation, which was found in God's liberating deeds in the Old Testament. This close relationship is also found in God sending his Son to live and die amongst the poor, sick and oppressed, and to be resurrected as the promise of eternal fullness of humanity.

> Christ is the Reconciler because he is first the Liberator. He was born in Bethlehem and "laid in a manger, because there was no place in the inn" (Luke 2:7 RSV). He was baptized with the sinners, the poor and the oppressed, because he was the Oppressed One sent from God to give wholeness to broken and wretched lives. Christ lived and worked among them, and on the cross he died for them. In him God entered history and affirmed the condition of the oppressed as his own existence, thereby making clear that poverty and sickness contradict the divine intentions for humanity. The cross and the resurrection are God's defeat of slavery. (Cone 1975:230)

Surely, if Christ was born and lived with the oppressed, then he also is to be found among the oppressed here in Australia. Christ says in the Gospel:

> . . . for I was hungry and you gave me food, I was thirsty and you gave me something to drink, I was a stranger and you welcomed me, I was naked and you gave me clothing, I was sick and you took care of me, I was in prison and you visited me. (Matt. 25:35–36)

How would Christians in Australia respond if Christ said these words to them today? Surely contemporary Australian Christians would ask the same question as in the rest of this passage.

> Then the righteous will answer him, "Lord, when was it that we saw you hungry and gave you food, or thirsty and gave you something to drink? And when was it that we saw you a stranger and welcomed you, or naked and gave you

clothing? And when was it that we saw you sick or in prison and visited you?"
And the King will answer them, "Truly I tell you, just as you did it to one of the
least of these who are members of my family, you did it to me." (Matt. 25:37–
40)

Aboriginal Christians have to wonder if Euro-Australian Christians
consider "the least" in Australia to be the Aboriginals, and if so, would
they consider them to be a part of the family about which Christ speaks?
If Christ is seen in the least, then why is it that the Aboriginal People still
suffer malnutrition, and live in "fourth-world" poverty in this first-world
country, with no housing, or running water, and we are sick and dying
because of the poor health conditions in which we are made to live? Why
is it that we are still dying in police and prison custody? Do not Euro-
Australian Christians identify the Aboriginal People as the least in this so-
called "lucky country," and do they not see Christ in this poor,
dehumanized people?

It could be said that Australian Christians' salvation is also dependent
on their just relationship with the Aboriginal People. Christ continues, in
Matthew 25:46, to condemn those who have failed to see him in the least
to eternal punishment, and to send the righteous into eternal life. What
would be the answer for some of the Christians in our society as to their
treatment of the least (the Aboriginal People)? Have they been faithful to
Christ's word, or have they simply overlooked this Scripture as a
precondition for reconciliation?

Christ Condemns the Religious Leaders

Some Aboriginal People say that if Christ walked this earth today and
saw the oppression of the Aboriginal People, he would criticize the
religious leaders and churches, just as he condemned the scribes and
Pharisees of his time for being hypocrites.

Woe to you, scribes and Pharisees, hypocrites! . . . You snakes, you brood of
vipers! How can you escape being sentence to hell? (Matt. 23:29, 33)

As history shows us, the church certainly has been a central part of the
dehumanizing oppression in which Aboriginal People find themselves
today. Through the racist practices of segregation, missionization and
then assimilation, the church wreaked havoc upon the Aboriginal People
over the past two centuries. We find that European and Euro-Australian
theological scholars have not made this connection between liberation
and reconciliation in their theological thought processes.

Unfortunately this essential connection between liberation and reconciliation is virtually absent in the history of Christian thought. Theologians emphasized the objectivity of reconciliation, but they lost sight of the fact that reconciliation is grounded in history. This tendency is undoubtedly due partly to the influence of Greek thought and the Church's political status after Constantine. The former led to rationalism and the latter produced a "gospel" that was politically meaningless for the oppressed. Reconciliation was defined on timeless "rational" grounds and was thus separated from God's liberating deeds in history. The political status of the post-Constantinian church, involving both alliance and competition with the state, led to definitions of the atonement that favoured the powerful and excluded the interests of poor. (Cone 1975:230–31; cf. Adler 1974:66)

It is in the incontrovertible *facts* of history, then, that Aboriginal People see the failures of the church to reconcile white and black. The church said one thing: "love"; yet it practised another: socio-political ambition, through destructive collusion with the government, which led to racist hostility. The church's two centuries of failures betrayed its hypocrisy, and its insincere pursuit of "reconciliation."

In a society dominated by white people, what does Paul mean when he says that Christ is "our peace, who has made us . . . one, and has broken down the dividing wall of hostility," reconciling us to God "in one body through the cross, thereby bringing the hostility to an end" (Eph. 2:14–15 RSV)? Are we to conclude that the hostility between blacks and whites has been brought to an end?" (Cone 1975:227)

This certainly has not been the reality in Australia for the Aboriginal People and the invading Euro-Australians, because the latter's practices show clearly that this hostility have not come to an end. Even today Aboriginal People and Euro-Australians are not reconciled, and the racist white Australians are still oppressing and denying the Indigenous People of this land their right to a full humanity. And, still, we see the racism of the white politicians who, being elected to serve the interests of the broader Australian society, continue to rationalize their subjugation and dehumanization of the Aboriginal People. Is the silence of the white churches, with all their liberalism, to be taken as silent support of this racial oppression as their defence of the status quo? How can the white church preach of the unity in Christ Jesus, when Aboriginal People's reality shows us a different experience of disunity? How can they possibly expected us to take them seriously?

These are the questions that must inform a black theological analysis of reconciliation, and they cannot be answered by spiritualizing Christ's emphasis on love, as if his love is indifferent to social and political justice. We black theologians must refuse to accept a view of reconciliation that pretends that slavery never existed, that we were not lynched and shot, and that we are not *presently* being cut to the core of our physical and mental endurance. (Cone 1975:227)

This is also the case for Aboriginal People—because of our historical experiences and epistemological differences, we also are unable to accept reconciliation being defined and structured by white Australians, based on their values. This alone excludes the participation of the Aboriginal People. If there is to be complete liberation, then the epistemological differences have to be the starting point of determining any and all stages and structures of this process. For Aboriginal People to not have input to the beginning of this dialogue means there can never be a beginning to reconciliation at all. If whites are not prepared to challenge the bases of their own racism and feelings of supremacy, then change will never come, and neither will liberation or reconciliation.

Australia's Original Sin

If the Australian churches are going to deal justly with the Aboriginal People, then they must begin with their original sin. If they are to have any credibility or integrity amongst the Aboriginal People and in the international Christian community, then what must happen?

We have sadly to recognize that in spite of the battle that has been fought against racism by churches, mission agencies and Council of Churches (. . .) racism is now a worse menace than ever. We have also sadly to confess that churches have participated in racial discrimination. Many religious institutions of the white northern world have benefited from racially exploitative economic systems. Lacking information about institutionalized racism and about the possibility of developing sophisticated strategies to secure racial justice, Christians often engage in irrelevant and timid efforts to improve race relations—too little and too late. (Adler 1974:3)

As reflected in this work, the history of the churches and their practice of missionization are far from honourable. Aboriginal People have to ask if the churches are serious about their commitment to the Aboriginal People. If the Australian churches are deeply committed to their relationship with God, extending to how they express their faith and worship, then

... combating racism is a matter not only of Christian social and political responsibility but also of the integrity of faith in Jesus Christ. Racism is a blatant denial of the Christian faith. (Adler 1974:4)

Yet, the churches say that they have more important issues on which to focus than their relationship with Aboriginal People. We Aboriginal People have to ask how they could have a relationship with God when their relationship with the Aboriginal People (in this case identified by Christ Jesus as "the least") is so shattered. The fall, or what we could call "Original Sin," for white Australia begins with their invasion, which continues right up to the present day. Euro-Australian Christians have never felt it necessary to address their Sins, in the light of their on-going relationship with God.

... racism is seen as a heresy, as an offence against God and the calling of the Church to witness to Christ who died for all men [sic]. (Adler 1974:9)

They never considered that their relationship with God is in question, because they believed that God was on "their side" and commissioned them to go out and steal other Peoples' land and to commit genocide, as they were the righteous ones (cf. Reynolds 1989:5–9). How do Australians have a full relationship with God when they have never identified their Original Sin, let alone repented of these Sins? How can they consider— let alone think—that their relationship with God is on solid ground? Have they not been blinded by their greed and lust for power and domination and foolish pride—to be so oblivious to the fact that their Original Sin has prevented them from entering into a full and obedient relationship with God?

The Original Sin is the source of the Aboriginal oppression, and it seems that no matter how committed the Council for Aboriginal Reconciliation or the churches are to solving the oppression and poverty of Aboriginal People, their hard work and endeavours seem to be seen as a waste of time because they continue to focus on the symptoms of injustice and never on the sources of injustice. The root of the injustice and oppression is white Australians' failure to come to terms with their Original Sin.

The problem confronting contemporary Australians is their denial of the status and privilege they have inherited from their forebears, and their failure to identify that the Sins of their forebears have now passed on to their children. The most popular statements made over and over again by white Australians are, "I cannot be held responsible for what my forefathers did to the Aboriginal People"; or, "We white Australians cannot be made to feel guilty for what our forefathers have done to the Aboriginal People." Australia's failure to repent and convert is the continuation of their sinning.

Nobody who was at Uppsala will ever forget James Baldwin, speaking "as one of God's creatures whom the Christian Church had most betrayed" and saying to his Christian audience:

"I wonder if there is left in Christian civilization the moral energy, the spiritual daring, to atone, to repent, to be born again." (Adler 1974:7)

Bibliography

The bibliography entries are listed in the following priority order: type (archival material, bibliographies, books, chapters, articles, addresses, audio-visual material, oral testimony, etc.), author (first alphabetically, then chronologically), and title (if no author is listed).

Archival Material

Anglican Church of Australia. Minutes of Australian Board of Mission, Aboriginal Advisory Committee Meetings, 1989–92.

Anglican Church of Australia. Minutes of National Aboriginal Anglican Council Meetings, 1992– .

Australian Board of Mission. Archives. Mitchell Library, Sydney.

Australian Council for the World Council of Churches. Archives, 1946–60.

Australian Council for the World Council of Churches. Minutes of Meetings, 1946–60.

Australian Council of Churches. Aboriginal & Islander Commission. Archives, 1989–94.

Australian Council of Churches. Aboriginal & Islander Commission. Minutes of National Meetings, 1989–94.

Australian Council of Churches. Archives, 1960–94.

Australian Council of Churches. Minutes of General Meetings, 1960–94.

Australian Council of Churches. Minutes of Executive Meetings, 1989–94.

National Council of Churches in Australia. Aboriginal & Islander Commission. Minutes of National Meetings, 1994– .

National Council of Churches in Australia. Minutes of Executive Meetings, 1994– .

National Council of Churches in Australia. Minutes of National Forums, 1994– .

National Missionary Council of Australia. Minutes of Meetings, 1926–65.

Taplin, George. *The Journal of George Taplin*. Mortlock Library, Adelaide, PR6 186/1/3, Janaury 1860.

Threlkeld, Lancelot. *The Journal of Lancelot Threlkeld*. Mitchell Library, Sydney.

Threlkeld/MLS [Threlkeld, Lancelot]. Papers, held in Mitchell Library, Sydney, MS A382.

Uniting Aboriginal and Islander Christian Congress. Minutes of National Meetings, 1985– .

Uniting Aboriginal and Islander Christian Congress. Minutes of New South Wales State Regional Council Meetings, 1985– .

Uniting Church in Australia. Minutes of National Assemblies, 1977– .

Uniting Church in Australia. Synod of N.S.W. Minutes of Meetings, 1977– .

Uniting Church in Australia. Synod of N.S.W., Board of Mission. Minutes of Meetings, 1990– .

Bibliographies/Catalogues—Specific

Aboriginal Land Rights NSW: A Preliminary Bibliography. Occasional Paper No. 3. Sydney: Ministry of Aboriginal Affairs (New South Wales), n.d.

Aboriginal Resources: Helping Each Other to Understand Aboriginal People and Their Issues. Melbourne: Division of Social Justice, Victorian Synod, Uniting Church in Australia, 1987, 20 pp.

Allen, L. M., Altman, J. C., and Owen, E. (with assistance from Arthur, W. S.). *Aborigines in the Economy: A Select Annotated Bibliography of Policy-Relevant Research 1985–90.* Research Monograph No. 1. Canberra: Centre for Aboriginal Economic Policy Research, Australian National University, 1991, xxii + 242 pp.

Australian Institute of Aboriginal Studies Bibliography. Canberra: Australian Institute of Aboriginal Studies, 1961– .

Barlow, Alex. *Aboriginal Studies Resource List* Canberra: Australian Institute of Aboriginal Studies, 1983.

Blackbooks Catalogue 1992. Glebe [Sydney], N.S.W., Australia: Tranby Aboriginal Cooperative College, 1992.

A Catalogue of Books. Sydney: Ministry of Aboriginal Affairs (New South Wales), n.d.

Centre for Black Books: Catalogue 1984. Glebe [Sydney], N.S.W., Australia: Tranby Aboriginal Cooperative College, [1984].

Coppell, William G[eorge]. *World Catalogue of Theses and Dissertations about the Australian Aborigines and Torres Strait Islanders.* Sydney: Sydney University Press, 1977, 113 pp.

Coppell, W[illiam] G[eorge]. *Austronesian and Other Languages of the Pacific and Southeast Asia: An Annotated Catalogue of Theses and Dissertations.* Pacific Linguistics, Series C, Books, No. 64. Canberra, Australia: Department of Linguistics, Research School of Pacific Studies, The Australian National University, 1981, 15 pp.

Coppell, William G., and Mitchell, Ian S. *Education and Aboriginal Australians 1945–1975: A Bibliography.* Sydney: Centre for Advancement of Teaching, Macquarie University, 1977.

Coppell, William G., ed. *Audio-Visual Resource Materials Relating to the Aboriginal Australians.* Canberra: Curriculum Development Centre, 1978.

Craig, Beryl F., comp. *Arnhem Land Peninsula Region (Including Bathurst and Melville Islands.* Occasional Papers in Aboriginal Studies, No. 8. Canberra: Australian Institute of Aboriginal Studies, 1966, 205 pp.

Craig, Beryl F., comp. *Central Australian and Western Desert Regions: An Annotated Bibliography.* Australian Aboriginal Studies, No. 31. Canberra: Australian Institute of Aboriginal Studies, 1969, 351 pp.

Craig, Beryl F., comp. *North-West-Central Queensland: An Annotated Bibliography.* Australian Aboriginal Studies No. 41, Bibliography Series, No. 6. Canberra: Australian Institute of Aboriginal Studies, 1970, 137 pp.

Ethnic Studies Bibliography. Vol. 1– . Pittsburgh, PA.: University of Pittsburgh, University Center for International Studies, 1977– ; annual.

Greenway, John. *Bibliography of the Australian Aborigines and the Native Peoples of Torres Strait to 1959.* [Sydney]: Angus and Robertson, [1963], 420 pp.

Hill, Marji, and Barlow, Alex, eds. *Black Australia: An Annotated Bibliography and Teacher's Guide to Resources on Aborigines and Torres Strait Islanders.* Canberra: Australian Institute of Aboriginal Studies, 1978, 1984; Volume I, up to 1977, 200 pp.; Volume II, 1977–82, 96 pp.

Kehr, Helen, comp. and ed. *Prejudice: Racist—Religious—Nationalist.* Weiner Library, Catalogue Series, No. 5. London: Valentine, Mitchell for the Institute of Contemporary History, 1971.

Kimber, R. G. *Aboriginal Studies—Literature and Other Resources: A Bibliography.* Darwin, N.T., Australia: Media Services, Northern Territory Division, Department of Education, 1977.

Massola, Aldo. *Bibliography of the Victorian Aborigines from the Earliest Manuscripts to 31 December, 1970.* Melbourne: Hawthorn Press, 1971, 95 pp.

Mayne, Tom, comp. and ed. *Aborigines and The Issues: Information and Resource Catalogue.* Sydney: Australian Council of Churches, 1986, 276 pp.

Mills, Carol M., comp. *Chronologies Relating to Northern Territory History.* Historical Bibliography Monograph No. 1. Sydney: Australia 1788–1988: A Bicentennial History, 1981, 19 pp.

Odubho, Constance E. *Black-White Racial Attitudes: An Annotated Bibliography.* Westport, CT: Greenwood Press, 1976.

Pilling, Arnold R. *Aborigine Culture History: A Survey of Publications, 1954–1957.* Wayne State University Studies, No. 11. Detroit, MI.: Wayne State University Press, 1962, 217 pp.

Reed, L[es], and Parr, eds. *The Keeping Place: An Annotated Bibliography and Guide to the Study of the Aborigines and Aboriginal Culture in Northeast New South Wales and Southeast Queensland.* Lismore, N.S.W.: North Coast Institute for Aboriginal Community Education, [1988], 157 pp.

Sage Race Relations Abstracts. Vol. 1– . London: Sage Publications for the Institute of Race Relations, 1976– ; quarterly.

Swain, Tony. *Aboriginal Religions in Australia: A Bibliographic Survey.* Bibliographies and Indexes in Religious Studies. Westport, CN.: Greenwood Press, 1991, 325 pp.

Thomson, Neil and Merrifield, Patricia. *Aboriginal Health: An Annotated Bibliography.* Canberra: Australian Institute of Aboriginal Studies and Australian Institute of Health, 1989.

Bibliographies/Catalogues—General

Ahrens, Theodor. "Die theologische Szene in Oceanien." *Verkündigung und Forschung* 37 2 (1992):67–91.

Annual Catalogue of Australian Publications. Vols. 1–25. Canberra: Australian National Library, 1936–1960. [Continued by: *Australian National Bibliography.*]

Australasian Religion Index. Annual Cumulation Volume 1– . Wagga Wagga, N.S.W., Australia: Australian and New Zealand Theological Library Association and Centre for Information Studies, Charles Sturt University, 1989– .

Australian National Bibliography. Canberra: Australian National Library, 1960– . [Continues: *Annual Catalogue of Australian Publications.*]

"Australian Publications in Religion/s." *Australian Religious Studies Review* 2,1 (April 1989): 43–57.

"Australian Publications in Religion/s: Supplementary List." *Australian Religious Studies Review* 2,2 (August 1989): 71–72.

Bibliography of Urban Studies in Australia.

Coppell, W[illiam] G[eorge], and Stratigos, S. *A Bibliography of Pacific Island Theses and Dissertations.* [Canberra, Australia]: Research School of Pacific Studies, Australian

National University in conjunction with the Institute for Polynesian Studies, Brigham Young University-Hawaii Campus, Honolulu, Hawaii: University of Hawaii Press, c1983, 520 pp.

Howard, Irwin, Vinacke, W. Edgar, [and] Maretzki, Thomas, comps. *Culture & Personality in the Pacific Islands: A Bibliography.* Honolulu: [Published for] Anthropological Society of Hawaii [by] University of Hawaii Library, 1963, 110 pp.

Robert, Willem Carel Hendrik. *Contributions to a Bibliography of Australia and the South Sea Islands. Supplement.* Vols. 1–4. Amsterdam: Philo Press, 1968–75.

Books/Monographs—In an Aboriginal Language

Godku Dhäruk Nininygukunhara Nherranara: Yutana Gal'ngu ngunhi dhawu' [The New Testament in Gumatj]. Canberra: Bible Society in Australia, 1985, ix + 1,971 pp.; in Gumatj.

Marika-Mununggiritj, Raymattja. *Rirratjingu Matha.* Yirrkala: Yirrkala Literature Production Centre, 1990, 11 pp.

[The New Testament in Warlpiri]. Canberra: Bible Society in Australia, 1992; in Warlpiri.

Ngurrju Maninja Kurlangu: Nyurnu Yapa Kurlangu: Bush Medicine. Yuendemu, N.T.: Warlpiri Literature Production Centre, 1980, 25 pp.; in Warlpiri.

Pitjantjatjara Hymnbook and Catechism—with English Hymn Supplement. Ernabella, S.A.: Pitjantjatjara Church Council, 1978, pp.; in Pitjantjatjara.

Books/Monographs

Abernathy, Ralph. *And the Walls Came Tumbling Down: An Autobiography.* New York: Harper & Row, 1989, 638 pp.

Aboriginal Consultative Group. *Education for Aborigines: Report to the Schools Committee by the Aboriginal Consultative Group, June 1975.* [Canberra]: Aboriginal Consultative Group, 1975, 40 pp.

Aboriginal Film & Video Guide. [Canberra]: Awareness Through Film Group, 1988. 56 pp.

Aboriginal Heroes and Heroines of the Resistance. Surry Hills, N.S.W.: Action for World Development, 1988, 46 pp.; Second edition, 1993.

Aboriginal Provisional Government [APG]. *The APG Papers.* Vol. 1. Hobart, Tas.: Deep South Sovereign, 1992, 45 pp.; Vol. 2, 1992, [29] pp.

Aboriginal Provisional Government. *The Australian Constitution: An Aid to Justice or an Accomplice to Oppression.* APG Papers, Vol. 3. Hobart, Tas.: Deep South Sovereign, 1993, 26 pp.

Aboriginal Provisional Government. *Mabo: The Aboriginal Provisional Government Perspective.* APG Papers, Vol. 4. Hobart, Tas.: Deep South Sovereign, 1993, 42 pp.

Aborigines: A Statement of Concern. Surry Hills, N.S.W.: Catholic Commission for Justice and Peace for the Catholic Bishops of Australia, 1978, 22 pp.

Aborigines' Friends' Association. *A National Policy for the Australian Aborigines.* n.p.: Aborigines' Friends' Association, n.d.

Adler, Elisabeth. *A Small Beginning: An Assessment of the First five Years of the Programme to Combat Racism.* Geneva: World Council of Churches, 1974, 102 pp.

Adult Education Department, University of New England. *Proceedings of Conference on N.S.W. Aborigines, Armidale—May 1959.* Armidale: Adult Education Department, University of New England, 1959, 124 pp.

Allport, Gordon. *The Nature of Prejudice.* Reading, MA.: Addison-Wesley, 1954.

Altman, J[on] C., ed. *Aboriginal Employment Equity by the Year 2000.* Research Monograph, No. 2. Canberra: Centre for Aboriginal Economic Policy Research, Australian National University, 1991, 177 pp.

Altman, J[on] C., ed. *A National Survey of Indigenous Australians: Options and Implications.* Research Monograph, No. 3. Canberra: Centre for Aboriginal Economic Policy Research, Australian National University, 1992, 170 pp.

Amnesty International. *Amnesty International Report 1992.* New York: Amnesty International, 1992.

Amnesty International. *Australia: A Criminal Justice System Weighted Against Aboriginal People.* Sydney: Amnesty International, 1993, 31 pp.

Anderson, Ian. *Koorie Health in Koorie Hands: An Orientation Manual in Aboriginal Health for Health Care Providers.* Melbourne: Koorie Health Unit, Health Department Victoria, 1988, 149 pp.

Anglican Church of Australia. *Yearbook of the Diocese of Sydney 1991.* Sydney: Anglican Church of Australia, 1991.

Ansara, Martha. *Always Was, Always Will Be: The Sacred Grounds of the Waugal, Kings Park, Perth, W.A.* Balmain, N.S.W.: Jequerity Pty. Ltd., 1989, 121 pp.

Archbishop and Bishops of the Church of England in Australia and Tasmania. *A Pastoral Letter from the Archbishop and Bishops to the Church of England in the Commonwealth of Australia.* Canberra: Archbishop and Bishops of the Church of England in Australia and Tasmania, 1910, 9 pp.

Ariarajah, S. Wesley. *The Bible and People of Other Faiths.* Risk Book Series, 26. Geneva: World Council of Churches, 1985, 71 pp.

Armstrong, Robert E. M. *The Kalkadoons.* Brisbane: William Brooks, 1980.

Armstrong, Sally. *Sentenced To Silence: Have Prison Cells Become Death Chambers for Australia's Aborigines?* [Sydney]: Uniting Church in Australia, 1987, 33 pp.

Arthur, George. *Van Diemen's Land: Copies of All Correspondence Between Lieutenant-Governor Arthur and His Majesty's Secretary of State for the Colonies, on the Subject of the Military Operations Lately Carried on Against the Aboriginal Inhabitants of Van Diemen's Land.* Hobart: Tasmanian Historical Research Association, 1971.

Attwood, Bain. *The Making of the Aborigines.* Sydney: Allen & Unwin, 1989, 181 pp.

Australian Council for Overseas Aid. *Australian Aid: Make It Work for the Poor.* Canberra: Australian Council for Overseas Aid, 1991, 14 pp.

Australian Council for Overseas Aid. *Annual Report 1992.* Canberra: Australian Council for Overseas Aid, 1992, 24 pp.

Australian Council of Churches [ACC]. *Racism in Australia: Tasks for General and Christian Education—Report of Conference at Southport, Queensland, November 19–24, 1971.* Melbourne: Australian Council of Churches, Division of Christian Education, 1971.

ACC. *Justice for Aboriginal Australians . . . Continuing the Journey.* Sydney: Australian Council of Churches, 1982, 63 pp.

ACC. *Justice for Aboriginal Australians: Report of the World Council of Churches Team Visit to the Aborigines June 15 to July 3, 1981.* Sydney: Australian Council of Churches, 1981, 91 pp.

ACC. *Report of the ACC's Anti-Discrimination Task Group.* Sydney: Australian Council of Churches, 1993, 16 pp.

ACC and Catholic Commission for Justice and Peace. *Your Church and Land Rights.* Sydney: Australian Council of Churches and Catholic Commission for Justice and Peace, 1980.

Australian Mining Industry Council [AMIC]. "Mining—The Backbone of Australia." *Mining and Access to Aboriginal Land, An Issue of National Importance.* Canberra: The Australian Mining Industry Council, [1984].

Barndt, Joseph [R]. *Dismantling Racism: The Continuing Challenge to White America.* Minneapolis: Augsburg, 1991, 179 pp.

Barrett, John. *That Better Country: The Religious Aspect of Life in Eastern Australia, 1835–1850.* Melbourne: Melbourne University Press, 1966.

Barwick, Diane, and Reece, Robert, eds. *Aboriginal History.* Volume 1. Canberra: Australian National University Press, 1977. Vol. 2, 1978; Vol. 3, 1979.

Battung, Mary Rosario; Bautista, Liberato C.; Lizares-Bodegon, Ma. Sophia; and, Guillermo, Alice G., eds. *Religion and Society: Towards a Theology of Struggle.* Book 1. Manila: Forum for Interdisciplinary Endeavors and Studies, 1988, 267 pp.

Beckett, Jeremy R., ed. *Past and Present: The Construction of Aboriginality.* Canberra: Aboriginal Studies Press, 1988, 217 pp.

Bell, Derrick. *Faces at the Bottom of the Well: The Permanence of Racism.* New York: Basic Books, 1992, 222 pp.

Bell, Diane. *Daughters of the Dreaming.* Melbourne/Sydney: McPhee Gribble/George Allen & Unwin, 1983.

Benedict, Ruth. *Race and Racism.* London: Routledge & Kegan Paul, 1942, 175 pp.

Bennett, Scott. *Aborigines and Political Power.* Sydney: Allen & Unwin, 1989, 167 pp. + photographs.

Bentley, Peter, Blombery, 'Tricia, and Hughes, Philip J. *A Yearbook for Australian Christian Churches 1992.* Sydney: Christian Research Association, 1991, 221 pp.

Bentley, Peter, Blombery, 'Tricia, and Hughes, Philip J. *A Yearbook for Australian Christian Churches 1993.* Sydney: Christian Research Association, 1992, 221 pp.

Berndt, Ronald M. *An Adjustment Movement in Arnhem Land, Northern Territory of Australia.* Paris: Mouton, 1962.

Berndt, Ronald M., ed. *Aborigines and Change: Australia in the '70s.* Social Anthropology Series, No. 11. Canberra: Australian Institute of Aboriginal Studies; [Atlantic Highlands], N.J.: Humanities Press, 1977, 424 pp.

Berndt, Ronald M., and Berndt, Catherine H. *Arnhem Land: Its History and Its People.* Melbourne: F. W. Cheshire, 1953.

Berndt, Ronald M., and Berndt, Catherine H. *End of an Era: Aboriginal Labour in the Northern Territory.* Canberra: Australian Institute of Aboriginal Studies, 1987, 310 pp. + maps, tables, diagrams and photographs.

Berndt, Ronald M., and Berndt, Catherine H. *The Speaking Land: Myth and Story in Aboriginal Australia.* Ringwood, Vic.: Penguin Books, 1989, xxiv + 438 pp.

Berndt, Ronald M., and Berndt, Catherine H. *The World of the First Australians: Aboriginal Traditional Life: Past and Present.* Canberra: Aboriginal Studies Press, 1992, xxiv + 608 pp.

Best, Thomas F., ed. *Vancouver to Canberra 1983–1990: Report of the Central Committee of the World Council of Churches to the Seventh Assembly*. Geneva: World Council of Churches, 1990, 275 pp.

The Bible. New English Bible. [London]: Oxford University Press and Cambridge University Press, 1970.

The Bible. New Revised Standard Version. New York: Division of Christian Education, National Council of the Churches of Christ in the U.S.A., 1989.

The Bible. Revised Standard Version. New York: National Council of the Churches of Christ in the U.S.A., 1946, 1952.

Black, Alan, ed. *Religion in Australia: Sociological Perspectives*. Sydney: Allan & Unwin, 1991.

Black Deaths In Custody Resource Kit. Sydney: Action for World Development, 1987.

Black Theology and the Black Struggle: Conference Report, St Francis Xavier, Cape Town, 10th–14th September 1984. Braamfontein: Institute for Contextual Theology, 1984, 143 pp.

Blomfield, Geoffrey. *Baal Belbora: The End of the Dancing—The Agony of the British Invasion of the Ancient People of the Three Rivers: The Hastings, the Manning and the Macleay, in New South Wales*. Chippendale, N.S.W.: APCOL, 1981, 1986, 151 pp.

Boff, Clodovis. *Theology and Praxis: Epistemological Foundations*. Trans. (from the Portuguese) by Robert R. Barr. Maryknoll, N.Y.: Orbis Books, 1987.

Boff, Leonardo. *Faith on the Edge: Religion and Marginalized Existence*. Translated (from the Portuguese) by Robert R. Barr. San Francisco: Harper & Row, 1989.

Boff, Leonardo. *Nova Evangelização: Perspectiva dos Oprimidos*. Fortaleza: Editora Vozes, 1990; *New Evangelization: Good News to the Poor*. Translated (from the Portuguese) by Robert R. Barr. Maryknoll, N.Y.: Orbis Books, 1991, 128 pp.

Bollen, J. D. *Protestantism and Social Reform in New South Wales 1890–1910*. Melbourne: Melbourne University Press, 1972, 199 pp.

Bolton, Geoffrey. *Spoils and Spoilers: Australians Make Their Environment 1788–1980*. Sydney: George Allen & Unwin, 1981, 197 pp.; Second edition, 1992.

Brain, Robert. *Rites in Black and White*. Harmondsworth, U.K.: Penguin Books, 1979, x + 228 pp.

Brennan, Frank. *Too Much Order with Too Little Law*. St. Lucia, Queensland: University of Queensland Press, 1983, 303 pp.

Brennan, Frank. *Sharing the Country: The Case for an Agreement Between Black and White Australians*. Ringwood, Victoria: Penguin Books, 1991, 176 pp.

Brennan, Frank. *Land Rights Queensland Style: The Struggle for Aboriginal Self-Management*. Brisbane: University of Queensland Press, 1992a, 182 pp.

Brennan, Frank, ed. *Reconciling Our Differences: A Christian Approach to Recognising Aboriginal Land Rights*. Richmond/Brunswick, Vic.: Aurora Books/David Lovell Publishing, 1992b, 117 pp.

Brennan, Frank, Egan, John, and Honner, John. *Finding Common Ground: An Assessment of the Bases of Aboriginal Land Rights*. Blackburn, Victoria: Dove Communications, [1985], 79 pp.; with William Daniel, Revised edition, 1986, 122 pp.

Breward, Ian. *Australia: The Most Godless Place on Earth?* Melbourne: Beacon Hill, 1988.

Breward, Ian. *A History of the Australian Churches*. Sydney: Allen & Unwin, 1993, 305 pp.

British Museum. *Guide to the Specimens Illustrating the Races of Mankind (Anthropology) Exhibited in the Department of Zoology, British Museum (Natural History), Cromwell Road, London.* 4th edition. London: British Museum, 1921, 36 pp.

Brook, Jack, and Kohen, James L. *The Parramatta Native Institution and the Black Town: A History.* Modern History Series, 15. Sydney: New South Wales University Press, 1991, x + 295 pp.

Broome, Richard. *Aboriginal Australians: Black Responses to White Dominance 1788–1980.* The Australian Experience, 4. Sydney: George Allen & Unwin, 1982.

Brown, John P. *With Jesus at the Fringes: A Collection of Addresses and Studies on Mission Theology and Practice.* Seoul: Nulbot Press, 1993, 444 pp.

Budden, Chris. *Reconciliation, Celebration and Aboriginal People: Five Bible Studies on Issues Raised for the Australian Christian Community in 1988.* Sydney: Uniting Church in Australia, 1988.

Butlin, Noel George. *Our Original Aggression: Aboriginal Populations of Southeastern Australia, 1788–1850.* Sydney: Allen & Unwin, 1983.

Byrnes, Jill. *Aboriginal Economic Independence: A Report on Some Canadian Initiatives.* TRDC Publication, 167. Armidale, N.S.W.: Rural Development Centre (University of New England-Armidale), 1990, 74 pp.

Camron, Michael. *Who Killed the Koories?* Melbourne: William Heinemann Australia, 1990, 295 pp. [Republished as: *Black Land, White Land.* Melbourne: Minerva, 1993.]

Cannon, Katie G. *Black Womanist Ethics.* American Academy of Religion Academy Series, 60. Atlanta: Scholars Press, 1988, 183 pp.

Carne, Derek. *Land Rights: A Christian Perspective.* Chippendale, N.S.W.: Australian Council of Churches and Catholic Commission for Justice and Peace, 1980, 159 pp.

Central Land Council and Northern Land Council. *Our Land, Our Life: Aboriginal Land Rights in Australia's Northern Territory.* Alice Springs and Winnellie, N.T.: Central Land Council and Northern Land Council, 1991, 32 pp.

Chambers, Barbara, and Pettman, Jan. *Anti-Racism: A Handbook for Adult Educators.* Human Rights Commission Education Series, 1. Canberra: Australian Government Publishing Service, 1986, 101 pp.

Charlesworth, Max, Kimber, Richard, and Wallace, Noel. *Ancestor Spirits: Aspects of Australian Aboriginal Life and Spirituality.* Geelong, Vic.: Deakin University Press, 1990, iii + 92 pp.

Chikane, Frank. *No Life of My Own: An Autobiography.* Braamfontein, S.A.: Skotaville Publishers, 1988; London: Catholic Institute for International Relations, 1988; Maryknoll, N.Y.: Orbis Books, 1989, 132 pp.

Christie, M. F. *Aborigines in Colonial Victoria 1835–86.* Sydney: Sydney University Press, 1979, 224 pp.

Christie Palmerston: Explorer of the Rainforest. Second edition. Eacham, Qld.: Eacham Historical Society, 1985, 52 pp.

A Church Leaders' Statement for 1990. Auckland: Conference of Churches in Aotearoa New Zealand, 1990.

A Church Leaders' Statement for 1990: A Backgrounder—150 Years After the Signing of the Treaty of Waitangi. Auckland: Conference of Churches in Aotearoa New Zealand, 1990.

Clark, Manning. *A History of Australia.* Melbourne: Melbourne University Press, 1962.

Cleage, Albert B. *Black Christian Nationalism: New Directions for the Black Church*. Detroit, MI.: Luxor Publishers, [1972] 1987, 312 pp.

Cleage, Albert B., Jr. *The Black Messiah*. Trenton: Africa World Press, 1989, 278 pp.

Clouten, K. H. *Reid's Mistake*. Sydney: Macquarie Shire Council, 1967.

Cole, Keith. *Perriman in Arnhem Land: A Biography of Harry Leslie Perriman, Pioneer Missionary Among Aborigines at Roper River, Groote Eylandt and Oenpelli in Arnhem Land*. Great Australian Missionaries No. 5. Melbourne: Church Missionary Historical Publications, 1973.

Cole, Keith. *Nungalinya College*. Darwin, N.T.: Nungalinya Publications, 1978.

Cole, Keith. *The Aborigines of Arnhem Land*. Adelaide, S.A.: Rigby Publishers Ltd., 1979.

Cole, Keith. *Arnhem Land: Places and People*. Adelaide, S.A.: Rigby Publishers Ltd., 1980.

Comblin, José. *The Church and the National Security State*. Maryknoll, N.Y.: Orbis Books, 1979.

Commission for Racial Justice, United Church of Christ. *Toxic Waste and Race in the United States: A National Report on the Racial and Socio-Economic Characteristics of Communities with Hazardous Waste Sites*. New York: Public Data Access, 1987, 69 pp.

Commission for Racial Justice, United Church of Christ. *Program Guide: The First National People of Color Environmental Leadership Summit, The Washington Court on Capitol Hill, Washington, D.C., October 24–27, 1991*. Washington, D.C.: Commission for Racial Justice, United Church of Christ, 1991, 93 pp.

Commission on Theological Concerns of the Christian Conference of Asia. *Minjung Theology: People as the Subjects of History*. London/Maryknoll, N.Y./Singapore: Zed Press/Orbis Books/Christian Conference of Asia, 1981, 200 pp.

Cone, James H. *The Spirituals and the Blues: An Interpretation*. New York: Seabury Press, 1972, 152 pp.

Cone, James H. *God of the Oppressed*. New York: Seabury Press, 1975, 280 pp.

Cone, James H. *A Black Theology of Liberation*. 20th Anniversary Edition. Maryknoll, N.Y.: Orbis Books, [1986] 1990, 214 pp.

Cone, James H. *Speaking the Truth: Ecumenism, Liberation, and Black Theology*. Grand Rapids, MI.: William B. Eerdmans Publishing Co., 1986, 167 pp.

Cone, James H. *Black Theology & Black Power*. New York: Seabury, 1969; San Francisco: Harper & Row, 1989, 165 pp.

Cone, James H. *Martin & Malcolm & America: A Dream or a Nightmare*. Maryknoll, N.Y.: Orbis Books, 1991, 358 pp.

Cone, James H., and Wilmore, Gayraud S., ed. *Black Theology: A Documentary History*. Volume 1: 1966–1979. Maryknoll, N.Y.: Orbis Books, 1993a, 462 pp.

Cone, James H., and Wilmore, Gayraud S., ed. *Black Theology: A Documentary History*. Volume 2: 1980–1992. Maryknoll, N.Y.: Orbis Books, 1993b, 450 pp.

Coombs, H[erbert] C[ole]; H[elen] McCann; H[elen] Ross; and N[ancy] M. Williams, eds. *Land of Promises*. Canberra: Centre for Resource and Environmental Studies, Australian National University and Aboriginal Studies Press, Australian Institute of Aboriginal Studies, 1989, 165 pp.

Copher, Charles B. *Black Biblical Studies: Biblical and Theological Issues on the Black Presence in the Bible: An Anthology of Charles B. Copher*. Chicago: Black Light Fellowship, 1993, 150 pp.

Corbett, Helen. *Position Paper on the Situation of Aboriginal Deaths in Australian Custody, Presented to the United Nations Working Group on Indigenous People and to Our*

Indigenous Sisters and Brothers Throughout the World, August, 1989. [Sydney]: Committee to Defend Black Rights, 1989, [24] pp.

Critchett, Jan. *Our Land Till We Die: A History of the Framlingham Aborigines.* Australia Felix Series No. 1. Warrnambool, Vic.: Warrnambool Institute Press, 1980, pp.

Croatto, J. Severino. *Biblical Hermeneutics: Toward a Theory of Reading as the Production of Meaning.* Translated (from the Spanish) by Robert R. Barr. Maryknoll, N.Y.: Orbis Books, 1987, 94 pp.

Cruz, Virgil, and Cooley, Jean. *Breaking Down the Walls: Responding to the Racism that Divides Us.* Louisville, KY.: Presbyterian Church (U.S.A.), 1991, [13] pp.

CSW/ACC/NSW [Commission on the Status of Women, Australian Council of Churches, New South Wales State Council]. *Report of the Enquiry into the Status of Women in the Church.* Sydney: CSW/ACC/NSW, 1974.

Cummings, Barbara. *Take This Child . . . From Kahlin Compound to the Retta Dixon Children's Home.* Canberra: Aboriginal Studies Press, 1990, 139 pp.

Cunneen, Chris. *A Study of Aboriginal Juveniles and Police Violence.* Report Commissioned by the National Inquiry into Racist Violence. Sydney: Human Rights and Equal Opportunity Commission, 1990.

Cunneen, Chris, and Robb, Tom. *Criminal Justice in North-West New South Wales.* Sydney: N.S.W. Bureau of Crime Statistics and Research, 1987, 274 pp.

Darwin, Charles. *On the Origin of the Species by Means of Natural Selection, or the Preservation of Favoured Races in the Struggle for Life.* London: [John Murray, 1872] Penguin, 1982.

Daylight, Phyllis, and Johnstone, Mary. *Women's Business: Report of the Aboriginal Women's Task Force.* Canberra: Australian Government Publishing Service, 1986.

de las Casas, Bartolomé. *Brevísima relación de la destrucción de las Indias.* Buenos Aires: EUDEBA, 1966.

Debt Crisis and People's Struggle. Hong Kong/Singapore: DAGA, 1987, 110 pp.

Deloria, Vine, Jr. *Custer Died for Your Sins.* New York: Macmillan, 1969; Norman: University of Oklahoma Press, 1988, 278 pp.

The Demands of Justice: Compensation, Land Rights and Self-Determination for Victorian Aborigines. [Melbourne]: Working Group on Aboriginal Matters, Anglican Province of Victoria and Aboriginal Affairs Committee, Synod of Victoria, Uniting Church in Australia, 1984, 98 pp.

Des Pres, T[errence]. *The Survivors: An Anatomy of Life in the Death Camps.* New York: Oxford University Press, 1976.

Desmond, Adrian, and Moore, James. *Darwin.* London: Penguin Books, 1992, 808 pp.

Dewar, Mickey. *The 'Black War' in Arnhem Land: Missionaries and the Yolngu 1908–1940.* Darwin: Australian National University, North Australia Research Unit, 1992, 107 pp.

Dewdney, Andrew, and Michels, Debby. *More Than Black and White: Racism and Everyday Life.* Sydney: Inner City Education Centre, 1988, 94 pp.

Dickinson, Richard D. N. *To Set At Liberty the Oppressed: Towards an Understanding of Christian Responsibilities for Development/Liberation.* Geneva: World Council of Churches, Commission on the Churches' Participation in Development, 1975, 193 pp.

Dickinson, Richard D. N. *Poor, Yet Making Many Rich.* Geneva: World Council of Churches, Commission on the Churches' Participation in Development, 1983, 219 pp.

Dingle, T. *Aboriginal Economy: Patterns of Experience*. Melbourne: McPhee Gribble/Penguin, 1988.

Downe, Tobias, and Rollason, Russell. *Every Right: Australia and Global Human Rights*. Canberra: Australian Council for Overseas Aid, 1988, 20 pp.

Downing, Jim. *The Great Northern Territory Myths*. Alice Springs: Cross-Culture Group, 1973, 12 pp.

Drysdale, Ingrid, and Durack, Mary. *The End of Dreaming*. Sydney: Rigby, 1978.

Duguid, Charles. *No Dying Race*. Sydney: Rigby, 1963.

Duguid, Charles. *Doctor Goes Walkabout*. Sydney: Rigby, 1972.

Dunbar Orti, Roxanne. "Indigenous People Battle for their Rights." *Third World Network Features* (10 October 1992): 1–6.

Durkheim, Emile. *The Elementary Forms of the Religious Life*. Translated (from the French) by Joseph Ward Swain. New York: Free Press, [1915] 1965, 507 pp.

Durkheim, Emile, and Mauss, Marcel. *Primitive Classification*. Trans. (from the French) by Rodney Needham. London: Cohen & West, 1963, 96 pp.

Dussel, Enrique. *A History of the Church in Latin America: Colonialism to Liberation*. Translated (from the Spanish) and revised by Alan Neely. Grand Rapids, MI.: William B. Eerdmans Publishing Co., 1981, 360 pp.

Dutney, Andrew. *Manifesto for Renewal: The Shaping of a New Church*. Melbourne: Uniting Church Press, 1986.

Dutney, Andrew, ed. *From Here to Where: Australian Christians Owning the Past — Embracing the Future*. Melbourne: Uniting Church Press, 1988, 156 pp.

Dutney, Andrew. *Food, Sex and Death: A Personal Account of Christianity*. Melbourne: Uniting Church Press, 1993, 176 pp.

Dwyer, Peter. *How Lucky are We? Australia in the 1970s*. Melbourne: Pitman Publishing for the Australian Council of Churches, 1977, 69 pp.

Edwards, Coral, and Read, Peter, eds. *The Lost Children*. Sydney: Doubleday, 1989, 198 pp.

Edwards, W. H. *An Introduction to Aboriginal Societies*. Wentworth Falls, N.S.W.: Social Science Press, 1988, 121 pp.

Elder, Bruce. *Blood on the Wattle: Massacres and Maltreatment of Australian Aborigines since 1788*. Brookvale, N.S.W.: National, 1988, 208 pp.

Elder, J. R. *The Letters and Journals of Samuel Marsden 1765–1838*. Dunedin: Otago University Council, 1932.

Eliade, Mircea. *Aboriginal Religions: An Introduction*. Ithaca, N.Y., and London: Cornell University Press, 1973.

Elkin, A[dolphus]. P. *Studies in Australian Totemism*. Oceania Monographs, 2. Sydney: Australian National Research Council, 1933, 147 pp.

Elkin, A[dolphus] P. *The Australian Aborigines*. Rev. Ed. Sydney: Angus & Robertson, [1938] 1974, 397 pp.

Elkins, Stanley M. *Slavery: A Problem in American Institutional and Intellectual Life*. Chicago: University of Chicago Press, 1959.

Engel, Frank G. *The Land Rights of Australian Aborigines*. Sydney: Australian Council of Churches, 1965, 15 pp.

Engel, Frank G. *Turning Land Into Hope*. Sydney: Australian Council of Churches, 1968, 23 pp.

Engel, Frank G. *The Position of The Australian Aborigines: Two Centuries of Injustice and Some Recent Steps Towards Justice.* Sydney: Australian Council of Churches, 1978, [31] pp.

Engel, Frank [G.], and Skuse, Jean. *Some Main Actions in Support of the Aboriginal Cause taken by the National Missionary Council of Australia, 1926–1965, and by the Australian Council of Churches, 1965–1989.* [Sydney: Australian Council of Churches, 1989], 10 pp.

Enroth, Ronald M. *Churches That Abuse.* Grand Rapids, MI.: Zondervan Publishing House, 1992, 231 pp.

Evans, Raymond, Saunders, Kay, and Cronin, Katheryn. *Exclusion, Exploitation and Extermination: Race Relations in Colonial Queensland.* Sydney: Australia and New Zealand Book Company, 1975, 446 pp.

Evans, Robert A., and Evans, Alice F. *Human Rights: A Dialogue Between the First and Third World.* Maryknoll, N.Y.: Orbis Books, 1983.

Fanon, Frantz. *Black Skin, White Masks.* Translated by Charles Lam Markmann. London: Paladin, [1968] 1970, 174 pp.

Felder, Cain Hope. *Troubling Biblical Waters: Race, Class, and Family.* The Bishop Henry McNeal Turner Studies in North American Black Religion, Vol. 3. Maryknoll, N.Y.: Orbis Books, 1989, 233 pp.

Felder, Cain Hope, ed. *Stony the Road We Trod: African American Biblical Interpretation.* Minneapolis: Fortress Press, 1991, 260 pp.

Fey, Harold C., ed. *The Ecumenical Advance: A History of the Ecumenical Movement, Volume 2, 1948–1968.* Third edition. Geneva: World Council of Churches, 1993, xix + 571 pp.

Final Submission on behalf of Aboriginal Groups and Individuals [to the Royal Commission into British Nuclear Tests in Australia] [FS], 16 September 1985.

Fiorenza, Elizabeth Schüssler. *In Memory of Her: A Feminist Theological Reconstruction of Christian Origins.* New York: Crossroad, 1983.

Fiorenza, Elizabeth Schüssler. *Bread Not Stone: The Challenge of Feminist Biblical Interpretation.* Boston: Beacon Press, 1984, 182 pp.

Flynn, James R. *Race, IQ and Jensen.* London: Routledge and Kegan Paul, 1980, 313 pp.

Forbes, Jack D. *Africans and Native Americans: The Language of Race and the Evolution of Red-Black Peoples.* Second Edition. Urbana: University of Illinois Press, 1993, 344 pp.

Foundation for Aboriginal and Islander Research Action (FAIRA). *The Mabo Case: An Easy Guide.* [Brisbane]: FAIRA, 1992.

Franklin, Margaret Ann. *Black and White Australians: An Inter-racial History 1788–1975.* Melbourne: Heinemann Educational Australia, 1976, 248 pp.

The Future of Aboriginal Missions. Sydney: Division of Mission of the Australian Council of Churches, 1967, 11 pp.

Galbraith, Douglas, ed. *Worship in the Wide Red Land.* Melbourne: Uniting Church Press, 1985, 108 pp.

Gale, Fay, ed. *Woman's Role in Aboriginal Society.* Third edition. Canberra: Australian Institute of Aboriginal Studies, 1978, 84 pp.

Gale, Fay, and Brockman, Alison. *Race Relations in Australia: The Aborigines.* Sydney: McGraw Hill, 1975.

Gerard, A. E. *History of UAM.* Melbourne: United Aborigines Mission, n.d.

Gifford, Paul. *The Religious Right in Southern Africa.* Harare: Baobab Books and University of Zimbabwe Publications, 1988, 118 pp.

Gifford, Paul, ed. *New DImensions in African Christianity.* Africa Challenge Series, 3. Nairobi: All Africa Conference of Churches, 1992, 215 pp.

Gilbert, Kevin. *Living Black: Blacks Talk to Kevin Gilbert.* London: Penguin Books, 1971, 1978; Melbourne: Penguin Books, 1977; 305 pp.

Gilbert, Kevin. *Because a White Man'll Never Do It.* Sydney: Angus & Robertson, [1973] 1993.

Gilbert, Kevin. *People Are Legends.* Brisbane: University of Queensland Press, 1979, 70 pp.

Gilbert, Kevin. *Aboriginal Sovereignty, Justice, The Law and Land.* Canberra: Treaty '88!, 1988a, 69 pp.

Gilbert, Kevin. *The Cherry Pickers.* Canberra: Burrambinga, 1988b, 80 pp.

Gilbert, Kevin, ed. *Inside Black Australia: An Anthology of Aboriginal Poetry.* Ringwood, Vic.: Penguin Books, 1988c, 213 pp.

Gilbert, Kevin. *The Blackside: People Are Legends and Other Poems.* Melbourne: Hyland House Publishing, 1990, 118 pp.

Gilbert, Kevin. *Black From the Edge.* South Melbourne: Hyland House, 1994, 97 pp.

Gill, David, ed. *Gathered for Life: Official Report, VI Assembly, World Council of Churches, Vancouver, Canada, 24 July–10 August 1983.* Geneva/Grand Rapids, MI.: World Council of Churches/William B. Eerdmans Publishing Co., 1983, 355 pp.

Goba, Bonganjalo. *An Agenda for Black Theology: Hermeneutics for Social Change.* Johannesburg: Skotaville Publishers, 1988, 126 pp.

Gómez, Medardo Ernesto. *Fire Against Fire: Christian Ministry Face-to-Face with Persecution.* Translated (from the Spanish) by Mary M. Solberg. Minneapolis: Augsburg Press, 1989, 94 pp.

Gondarra, Djiniyini. *Let My People Go—Series of Theological Reflections of Aboriginal Theology: Four Reflections Based on Church Renewal, Christian Theology of the Land, Contextualization and Unity.* [Darwin, N.T.]: Bethel Presbytery, Northern Synod, Uniting Church in Australia, 1986, 35 pp.

Gondarra, Djiniyini. *Father, You Gave Us The Dreaming.* Darwin, N.T.: Bethel Presbytery, Northern Synod, Uniting Church in Australia, 1988, [9 pp.].

Goodfellow, E. *Five Cottages.* Melbourne: United Aborigines Mission, n.d.

Gottwald, Norman K. *The Tribes of Yahweh: A Sociology of the Religion of Liberated Israel 1250–1050 B.C.E.* London: SCM Press, 1980, 916 pp.

Gould, Stephen Jay. *The Mismeasure of Man.* New York: Norton, 1981; Harmmondsworth, U.K.: Penguin Books, 1984, 352 pp.

Grainger, Alan. *The Threatening Desert: Controlling Desertification.* London: Earthscan Publications, 1990, 369 pp.

Grant, Jacquelyn. *White Women's Christ and Black Women's Jesus: Feminist Christology and Womanist Response.* American Academy of Religion Academy Series, 64. Atlanta: Scholars Press, 1989, 264 pp.

Grant, James P. *The State of the World's Children 1992.* Oxford: Oxford University Press, 1992.

Grey, George. *Journals of Two Expeditions of Discovery in North-West and Western Australia, During the Years 1837, 38, and 39, Under the Authority of Her Majesty's Government.* 2 Vols. London: T. and W. Boone, 1841, 412 and 482 pp.

Gribble, Ernest Richard Bulmer. *Forty Years with the Aborigines.* Sydney: Angus & Robertson, 1930, 228 pp.

Gribble, J. R. *Dark Deeds in a Sunny Land* or *Blacks and Whites in North West Australia*. London: Morgan & Scott, 1886.

Gsell, François-Xavier. *The Bishop with 150 Wives: Fifty Years as a Missionary*. London: Angus and Robertson, 1955, 175 pp.

Gumbert, M. *Neither Justice Nor Reason: A Legal and Anthropological Analysis of Aboriginal Land Rights*. Brisbane: University of Queensland Press, 1984.

Gunsen, N., ed. *Australian Reminiscences and Papers of L. E. Threlkeld—Missionary to the Aborigines, 1824–1859*. 2 Vols. Canberra: Australian Institute of Aboriginal Studies, 1974.

Guthrie, Shirley C., Jr. *Christian Doctrine: Teachings of the Christian Church*. Atlanta: John Knox Press, 1968, 420 pp.

Gutiérrez, Gustavo. *A Theology of Liberation: History, Politics and Salvation*. Translated (from the Spanish) by Caridad Inda and John Eagleson. Maryknoll, N.Y.: Orbis Books, 1973.

Gutiérrez, Gustavo. *El Dios de la vida*. Rimac/Lima: Instituto Bartolomé de las Casas/Centro de Estudios y Publicaciones, 1982, 1989; *The God of Life*. Translated (from the Spanish) by Matthew J. O'Connell. Maryknoll, N.Y.: Orbis Books, 1991, 214 pp.

Habel, Norman C., ed. *Religion and Multiculturalism in Australia: Essays in Honour of Victor C. Hayes*. Special Studies in Religions Series, 7. Adelaide: Australian Association for the Study of Religion, 1992.

Hall, Robert A. *The Black Diggers: Aborigines and Torres Strait Islanders in the Second World War*. Sydney: Allen & Unwin, 1989, 228 pp.

Hanks, Peter, and Keon-Cohen, Bryan, eds. *Aborigines & the Law*. Sydney: George Allen & Unwin, 1984, 366 pp.

Harding, Vincent. *There is a River: The Black Struggle for Freedom in America*. New York: Vintage Books, 1981, 416 pp.

Harris, John. *One Blood—200 Years of Aboriginal Encounter with Christianity: A Story of Hope*. Sutherland, N.S.W.: Albatros Books, 1990, 956 pp.

Hart, Max. *Kulila: On Aboriginal Education*. Sydney: Australia and New Zealand Book Company, 1974, 134 pp.

Hart, Max. *A Story of Fire: Aboriginal Christianity*. Blackwood, S.A.: New Creation Publications, 1988, 253 pp.

Hasluck, Paul M. C. *Black Australians: A Survey of Native Policy in Western Australia 1829–1897*. Melbourne: Melbourne University Press, 1942, 229 pp.

Hasluck, Paul M. C. *Native Welfare in Australia: Speeches and Addresses by the Hon. Paul Hasluck, M.P., Minister for Territories*. Perth: Patterson Broken Sha, 1953, 59 pp.

Hasluck, Paul M. C. *Shades of Darkness: Aboriginal Affairs 1925–1965*. Melbourne: Melbourne University Press, 1988, 154 pp.

Hayes, John H., and Holladay, Carl R. *Biblical Exegesis: A Beginner's Handbook*. London: SCM Press, 1983, 132 pp.

Hayes, Victor C., ed. *Toward Theology in an Australian Context*. Adelaide: Australian Association for the Study of Religions, 1979.

Heppell, M., and Wigley, J[ulian] J. *Black Out in Alice: A History of the Establishment and Development of Town Camps in Alice Springs*. Development Studies Centre, No. 26. Canberra; Miami, FL.: Australian National University, 1981, 216 pp.

Hines, Donald M. *Ghost Voices: Yakima Indian Myths, Legends, Humor, and Hunting Stories*. Issaquah, WA.: Great Eagle Publishing, 1992, 435 pp.

The History of Christianity. Oxford: Lion Publishing, 1977; Revised ed., 1990.

Hocking, Barbara. *International Law and Aboriginal Human Rights.* Sydney: The Law Book Co., 1988, 195 pp.

Hodgson, Janet, and Kothare, Jay. *Vision Quest: Native Spirituality and the Canadian Church in Canada.* Toronto: Anglican Book Centre, 1990, 213 pp.

Holmer, N. M., and Holmer, V. E. *Stories from Two Native Tribes of Eastern Australia.* Uppsala: A.-B. Lundequistska, 1969.

Hooks, Bell. *Feminist Theology: From Margin to Center.* Boston: South End Press, 1984.

Hoornaert, Eduardo. *The Memory of the Christian People.* Theology and Liberation Series, No. 3. Translated (from the Portuguese) by Robert R. Barr. Maryknoll, N.Y.: Orbis Books, 1988, 304 pp.

Houston, Jim, ed. *The Cultured Pearl: Australian Readings in Cross-Cultural Theology and Mission.* Melbourne: Joint Board of Christian Education, 1988, 294 pp.

Howe, Morgan B. *Aborigines and Christians: An Introduction to Some of the Issues Involved.* Brisbane: Foundation for Aboriginal and Islander Research Action, 1977, 56 pp.

Howitt, A. W. *The Native Tribes of South-east Australia.* London: Macmillan, 1904, 819 pp.

Human Rights Watch: Annual Report 1987. [Washington, D.C.:] Human Rights Watch, 1987, 90 pp.

Identity and Belonging in Aboriginal Foster Care: A Study of Aboriginal Children in Long Term Foster Care, Their Foster Families and Natural Families. n.p.: S[outh] A[ustralia] Aboriginal Child Care Agency Forum, 1988, 49 pp.

Immigration Reform Group. *Immigration: Control or Colour Bar? The Background to 'White Australia' and a Proposal for Change,* ed. by Kenneth Rivett. Australian edition. Melbourne: Melbourne University Press, [1960] 1962, 171 pp.

Jackomos, Alick, and Fowell, Derek. *Living Aboriginal History of Victoria: Stories in the Oral Tradition.* Cambridge: Cambridge University Press, 1991, 203 pp.

Johnson, Phillip E. *Darwin on Trial.* 2nd ed. Downers Grove, IL.: InterVarsity Press, 1993, 220 pp.

Johnstone, Richard, and Richardson, Peter. *Australia's South African Connection: A Case for Economic Sanctions Against Apartheid?* Development Dossier No. 17. Canberra: Australian Council for Overseas Aid, 1986, pp.

Jones, F. Lancaster. *The Structure and Growth of Australia's Aboriginal Population.* Aborigines in Australian Society, 1. Canberra: Australian National University Press, 1970.

A Just & Proper Settlement. Blackburn, Victoria: Collins Dove, 1987, 55 pp. [Prepared by the Australian Council of Churches' Commission for Church and Society, the Catholic Commission for Justice and Peace, and the Uniting Church in Australia Social Responsibility and Justice Committee]

Justice, Peace and the Integrity of Creation Resource Materials. Geneva: World Council of Churches, 1988– .

The Kalkadoons of North-west Queensland. Brisbane: Archaeology Branch, Department of Community Services, n.d., 10 pp. [Based on ("Date obtained from"): Roth, W. E. *North West Central Queensland Aborigines.* Brisbane: Government Printer, 1897.]

Karamaga, André, comp. *Problems and Promises of Africa: Towards and Beyond the Year 2000.* Second edition. Nairobi: All Africa Conference of Churches, 1993, 90 pp.

Katz, J. *White Awareness.* Norman, OK.: University of Oklahoma, 1982.

Katz, William Loren. *Black Indians: A Hidden Heritage.* New York: Atheneum, 1986, 198 pp.

Keen, Ian, ed. *Being Black: Aboriginal Cultures in 'Settled' Australia.* Canberra: Aboriginal Studies Press, 1988, 273 pp.

Kelsey, George D. *Racism and the Christian Understanding of Man.* New York: Charles Scribner's Sons, 1965, 178 pp.

Keneally, Thomas. *The Chant of Jimmy Blacksmith.* Sydney: Angus & Robertson, 1972.

King, Martin Luther, Jr. *Where Do We Go From Here: Chaos or Community?* Boston: Beacon Books, 1967, 209 pp.

King, Martin Luther, Jr. *The Essential Writings and Speeches of Martin Luther King, Jr.,* ed. by James M. Washington. New York: HarperCollins, 1986, 702 pp.

Kinnamon, Michael, ed. *Signs of the Spirit: Official Report, Seventh Assembly, Canberra, Australia, 7–20 February 1991.* Geneva/Grand Rapids, MI.: World Council of Churches/William B. Eerdmans 1991, 396 pp.

Kinsler, F. Ross, ed., *Ministry By the People: Theological Education by Extension.* Geneva/Maryknoll, N.Y.: World Council of Churches/Orbis Books, 1983, 332 pp.

Kirk, R. L., and Thorne, A. G., eds. *The Origins of the Australians.* Human Biology Series, 6. Canberra: Australian Institute of Aboriginal Studies, 1976, 449 pp.

Kolig, Erich. *The Silent Revolution: The Effects of Modernization on Australian Aboriginal Religion.* Philadelphia, PA.: Institute for the Study of Human Issues, 1981, 192 pp.

Kovel, Joel. *White Racism: A Psychohistory.* New York: Columbia University Press, 1984, 301 pp.

Labumore (Elsie Roughsey). *An Aboriginal Mother Tells of the Old and the New.* Melbourne: McPhee Gribble/Penguin Books, 1984, 245 pp.

Lamilami, Lazarus. *Lamilami Speaks.* Sydney: Ure Smith, 1974.

Land Is Our Life: Global Consultation [on] Land Rights, Darwin, Australia. Geneva: Programme to Combat Racism, World Council of Churches, 1989, 25 pp.

Land Rights for Indigenous People. Geneva: Programme to Combat Racism, World Council of Churches, 1983, 91 pp.

Langford, Ruby. *Don't Take Your Love to Town.* Melbourne: Penguin Books, 1988.

Larnach, S. L. *Australian Aboriginal Craniology.* Oceania Monographs, 21. 2 Vols. Sydney: Oceania Publications, 1978, 345 pp.

Libby, Ronald T. *Hawke's Law: The Politics of Mining and Aboriginal Land Rights in Australia.* Nedlands, W.A.: University of Western Australia Press, 1989, 175 pp.

Lincoln, C. Eric. *Race, Religion and the Continuing American Dilemma.* New York: Hill and Wang, 1986.

Lindsay, Ian, with Miles, Howard. *Bringing Christ to Aboriginal Australia.* Lawson, N.S.W.: Mission Publications of Australia, 1989, 20 pp.

Lippmann, Lorna. *The Aim is Understanding: Educational Techniques for a Multicultural Society.* Second edition. Sydney: ANZ Book Co., 1977, viii + 59 pp.

Lippmann, Lorna. *Generations of Resistance: The Aboriginal Struggle for Justice.* Melbourne: Longman Cheshire, 1981, 243 pp.; Second Edition, 1991, 185 pp.

Long, Charles H. *Significations: Signs, Symbols, and Images in the Interpretation of Religion.* Philadelphia: Fortress Press, 1989, 207 pp.

Long, R. *Providential Channels.* Sydney: Aborigines Inland Mission, 1935.

Loos, Noel. *Invasion and Resistance: Aboriginal-European Relations on the North Queensland Frontier 1861–1897.* Canberra: Australian National University Press, 1982, xix + 325 pp.

Luzbetak, Louis J. *The Church and Cultures: New Perspectives in Missiological Anthropology.* American Society of Missiology Series, No. 12. Maryknoll, N.Y.: Orbis Books, 1988, 464 pp.

Lyon, P., and Parsons, M. *We Are Staying: The Alyawarra Struggle for Land at Lake Nash.* Alice Springs: Institute for Aboriginal Development Press, 1988.

MacFarlane, Alan. *Reconstructing Historical Communities.* London: Cambridge University Press, 1977, 222 pp.

Maglaya, Felipe E. *Organizing for People Power: A Manual for Organizers.* Hong Kong: Asian Committee for People's Organization, 1987, 68 pp.

Maimela, Simon S. *Proclaim Freedom to My People: Essays on Religion and Politics.* Johannesburg: Skotaville Publishers, 1987, 152 pp.

Maimela, Simon S. *Modern Trends in Theology.* Johannesburg: Skotaville Publishers, 1990, 208 pp.

Maimela, Simon S., and Hopkins, Dwight N., eds. *We Are One Voice.* Johannesburg: Skotaville Publishers, 1989, 166 pp.

Malcolm, Arthur. *Love Speaks Out: Meditations and Studies for Lent and for Other Times.* Sydney: Anglican Information Office, 1989, 71 pp.

Maris, Hyllus, and Borg, Sonia. *Women of the Sun.* Sydney: Currency Press, 1983, xiii + 234 pp.

Markus, Andrew. *Governing Savages: the Commonwealth and Aborigines, 1911–1939.* Sydney: Allen & Unwin, 1990, 214 pp.

Mason, H. G. B. *Darkest Western Australia: A Treatise Bearing on the Habits and Customs of the Aborigines and the Solution of the Native Question."* Kalgoorlie, W.A.: Hocking & Co., 1909; Facsimile edition, Victoria Park, W.A.: Hesperian Press, 1980, 68 pp.

Matheson, Alan. *Racism Australia 1989—More or Less?* No. D.60/90. Melbourne: Australian Council of Trade Unions, 1990, 68 pp.

Matheson, Alan. *What If We are Winning!: An Overview of Racism and Antisemitism in 1992.* No. D.8/1993. Melbourne: Australian Council of Trade Unions, 1993.

Mattingley, Christobel, and Hampton, Ken, eds. *Survival in Our Own Land: "Aboriginal" Experiences in "South Australia" Since 1836.* Sydney: Aboriginal Literature Development Assistance Association and Hodder & Stoughton, 1988.

Maushart, Susan. *Sort of a Place Like Home: Remembering the Moore River Native Settlement.* South Freemantle: Freemantle Arts Centre Press, 1993, 351 pp.

Mayne, Tom. *A Submission to the Western Australia Government Aboriginal Land Inquiry (The Seaman Inquiry).* Sydney: Australian Council of Churches, 1983.

McCall, T. Bruce. *Blood & Race: A Study of the Colour Problem.* Sydney: Anglican Truth Society, 1957, 469 pp.

McConnochie, Keith, Hollinsworth, David, and Pettman, Jan. *Race and Racism in Australia.* Wentworth Falls, N.S.W.: Social Science Press, 1989, 259 pp.

McKenzie, Maisie. *Mission to Arnhem Land.* Adelaide: Rigby Limited, 1976, 260 pp.

McLeod, D[onald] W[illiam]. *How the West Was Lost: The Native Question in the Development of Western Australia.* Port Hedland, W.A.: n.p., 1984, 156 pp.

McMichael, Philip. *Settlers and the Agrarian Question: Capitalism in Colonial Australia.* Cambridge: Cambridge University Press, 1984, 304 pp.

Mickler, Steve. *Gambling on the First Race: A Comment on Racism and Talk-Back Radio—6PR, the TAB, and the WA Government.* [Perth], W.A.: Louis St John Johnson Memorial Trust Fund, 1992, 69 pp.

Míguez Bonino, José. *Toward a Christian Political Ethics.* Philadelphia: Fortress Press, 1983, 126 pp.

Mining and Access to Aboriginal Land, An Issue of National Importance. Canberra: Australian Mining Industry Council, [1984].

Mol, Hans. *The Firm and the Formless: Religion and Identity in Aboriginal Australia.* Waterloo, Ont., Canada: Wilfred Laurier University Press, 1982, 103 pp.

Montagu, Ashley. *Statement on Race: An Annotated Elaboration and Exposition of the Four Statements on Race Issued by the United Nations Educational, Scientific, and Cultural Organization.* 3rd edition. London: Oxford Univeristy Press, 1972, 278 pp.

Moody, Roger. *Plunder!* London/Christchurch: PARTiZANS/CAFCA, 1991, 196 pp.

Morgan, Margaret. *Mt Margaret: A Drop in a Bucket.* Melbourne: By the Author, 1986, vi + 304 pp.

Mosala, Itumeleng J. *Biblical Hermeneutics and Black Theology in South Africa.* Grand Rapids, MI.: William B. Eerdmands Publishing Co., 1989, 218 pp.

Mowaljarlai, David, with Malnic, Jutta. *Yorro Yorro: Spirit of the Kimberley-Everything Standing Up Alive.* Broome, W.A.: Magabala Books, 1993, xxii + 216 pp.

Nabokov, Peter, ed. *Native American Testimony: A Chronicle of Indian-White Relations from Prophecy to the Present, 1492–1992.* New York: Penguin, 1978, 1991, 474 pp.

National Aborigines Conference. *Land Rights: Aboriginal Land Rights and the Need for a National Policy.* Canberra: National Aborigines Conference, n.d.

National Aboriginal Health Strategy Working Party [NAHSWP]. *A National Aboriginal Health Strategy.* [Sydney?]: National Aboriginal Health Strategy Working Party, 1989, 320 pp.

National Education Association. *Education and Racism: An Action Manual.* Washington, D.C.: National Education Association, 1973.

National Missionary Conference. *The Aborigines: Report Prepared for Presentation to the Conference.* Sydney: National Missionary Conference, 1937.

National Missionary Council of Australia. *General Policy on Aborigines.* Sydney: National Missionary Council of Australia, 1959, 8 pp.

National Seminar on Aboriginal Antiquities in Australia, Canberra, Australia, 1972. *he Preservation of Australia's Aboriginal Heritage: Report of National Seminar on Aboriginal Antiquities in Australia, May 1972.* Ed. by Robert Edwards. Prehistory and Material Culture Series, No. 11. Australian Aboriginal Studies, No. 54. Canberra [Australia]: Australian Institute of Aboriginal Studies, 1975, 237 pp.

The National Trachoma & Eye Health Program of the Royal Australian College of Opthalmologists. Sydney: Royal Australian College of Opthalmologists, 1980, 236 pp.

Naulty, Barbara, comp. *Murawina—Multi-Purpose Aboriginal Education Centre: Information Booklet.* Redfern, [Sydney,] N.S.W.: Murawina Limited, 1989, [18] pp.

Neate, Graeme. *Aboriginal Land Rights Law in the Northern Territory.* 2 Vols. Chippendale, N.S.W.: Alternative Publishing Cooperative Ltd. (APCOL), 1989.

Nettheim, Garth. *Victims of the Law: Black Queenslanders Today.* Sydney: George Allen & Unwin/International Commission of Jurists-Australian Section, 1981, 199 pp.

Neville, John W. *The Root of All Evil: Essays on Economics, Ethics and Capitalism.* Sydney: Australian Council of Churches, 1979, 74 pp.

The New Oxford Annotated Bible with the Apocrypha, ed. by Bruce M. Metzger and Roland E. Murphy. New Revised Standard Version. New York: Oxford University Press, 1989.

Newbigin, Leslie. *The Gospel in a Pluralist World.* Grand Rapids, MI.: William B. Eerdmans Publishing Co., 1989, 244 pp.

Niebuhr, Reinhold. *Moral Man and Immoral Society: A Study in Ethics and Politics.* New York: Charles Scribner's Sons, 1932.

Niebuhr, Reinhold. *The Essential Reinhold Niebuhr.* Edited by Robert McAfee Brown. New Haven, CT.: Yale University Press, 1986, 299 pp.

Niles, Preman, comp. *Between the Flood and the Rainbow: Interpreting the Conciliar Process of Mutual Commitment (Covenant) to Justice, Peace and the Integrity of Creation.* Geneva: World Council of Churches, 1992, 192 pp.

Nolan, Albert. *God in South Africa: The Challenge of the Gospel.* Capetown: David Philip, 1988, 241 pp.

Nungalinya College, Darwin, Handbook 1990. Darwin, N.T.: Nungalinya College, 1990, 95 pp.

Oldfield, Audrey. *Woman Suffrage in Australia: A Gift or a Struggle?* Cambridge: Cambridge University Press, 1992, 263 pp.

Oldham, J. H. *Christianity and the Race Problem.* London: S.C.M. Press, 1924.

Oldham, J. H., ed. *The Churches Survey Their Task: The Report of the Conference at Oxford, July 1937, on Church, Community, and State.* Church, Community, and State Series, 8. London: George Allen & Unwin, 1937, 314 pp.

Olsen, John. "Speech on the Second Reading of the Maralinga Tjarutja Land Rights Act." *Liberal Party Policy on Maralinga Lands.* n.p.: n.p., [1983].

Ormerod, Neil. *Introducing Contemporary Theologies: The What and the Who of Theology Today.* Sydney: E. J. Dwyer, 1990, 180 pp.

O'Shane, Pat. *The Queensland Acts: Australia's Apartheid Laws?* Sydney: Australian Council of Churches, 1979, 37 pp.

Paine, Robert. *The White Arctic: Anthropological Essays on Tutelage and Ethnicity.* Newfoundland Social and Economic Papers, No. 7. Toronto, Canada: Institute of Social and Economic Research, Memorial University of Newfoundland, 1977.

Parbury, Nigel. *Survival: A History of Aboriginal Life in New South Wales.* Sydney: Ministry of Aboriginal Affairs (New South Wales), 1986, 160 pp.

Paris, Peter J. *Black Religious Leaders: Conflict in Unity.* Rev. ed. Louisville, KY.: Westminster/John Knox Press, 1991, 326 pp.

Pattel-Gray, Anne. *Through Aboriginal Eyes: The Cry from the Wilderness.* Geneva: World Council of Churches, 1991a, 159 pp.

Pattel-Gray, Anne, ed. *Cry for Justice: The Aboriginal and Islander Contribution to the World Council of Churches 7th Assembly.* Sydney: Aboriginal & Islander Commission of the Australian Council of Churches, 1991b, 21 pp.

Pattel-Gray, Anne, ed. *Towards an Active Partnership.* Sydney: Aboriginal & Islander Commission of the Australian Council of Churches, 1992, 58 pp.

Pattel-Gray, Anne, ed. *Aboriginal Spirituality: Past, Present, Future.* Melbourne: HarperCollins*Religious*, 1996, 127pp.

Pattel-Gray, Anne, ed. *Martung Upah: Black and White Australians Seeking Partnership.* Melbourne: HarperCollins*Religious*, 1996, 340 pp.

Peck, M. Scott. *The Road Less Travelled.* London: Arrow Books, [1978] 1990, 342 pp.

Peck, M. Scott. *People of the Lie: The Hope for Healing Human Evil.* New York: Simon & Schuster, 1983, 269 pp.

Perkins, John. *A Call to Wholistic Ministry.* St. Louis, MO.: Open Door Press, 1980, 59 pp.

Perkins, John. *Let Justice Roll Down: John Perkins Tells His Own Story.* Ventura, CA.: Regal Books, 1976, 223 pp.

Perkins, John. *With Justice for All.* Ventura, CA.: Regal Books, 1982, 211 pp.

Peterson, Nicolas, ed. *Land Rights Handbook.* Canberra: Australian Institute of Aboriginal Studies, 1981, 300 pp.

Peterson, Nicolas, and Langton, Marcia, eds. *Aborigines, Land, and Land Rights.* AIAS New Series, No. 42. Canberra: Australian Institute of Aboriginal Studies; Atlantic Highlands, N.J.: Humanities Press, 1983, 468 pp.

Pettman, Jan. *Living in the Margins: Racism, Sexism and Feminism in Australia.* Sydney: Allen & Unwin, 1992, x + 187 pp.

Pickford, Pauline. *The Hopevale Mission Flogging.* Brisbane: Unitarian Church, 1962.

Pilger, John. *A Secret Country.* London: Vintage, 1989, 1992, xv + 409 pp.

Pittock, A. Barrie. *Aboriginal Land Rights.* IWGIA Document No. 3. Copenhagen, [Denmark]: International Working Group Indigenous Affairs, 1972, 23 pp.

Pittock, A. Barrie. *Australian Aborigines: The Common Struggle for Humanity.* IWGIA Document No. 39. Copenhagen, [Denmark]: International Working Group Indigenous Affairs, 1979.

Poignant, Axel. *Piccaninny Walkabout: A Story of Two Aboriginal Children.* Sydney: Angus and Robertson, 1957, 49 pp.

Pontificial Commission "Iustitia et Pax." *The Church and Racism: Towards a More Fraternal Society* Vatican City: Pontificial Commission "Iustitia et Pax," 1988, [45] pp.

Porter, Muriel. *Land of the Spirit? The Australian Religious Experience.* Geneva/Melbourne: World Council of Churches/Joint Board of Christian Education, 1990, 112 pp.

Porteus, Stanley David. *The Psychology of a Primitive People: A Study of the Australian Aborigine.* New York: Longmans, Green & Co.; London: E. Arnold & Co., [1931], 438 pp.

Prentis, Malcolm D. *A Study in Black and White: The Aborigines in Australian History.* Second edition. Wentworth Falls, N.S.W.: Social Sciences Press, 1988, 119 pp.

Price, Grenfell. *White Settlers and Native Peoples: An Historical Study of Racial Contacts Between English Speaking White and Aboriginal Peoples in U.S.A., Canada and New Zealand.* n.p.: Georgian House, 1949.

Prison-The Last Resort: A Christian Response to Australian Prisons. Melbourne: Collins Dove, 1991, 47 pp.

Pybus, Cassandra. *Community of Theives.* Melbourne: Minerva Australia, 1992, 198 pp. + photographs and maps.

Racism Australia 1989—More or Less? n.p.: ACTU, 1989.

Rae-Ellis, Vivienne. *Black Robinson: Protector of Aborigines.* Melbourne: Melbourne University Press, 1988, 295 pp.

Recognition: The Way Forward. Melbourne: Collins Dove, 1993, 42 pp.

Reid, Gordon. *A Picnic with the Natives: Aboriginal-European Relations in the Northern Territory to 1910.* Melbourne: Melbourne University Press, 1990, xii + 220 pp.

Reynolds, Henry. *The Other Side of the Frontier: Aboriginal Resistance to the European Invasion of Australia.* Melbourne: Penguin Books, 1981, 255 pp.

Reynolds, Henry. *Frontier: Aborigines, Settlers, and Land.* Sydney: Allen & Unwin, 1987a, 234 pp.

Reynolds, Henry. *The Law of the Land.* Melbourne: Penguin Books, 1987b, 224 pp.

Reynolds, Henry. *Aboriginal Land Rights in Colonial Australia.* Canberra: National Library of Australia, 1988, 20 pp.

Reynolds, Henry, comp. *Dispossession: Black Australia and White Invaders.* Sydney: Allen & Unwin, 1989, 226 pp.

Reynolds, Henry. *With the White People.* Melbourne: Penguin Books, 1990, 288 pp.

Rintoul, Stuart. *The Wailing: A National Black Oral History.* Melbourne: William Heinemann Australia, 1993, 422 pp.

Roberts, J. *The Mapoon Story by the Mapoon People.* Volume 1. Fitzroy, Vic.: International Development Action, 1975.

Roberts, Jan[ine]. *Massacres to Mining: The Colonization of Aboriginal Australia.* London: War on Want, 1978, 212 pp.; Blackburn, Victoria: Dove Communications, 1981.

Roberts, J., Parsons, M., and Russell, B., eds. *The Mapoon Story According to the Invaders: Church Mission, Queensland Government and Mining Company.* Volume 2. Fitzroy, Vic.: International Development Action, 1975, 113 pp.

Rollason, Russell, ed. *Racism in Australia in the 1980's: Challenge to the Churches.* Sydney: Australian Council of Churches, 1981, 100 pp.

Rollason, Russell. *Human Rights and Development.* Canberra: Australian Council for Overseas Aid, 1987, 14 pp.

Rose, Deborah Bird. *Hidden Histories: Black Stories from Victoria River Downs, Humbert River and Wave Hill Stations.* Canberra: Aboriginal Studies Press, 1991, 268 pp.

Rose, Deborah Bird. *Dingo Makes Us Human: Life and Land in an Australian Aboriginal Culture.* Cambridge: Cambridge University Press, 1992, xii + 249 pp.

Rose, Willie Lee. *Rehearsal for Reconstruction: The Port Royal Experiment.* Indianapolis: Bobbs-Merrill Co., 1964, 442 pp.

Rose, Willie Lee. *Slavery and Freedom.* Ed. by William W. Freehling. Oxford: Oxford University Press, 1982, 254 pp.

Rosser, Bill. *This Is Palm Island.* Canberra: Australian Institute of Aboriginal Studies, 1978, 91 pp.

Rosser, Bill. *Up Rode the Troopers: The Black Police in Queensland.* St Lucia: University of Queensland Press, 1990, 211 pp.

Roth, Walter E. *Ethnological Studies among the North West Central Queensland Aborigines.* Brisbane: Government Printer, 1897, 247 pp.

Rouse, Ruth, and Neill, Stephen C., eds. *A History of the Ecumenical Movement, 1517–1948.* Fourth edition. Geneva: World Council of Churches, 1993, xxvii + 838 pp.

Rousseau, Jean-Jacques. *The Social Contract and Discourses.* Trans. by G. D. H. Cole. London: J. M. Dent; Rutland, VT.: Charles E. Tuttle Co., 1973, 362 pp.

Rowley, C[harles] D. *The Destruction of Aboriginal Society: Aboriginal Policy and Practice.* Canberra: Australian National University Press, 1970; London: Penguin, 1972a, 430 pp.

Rowley, C. D. *Outcasts in White Australia: Aboriginal Policy and Practice-Volume II.* Aborigines in Australian Society, 6. Canberra: Australian National University Press, 1971a; London: Penguin, 1972b, 472 pp.

Rowley, C. D. *The Remote Aborigines.* Canberra: Australian National University Press, 1971b; London: Penguin, 1972c, 379 pp.

Rowley, C. D. *A Matter of Justice.* Canberra: Australian National University Press, 1981.

Rowley, C. D. *Recovery: The Politics of Aboriginal Reform.* Melbourne: Penguin, 1986, 169 pp.

Russell, Archer. *Gone Nomad: Twenty Years' Vagabond Wanderings in Three Continents.* Sydney: Angus & Robertson, 1936, 230 pp.

Ryan, Lyndall. *The Aboriginal Tasmanians.* Brisbane: University of Queensland Press, 1982.

Salvado, Rosendo. *The Salvado Memoirs,* trans. by E. J. Stormon. Perth, W.A.: University of Western Australia Press, 1977; rev. ed., 1991.

Sawer, Marian, and Simms, Marian. *A Woman's Place: Women and Politics in Australia.* 2nd edition. Sydney: Allen & Unwin, 1993.

Segal, Ronald. *The Race War: The World-wide Conflict of Races.* Harmondsworth, U.K.: Penguin Books, [1966] 1967, 458 pp.

Self Sufficiency, Not Dependency. Sydney: N.S.W. Aboriginal Land Council, 1989. [Resource Kit.]

Setiloane, Gabriel M. *African Theology: An Introduction.* Johannesburg: Skotaville Publishers, 1986, 50 pp.

Sharp, Ian G., and Tatz, Colin M., eds. *Aborigines in the Economy.* Brisbane: Jacaranda Press, 1966, 382 pp.

Sheils, Helen. *Australian Aboriginal Studies: A Symposium of Papers Presented at the 1961 Research Conference.* Melbourne: Oxford University Press, 1963, 505 pp.

Shelley, Nancy, ed. *Whither Australia? A Response to Australia's Current Defence Policy.* Sydney: Australian Council of Churches, Commission on International Affairs, 1990, 122 pp.

Simpson, Colin. *Adam in Ochre: Inside Aboriginal Australia.* Sydney: Angus & Robertson, 1951, 222 pp.

Sindab, Jean. *Blacks, Indigenous People and the Churches: 1992—Ending the Pain, Beginning the Hope.* Continental Consultation on Racism in the America— Background Paper. Geneva: World Council of Churches, Programme to Combat Racism, 1990.

Singer, R., comp. *Immigration Debate in the Press.* [Richmond, Vic.]: CHOMI [Clearing House on Migration Issues], 1985.

Sipka, Jarka, comp., *The 1984 Immigration Debate: The Myths and the Facts.* Occasional Papers, No. 4. Sydney: Ethnic Affairs Commission of N.S.W., (August) 1984.

Skelton, Kathy, and Kerr, Gillian. *Combating Prejudice in Schools: An In-Service Guide for Schools and Teacher Training Institutions.* Canberra: Curriculum Development Centre, 1989, 182 pp.

Skuse, Jean, Tulip, Marie, and Moore, Basil. *Liberation Theology and Feminism.* Sydney: Australian Council of Churches (N.S.W.), 1975.

Smith, Shirley. *Mum Shirl: An Autobiography.* Melbourne: William Heinemann 1981.

Snowden, Frank M., Jr. *Blacks in Antiquity: Ethiopians in the Greco-Roman Experience.* Cambridge, MA.: Harvard University Press, 1970.

Snyder, Louis L. *The Idea of Racialism: Its Meaning and History.* New York: Van Nostrand Reinhold Co., 1962, 191 pp.

South Australian Campaign Against Racism and Racial Discrimination Committee, United Nations Association of Australia. *Racism 1971.* [Adelaide]: United Nations Association of Australia, 1971, 16 pp.

South Commission. *The Challenge to the South: The Report of the South Commission.* Oxford: Oxford University Press, 1990.

Spencer, Baldwin. *Guide to the Australian Ethnographical Collection in the National Museum of Victoria.* Melbourne: Public Library, Museums and National Gallery, 1901.

Spencer, Baldwin, and Gillen, F. J. *The Native Tribes of Central Australia.* London: Macmillan, 1899, 671 pp.

Spencer, Baldwin, and Gillen, F. J. *The Northern Tribes of Central Australia.* London: Macmillan, 1904.

Spencer, Herbert. *Descriptive Sociology: Or, Groups of Sociological Facts.* London: Williams & Norgate, 1874.

Stackhouse, Max. *Creeds, Society and Human Rights.* Grand Rapids, MI.: William B. Eerdmans Publishing Co., 1984, 315 pp.

Stampp, Kenneth M. *The Peculiar Institution: Slavery in the Ante-Bellum South.* New York: Knopf, 1956.

Stanner, W. E. H. *On Aboriginal Religion.* Oceania Monographs, 11. Sydney: Sydney University Press, 1959–61, 171 pp.

Stanner, W. E. H. *After the Dreaming: Black and White Australians—An Anthropologist's View.* The Boyer Lectures, 1968. Sydney: Australian Broadcasting Commission, [1969] 1993, 64 pp.

Stanner, W. E. H. *White Man Got No Dreaming: Essays 1938–1973.* Canberra: Australian National University Press, 1979, 376 pp.

Starr, Mark. *Lies and Hate in Education.* London: Hogarth Press, 1929, 197 pp.

Stephenson, Margaret A., and Ratnapala, Suri, eds. *Mabo: A Judicial Revolution-The Aboriginal Land Rights Decision and Its Impact on Australian Law.* Brisbane: University of Queensland Press, 1993, 225 pp.

Stevens, Frank [S]. *Equal Wages for Aborigines.* Melbourne: Federal Council for the Advancement of Aborigines, 1968, 71 pp.

Stevens, F[rank] S., ed. *Racism: The Australian Experience—A Study of Race Prejudice in Australia.* Sydney: Australia and New Zealand Book Company, 1971; Volume 1: Prejudice and Xenophobia, 193 pp.; Volume 2: Black and White; Volume 3: Colonialism.

Stevens, Frank [S]. *Aborigines in the Northern Territory Cattle Industry.* Canberra: Australian National University Press, 1974, 230 pp.

Stevens, Frank [S]. *A Survey of the Impact of Racism on Education and Information Systems in Australia.* Paris: UNESCO, 1976, 155 pp.

Stevens, Frank [S]. *The Politics of Prejudice.* Sydney: Alternative Publishing Co-Operative Limited, 1980, 220 pp.

Stevens, Frank [S]. *Black Australia.* Sydney: Alternative Publishing Co-Operative Limited, 1981, 248 pp.

Stewart, Alf. *The Years Between.* Atherton, Qld.: Atherton Shire Council, 1992.

Stone, Sharman N., comp. and ed. *Aborigines in White Australia: A Documentary History of the Attitudes Affecting Official Policy and the Australian Aborigine, 1697–1973.* Melbourne: Heinemann Educational Books, 1974, 253 pp.

Story, J. Lyle, and Story, Cullen I. K. *Greek to Me.* San Francisco: Harper & Row, 1979, 340 pp.

A Submission to the Western Australian Government Aboriginal Land Inquiry. Sydney: Australian Council of Churches, 1983, [36] pp.

Suh, David Kwang-sun. *The Korean Minjung in Christ.* Hong Kong: Christian Conference of Asia (Commission on Theological Concerns), 1991, 198 pp.

Summers, Anne. *Damned Whores and God's Police.* Melbourne: Penguin Books, 1994.

Suter, Keith D., and Stearman, Kaye. *Aboriginal Australians.* Report No. 35. London: Minority Rights Group, 1988, 22 pp.

Sutton, Peter. *Aboriginal Languages.* n.p.: Inma Press, n.d., 8 pp.

Swain, Tony. *Interpreting Aboriginal Religion: An Historical Account.* Adelaide: Australian Association for the Study of Religion, 1985a, 156 pp.

Swain, Tony. *On 'Understanding' Australian Aboriginal Religion.* Young Australian Scholar Lecture Series, No. 6. Adelaide: Charles Strong Trust, 1985b, 14 pp.

Swain, Tony. *A Place for Strangers: Towards a History of Australian Aboriginal Being.* Sydney: Cambridge University Press, 1993.

Swain, Tony, and Rose, Deborah Bird, eds. *Aboriginal Australians and Christian Missions: Ethnographic and Historical Studies.* Adelaide: Australian Association for the Study of Religion, 1988, 489 pp.

Tall Timber and Golden Grain: Atherton 1885–1985. Atherton, Qld.: Atherton Centenary Committee, 1985, 107 pp.

Tatz, Colin, ed. *Black Viewpoints: The Aboriginal Experience.* Sydney: A.N.Z. Book Company, 1975.

Tatz, Colin. *Race Politics in Australia.* Armidale: University of New England Publishing Unit, 1979, 118 pp.

Tench, Watkin. *Sydney's First Four Years: A Narrative of the Expedition to Botany Bay and a Complete Account of the Settlement at Port Jackson 1788–1791.* Sydney: Royal Australian Historical Society, [1790] 1979.

Thistlethwaite, Susan Brooks. *Sex, Race and God: Christian Feminism in Black and White.* London: Geoffrey Chapman, 1990.

Thomson, Donald F. *Economic Structure and the Ceremonial Exchange Cycle in Arnhem Land.* Melbourne: Macmillan, 1949.

Thomson, Donald F. *Donald Thomson in Arnhem Land,* comp. by N. Peterson. Melbourne: Currey O'Neill, 1983.

Thomson, Judy, ed. *Reaching Back: Queensland Aboriginal People Recall Early Days in Yarrabah Mission.* Canberra: Aboriginal Studies Press, 1989.

Thomson, Neil, and Briscoe, Norma. *Overview of Aboriginal Health Status in Western Australia.* Australian Institute of Health: Aboriginal and Torres Strait Islander Health Series, 1. Canberra: Australian Government Publishing Service, 1991. [No. 2, Northern Territory; No. 3, South Australia; No. 4, Queensland; and No. 5, New South Wales.]

Thonemann, H. E. *Tell the White Man: The Life Story of an Aboriginal Lubra.* London: Collins, 1949, 190 pp.

Thurman, Howard. *The Growing Edge.* Richmond, IN.: Friends United Press, 1956.

Thurman, Howard. *Deep River* and *The Negro Spiritual Speaks of Life and Death.* Richmond, IN.: Friends United Press, 1975, 95/56 pp.

Thurman, Howard. *Jesus and the Disinherited.* Richmond, IN.: Friends United Press, [1976] 1981, 112 pp.

Tindale, N. B. *Aboriginal Tribes of Australia: Their Terrain, Environmental Controls, Distribution, Limits and Proper Names.* Berkeley: University of California Press, 1974.

Tinker, George E. *Missionary Conquest: The Gospel and Native American Cultural Genocide.* Minneapolis: Fortress Press, 1993, 182 pp.

Toohey, Edwina. *Tumbling Waters: Tumoulin on the Evelyn Tableland in Days Gone By.* Tumoulin, Qld.: By the Author, 1991, 79 pp.

Townes, Emilie M., ed. *A Troubling in My Soul: Womanist Perspectives on Evil and Suffering.* Bishop Henry McNeal Turner Studies in North American Black Religion, 8. Maryknoll, N.Y.: Orbis Books, 1993, 257 pp.

Townsend, Kathleen. *Issues on Australia's Doorstep.* Perth, W.A.: One World Centre, 1989, 220 pp.

Toyne, Phillip, and Vachon, Daniel. *Growing Up the Country: The Pitjantjatjara Struggle for Their Land.* Harmondsworth, U.K.: Penguin/McPhee Gribble, 1984.

Trigger, David S. *Whitefella Comin': Aboriginal Responses to Colonialism in Northern Australia.* Cambridge: Cambridge University Press, 1992, 250 pp.

Trompf, Garry W. *Friedrich Max Mueller As a Theorist of Comparative Religion.* Bombay: Shakuntala Publishing House, 1978, 99 pp.

Trompf, Garry W., ed. *The Gospel is Not Western: Black Theologies from the Southwest Pacific.* Maryknoll, N.Y.: Orbis Books, 1987, 213 pp.

Trompf, Garry W. *In Search of Origins.* Studies in World Religions Series, 1, ed. by Kapil Tiwari and Garry W. Trompf. London: Oriental University Press, 1990a, 219 pp.

Trompf, Garry W., ed. *Cargo Cults and Millenarian Movements.* Religion and Society, 29. Berlin: De Gruyter, 1990b.

Trompf, Garry W. *Payback: The Logic of Retribution in Melanesian Religions.* Cambridge: Cambridge University Press, 1994, 535 pp.

Tucker, Margaret [Lilardia]. *If Everyone Cared: Autobiography of Margaret Tucker M.B.E.* London: Grosvenor Books; Sydney: Ure Smith, 1977, 205 pp.

Turnbull, Clive. *Black War-The Extermination of the Tasmanian Aborigines.* Melbourne: Sun Books [1948] 1974; F. W. Cheshire, 1956.

Turner, George W., ed. *The Australian Pocket Oxford Dictionary.* Second edition. Melbourne: Oxford University Press, 1984; p. 327, s.v. "heresy."

Turner, R. *The Eye of the Needle.* Braamfontein: Christian Institute, 1972.

Tyson, Sarah, comp. and ed. *A Family History and Genealogy of the Mimi Family from the Gayndah Area (Upper Burnett) as Told to Sarah Tyson.* n.p. (Qld.): n.p., 1990, 64 pp.

Uniapon, David. *Native Legends.* Adelaide: Hunkins, Ellis and King, n.d., 15 pp.

United Nations [UN]. *Human Rights: A Compilation of International Instruments.* New York: United Nations, 1988, 416 pp.

United Nations. *The Effects of Racism and Racial Discrimination on the Social and Economic Relations Between Indigenous People and States: Report of a Seminar, Geneva (Switzerland), 16–20 January 1989.* New York: Centre for Human Rights, United Nations, 1989.

United Nations. *Human Rights: Status of International Instruments-Chart of Ratifications as at 31 July 1992.* New York: United Nations, 1992, 11 pp. [Document: ST/HR/4/Rev.6]

United Nations, Working Group on Indigenous Populations. *Draft Declaration on Indigenous Rights.* Geneva: United Nations, 1988. [Document: E/CN.4/Sub.2/1988/2S]

United States, Congress, House, Committee on Interior and Insular Affairs. *Establishing the Aboriginal Hawaiian Claims Settlement Study Commission and for Other Purposes: Report to Accompany S.J. Res. 4.* [Washington, D.C.: United States Government Printing Office, 1978], 14 pp. [No. 95–2:H.rp.860; House report–95th Congress, 2d session, no. 95–860; Issued January 31, 1978.]

United States Commission on Civil Rights. *Indian Tribes: A Continuing Quest for Survival.* Washington, D.C.: United States Government Printing Office, 1981, 192 pp.

Uniting Church in Australia [UCA]. *Minutes of the Fifth Assembly, August, 1988.* Sydney: Uniting Church in Australia, 1988.

UCA. *Theological Reflections on Australian Society and the Mission Task of the Church.* Sydney: Uniting Church in Australia, 1989.

UCA. *Constitution and Regulations and the Basis of Union and Standing Orders and Rules of Debate: The Uniting Church in Australia.* Melbourne: Uniting Church Press, 1990.

UCA. *Minutes of the Sixth Assembly, July 14–20, 1991.* Sydney: Uniting Church in Australia, 1991.

UCA. *Reports to the Seventh Assembly, July, 1994.* Sydney: Uniting Church in Australia, 1994.

Urban Rural Mission. *Resistance as a Form of Christian Witness.* Geneva: World Council of Churches, 1985, 49 pp.

Urban Rural Mission. *We Discovered the Good News: Brazilian Workers Reread the Bible.* Geneva: World Council of Churches, 1988, 81 pp.

Urban Rural Mission. *People of God (The) Church: A URM Perspective.* Geneva: World Council of Churches, 1990, 108 pp.

Urban Rural Mission-Christian Conference of Asia [URM-CCA]. *Captives on the Land: Report of a Consultation on Land, Colombo, February 1976.* Tokyo: URM-CCA, 1977a, 69 pp.

URM-CCA. *Identity and Justice.* Tokyo: URM-CCA, 1977b, 64 pp.

URM-CCA. *Set Free To Struggle for Freedom.* Hong Kong: URM-CCA, 1985, 115 pp.

URM-CCA. *Stories of Faith from the Grassroots.* Hong Kong: URM-CCA, 1987, 26 pp.

URM-CCA. *Crossing Borders for Justice.* Hong Kong: URM-CCA, 1990, 115 pp.

URM-CCA. *Thinking Ahead.* URM Series 3. Hong Kong: URM-CCA, 1992, 69 pp.

van der Bent, Ans J., ed. *Breaking Down the Walls: World Council of Churches Statements and Actions on Racism, 1948–1985.* PCR Information: Special Report. Geneva: World Council of Churches, 1986.

Various. *Teología y liberación: escritura y espiritualidad—ensayos en torno a la obra de Gustavo Gutiérrez.* Vol. 1, CEP 109. Lima: Instituto Bartolomé de las Casas y Centro de Estudios y Publicaciones, 1990.

Vincent, John. *The Race Race.* London: SCM Press, 1970, 116 pp.

Wallis, Jim. *Agenda for Biblical People.* New edition. San Francisco: Harper & Row, 1984a, 109 pp.

Wallis, Jim. *The Call to Conversion.* San Francisco: Harper & Row, 1984b, 190 pp.

Wallis, Jim, ed. *The Rise of Christian Conscience: The Emergence of a Dramatic Renewal Movement in Today's Church.* San Francisco: Harper & Row, 1987, 290 pp.

Walter, George. *Australia: Land, People, Mission.* Translated (from the German) by Inge Danaher. Limburg: Lahn-Verlag, 1982. [Original—Limburg: Pallotine Society, 1928.]

Ward, Glenyse. *Wandering Girl.* Broome, W.A.: Magabala Books, 1987, 159 pp.

Weems, Renita J. *Just a Sister Away: A Womanist Vision of Women's Relationships in the Bible.* San Diego: LuraMedia, 1988, 147 pp.

Weller, Archie. *The Day of the Dog.* Sydney: Allen & Unwin, [1981] 1992.

Wellman, David T. *Portraits of White Racism*. 2nd ed. Cambridge: Cambridge University Press, [1977] 1993, 270 pp.

Welsing, Frances Cress. *The Isis (Yssis) Papers*. Chicago: Third World Press, 1991, 301 pp.

West, Cornel. *Race Matters*. Boston: Beacon Press, 1993.

West, Ida. *Pride Against Prejudice: Reminiscences of a Tasmanian Aborigine*. Canberra: Australian Institute of Aborginal Studies, 1984.

White, Erin, and Tulip, Marie. *Knowing Otherwise: Feminism, Women and Religion*. Melbourne: David Lovell Publishing, 1991.

White, Isobel; Barwick, Diane, and Mechan, Betty, eds. *Fighters and Singers: The Lives of Some Aboriginal Women*. Sydney: George Allen & Unwin, 1985, 226 pp.

The White Invasion Booklet. Torrensville, S.A.: White Invasion Diary Collective, 1986, [41] pp.

Williams, Nancy M. *The Yolngu and their Land: A System of Land Tenure and the Fight for its Recognition*. Canberra: Australian Institute of Aboriginal Studies, 1986, xvi + 264 pp.

Williams, Nancy M. *Two Laws: Managing Disputes in a Contemporary Aboriginal Community*. Canberra: Australian Institute of Aboriginal Studies, 1987, xiv + 176 pp.

Willis, Sabine, ed. *Women, Faith and Fetes: Essays in the History of Women and the Church in Australia*. Melbourne: Dove Communications/Australian Council of Churches (N.S.W.), 1977.

Willmot, Eric. *Pemulwuy: The Rainbow Warrior*. McMahons Point, N.S.W.: Weldons Pty. Ltd., 1987, 310 pp.

Wilmore, Gayraud S. *Black Religion and Black Radicalism: An Interpretation of the Religious History of Afro-american People*. C. Eric Lincoln Series on Black Religion. New York: Anchor Press/Doubleday, 1973. Second edition, Maryknoll, N.Y.: Orbis Books, 1983, 288 pp.

Wilmore, Gayraud S., ed. *Black Men in Prison: The Response of the African American Church*. Black Church Scholars Series, 2. Atlanta: ITC Press, 1990, 169 pp.

Wilson, Frederick R., ed. *The San Antonio Report: Your Will Be Done Mission in Christ's Way*. Geneva: World Council of Churches, 1990, 214 pp.

Wilson, Paul R. *Black Deaths-White Hands*. Revised edition. Sydney: George Allen & Unwin, [1982] 1985.

Witvliet, Theo. *The Way of the Black Messiah: The Hermeneutical Challenge of Black Theology as a Theology of Liberation*. Trans. (from the Dutch) by John Bowden. Oak Park, IL.: Meyer Stone Books, 1987, 332 pp.

Wright, Don, and Clancy, Eric. *The Methodists: A History of Methdism in New South Wales*. Sydney: Allen & Unwin, 1993, 276 pp.

Wright, Judith. *Cry for the Dead*. Melbourne: Oxford University Press, 1981.

Wright, Judith. *We Call for a Treaty*. Sydney: Fontana, 1985.

X, Malcolm. *Malcolm X: The Last Speeches*. Ed. by Bruce Perry. New York: Pathfinder Press, 1989, 189 pp.

Yarwood, A. T. *Samuel Marsden: The Great Survivor*. Melbourne: Melbourne University Press, 1977, 341 pp.

Yule, Ian R., ed. *My Mother The Land*. Galiwin'ku, N.T.: Galiwin'ku Parish, 1980, 43 pp.

Dissertations/Theses

Blaskett, Beverly A. *The Development of Mission Policy for Aborigines: With Particular Reference to the Education Policy of the Roman Catholic Missions.* Melbourne: LaTrobe University, Master of Education thesis, 1983.

Bos, Robert. *Jesus and the Dreaming: Religion and Social Change in Arnhem Land.* Brisbane: University of Queensland, Doctor of Philosophy dissertation, 1988, 398 pp.

Budden, Chris [G]. *A Place in Society? Biblical Reflections on the Shape of Australian Society at the Time of the Bicentennial.* San Anselmo, CA.: San Francisco Theological Seminary, Doctor of Ministry dissertation, 1989, 119 pp.

Dawia, Alex. *The Emergence of Black Theology in Aboriginal Australia.* Port Moresby: University of Papua New Guinea, Bachelor of Arts (Honours) thesis, 1986, 78 pp.

Gilbert, Stephanie Louise. *Colonisation at Work: An Analysis of the Legislative Basis for the Oppression of Aborigines and their Children in Queensland.* Townsville, Qld.: James Cook University of North Queensland, Bachelor of Social Work (Honours) thesis, 1992.

Gross, Rita M. *Exclusion and Participation: The Role of Women in Aboriginal Australian Religions.* Chicago, IL.: University of Chicago, Doctor of Philosophy dissertation, 1975.

Hammer, David George Mervyn. *Central Subliminal Wants Among the Australian Aborigines: The Role of Christian Missions Towards Fulfillment.* South Pasedena, CA.: Fuller Theological Seminary, Doctor of Missiology dissertation, 1976.

Leske, Percy E. *An Indigenous Church in Aboriginal Society.* Melbourne: n.p., 1980.

McDonald, H. *Two Ways: A Study of the Incorporation of European Christianity into Traditional Aboriginal Religion.* Brisbane: University of Queensland, Bachelor of Arts (Honours) thesis, 1987.

Malone, Colleen. *Widening the Track: The Josephite Journey Towards an Eclectic Missiology.* Sydney: University of Sydney, School of Studies in Religion, Master of Philosophy dissertation, 1991, 214 pp.

Morris, Christine. *The Western Construction of Aboriginal Religion.* Brisbane: University of Queensland, Bachelor of Arts (Honours) thesis, 1992.

Swain, Tony. *A Place for Strangers.* Sydney: University of Sydney, Doctor of Philosophy dissertation, 1991.

Government Documents

Aboriginal Affairs Planning Authority. *Annual Report [1988].* West Perth, W.A.: Aboriginal Affairs Planning Authority, 1988, 63 pp.

Aboriginal and Torres Strait Islander Commission [ATSIC]. *Annual Report 5 March 1990–30 June 1990.* Canberra: Australian Government Publishing Service, 1991a.

ATSIC. *Programs for Indigenous Australians: An Introduction.* Canberra: ATSIC, 1991b, 24 pp.

ATSIC. *Aboriginal and Torres Strait Islander Commission Corporate Plan 1992–1996.* Canberra: ATSIC, 1992a.

ATSIC. *Aboriginal and Torres Strait Islander Women: Part of the Solution—National Conference, Canberra, ACT, 6–10 April 1992.* Canberra: ATSIC, 1992b, 40 pp.

ATSIC. *Aboriginal Australia [Kit].* Canberra: ATSIC, 1992c.

Bibliography

269

ATSIC. *Aboriginal Employment Development Policy: Annual Report 1990–91.* Canberra: ATSIC, 1992d, 51 pp.

ATSIC. *The First Step: A Report on the Initial Community Consultations on the Royal Commission into Aboriginal Deaths in Custody.* Canberra: ATSIC, 1992e, 41 pp.

ATSIC. *25 Years On: Parliamentary Speeches Marking the Anniversary of the Aboriginal Referendum of 27 May 1967.* Canberra: ATSIC, 1992f, 32 pp.

ATSIC. *UN Working Group on Indigenous Populations, Tenth Session, 20–31 July 1992, Geneva, Switzerland: The Australian Contribution.* Canberra: Aboriginal and Torres Strait Islander Commission, 1992g, 113 pp.

ATSIC. *Current Issues: The Mabo Judgement.* Canberra: ATSIC, 1994, 8 pp.

ATSIC, Royal Commission into Aboriginal Deaths in Custody Government Response Monitoring Unit. *Response to the Recommendations of the Royal Commission into Aboriginal Deaths in Custody: Commonwealth Funded Initiatives.* Canberra: ATSIC, 1992, 70 pp.

ATSIC, Council for Aboriginal Reconciliation [CAR], and Aboriginal and Torres Strait Islander Social Justice Commissioner [ATSISJC]. *Towards Social Justice? An Issues Paper.* [Canberra]: ATSIC, CAR, ATSISJC, 1994, 20 pp.

Aboriginal Development Commission. *1987 Aboriginal and Torres Strait Islander Housing and Accommodation Needs Survey.* Canberra: Australian Government Publishing Service, February 1988a.

Aboriginal Development Commission. *Annual Report 1986–87.* Canberra: Australian Government Publishing Service, 1988b, 172 pp.

Aboriginal Development Commission. *Annual Report 1987–88.* Canberra: Australian Government Publishing Service, 1989, 184 pp.

Aboriginals in Victoria. Melbourne: Commonwealth Government Printing Unit, [1973], [13] pp. [Reprinted from: *Victorian Year Book 1973.*]

Australian Bureau of Census and Statistics. *Official Year Book of the Commonwealth of Australia, No. 54, 1968.* Canberra: Commonwealth Bureau of Census and Statistics, 1968.

Australian Bureau of Statistics [ABS]. *ABS Census of Population and Housing 1986: Aboriginals, Torres Strait Islanders, Australia, States and Territories.* Catalogue No. 2499.0. Canberra: Australian Government Publishing Service, 1988.

Australian Institute of Aboriginal Studies. *Annual Report 1989–90.* Canberra: Australian Government Publishing Service, 1990.

Australian Institute of Aboriginal and Torres Strait Islander Studies. *Annual Report 1990–91.* Canberra: Australian Government Publishing Service, 1991.

Australian Institute of Aboriginal and Torres Strait Islander Studies. *Annual Report 1991–92.* Canberra: Australian Government Publishing Service, 1992.

Australian Institute of Criminology. "Aboriginal Deaths in Custody." *Trends and Issues in Crime and Criminal Justice No. 12.* [Canberra: Australian Institute of Criminology,] May 1988. [Compiled by Peter Grabosky, Anita Scandia, Kayleen Hazelhurst, and Paul Wilson.]

Bray, Greg. "New South Wales Government Finances: Budget Sector." *Monthly Summary of Statistics: New South Wales: February 1992.* Canberra: Australian Bureau of Statistics, 1992.

Byrne, Denis. *The Mountains Call Me Back: A History of the Aborigines and the Forests of the Far South Coast of New South Wales.* Occasional Paper No. 5. Sydney: N.S.W. Ministry of Aboriginal Affairs, 1984, 32 pp.

Commonwealth of Australia [CoA]. *Constitution of Australia.* Canberra: Australian Government Publishing Service, 1901.

Commonwealth of Australia. *Aboriginal Welfare: Initial Conference of Commonwealth and States Aboriginal Authorities.* Canberra: Commonwealth Government Printer, 1937.

Commonwealth of Australia. *Aboriginal Employment Policy Statement: Policy Paper No. 1.* Canberra: Australian Government Publishing Service, 1987.

Commonwealth of Australia. *Native Welfare: Meeting of Commonwealth and State Ministers held at Canberra, 3rd and 4th September, 1951.* Canberra: Commonwealth Government Printer, 1951.

Commonwealth of Australia. *Mabo: The High Court Decision on Native Title: Discussion Paper, June 1993.* Canberra: Australian Government Publishing Service, 1993, 106 pp.

Commonwealth of Australia. Bureau of Census and Statistics. *Official Year Book of the Commonwealth of Australia, No. 54, 1968.* Canberra: Commonwealth Bureau of Census and Statistics, 1968.

Department of Aboriginal Affairs [DAA]. *Aboriginal Land Rights in the Northern Territory: What It Means and How It Will Work.* Canberra: Australian Government Printing Service, 1979, 24 pp.

DAA. *Aboriginal Statistics 1986.* Canberra: Australian Government Publishing Service, 1987a.

DAA. *The Australian Aboriginals 1987.* Canberra: Australian Government Printing Service, 1987b, 16 pp.

DAA. *Annual Report 1987–88.* Canberra: Australian Government Printing Service, 1988, 134 pp.

DAA. *Aboriginal Australia—Culture and Society: Australian Languages.* [Canberra: Australian Government Printing Service,] 1989, 8 pp.

DAA. *Annual Report 1 July 1989–4 March 1990.* Canberra: Australian Government Publishing Service, 1990.

Department of Education, Employment and Training. *Report of the Aboriginal Education Policy Task Force.* Canberra: Australian Government Publishing Service, 1988.

Department of Employment and Industrial Relations. *CES [Commonwealth Employment Service] Review of Aboriginal Unemployed.* [Canberra: Australian Government Publishing Service,] December 1983. [manuscript]

Department of Foreign Affairs and Trade [CoA-DFAT]. "Hope for Global Solutions on Environment." *Environment* 1 ([June] 1991), pp. 1–2.

CoA-DFAT. "Shaping Up for the Rio Summit," *Environment* 2 (September 1991), p. 3.

Department of the Prime Minister and Cabinet, Aboriginal Reconciliation Unit. *Council for Aboriginal Reconciliation: An Introduction.* Canberra: Australian Government Publishing Service, 1991, 11 pp.

Department of the Prime Minister and Cabinet, Office of the Status of Women. *Women's Business: Report of the Aboriginal Women's Task Force.* Canberra: Australian Government Publishing Service, 1986.

Department of the Prime Minister and Cabinet, Resource Assessment Commission [DPMC-RAC]. *Kakadu Conservation Zone [Inquiry]: Background Paper.* 2 Vols. Canberra: Australian Government Publishing Service, June 1990.

Bibliography

Bibliography 271

Department of Resources and Energy, Bureau of Resource Economics. *Processing of Australia's Mineral Exports: An Overview*. Occasional Paper [No.] 1. Canberra: Australian Government Publishing Service, 1987.

Law Reform Commission. *The Recognition of Aboriginal Customary Laws: Summary Report*. Report No. 31. Canberra: Australian Government Printing Service, 1986, 104 pp.

Minister for Territories [CoA-MT]. *Assimilation of Our Aborigines*. Canberra: Commonwealth Government Printer, 1958a, 16 pp.

Minister for Territories. *Progress Towards Assimilation: Aboriginal Welfare in the Northern Territory*. Canberra: Commonwealth Government Printer, 1958b, 58 pp.

Minister for Territories. *Fringe Dwellers*. Canberra: Commonwealth Government Printer, 1959, 32 pp.

Minister for Territories. *The Skills of Our Aborigines*. Canberra: Commonwealth Government Printer, 1960, 32 pp.

Minister for Territories. *One People*. Canberra: Commonwealth Government Printer, 1961, 32 pp.

Minister for Territories. *Our Aborigines*. Canberra: Commonwealth Government Printer, 1962, 32 pp.

Task Force on Aboriginal and Islander Broadcasting and Communications. *Out of the Silent Land: Report of the Task Force on Aboriginal and Islander Broadcasting and Communications/Department of Aboriginal Affairs*. Canberra: Australian Government Publishing Service, [1984], 171 pp.

Conference of Commonwealth and State Aboriginal Authorities. *Resolutions Passed by the Conference of Commonwealth and State Aboriginal Authorities held at Parliament House, Canberra, on 3rd and 4th February, 1948*. Canberra: n.p., 1948, 4 pp.

Council for Aboriginal Reconciliation [CAR]. *Addressing the Key Issues for Reconciliation*. Canberra: Australian Government Publishing Service, 1993a, 70 pp.

Council for Aboriginal Reconciliation. *Making Things Right: Reconciliation After the High Court Decision on 'Native Title'*. Canberra: Council for Aboriginal Reconciliation, 1993b, 27 pp.

Dewdney, Andrew, and Michels, Debby. *More Than Black and White: Racism and Everyday Life*. Sydney: Inner City Education Centre, 1988, 94 pp.

Dodson, Michael. *Aboriginal and Torres Strait Islander Social Justice Commission: First Report 1993*. Canberra: Australian Government Publishing Service, 1993, 160 pp.

Electoral and Administrative Review Commission (Queensland) [EARC/Q]. *Report on Review of the Preservation and Enhancement of Individual Rights and Freedoms*. Brisbane: Electoral and Administrative Review Commission, 1993, 487 pp.

Ethnic Affairs Commission of N.S.W. *Ethnic Affairs Policy Statement of the Ethnic Affairs Commission of NSW*. [Sydney]: Ethnic Affairs Commission of N.S.W., 1986.

Ethnic Affairs Commission of N.S.W. *Submission Review of the Racial Vilification Amendments to the NSW Anti-Discrimination Act 1977*. Sydney: Ethnic Affairs Commission of N.S.W., 1992.

Evans, Gareth, Sen. The Hon (Federal Minister for Foreign Affairs and Trade). *Australia's Overseas Aid Program 1990–1991*. Budget Related Paper No. 4. Canberra: Australian Government Publishing Service, 1990, 58 pp.

Hallahan, Kay, The Hon. (Federal Minister for Community Services). [*Ministerial Statement to Parliament on Juvenile Justice*. Canberra: Australian Government Publishing Service,] December 1987.

Hand, Gerry, MP. *Aboriginal and Torres Strait Islander Commission Bill 1988: Second Reading Speech.* Canberra: Australian Government Printing Service, (24 August) 1988, 11 pp.

Hasluck, Paul M. C. *The Policy of Assimilation: Native Welfare Conference.* Canberra: Commonwealth Government Printer, 1961, 8 pp.

Historical Records of New South Wales. Vol. I, Part I—Cook 1762–1780. Sydney: Charles Potter, Government Printer, 1893.

Historical Records of New South Wales. Vol. I, Part II—Phillip 1783–1792. Sydney: Charles Potter, Government Printer, 1892.

Human Rights and Equal Opportunity Commission [HREOC]. HREOC. *Aboriginal Reserves By-laws and Human Rights.* Occasional Paper, 5. Canberra: Australian Government Publishing Service, 1983a, 93 pp.

HREOC. *Racism: Human Rights for Humankind.* Canberra: Australian Government Publishing Service, 1983b, [22] pp.

HREOC. *Community Services (Aborigines) Act 1984.* Report, 9. Canberra: Australian Government Publishing Service, 1985, 22 pp.

HREOC. *Toomelah Report: Report on the Problems and Needs of Aborigines Living on the NSW-Queensland Border, June 1988.* Sydney: HREOC, 1988, 79 pp.

HREOC. *Our Homeless Children: Report of the National Inquiry into Homeless Children.* Canberra: Australian Government Publishing Service, February 1989.

HREOC. *Racist Violence: Report of the National Inquiry into Racist Violence in Australia.* Canberra: Australian Government Publishing Service, 1991, 535 pp.

HREOC. *Mornington: A Report by the Federal Race Discrimination Commissioner.* Canberra: Australian Government Publishing Service, 1993, 113 pp.

HREOC-Federal Race Discrimination Commissioner. *Water: A Report on the Provision of Water and Sanitation in Remote Aboriginal and Torres Strait Islander Communities.* Sydney: Australian Government Publishing Service, 1994, 487 pp.

Juvenile Justice Advisory Council of N.S.W. *Green Paper: Future Directions for Juvenile Justice in New South Wales.* Sydney: Juvenile Justice Advisory Council of N.S.W., 1993, 278 pp.

McEwen, J. [Minister for the Interior]. *The Northern Territory of Australia: Commonwealth Government Policy with Respect to Aboriginals.* Canberra: Commonwealth Government Printer, (February) 1939, 6 pp.

National Aboriginal Education Committee. *Policy Statement on Tertiary Education for Aborigines and Torres Strait Islanders.* Canberra: Australian Government Publishing Service, 1986.

N.S.W. Anti-Discrimination Board. *Study of Street Offences by Aborigines.* Sydney: N.S.W. Anti-Discrimination Board, 1982, 245 pp.

N.S.W. Department of Education, Directorate of Special Programs [NSWDOEDSP]. *Aboriginal Education Policy.* Support Document No. 1. [Sydney]: N.S.W. Department of Education, Directorate of Special Programs, 1982a, 10 pp.

NSWDOEDSP. *Strategies for Teaching Aboriginal Children.* Support Document No. 5. [Sydney]: N.S.W. Department of Education, Directorate of Special Programs, 1982b, 11 pp.

NSWDOEDSP. *Intercultural Education: A Support Document to the Multicultural Education Policy 1983.* [Sydney]: N.S.W. Department of Education, Directorate of Special Programs, 1983a, 15 pp.

NSWDOEDSP. *Multicultural Education Policy Statement.* [Sydney]: N.S.W. Department of Education, Directorate of Special Programs, 1983b, 4 pp.

NSWDOEDSP. *Our Multicultural Society.* [Sydney]: N.S.W. Department of Education, Directorate of Special Programs, 1983c, 165 pp.

N.S.W. Office of Juvenile Justice. *A Synopsis of the Green Paper: Future Directions for Juvenile Justice in New South Wales.* Sydney: N.S.W. Office of Juvenile Justice, 1993, 15 pp.

N.S.W. Office of Juvenile Justice. *Breaking the Crime Cycle: New Directions for Juvenile Justice in NSW.* White Paper. Sydney: N.S.W. Office of Juvenile Justice, 1994, 27 pp.

New South Wales Police Service [NSWPS]. *Aboriginal Policy Statement.* [Sydney]: NSWPS, 1992, 3 pp.

NSWPS. *Aboriginal Strategic Plan.* [Sydney]: NSWPS, n.d., 8 pp.

Nugent, Peter, MP. Principal Portfolio Speeches and Press Releases, May-December 1993. Canberra: Shadow Minister for Aboriginal and Torres Strait Islander Affairs, 1993.

Office of the Commissioner for Community Relations [OCCR]. *Let's End the Slander: Combating Racial Prejudice in Teaching Materials.* Canberra: OCCR, 1979, 124 pp.

OCCR. *Discrimination Against Aboriginals and Islanders in Queensland.* Community Relations Paper No. 17. Canberra: OCCR, 1981a, 111 pp.

OCCR. *Discrimination Against Aboriginals in Country Towns of New South Wales.* Community Relations Paper No. 11. Canberra: OCCR, 1981b, 44 pp.

OCCR. *World Perceptions of Racism in Australia.* Community Relations Paper No. 12. Canberra: OCCR, 1981c, 26 pp.

Office of the New South Wales Ombudsman. *Race Relations & Our Police: A Discussion Paper.* Sydney: Office of the New South Wales Ombudsman, 1994, 54 pp.

Parliament of the Commonwealth of Australia, House of Representatives. *Aboriginal and Torres Strait Islander Commission Bill 1988.* Canberra: Australian Government Printing Service, 1988a, viii + 103 pp.

Parliament of the Commonwealth of Australia, House of Representatives. *Aboriginal and Torres Strait Islander Commission Bill 1988-Explanatory Memorandum.* Canberra: Australian Government Printing Service, 1988b, ii + 97 pp.

Parliament of the Commonwealth of Australia, House of Representatives. *Native Title Bill 1993: Explanatory Memorandum, Part A.* Canberra: Australian Government Printing Service, 1993, 9 pp.

Parliament of the Commonwealth of Australia, House of Representatives. *Native Title Bill 1993: Explanatory Memorandum, Part B.* Canberra: Australian Government Printing Service, 1993, 109 pp.

Parliament of the Commonwealth of Australia, House of Representatives. *ATSIC Amendment (Indigenous Land Corporation and Land Fund) Bill 1994.* Canberra: Australian Government Printing Service, 1994a, iv + 51 pp.

Parliament of the Commonwealth of Australia, House of Representatives. *ATSIC Amendment (Indigenous Land Corporation and Land Fund) Bill 1994-Explanatory Memorandum, Part A.* Canberra: Australian Government Printing Service, 1994b, 6 pp.

Parliament of the Commonwealth of Australia, House of Representatives. *ATSIC Amendment (Indigenous Land Corporation and Land Fund) Bill 1994-Explanatory*

Memorandum, Part B. Canberra: Australian Government Printing Service, 1994c, 31 pp.

Parliament of the Commonwealth of Australia, Senate. *Native Title Bill 1993: Report by the Senate Standing Committee on Legal and Constitutional Affairs*. Canberra: Australian Government Printing Service, December 1993, iv + 107 pp.

Read, Peter. "The Stolen Generations: The Removal of Aboriginal Children in New South Wales 1883 to 1969." *New South Wales Ministry of Aboriginal Affairs, Occasional Paper (No. 1)*. Sydney: Ministry of Aboriginal Affairs (NSW), n.d.

Royal Commission into Aboriginal Deaths in Custody (RCADC). *National Report, Research Paper No. 1– *. Canberra: RCADC, 1988.

Royal Commission into British Nuclear Tests in Australia. *Report of the Royal Commission into British Nuclear Tests in Australia*. Canberra: Australian Government Publishing Service, 1985.

Schmider, Joann. *Economic and Social Relations Between States and Indigenous Peoples: Inclusion of Indigenous Perspectives in the United Nations Environment and Development Processes*. Canberra: Department of Foreign Affairs and Trade, [1991].

Select Committee Appointed to Inquire into Native Welfare Conditions in the Laverton-Warburton Range Area, Western Australia [SCWA], Report, 22nd Parliament, 1st Session, Perth, Western Australia, 12 December 1956.

Select Committee of the Legislative Council on the Aborigines Bill 1899, Minutes of Evidence and Appendices, South Australia, No. 77 of 1899, Witness the Government Resident and Judge of the Northern Territory.

Tickner, Robert, MP. *Council for Aboriginal Reconciliation Bill 1991: Second Reading Speech*. Canberra: Australian Government Printing Service, 1991a, 10 pp.

Tickner, Robert, MP. *Social Justice for Indigenous Australians, 1992–93*. Budget Related Paper, No. 7. Canberra: Australian Government Printing Service, 1992, 191 pp.

Western Australian Parliamentary Debates. Vol. 102 (1939).

Western Australian Parliamentary Debates. Vol. 140 (1954).

Walker, Frank. *Green Paper on Aboriginal Land Rights in New South Wales*. 22 December 1982, 66 pp. [Frank Walker, Q.C., M.P., then-N.S.W. Minister for Aboriginal Affairs.]

Legal Documents

Australian Legislation

Aboriginal and Torres Strait Islander Commission Act 1988.

Aboriginal Land Rights Act (NSW) 1983.

Aboriginal Land Rights (Northern Territory) Act 1976.

Aborigines Act (Qld.) 1971.

Anti-Discrimination Act (NSW) 1977.

Children's Protection Act (S.A.) 1993.

Commonwealth of Australia Constitution Act 1900.

Community Services (Aborigines) Act 1984.

Constitution Alteration (Aboriginals) Act 1967.

Council for Aboriginal Reconciliation Act 1991.

Human Rights and Equal Opportunity Legislation Amendment Act (No. 2) 1992.

Native Title Act 1993.

Racial Discrimination Act 1975.

Australian Cases

Coe v. Commonwealth (1978) 18 A.L.R. 592.
Coe v. Commonwealth (1978) 24 A.L.R. 118.
Koowarta v. Bjelke Peteresen (1982) 56 A.L.J.R. 625.
Mabo v. Queensland (1988) 166 C.L.R. 186.
Mabo v. Queensland (1992) 175 C.L.R. 1–217.
Milirrpum v. Nabalco Pty. Ltd. (1971) 17 F.L.R. 141.

International Instruments

Universal Declaration of Human Rights (1948).
Convention relating to the Status of Stateless Persons (1954).
Convention on the Reduction of Statelessness (1961).
United Nations Declaration on the Elimination of All Forms of Racial Discrimination (1963).
International Convention on the Elimination of All Forms of Racial Discrimination (1965).
International Covenant on Civil and Political Rights (1966).
United Nations (Draft) Declaration on the Rights of Indigenous Peoples (1993).

Non-Government Reports

Central Land Council. *Central Land Council Annual Report 1987–88.* Alice Springs: Central Land Council, 1988, 50 pp.

Cunneen, Chris, and Behrendt, Jason. *Aboriginal and Torres Strait Islander Custodial Deaths Between May 1989 and January 1994: A Report to the National Committee to Defend Black Rights.* Sydney: n.p., 1994, 61 pp.

Nganampa Health Council, Inc., SA Health Commission & Aboriginal Health Organisation of SA. *Report of Uwankara Palyanyku Kanyintjaku: An Environmental and Public Health Review Within the Anangu Pitjantjatjara Lands.* n.p.: Nganampa Health Council, 1987.

QEA Aboriginal and Islander Community. *Report to the QEA Aboriginal and Islander Community: Results of 1985 QEA Black Community Housing Survey.* Queensland: QEA Aboriginal and Islander Community, 1986.

Tangentyere Council. Tangentyere Council Annual Report 1987–88. Tangentyere, N.T.: Tangentyere Council, 1988, 36 pp.

Tangentyere Council. Tangentyere Council Annual Report 1989–90. Tangentyere, N.T.: Tangentyere Council, 1990, 32 pp.

Thomson, Donald F. Interim General Report of Preliminary Expedition to Arnhem Land, Northern Territory of Australia 1935–6. Submitted to the Minister of the Interior, 9 April 1936. Typescript.

Thomson, Donald F. *Report on Expedition to Arnhem Land, 1936–37.* Canberra: Published under the Authority of the Minister for the Interior, 1939.

Yipirinya School Council. *Yipirinya School Council Annual Report 1993–94.* Alice Springs: Yipirinya School Council, 1994, 36 pp.

World Council Of Churches Documents (In Chronological Order)

World Council of Churches [WCC]. *Ecumenical Statements on Race Relations: Development of Ecumenical Thought on Race Relations 1937–1964.* Geneva: World Council of Churches, 1965, 47 pp.

WCC. World Conference on Church and Society, "Christians in the Technical and Social Revolutions of our Time," Geneva, 1966, pp. 204–5 (Section III, n. 34, 36).

WCC. Statement from the Fourth Assembly of the World Council of Churches, Uppsala, 1968, pp. 65–66 (Section IV, n. 28a), 241–42 (n. 7).

WCC. Statement from Central Committee, Canterbury, 1969, pp. 270–75 (part II).

WCC. *Aboriginal Issues: Racism in Australia.* Geneva: World Council of Churches, Programme to Combat Racism, 1971a, 29 pp.

WCC. *Aboriginal Issues: Racism in Australia—More Facts and Figures.* Geneva: World Council of Churches, Programme to Combat Racism, 1971b, 37 pp.

WCC. *Racism in Theology and Theology Against Racism: Report of a Consultation Organized by the Commission on Faith and Order and the Programme to Combat Racism [Geneva, 14–20 September 1975].* Geneva: World Council of Churches, 1975, 21 pp.

WCC. *Racism in Children's and School Textbooks.* Geneva: World Council of Churches, Programme to Combat Racism, 1979. [From Workshop, Evangelische Akademie Arnoldshain, FRG, 13–18 October 1978.]

WCC. "Australia." *PCR Information: Reports and Background Papers* 8 (June 1980): pt. 4, 55–60. [Special Issue: " Churches Responding to Racism in the 1980s."]

WCC. "Action in Solidarity with the Aborigines of Australia" [Statement from the Conference on World Mission and Evangelism, Melbourne, Australia, 12–24 May 1980]. *International Review of Mission* 69,275 (July 1980): 326–28.

WCC. *We the Women, We the World: Report on the Programme to Combat Racism's "Women Under Racism" Consultation, 10–13 November 1986,* ed. by Cherrie Waters. Geneva: World Council of Churches, (November) 1986.

WCC. *Urban Rural Mission Reflections.* Geneva: World Council of Churches, Commission on World Mission and Evangelism, (July) 1986, 28 pp.

WCC. "Statement of Team Visits to Aboriginal Communities." World Council of Churches Seventh Assembly, Canberra, 4 February 1991a, p. 1.

WCC. *Between Two Worlds: Report of a WCC Team Visit to Aboriginal Communities in Australia.* PCR Information, 28. Geneva: World Council of Churches, 1991b.

WCC. *Sisters in Struggle to Eliminate Racism: Global Gathering of Women Under Racism, Trinidad & Tobago, 25–30 October 1992.* Geneva: World Council of Churches, 1992a.

WCC. "Recommendations to WCC." *Global Gathering of Women Under Racism.* Geneva: World Council of Churches, 1992b.

WCC. *Christian Faith and the World Economy Today: A Study Document from the World Council of Churches.* Geneva: World Council of Churches, 1992c, 72 pp.

WCC. *Stories of the Land: WCC Team Visit ot Australia,* ed. by Brenda Fitzpatrick. Geneva: World Council of Churches, November 1993, 66 pp.

Chapters in Books

Amnesty International. "Australia." In *Amnesty International Report 1992.* New York: Amnesty International, 1992, pp. 59–60.

"Australia URM [Urban Rural Mission] Report." In *Proceedings 1992: 23rd CCA-URM Committee Meeting, February 11–15, 1992, Colombo, Sri Lanka.* Hong Kong: Chrisitian Conference of Asia-Urban Rural Mission, 1992, pp. 164–71.

"Australian Aboriginal Issues." In *Seoul 1989: Proceedings of the 22nd General Council of the World Alliance of Reformed Churches (Presbyterian and Congregational), Held at Seoul, Republic of Korea, August 15–26, 1989,* ed. by Edmond Perret. Geneva: World Alliance of Reformed Churches, 1990, pp. 49–50, 270–71.

Beckett, Jeremy. "The Past in the Present; the Present in the Past: Constructing a National Aboriginality." In *Past and Present: The Construction of Aboriginality,* ed. by Jeremy R. Beckett. Canberra: Aboriginal Studies Press, 1988, pp. 191–212.

Behrendt, Paul. "Aboriginal Australians: A Mirror of Attitude and National Conscience." In *Martung Upah: Black and White Australians Seeking Partnership,* ed. by Anne Pattel-Gray. Melbourne: HarperCollins*Religious*, 1996, pp. 6–15.

Brady, Don. "Sermon Quotes." In *Racism in Australia: Tasks for General and Christian Education—Report of Conference at Southport, Queensland, November 19–24, 1971.* Melbourne: Australian Council of Churches, Division of Christian Education, 1971, p. 39.

Brennan, Frank, S.J. "Aboriginal Aspirations to Land: Unfinished History and an Ongoing National Responsibility." In *International Law and Aboriginal Human Rights,* ed. by Barbara Hocking. Sydney: The Law Book Company, Ltd., 1988, pp. 148–77.

Brown, Wendy R. "Strategy Group Workshop: Law." In *Program Guide: The First National People of Color Environmental Leadership Summit, The Washington Court on Capitol Hill, Washington, D.C., October 24–27, 1991,* by Commission for Racial Justice, United Church of Christ. Washington, D.C.: Commission for Racial Justice, United Church of Christ, 1991, pp. 31–33.

Chryssavgis, John. "Bible Study." In *WCC Seventh Assembly, South-East Asia Pre-Assembly Regional Meeting, Dhyana Pura Training Center, Bali, Indonesia, 1–4 May 1990,* ed. by Bob Scott. Geneva: World Council of Churches, Programme to Combat Racism, 1990, pp. 34–39.

Clarke, Bernard A., and Hunt, Arnold D. "Multiculturalism and the Uniting Church." In *Religion and Multiculturalism in Australia: Essays in Honour of Victor C. Hayes,* ed. by Norman C. Habel. Special Studies in Religions Series, 7. Adelaide: Australian Association for the Study of Religion, 1992, pp. 225–38.

Cole, Keith. "A Critical Appraisal of Anglican Mission Policy and Practice in Arnhem Land, 1907–1939." In *Aborigines and Change: Australia in the 70s,* ed. by R. M. Berndt. Canberra: Australian Institute of Aboriginal Studies; [Atlantic Highlands], N.J.: Humanities Press, 1977, pp. 177–98.

Cook, James. "Lieutenant Cook's Private Log: Sunday, 29th April, to Saturday, 5th May, 1770." In *Historical Records of New South Wales.* Vol. I, Part I—Cook 1762–1780. Sydney: Charles Potter, Government Printer, 1893, p. 97.

Corbett, Helen. "Statement on Behalf of the National Committee to Defend Black Rights (NCDBR)." In *UN Working Group on Indigenous Populations, Tenth Session, 20–31 July 1992, Geneva, Switzerland: The Australian Contribution.* Canberra: Aboriginal and Torres Strait Islander Commission, 1992, pp. 56–59.

Daly, Anne E. "Aboriginal Women in the Labour Market." In *Aboriginal Employment Equity by the Year 2000,* ed. by J[on] C. Altman. Research Monograph, No. 2.

Canberra: Centre for Aboriginal Economic Policy Research, Australian National University, 1991, pp. 91–100.

Dicker, Gordon S. "Kerygma and Australian Culture: The Case of the Aussie Battler." In *Toward Theology in an Australian Context,* ed. by Victor C. Hayes. Adelaide: Australian Association for the Study of Religions, 1979, pp. 46–52.

Dodson, Michael. "Land Rights: A Question of Social Justice." In *Martung Upah: Black and White Australians Seeking Partnership,* ed. by Anne Pattel-Gray. Melbourne: HarperCollins*Religious,* 1996, pp. 45–56.

Dodson, Pat. "Preface." In *Addressing the Key Issues for Reconciliation,* by the Council for Aboriginal Reconciliation, v-vi. Canberra: Australian Government Publishing Service, 1993.

Dunn, Michael. "Early Australia: Wage Labour or Slave Society?" In *Essays in the Political Economy of Australian Capitalism,* ed. by E. L. Wheelwright and Ken Buckley. Sydney: ANZ Book Company, 1975, vol. 1, pp. 33–46.

Dunstan, Don. "Racism in Australia." In *Racism in Australia in the 1980's: Challenge to the Churches,* ed. by Russell Rollason. Sydney: Australian Council of Churches, [1980], pp. 5–13.

Dussel, Enrique. "Towards a History of the Church in the World Periphery: Some Hypotheses." In *Towards a History of the Church in the Third World,* ed. by Lukas Vischer. Veröffentlichung No. 3. Bern: Evangelische Arbeitsstelle Oekumene Schweiz, 1985, pp. 110–30.

Dutney, Andrew. "Teaching the Teacher: A Third Phase in Theological Education of Aboriginal People in the Uniting Church in Australia." In *Martung Upah: Black and White Australians Seeking Partnership,* ed. by Anne Pattel-Gray. Melbourne: HarperCollins*Religious,* 1996, pp. 248–62.

Eddy, John. "Australian Historical Studies as Resouces for Theological Reflection." In *Toward Theology in an Australian Context,* ed. by Victor C. Hayes. Adelaide: Australian Association for the Study of Religions, 1979, pp. 53–58.

Einfeld, (Justice) Marcus R. "The Lond March to Aboriginal Equity." In *Martung Upah: Black and White Australians Seeking Partnership,* ed. by Anne Pattel-Gray. Melbourne: HarperCollins*Religious,* 1996, pp. 195–211.

Elkin, A[dolphus] P. "Historical Background to the Present Problems." In *Proceedings of Conference on N.S.W. Aborigines, Armidale—May 1959,* by the Adult Education Department, University of New England. Armidale: Adult Education Department, University of New England, 1959, pp. 3–27.

Encel, S. "The Nature of Race Prejudice in Australia." In *Racism: The Australian Experience—A Study of Race Prejudice in Australia,* ed. by F[rank] S. Stevens. Volume 1: Prejudice and Xenophobia. Sydney: Australia and New Zealand Book Company, 1971, pp. 30–40.

Engel, F[rank]. "The Protestant Church and Race Prejudice." In *Racism: The Australian Experience—A Study of Race Prejudice in Australia,* ed. by F[rank] S. Stevens. Volume 1: Prejudice and Xenophobia. Sydney: Australia and New Zealand Book Company, 1971, pp. 175–88.

Felder, Cain Hope. "Cultural Ideology, Afro-Centrism and Biblical Interpretation." In *Black Theology: A Documentary History,* ed. by James H. Cone and Gayraud S. Wilmore. Volume 2: 1980–1992. Maryknoll, N.Y.: Orbis Books, 1993, pp. 184–95.

Fesl, Eve Mungwa D. "Religion and Ethnic Identity: A Koorie View." In *Religion and Ethnic Identity: An Australian Study (Volume II),* ed. by A. Ata. Burwood, Vic.: VICTRACC Publication, 1989.

Gale, Fay. "Introduction." In *Woman's Role in Aboriginal Society,* ed. by Fay Gale, 1–3. 3rd ed. Canberra: Australian Institute of Aboriginal Studies, 1978.

Geary, Judith. "Aboriginal Family Education Centres." In *Bygee: A Collection of Writings Describing Minority Group Movements in Australia and North America.* Townsville, Qld.: Townsville College of Advanced Education, 1980, pp. 24–25.

Gilbert, Kevin. "Kevin Gilbert." In *Imaging the Real: Australian Writing in the Nuclear Age,* ed. by D. Green and D. Headon. Sydney: Australian Broadcasting Commission, 1987.

Gilbert, Kevin. "God at the Campfire and that Christ Fella." In *Aboriginal Spirituality: Past, Present, Future,* ed. by Anne Pattel-Gray. Melbourne: HarperCollins*Religious,* 1996, pp. 54–65.

Gondarra, Djiniyini. "'Father, You Gave Us the Draming . . .': Aboriginal Theology and the Future." In *From Here to Where: Australian Christians Owning the Past — Embracing the Future,* ed. by Andrew Dutney. Melbourne: Uniting Church Press, 1988, pp. 149–53. [Adaptation of book by same title.]

Gondarra, Djiniyini. "Overcoming the Captivities of the Western Church Context." In *The Cultured Pearl: Australian Readings in Cross-Cultural Theology and Mission,* ed. by Jim Houston. Melbourne: Joint Board of Christian Education, 1988, pp. 176–82.

Gondarra, [Djiniyini] Terry, and Carrington, Don. "Commentary on 'Sacred Sites.'" In *Human Rights: A Dialogue Between the First and Third World,* by Robert A. Evans and Alice F. Evans. Maryknoll, N.Y.: Orbis Books, 1983, pp. 113–18.

Hall, R. V. "Racism and the Press." In *Racism: The Australian Experience—A Study of Race Prejudice in Australia,* ed. by F[rank] S. Stevens. Volume 1: Prejudice and Xenophobia. Sydney: Australia and New Zealand Book Company, 1971, pp. 123–35.

Hanks, Peter. "Aborigines and Government: The Developing Framework." In *Aborigines & the Law,* ed. by Peter Hanks and Bryan Keon-Cohen. Sydney: George Allen & Unwin, 1984, pp. 19–49.

Harding, Vincent. "In the Company of the Faithful: Journeying Toward the Promised Land." In *The Rise of Christian Conscience: The Emergence of a Dramatic Renewal Movement in Today's Church,* ed. by Jim Wallis. San Francisco: Harper & Row, 1987, pp. 273–84.

Harris, Charles. "Guidelines for So-Called Western Civilization and Western Christianity." In *Aboriginal Spirituality: Past, Present, Future,* ed. by Anne Pattel-Gray. Melbourne: HarperCollins*Religious,* 1996, pp. 66–78.

Harrison, Patricia J. "A Rural Australian Experiment in Training Church Leaders." In *Ministry By the People: Theological Education by Extension,* ed. by F. Ross Kinsler. Geneva/Maryknoll, N.Y.: World Council of Churches/Orbis Books, 1983.

Hobsbawm, Eric. "The Losers." In *Introduction to the Sociology of "Developing Societies,"* ed. by Hamza Alazi and Teodor Shanin. New York: Monthly Review Press, 1982, pp. 78–80.

Johanson, David. "History of the White Australia Policy." In *Immigration: Control or Colour Bar? The Background to 'White Australia' and a Proposal for Change,* by Immigration Reform Group, ed. by Kenneth Rivett. Australian edition. Melbourne: Melbourne University Press, [1960] 1962, pp. 1–27.

Keating, Paul. "Speech by the Hon P J Keating MP, Prime Minister, Redfern, Sydney, 10 December 1992." In *International Year Speeches: 1993 International Year of the*

World's Indigenous People. Canberra: Aboriginal and Torres Strait Islander Commission, 1992, pp. 5–6.

Kelly, Anthony. "Theology in an Australian Context: Towards 'a Framework of Collaborative Creativity.'" In *Toward Theology in an Australian Context,* ed. by Victor C. Hayes. Adelaide: Australian Association for the Study of Religions, 1979, pp. 29–37.

Keon-Cohen, B. A. "Some Problems of Proof: The Admissibility of Traditional Evidence." In *Mabo: A Judicial Revolution-The Aboriginal Land Rights Decision and Its Impact on Australian Law,* ed. by Margaret A. Stephenson and Suri Ratnapala. Brisbane: University of Queensland Press, 1993, pp. 185–205.

Kolig, E. "Mission Not Accomplished: Christianity in the Kimberleys." In *Aboriginal Australians and Christian Missions: Ethnographic and Historical Studies,* ed. by Tony Swain and Deborah Bird Rose. Adelaide: Australian Association for the Study of Religion, 1988, pp. 376–90.

Langton, Marcia. "Aboriginals: The Phantoms of the Northern Militarisation." In *The New Australian Militarism: Undermining Our Future Security,* ed. by Graeme Cheeseman and StJohn Kettle. Sydney: Pluto Press, 1990, pp. 169–74.

Lippmann, Lorna. "Racism in Australian Children's Books." In *The Slant of the Pen: Racism in Children's Books,* ed. by Roy Preiswerk. Geneva: World Council of Churches, 1980, pp. 61–71.

Litster, Glynn. "The Aborigines." In *Seventh-day Adventists in the South Pacific 1885–1985: Australia, New Zealand, South-Sea Islands,* ed. by Noel Clapham. Sydney: Signs Publishing Co., 1985[?], pp. 186–97.

Lyng, Jens. "Racial Composition of the Australian People." In *The Peopling of Australia,* ed. by Philip David Phillips and Gordon Leslie Wood. Melbourne: Macmillan, 1928, pp. 145–55.

Mackinolty, C., and Wainburranga, Paddy. "Too Many Captain Cooks." In *Aboriginal Australians and Christian Missions: Ethnographic and Historical Studies,* ed. by Tony Swain and Deborah Bird Rose. Adelaide: Australian Association for the Study of Religion, 1988.

McGuinness, Bruce. "Black Power in Australia." In *Racism: The Australian Experience—A Study of Race Prejudice in Australia,* ed. by F[rank] S. Stevens. Volume 2: Black Versus White. Sydney: Australia and New Zealand Book Company, 1971, pp. 150–56.

Mesters, Carlos. "La profesía durante y después del cautiverio." In *Teología y liberación: escritura y espiritualidad—ensayos en torno a la obra de Gustavo Gutiérrez,* ed. by Various. Vol. 1, CEP 109. Lima: Instituto Bartolomé de las Casas y Centro de Estudios y Publicaciones, 1990.

Morris, Christine. "The Oral Tradition Under Threat." In *Aboriginal Spirituality: Past, Present, Future,* ed. by Anne Pattel-Gray. Melbourne: HarperCollins*Religious*, 1996, pp. 22–36.

Mulvaney, D., and White, P. "How Many People?" In *Australians to 1788,* ed. by D. Mulvaney and P. White. Sydney: Fairfax, Syme and Weldon Associates, 1987.

Needham, Rodney. "Introduction." In *Primitive Classification,* by Emile Durkheim and Marcel Mauss. Trans. (from the French) by Rodney Needham. London: Cohen & West, 1963, pp. vii-xlviii.

Nettheim, Garth. "The Relevance of International Law." In *Aborigines & the Law,* ed. by Peter Hanks and Bryan Keon-Cohen. Sydney: George Allen & Unwin, 1984, pp. 50–73.

Palfreeman, A. C. "The White Australia Policy." In *Racism: The Australian Experience—A Study of Race Prejudice in Australia,* ed. by F[rank] S. Stevens. Volume 1: Prejudice and Xenophobia. Sydney: Australia and New Zealand Book Company, 1971, pp. 136–44.

Passi, Dave. "From Pagan to Christian Priesthood." In *The Gospel is Not Western: Black Theologies from the Southwest Pacific,* ed. by Garry W. Trompf. Maryknoll, N.Y.: Orbis Books, 1987, pp. 45–48.

Pattel-Gray, Anne. "The Text of the Land Rights Plenary." In *PCR Information: Between Two Worlds: Report of a WCC Team Visit to Aboriginal Communities in Australia,* ed. by Jean Sindab. Geneva: World Council of Churches, Programme to Combat Racism, 1991, pp. 81–97.

Pattel-Gray, Anne. "The Australian Education System Contributes to Racism." In *Aboriginal Studies: A National Priority,* ed. by Damien Coghlan, Rhoda Craven and Nigel Parbury. Sydney: Aboriginal Studies Association, 1992, Vol. 2, pp. 355–65.

Pattel-Gray, Anne. "Aboriginal People, Multiculturalism and Immigration." In *Immigration,* ed. by Catherine Hannon. Sydney: Australian Catholic Social Justice Council, 1998 (forthcoming).

Pattel-Gray, Anne. "Dreaming: An Aboriginal Interpretation of the Bible." In *Text & Experience: Toward a Cultural Exegesis of the Bible,* ed. by Daniel Smith-Christopher. Sheffield: Sheffield Academic Press, 1996, pp. 228–42.

Pattel-Gray, Anne. "One Mob, One Land: Australian Aboriginals Die Fighting for Land Rights." In *PCR Information: Women Under Racism and Casteism—Global Gathering,* ed. by Marilia Schuller. Geneva: World Council of Churches, Programme to Combat Racism, 1994c.

Pearson, Noel. "204 Years of Invisible Title: From the Most Vehement Denial of a People's Rights to Land to a Most Cautious and Belated Recognition." In *Mabo: A Judicial Revolution-The Aboriginal Land Rights Decision and Its Impact on Australian Law,* ed. by Margaret A. Stephenson and Suri Ratnapala. Brisbane: University of Queensland Press, 1993, pp. 75–95.

Phillip, Arthur. "Phillip's Views on the Conduct of the Expedition and the Treatment of Convicts." In *Historical Records of New South Wales,* Vol. I, Part II—Phillip 1783–1892. Sydney: Charles Potter, Government Printer, 1892, p. 53.

Roberts, Frank. "Being an Aboriginal in Australian Society." In *Racism in Australia: Tasks for General and Christian Education—Report of Conference at Southport, Queensland, November 19–24, 1971.* Melbourne: Australian Council of Churches, Division of Christian Education, 1971, pp. 19–20.

Robinson, G. A. "Narrative of Mr. G. A. Robinson." In *Thirty-three Years in Tasmania and Victoria,* by G. T. Lloyd. London: T. and W. Boone, 1962.

Rowan, Cynthia B. "Aboriginal Spirituality: A Sense of Belonging." In *Aboriginal Spirituality: Past, Present, Future,* ed. by Anne Pattel-Gray. Melbourne: HarperCollins*Religious,* 1996, pp. 11–21.

Rowley, C[harles] D. "Foreword." In *The Other Side of the Frontier: Aboriginal Resistance to the European Invasion of Australia,* by Henry Reynolds. Melbourne: Penguin Books, 1982, pp. vii-viii.

Sindab, Jean. "Strategy Group Workshop: Religion." In *Program Guide: The First National People of Color Environmental Leadership Summit, The Washington Court on Capitol Hill, Washington, D.C., October 24–27, 1991,* by Commission for Racial

Justice, United Church of Christ. Washington, D.C.: Commission for Racial Justice, United Church of Christ, 1991, pp. 42–44.

Spivey, Charles. "Australian White Racism." In *Racism in Australia: Tasks for General and Christian Education—Report of Conference at Southport, Queensland, November 19–24, 1971.* Melbourne: Australian Council of Churches, Division of Christian Education, 1971, pp. 17–18.

Spykerboer, Hendrik. "Politics in the Pulpit." In *Worship in the Wide Red Land,* ed. by Douglas Galbraith. Melbourne: Uniting Church Press, 1985, pp. 79–82.

Stanner, W. E. H. "Religion, Totemism and Symbolism." In *Aboriginal Man in Australia: Essays in Honour of Emeritus Professor A. P. Elkin,* ed. by Ronald M. Berndt, and Cathrine H. Berndt. Sydney: Angus & Robertson, 1965, pp. 219–20.

Stevens, F[rank] S. "Parliamentary Attitudes to Aboriginal Affairs." In *Racism: The Australian Experience—A Study of Race Prejudice in Australia,* ed. by F[rank] S. Stevens. Volume 2: Black Versus White. Sydney: Australia and New Zealand Book Company, 1971, pp. 110–49.

Swain, Tony. "The Ghost of Space: Reflections on Warlpiri Christian Iconography and Ritual." In *Aboriginal Australians and Christian Missions: Ethnographic and Historical Studies,* ed. by Tony Swain and Deborah Bird Rose. Adelaide: Australian Association for the Study of Religion, 1988, pp. 452–69.

Tatz, Colin. "Education and Land Rights: Australian and South African Ideologies" [Paper presented to 43rd Australia and New Zealand Association for the Advancement of Science Conference, Brisbane]. In *Themes for a Change,* by Colin Tatz. n.p.: Abschol, [1971], pp. 1–11.

Trigger, David S. "Christianity, Domination and Resistance in Colonial Social Relations: The Case of Doomadgee, Northwest Queensland." In *Aboriginal Australians and Christian Missions: Ethnographic and Historical Studies,* ed. by Tony Swain and Deborah Bird Rose. Adelaide: Australian Association for the Study of Religion, 1988, pp. 213–35.

Uhr, Marie Louise. "Introduction." In *Changing Women, Changing Church,* ed. by Marie Louise Uhr. Sydney: Millenium Books, 1992, pp. 9–21.

Uniting Church in Australia. "Covenanting Statement." In *Reports to the Seventh Assembly, July, 1994,* by the Uniting Church in Australia. Sydney: Uniting Church in Australia, 1994, pp. 50–51.

Waters, John W. "Who Was Hagar?" In *Stony the Road We Trod: African American Biblical Interpretation,* ed. by Cain Hope Felder. Minneapolis: Fortress Press, 1991, pp. 187–205.

Whitlam, E. Gough. "State Rights Versus Human Rights." In *Martung Upah: Black and White Australians Seeking Partnership,* ed. by Anne Pattel-Gray. Melbourne: HarperCollins*Religious,* 1996, pp. 57–66.

Willis, Sabine. "Introduction." In *Women, Faith and Fetes: Essays in the History of Women and the Church in Australia,* ed. by Sabine Willis. Melbourne: Dove Communications/Australian Council of Churches (N.S.W.), 1977, pp. 9–18.

Yarwood, A. T. "Attitudes Toward Non-European Migrants." In *Racism: The Australian Experience—A Study of Race Prejudice in Australia,* ed. by F[rank] S. Stevens. Volume 1: Prejudice and Xenophobia. Sydney: Australia and New Zealand Book Company, 1971, pp. 145–55.

Yunupingu, Djungadjunga, and Yunupingu, Dhanggal. "Mungulk Dhalatj—A Calm Wisdom." In *Aboriginal Spirituality: Past, Present, Future,* ed. by Anne Pattel-Gray. Melbourne: HarperCollins*Religious,* 1996, pp. 94–98.

Articles

Aboriginal Affairs. "The Meaning of Mapoon." *On Aboriginal Affairs* 11 (February-June 1964): 2–5.

Adelaide Advertiser. "Push for Migrant Policy Approval." *Adelaide Advertiser,* 11 August 1988.

Age. "Landmark Ruling on Land Rights." *Age,* 4 June 1992, p. 10.

Alcorn, Gay. "Born To Lose." *Time,* 11 April 1994a, pp. 46–47, 49–51.

Alcorn, Gay. "Something to Build Upon." *Time,* 11 April 1994b, p. 48.

Alcorn, Gay. "NT Land Claim Hits Labor." *Sydney Morning Herald,* 4 June 1994a, p. 5.

Alcorn, Gay. "Election Deepens Racial Divide in NT Politics." *Sydney Morning Herald,* 6 June 1994b, p. 5.

Amjad-Ali, Charles. "The Future of Mission: A Subversive Memory of Jesus." *International Review of Mission* 79,315 (July 1990): 345–57.

"Anti-Racism Policy." *Duran Duran [Newsletter of the Aboriginal Education Council]* (May 1992): 4–6.

Armitage, Catherine. "Dawn of Dreamtime Awakening May Be Set in Stone." *Sydney Morning Herald,* 30 July 1992, p. 5.

"Assembly, Aboriginals, RC Relations, JPIC on WCC Agenda." *Ecumenical Press Service* 57,12 (1–5 April 1990): 4.11.

Atkinson, J. "Violence in Aboriginal Australia: Colonisation and Its Impact on Gender." *Aboriginal and Islander Health Care Worker Journal* 14,1 (1990): 2; 14,2 (1990): 3.

Atkinson, Judy. "Violence Against Aboriginal Women: Reconstitution of Community Law—the Way Forward." *Aboriginal Law Bulletin* 2,46 (October 1990): 6–9.

Austin, Greg, and AAP. "Aborigines Claim Old Parliament House as Embassy." *Sydney Morning Herald,* 28 January 1992, p. 3.

"Australia: Uniting Church Denies TV Report on Drug Kava." *Ecumenical Press Service* 57,11 (26–31 March 1990): 3.100.

Australian. "Racism Rebuke Over Casey." *Australian,* 18 May 1989, p. 2.

Australian. "Aborigines 'Skeptical' About Racism Reform." *Australian,* 6 March 1992b, p. 3.

Australian. "Blacks Decry Outbreak of Racism." *Australian,* 6 March 1992a, p. 1.

Australian. "Mr Perron's Land Rights Rhetoric." *Australian,* 16 May 1994, p. 8.

Australian Film Commission. "Aboriginal & Torres Strait Islander Employment Scheme Launched for Film & TV Industries." *AFC News* No. 119, September 1993, p. 1.

Australian Jewish News [AJN]. "Racist Cabbie Loses Licence." *Australian Jewish News,* 18 September 1992, p. 1.

Australian Mining Industry Council [AMIC]. "Native Title and Australia's Future." *Sydney Morning Herald,* 11 December 1993: 16.

"Australia's Largest Church." *Christian Century* 104,35 (November 25, 1987): 1057.

"Australia's Nuclear Connections: Uranium, Reactors, Facilities, Bases." Carlton South, Victoria: Pax Christi Australia, 1984.

Bailey, E. K. "The Anatomy of a Dream." *Princeton Seminary Bulletin* New Series 13,3 (November 1992): 311–19.

Banks, David. "Time for Full Debate on Immigration" [Editorial]. *Daily Telegraph Mirror,* 22 January 1991, p. 10.

Barnett, David. "Why I Am Right (Interview with John Howard)." *Bulletin,* 6 September 1988, p. 159.

Barrett, David B. "Annual Statistical Table on Global Mission: 1993." *International Bulletin of Missionary Research* (January 1993): 22–23.

Beale, Bob. "Outspoken Analyst Admits Stone Age Quip 'Frivolous.'" *Sydney Morning Herald,* 15 June 1993, p. 7.

Beatson, Jim. "European Dreaming." *The Bulletin* (12 November 1991), p. 37.

Beckett, Jeremy. "Aboriginality, Citizenship and Nation State." *Social Analysis* No. 24 (December 1988): 3–18.

Behrendt, Larissa, and Walsh, Stephen. "From Cairns to the Courtroom." *Polemic* 2,3 (1991), pp. 161–65.

Beier, U., and Johnson, Colin. "The Aboriginal Novelist Who Found Buddha." *Quadrant* (September 1985): 69–75.

Berndt, Ronald M. "Surviving Influence of Mission Contact in the Daly River, Northern Territory of Australia." *Neue Zeitschrift für Missionswissenschaft* 8 (1952): 1–20.

Best, Bruce. "Australia's Bicentenary: Who Counts?" *Christianity and Crisis* 48,17 (21 November 1988): 417–18.

Bevis, Stephen. [Untitled Letter to the Editor]. *Sydney Morning Herald,* 11 July 1992, p. 20.

Binnie, Craig; Ballantine, Derek; Champness, Boyd; and, Alberici, Emma. "Street Fury Over Yothu Ban." *Herald-Sun,* 6 March 1992, pp. 1–2.

Bishop, Karin. "Swearing-at-Police Law May Go." *Sydney Morning Herald,* 7 March 1992, p. 2.

Blainey, Geoffrey. "Race and Debate." *BIPR Bulletin* 11 (April 1994): 34–37.

Blunden, Verge. "Court Upholds Right to Native Title." *Sydney Morning Herald,* 4 June 1992, p. 3.

Bone, Pamela. "Human Rights Meeting a 'Sham.'" *Sydney Morning Herald,* 23 June 1993, p. 15.

Bonner, Peter. "Ranger Spills its Guts." *Aboriginal Law Bulletin* 2,42 (February 1990): 12–13.

Brady, Veronica. "Drums Throb for the Last Stand of the Palefaces." *Sydney Morning Herald,* 4 November 1993, p. 13.

Brennan, Frank. "Succeeding in a White Society (Address to Twelfth Annual Conference, Aboriginal & Islander Catholic Council, Rockhampton, 9 January 1985)." *Nelen Yubu* No. 23 (Winter 1985): 20–29.

Brennan, Frank. "Land Rights in 1985 and Beyond." *Nelen Yubu* 24 (Spring 1986): 24–28.

Brennan, Frank. "Waiting for the Resolution." *Australian Quarterly* 61,2 (Winter 1989): 242–50.

Brennan, Frank. "The Mabo Case and *Terra Nullius.*" *Uniya Occasional Paper Number 34.* Sydney: Uniya, [1992c], 20 pp.

Brennan, Frank. "2001: A Race Odyssey—A Target Date for Reconciliation." *Sydney Morning Herald,* 5 June 1992d, p. 13.

Brennan, Frank. "The Indigenous Year." *Uniya* (Autumn 1993a): 1.

Brennan, Frank. "Mabo: A Fair Deal But Not a Special Measure." *Uniya* (Summer 1993b): 7.

Brennan, Frank. "The Native Title Act." *Uniya* (Autumn 1994): 5.

Brolly, Mark. "The First Australians [Black & White History]." *One World* No. 156 (June 1990): 4–5.

Brown, John. "Racism, Migration and Land Rights." *UC National News Network (Supplement)* ([1984]), pp. 1–4.

Brown, John. "Property as Compensation." *Insights* 4,3 (April 1994): 2–3.

Brown, Malcolm. "States Blames for High Jail Rate." *Sydney Morning Herald*, 1 March 1994, p. 6.

Brown, Malcolm, and Burton, Tom. "No Excuses: Police Training Chief." *Sydney Morning Herald*, 6 March 1992, p. 2.

Brownley, Morris. "Racism in the West." *National Aboriginal Conference Newsletter* 1,3 (June 1981): 34–35.

Bryant, Val. "Documentation: Recovery of Spirituality." *International Review of Mission* 68,269 (January 1979): 62–63.

Burchill, Tony. "Imprisonment of Aborigines is 23 Times that of Whites: Study." *The Age*, 19 November 1987, p. 17.

Bureau of Immigration and Population Research. "The Yothu Yindi Family." *BIPR Bulletin* 11 (April 1994): 26–27.

Cannon, Katie G. "Doing Womanist Ethics." *Women in a Changing World* 27 (May 1989): 16–17.

Carnley, P. F., *et al.* "A Call for Reconciliation (Perth 1993)." *Faith and Freedom* 2,3 (September 1993): 3.

"Case Studies: Australia: Noonkanbah, Western Australia." *Land Rights for Indigenous People*. PCR Information, No. 16. Geneva: World Council of Churches, Programme to Combat Racism, March 1983, pp. 33–39.

Casimir, Jon, and Holmes, Peter. "Bandman from the Land." *Sydney Morning Herald*, 31 January 1992, p. 2s. [About Mandawuy Yunupingu of *Yothu Yindi*.]

Chamberlin, Paul. "Aborigines Quit House as Four Arrested." *Sydney Morning Herald*, 29 January 1992, p. 3.

Chamberlin, Paul. "Land Rights Campaigner Dies as Island Fight Goes On." *Sydney Morning Herald*, 1 February 1992, p. 21.

Chamberlin, Paul. "Aborigines Well Behind in Battle for Jobs: Study." *Sydney Morning Herald*, 26 February 1992, p. 4.

Chamberlin, Paul. "$150m Promised for Black Justice." *Sydney Morning Herald*, 11 March 1992, p. 3.

Chamberlin, Paul. "Minister in New Insult to Aborigines." *Sydney Morning Herald*, 14 March 1992a, p. 1.

Chamberlin, Paul. "Make This the Time to Change: Keating." *Sydney Morning Herald*, 14 March 1992b, p. 6.

Chamberlin, Paul. "It's Still Uphill on the Long, Hard Road." *Sydney Morning Herald*, 14 March 1992c, p. 7.

Chamberlin, Paul. "NT Anger as Tickner Blocks $20m Dam." *Sydney Morning Herald*, 21 March 1992, p. 6.

Chamberlin, Paul. "Call to Increase Jobs by 56,000." *Sydney Morning Herald,* 24 March 1992, p. 8.

Chamberlin, Paul. "States Attacked on Aboriginal Funding." *Sydney Morning Herald,* 28 March 1992, p. 24.

Chamberlin, Paul. "Fischer in Land Rights Outburst." *Sydney Morning Herald,* 13 January 1993, p. 1.

Chamberlin, Paul. "Fischer Stands by Comments on Japanese." *Sydney Morning Herald,* 14 January 1993, p. 12.

Chamberlin, Paul. "Fischer Fears Aboriginal Claim Will Cost Jobs." *Sydney Morning Herald,* 20 February 1993, p. 9.

Chamberlin, Paul. "Mining Chief Lashes Mabo." *Sydney Morning Herald,* 1 July 1993, pp. 1, 2.

Chamberlin, Paul. "Keating Caves In on Wik Claim." *Sydney Morning Herald,* 21 August 1993, pp. 1, 4.

Chamberlin, Paul. "Taps for Blacks a Waste: Fischer." *Sydney Morning Herald,* 28 April 1994, p. 3.

Chamberlin, Paul. "One Report That Should Not Be Watered Down." *Sydney Morning Herald,* 31 May 1994, p. 13.

Chamberlin, Paul. "Bureaucrats Blamed for Black Deaths Inaction." *Sydney Morning Herald,* 28 June 1994, p. 13.

Champion, Max. "The Uniting Church and Aborigines: A Laudable Commitment Spoiled by Paternalism and Misplaced Blame." *Stirring Times* (June 1994): 2–4.

"The Children WA Wants Locked Up" [Editorial]. *Sydney Morning Herald,* 10 February 1992, p. 12.

Clark, Manning. "What Do We Want To Be and What Should We Believe?" *Bulletin,* 26 January 1988, pp. 10–11.

Cole-Adams, Kate. "Land Returned After a 100-Year Wait." *Sydney Morning Herald,* 23 October 1992, p. 5.

Cole-Adams, Kate. "Help at Hand on the Long Road Home." *Sydney Morning Herald,* 13 January 1993, p. 13.

Cole-Adams, Kate. "For the Top End, Culture Is the Route to Asia." *Sydney Morning Herald,* 2 February 1993, p. 29.

Collins, Jock. "Do We Want Blainey's Australia?" *Australian Quarterly* (Autumn/Winter 1985): 55.

Cooper, Revel. "To Regain Our Pride." *Aboriginal Quarterly* 1,3 (1968): 20.

Cornwall, Deborah. "Harassment Increasing, Say Aborigines." *Sydney Morning Herald,* 6 March 1992, p. 2.

Cornwall, Deborah. "Redfern Police Support Boss." *Sydney Morning Herald,* 13 March 1992, p. 4.

Cornwall, Deborah. "Officers on Video Regret Perverse Humour." *Sydney Morning Herald,* 14 March 1992a, p. 7.

Cornwall, Deborah. "Police Transfer Threat Averted." *Sydney Morning Herald,* 14 March 1992b, p. 7.

Cornwall, Deborah. "Lauer Attacks Racism Survey." *Sydney Morning Herald,* 19 March 1992, pp. 1, 4.

Cornwall, Deborah. "Inspector Must Cop It Sweet Over TV's Peek." *Sydney Morning Herald,* 21 March 1992, p. 6.

Cornwall, Deborah; Garcia, Luis M.; and, Bishop, Karin. "Police Shake-Up Over TV Racism." *Sydney Morning Herald,* 6 March 1992, pp. 1–2.

Cornwall, Deborah, and Hewett, Tony. "Blacks Call for Inquiry into Raids." *Sydney Morning Herald,* 9 February 1990, p. 2.

Coultan, Mark. "Budget Deficit $1.5bn, Says Labor." *Sydney Morning Herald,* 28 March 1992, p. 7.

Coultan, Mark. "State Deficit to Hit $1.5bn—Greiner." *Sydney Morning Herald,* 8 April 1992, p. 3.

Coultan, Mark. "'Coons' Jibe Haunts New Nationals Leader." *Sydney Morning Herald,* 21 May 1993, p. 1.

Coultan, Mark, and Seccombe, Mike. "Fischer's Mabo Outburst: 'Not Even a Wheeled Cart.'" *Sydney Morning Herald,* 21 June 1993, p. 1.

Covenanting 6 (February 1994):1–10.

Cunneen, Chris. "Aboriginal Juveniles in Custody." *Currents in Criminal Justice* 3,2 (November 1991): 204–18.

Cunneen, Chris. "Aboriginal Imprisonment During and Since the Royal Commission into Aboriginal Deaths in Custody." *Current Issues in Criminal Justice* 3,3 (March 1992): 351–55. [Study reported on ABC-TV News, Sydney, 17 February 1992.]

Daily Telegraph Mirror [DTM]. "An Outrage Unites Our Leaders" [Editorial]. *Daily Telegraph Mirror,* 14 March 1992, p. 18.

DTM. "200 Prison Officers Have Records: Report." *Daily Telegraph Mirror,* 1 October 1993, p. 24.

Delvecchio, Julie. "Australians Wise Up to their Indigenous Elders." *Sydney Morning Herald,* 17 December 1993, p. 11.

Devine, Miranda. "A Race Against Time." *Daily Telegraph Mirror,* 14 March 1992, pp. 17–18.

Dhurrkay, [R]. "Through Struggle for Justice to Liberation: Story and Reflections of an Aboriginal Person." *International Review of Mission* 79,315 (July 1990): 285–87.

Diamond, Jared. "In Black and White." *Natural History* (October 1988): 8, 10, 12, 14.

Dias, Zwinglio Mota. "The Resurrection of the Church Amidst the People: Some Ecclesiological Implications from the San Antonio Section II Report." *International Review of Mission* 79,315 (July 1990): 339–44.

Dicker, Gordon. "Mission in Australia: A New Perspective." *International Review of Mission* 68,269 (January 1979): 36–43.

Dodson, Michael. "Rights, Not Benevolence." *Sydney Morning Herald,* 25 November 1993, p. 13.

Dodson, Pat. "Where Are We After 200 Years of Colonisation?" *Land Rights News* 2,6 (January 1988): 5–6.

Dodson, Pat. "The Land Our Mother, The Church Our Mother." *Compass Theology Review* 22 (1988): 1.

Dodson, Pat. "Statehood for NT." *Aboriginal Law Bulletin* 2,39 (August 1989): 14–16.

Doobov, Alan. "Racism in School Books." *Australian Quarterly* 46,2 (June 1974): 90–99.

Dow, Steve. "Black Vocalist Sings the Blues Over Colour Bar." *Australian,* 6 March 1992, p. 3.

Durrah, Betty J. "Triple Jeopardy: The Impact of Race, Sex and Class on Women of Color." *Church & Society* 82,1 (September/October 1991): 44–54.

Dussel, Enrique. "The Kingdom of God and the Poor." *International Review of Mission* 68,270 (April 1979): 115–30.

Easterbrook, Margaret. "Morgan Hits Joint Aboriginal Policy." *Age,* 30 January 1993, p. 16.

Elkin, A[dolphus] P. "Native Education, with Special Reference to the Australian Aborigines." *Oceania* 7,4 (June 1937): 459–500.

Elkin, A[dolphus] P. "Aboriginal Evidence and Justice in North Australia." *Oceania* 17 (1947): 173–210.

Elkin, A[dolphus] P. "The Aborigines: Australians." *Minister's Bulletin* 41 (June 1958): 1–4.

Elkin, A[dolphus] P. "Elements of Australian Aboriginal Philosophy." *Oceania* 40,2 (December 1969): 85–98.

Ellis, Stephen. "ANZ: Out of Africa and into Asia-Pacific." *Sydney Morning Herald,* 3 November 1992, p. 27.

Ellis, Stephen. "Joss Westpac's $7.8m Man." *Sydney Morning Herald,* 27 January 1993, p. 29.

Engel, Frank G. "Colonial Wrongs Need to be Rectified (Land Rights—1)." *Sydney Morning Herald,* 7 July 1965, p. 2.

Engel, Frank G. "National Honour at Stake (Land Rights—2)." *Sydney Morning Herald,* 8 July 1965, p. 2.

Engel, Frank G. "Australia: Its Aborigines and Its Mission Boards." *International Review of Mission* 59,235 (July 1970): 296–303.

Engel, Frank G. "We Bin Go Way-ee—The Aborigines: Outcasts in Their Own Country." *International Review of Mission* 68,269 (January 1979): 45–55.

Ethnos. "Ethnic Journalists Have Racism Role: Ray Martin Speaks Out on Racism and Journalism." *Ethnos* 85 (June 1992), p. 9.

Ewing, Tania. "Thalidomide Seen As Cancer Fighter." *Sydney Morning Herald,* 26 April 1994, p. 4.

Felder, Cain Hope. "Afrocentrism, the Bible, and the Politics of Difference." *Princeton Seminary Bulletin,* New Series 15,2 (1994): 131–42.

Fernández-Calienes, Raúl. "Racism: A Long Way to Go." *Ministry: Journal of Continuing Education* 4,2 (Summer 1993/94): 19–21; N.B. "Errata." *Ministry: Journal of Continuing Education* 4,3 (Fall 1994): 3.

Ferrari Justine, and Irving, Mark. "Dispute Over Number of Jailed Blacks." *Australian,* 19 February 1992, p. 4.

"First Aboriginal Woman as UCA Minister." *Nungalinya News* 65 (December 1991): 1, 4–5.

Foley, Gary. "The Barriers to a White/Black Accord." *Sydney Morning Herald,* 21 July 1993, p. 15.

Forman, David. "The Implications of the Mabo Decision." *Business Review Weekly,* 7 August 1992, pp. 48–49.

Freedman, Bernard. "RSL Will Fight Racial Vilification Laws." *Australian Jewish News,* 9 October 1992, p. 1.

Garcia, Luis M. "Greiner Willing to Use Race Law." *Sydney Morning Herald,* 14 March 1992, p. 6.

Garcia, Luis M. "Race Law Is Not Working, Govt Told." *Sydney Morning Herald,* 12 June 1992, p. 7.

Glover, Richard. "Language Law May Be a Joke—But Not for Blacks." *Sydney Morning Herald,* 7 March 1992, p. 2.

Glover, Richard. "Time to Share the Blame." *Sydney Morning Herald,* 6 March 1992, pp. 1–2.

Gondarra, Djiniyini. "Aboriginal and Christian—Developing an Indigenous Theology." *National Outlook* (February 1984): 11–12.

Gondarra, Djiniyini. "Aboriginal Christianity: Based on Indigenous Theology." *CTC Bulletin: Bulletin of the Commission on Theological Concerns, Christian Conference of Asia* 6,2–3 (January-April 1986): 36–39.

Gondarra, Djiniyini. "Father You Gave Us the Dreaming." *Compass Theology Review* 22 (1988): 6–8.

Gondarra, Djiniyini. "Djiniyini Gondarra: The Aboriginal Church." *Women in a Changing World* 28 (December 1989): 10–11.

Graham, Angus [Commissioner of N.S.W. Department of Corrective Services]. "Self-Control a Key to Black Freedom" [Letter to the Editor]. *Australian,* 20 February 1992, p. 8.

Graham, Duncan. "States Warned on Blacks in Custody." *Sydney Morning Herald,* 25 May 1994, p. 6.

Grant-Taylor, Tony. "Media Racist on Blacks: Hill." *Sydney Morning Herald,* 17 February 1993, p. 5.

Grattan, Michelle. "Police Crossword 'Racist.'" *Age,* 25 March 1992, p. 5.

Gunn, Michelle. "Church Acknowledges 'Deliberate Racism.'" *Australian,* 12 November 1992, p. 2.

Gurr, Ted Robert, and Scarritt, James R. "Minorities Rights at Risk: A Global Survey." *Human Rights Quarterly* 11,3 (1989): 375–405.

Hammond, Jane. "Aboriginal Outcry at Raid in No-Go Zone." *Australian,* 9 February 1990, p. 3.

Harris, Charles. "Reconciliation or Whitewash." *Koori Mail,* No. 15, 6 November 1991, p. 17.

Harris, Charles. "Indigenisation Key to Our Survival-Rev Harris." *Koori Mail,* No. 16, 18 December 1991, p. 11.

Harris, Charles. "Thinking for Ourselves: Rev Harris." *Koori Mail,* No. 17, 15 January 1992, pp. 18, 20.

Harris, Charles. "Western Christianity a Curse to Indigenous Spirituality." *Koori Mail,* No. 20, 26 February 1992, p. 19.

Harris, John. "Justice, Aboriginal Land Rights, and the Use and Abuse of Scripture." *Zadok Perspectives* No. 18 (June 1987): 3–10.

Hartcher, Peter. "Watch on Keating's Aboriginal Stance." *Sydney Morning Herald,* 27 March 1992, p. 11.

Hartcher, Peter. "Govt Asks: Who Owns Australia?" *Sydney Morning Herald,* 16 October 1992, p. 1.

Hartcher, Peter. "Govt to Act on 'Native Titles.'" *Sydney Morning Herald,* 28 October 1992, p. 1.

Harvey, Adam. "More Blacks End Up in Jail." *Sydney Morning Herald,* 28 February 1994, pp. 1, 6.

Harvey, Sandra. "'Racist' Raid Leaves Shiralee With a Burden of Fear." *Sydney Morning Herald,* 26 April 1994, p. 3.

Henderson, Gerard. "Lunar Right Rising." *Good Weekend,* 9 April 1994, pp. 70–74, 77–78, 81.

Henderson, Gregor. "Mapoon Celebrates Mission Centenary." *Insights* 2,2 (March 1992), p. 8.

Henry, Sarah. "Beyond the Fringe." *Good Weekend,* 9 April 1994, pp. 73–74, 77–78.

Herald-Sun. "In Black and White" [Editorial]. *Herald-Sun,* 6 March 1992, p. 12.

Hewett, Tony. "Provocation Feard at Black March." *Sydney Morning Herald,* 23 December 1987, p. 5.

Hewett, Tony. "Aboriginal Year of Mourning Dawns." *Sydney Morning Herald,* 25 January 1988a, p. 2.

Hewett, Tony. "Aborigines Add City March to Demonstrations." *Sydney Morning Herald,* 25 January 1988b, p. 7.

Hewett, Tony. "Black Leaders Row Over Redfern Protest March." *Sydney Morning Herald,* 26 January 1988, p. 2.

Hewett, Tony. "Jail Blacks Only as a Last Resort." *Sydney Morning Herald,* 9 May 1991, p. 1.

Hewett, Tony, and Monaghan, David. "Blacks Boo Royal Pair on Barge." *Sydney Morning Herald,* 27 January 1988, p. 2.

Hextall, Bruce. "Coronation Hill to Make or Break Industry: Miners." *Sydney Morning Herald,* 4 May 1991, pp. 34, 32.

Hextall, Bruce. "Coronation Hill Ban Challenged." *Sydney Morning Herald,* 11 February 1992, p. 24.

Hextall, Bruce. "South Africans Head This Way." *Sydney Morning Herald,* 23 October 1992, pp. 23, 26.

Hextall, Bruce. "Mining in Good Shape: AMIC." *Sydney Morning Herald,* 8 December 1994, p. 43.

Hirst, John. "Policy Dreamtime." *Weekend Australian,* 9–10 July 1994, p. 25.

Houweling, Suzanne, and AAP. "Aussie Whites as Gubbaoriginals." *Sunday Telegraph,* 17 January 1993, p. 27.

Howard, John. "Feelings of Guilt in the Racist Rantings." *Sunday Telegraph,* 17 January 1993, p. 47.

Howe, A. "Aboriginal Women in Custody: A Footnote to the Royal Commission." *Aboriginal Law Bulletin* 2,44 (1988): 30.

Howlett, Christine, and McDonald, David. "Australian Deaths in Custody 1992–93." *Deaths in Custody Australia* 6 (February 1994): 1–14.

Human Rights Australia [HRA]. "Toomelah Report." *Human Rights Australia* 1,2 (September 1988): 1.

Humphries, David. "WA to Get Tough on Juveniles." *Sydney Morning Herald,* 6 February 1992, p. 6.

Humphries, David. "Canberra May Stop WA Youth Crime Law." *Sydney Morning Herald,* 8 February 1992, p. 6.

"Indigenous Nations in Global Crisis [Darwin Declaration]." *Link* No. 4 (1989): 1, 6.

"Indigenous Populations Fund." *Human Rights Newsletter* 2,3 (October 1989): 4.

Insights. "1993—A New Journey." *Insights* 3,1 (February 1993): 9.

Insights. "Thursdays in Black." *Insights* 3,4 (May 1993): 3.

Insights. "It's Official: Wear Black to Beat Violence." *Insights* 3,6 (July 1993): 12.

Insights. "Aboriginal Communities 'Worse than Asia's Poorest.'" *Insights* 4,6 (July 1994): 5.

Jackson, Hugh. "'White Man Got No Dreaming': Religious Feeling in Australian History." *The Journal of Religious History* 15,1 (1988): 9.

Jeffrey, Paul. "No More Violence: Quechua Indian Women Speak Out." *Horizons* (July/August 1989): 6–7. [About Indigenous Quechua Women in northern Ecuador]

Jenkins, David. "Asians Have Come to Stay, Researchers Say." *Sydney Morning Herald,* 15 February 1992, p. 7.

Jones, Angela. "Down Under: Recovering an Aboriginal Hope." *Other Side* 24:7 (September 1988): 10–12.

Jones, Barry. "Modern Australians—Part 1: The Best and Worst." *Bulletin,* 8 January 1991, pp. 27–29.

Jones, Mark, and Bilkey, Marianne. "Police Tests 'Show Racism.'" *Herald-Sun,* 6 March 1992, p. 27.

Jones, E. Stanley. "Some Observations by a Visitor." *Minister's Bulletin* 2 (January 1943), pp. 5–6.

Journey. "UC Assembly Apologises to Mapoon people." *Journey* (September 1990), p. 16.

Jurman, Elizabeth. "Ombudsman's Aboriginal Report Wrong, Fahey Says." *Sydney Morning Herald,* 18 November 1992, p. 7.

Keirl, Steve. "Racism in Schools: Believing the Problem Can Be Solved." *Koori Mail,* 12 August 1992, p. 24.

Kirby, Michael. "What is a 'People.'" *Centre for Conflict Resolution Newsletter* 1,3 (November 1992): 7.

Kirk, Sigrid. "Asians See Racism in Immigrants Debate." *Sydney Morning Herald,* 28 January 1992, p. 4.

Kirk, Sigrid. "Blame Taken Off Migrants." *Sydney Morning Herald,* 11 February 1992, p. 5.

Kirk, Sigrid. "Hawke to Blame for Racism, Says Whitlam. *Sydney Morning Herald,* 11 March 1992, p. 5.

Kirk, Sigrid. "Families Say Apology Not Accepted." *Sydney Morning Herald,* 14 March 1992, p. 7.

Knight, Jeff. "[Cartoon: Racism Against Mandawuy Yunupingu]." *Sydney Morning Herald,* 6 March 1992, p. 10.

Kocken, Keith. [Untitled Letter to the Editor]. *Sydney Morning Herald,* 11 July 1992, p. 20.

Koori Mail [KM]. "Reconciliation Council Named." *Koori Mail* No. 16, 18 December 1991, p. 1.

KM. "Bombing, Vandalism Campaign Against Community Centre." *Koori Mail,* No. 19, 12 February 1992a, p. 4.

KM. "Harry's Ordination a First for Uniting Church in NSW." *Koori Mail,* No. 19, 12 February 1992b, p. 8. [About the Rev. Harry Walker's ordination.]

KM. "Two-Year Review for Harsh WA Juvenile Crime Laws." *Koori Mail,* No. 19, 12 February 1992c, p. 3.

KM. "25% Increase in Black Prision Population." *Koori Mail,* No. 20, 26 February 1992, p. 1.

KM. "An Historic Ordination that Began with a Corroboree." *Koori Mail*, No. 21, 11 March 1992a, pp. 12–13. [About the Rev. Harry Walker's ordination.]

KM. "A Time for Grown-Ups to Renew Acquaintances, Kids to Have Fun." *Koori Mail*, No. 21, 11 March 1992b, p. 16. [About the Rev. Harry Walker's ordination.]

KM. "Tickner Halts $20M Dam." *Koori Mail*, No. 22, 25 March 1992a, p. 1.

KM. "Teaching Survival Skills." *Koori Mail*, No. 22, 25 March 1992b, p. 11.

KM. "Dam Row Swamped in Accusations of Racial Slurs, Misinformation." *Koori Mail*, No. 22, 25 March 1992c, p. 14.

KM. "Mission Land to be Returned to Kimberley Aborigines." *Koori Mail*, No. 23, 8 April 1992, p. 7.

KM. "PM Admits Wrongs." *Koori Mail*, No. 41, 16 December 1992a, p. 1.

KM. "Indigenous People Treated as 'Cultural Curiosities.'" *Koori Mail*, No. 41, 16 December 1992, p. 3.

KM. "Lawrence to Address ATSIC Over Control of Health Funds." *Koori Mail*, No. 74, 20 April 1994, p. 1.

KM. "Health Budget Gutted." *Koori Mail*, No. 75, 4 May 1994, p. 1.

KM. "Funding a Huge Fraud: Foley." *Koori Mail*, No. 84, 7 September 1994, p. 3.

Lagan, Bernard. "Court Accused of Racism Over Referendum Call." *Sydney Morning Herald*, 12 July 1993, p. 3.

Lagan, Bernard. "Mabo's Legal Warrior." *Sydney Morning Herald*, 9 October 1993, p. 3A. [re: Noel Pearson.]

Land Rights News [LRN]. "Major Churches United on Aboriginal Rights." *Land Rights News* 2,6 (January 1988), p. 16.

LRN. "Kalkadoon Spirit." *Land Rights News* 2,7 (March 1988), p. 3.

LRN. "The Barunga Statement." *Land Rights News* 2,9 (July 1988), p. 26.

LRN. "60,000 Years is a Long, Long Time." *Land Rights News* 2,19 (June 1990), p. 11.

LRN. "Jawoyn Want Guratba in National Park." *Land Rights News* 2,21 (April 1991), p. 5.

Langsam, David. "Britain Falls to Burnum Burnum's Invasion Farce." *Sydney Morning Herald*, 27 January 1988, p. 2.

Lenthall, Kate. "Minorco Seeks Olympic Dam Role." *Sydney Morning Herald*, 9 November 1992, p. 30.

Leser, David. "The Aussie Pearl." *Bulletin*, 18 February 1992, p. 41.

Lyons, John. "Knight Moves." *Good Weekend: The Sydney Morning Herald Magazine*, 19 September 1992, pp. 12–13, 15–17, 19.

Lyons, John. "Redfern Wakes to Broken Doors and 128 Police." *Sydney Morning Herald* (9 February 1990), p. 2

Mackay, Hugh. "Seven Roads to Change." *Bulletin*, 8 January 1991, p. 36

MacKinolty, Chips. "Policeman Assaulted Aborigines, Claims MP." *Sydney Morning Herald*, 25 March 1992, p. 7.

MacKinolty, Chips. "NT Govt Chided on Access to Dam Site." *Sydney Morning Herald*, 27 March 1992, p. 4.

MacKinolty, Chips. "A Label that Mandawuy Will Wear with Pride." *Sydney Morning Herald*, 27 January 1993, p. 3.

Maley, Karen. "Duffy Joins Critics of WA Legislation." *Sydney Morning Herald*, 7 February 1992, p. 7.

Mansell, Michael. "Treaty Proposal: Aboriginal Sovereignty." *Aboriginal Law Bulletin* 2,37 (April 1989): 4–6.

Matthews, Philip. [Editorial]. *Faith and Freedom* 2,3 (September 1993): 2.

May, John D'Arcy. "Human Rights as Land Rights in the Pacific." *Pacifica* 6,1 (February 1993): 61–80.

McCarthy, Phillip. "Aust Envoy's Warning on New UN Role." *Sydney Morning Herald*, 10 March 1992, p. 10.

McGillion, Chris. "The Rich and Marginalised Seek Out the Poor and Marginalised." *Sydney Morning Herald*, 21 September 1993, p. 11.

Meade, Amanda. "Motion a Blow to Aboriginal Rights: Tickner." *Sydney Morning Herald*, 14 September 1992, p. 6.

Meade, Amanda. "Forget the Guilt, Fight Injustice: Hayden." *Sydney Morning Herald*, 22 September 1993, p. 8.

Meade, Amanda, and MacKinolty, Chips. "Uproar as NT Dam is Stopped." *Sydney Morning Herald*, 18 May 1992, p. 1.

Meade, Amanda, and Mostyn, Suzanne. "Ruling Aids Accord with Aborigines, says PM." *Sydney Morning Herald*, 5 June 1992, p. 9.

Miles, Bruce. "Resolve Land Title Uncertainties Speedily" [Letter to the Editor]. *Sydney Morning Herald*, 24 October 1992, p. 26.

Miller, Roy. "Migrant Fodder for the Dole Queue." *Sunday Telegraph*, 19 January 1992, p. 48.

Millett, Michael. "Coalition Is Racist: Keating." *Sydney Morning Herald*, 22 January 1991, p. 3.

Millett, Michael. "One Boatful May Be Just the Start." *Sydney Morning Herald*, 23 January 1992, p. 1.

Millett, Michael. "Race Slur: PM Won't Back Down." *Sydney Morning Herald*, 24 January 1992, p. 1.

Moffat, Donald K. "How Little Our Australian Indigenous People Have Featured in Discussions in *Church Scene*." *Church Scene* 4, 731 (17 December 1993): 4.

Monaghan, David. "Angel of Black Death." *Bulletin*, 12 November 1991, pp. 31–34, 38.

Morris, Linda. "Racism Rife in Police Force: Report." *Sydney Morning Herald*, 4 July 1994, p. 6.

Morrison, James, and Ferrari, Justine. "'Cowardly and Racist' Police Parody Sparks Outrage." *Australian*, 13 March 1992, p. 1.

Moss, Irene. "Racist Australia?" *RMS News* (August 1992): 5.

Mostyn, Suzanne. "Protest Over Newborn Baby Being Put in Care." *Sydney Morning Herald*, 13 March 1992, p. 4.

Muller, Denis. "Treatment of Aborigines Leads to Conflict: Survey." *Sydney Morning Herald*, 20 March 1992, p. 7.

Muller, Denis. "Most Say We Care About Aborigines." *Sydney Morning Herald*, 21 March 1992, p. 6.

Muller, Denis. "Two Out of Three Support a Treaty." *Sydney Morning Herald*, 24 March 1992, p. 8.

Mulvaney, D. J. "The Australian Aborigines 1606–1929: Opinion and Fieldwork." *Historical Studies of Australia and New Zealand* 8,30 (1958): 131–51; 8,31: 297–314.

Mydans, Seth. "Australia, at 200, Suffers an Attack of Self-Doubt." *New York Times,* 25 January 1988, p. 2.

Mydans, Seth. "Aborigines Cast a Cloud Over Australia's Party." *New York Times,* 26 January 1988, p. 2.

Nailon, Brigida. "Culture in a Crucible." *Nelen Yubu* No. 55 (1993): 13–29.

National Missionary Council of Australia. "A Day of Remembrance of the Aborigines." *Minister's Bulletin* 5 (January 1944): 5.

Nettheim, Garth. "Mabo and Beyond." *Alumni Papers* (Winter 1994): 1, 3.

New York Times. "Verbatim: Whose Party?: Gerry Hand." *New York Times,* 31 January 1988a, sec. 4, p. 3.

New York Times. "Verbatim: Whose Party?: Malcolm Fraser." *New York Times,* 31 January 1988b, sec. 4, p. 3.

New York Times. "Improve Aborigine Life, U.N. Urges Australia." *New York Times,* 7 August 1988, p. 15.

North Queensland Land Council. "Documentation: The North Queensland Land Council." *International Review of Mission* 68,269 (January 1979): 63–64.

Northern Land Council [NLC]. "NLC Boss Says Yothu Yindi are Cultural Heroes." Media Release, Northern Land Council, Casuarina, N.T., 5 March 1992.

Nungalinya News. "First Aboriginal Woman as UCA Minister," *Nungalinya News* 65 (December 1991): 1, 4–5.

O'Grady, Desmond. "Vatican Opens Aboriginal Collection to Researcher." *Sydney Morning Herald,* 22 September 1986, p. 31.

O'Grady, Desmond, and Jopson, Debra. "Aboriginal Religion to be Focus of Synod." *Sydney Morning Herald,* 25 July 1994, p. 3.

O'Neill, Elizabeth, and Chance, Bernadette. "The Indigenous Year: In Retrospect." *Uniya* (Summer 1993): 6.

Ormerod, Neil. "A Worrying 'Judaeo-Christian Mind-Set'" [Letter to the Editor]. *Sydney Morning Herald,* 11 July 1992, p. 20.

"Pacific Issues Spotlighted as Reformed Council Meets." *Ecumenical Press Service* 56,30 (1–5 September 1989): 6.

Parker, Kirstie. "120 Take to Streets to Protest Racist Attacks." *Koori Mail,* 25 March 1992a, p. 3.

Parker, Kirstie. "Apology for Aboriginal Parents in Kuranda." *Koori Mail,* No. 22, 25 March 1992b, pp. 15, 21.

Parker, Kirstie. "400 Leave Palm Island." *Koori Mail,* No. 23, 8 April 1992, p. 7.

Partamian, Hermine. "Thursdays in Black." *National Outlook* 15,5 (July 1993): 12–13.

Pattel, Jean. "Down, But Not Out!" *In God's Image* 13,2 (Summer 1994): 80–86.

Pattel-Gray, Anne. "Come Holy Spirit—Renew Your Whole Creation." *Youth* 14,2 (June 1990): 6.

Pattel-Gray, Anne. "1993: Year of the Half Hearted?" *Ministry* 3,3 (Autumn 1993): 19–21.

Pattel-Gray, Anne. "Australian Churches and Native Title." *In Unity* 41,1 (May 1994): 3.

Pattel-Gray, Anne, and Trompf, Garry W. "Styles of Australian Aboriginal and Melanesian Theology." *International Review of Mission* 82,326 (April 1993): 167–88.

Patten, J. T. "Calling All Aborigines: Straight Talk." *Australian Abo Call: The Voice of the Aborigines* 3 (June 1938): 1.

Pearson, George. "We Only Ask for an Opportunity." *Minister's Bulletin* No. 47 (June 1964), p. 3.

Penman, David. "Australia: A Multicultural Society? Cultural Pluralism—A Pattern for the Future." *International Review of Mission* 68,269 (January 1979): 4–11.

Perlez, Jane. "Life in Sun, Unclouded by Apartheid's Turmoil." *New York Times,* 27 January 1987, p. 4.

Pilkington, Edward. "Outback Battle of David and Goliah." *Guardian Weekly,* 20 March 1994, p. 25.

Pittock, Barrie. "Compare Overseas." *Crux* 68,3 (June-July 1965), p. 5.

Potter, Philip. "Mission as Reconciliation in the Power of the Spirit: Impulses from Canberra." *International Review of Mission* 80,319/320 (July/October 1991):305–14.

Powell, Sian. "Racist Reports Attacked." *Sydney Morning Herald,* 9 July 1992, p. 11.

Prior, Neale. "S. Africa Takes High Road: Anglo Chief." *Sydney Morning Herald,* 16 March 1994, p. 45.

"Problems Caused by Racism: A Response." *Church & Society* 82,1 (September/October 1991): 67–85.

"Racism's still rampant: Bush." *Sunday Telegraph,* 19 January 1992, p. 30.

Radcliffe-Brown, A. R. "Notes on the Social Organization of Australian Tribes." *Journal of the Royal Anthropological Institute* 48 (1918): 222–23.

Radcliffe-Brown, A. R. "The Social Organization of Australian Tribes." *Oceania* 1,1 (1930–31): 34–63; 1,2: 206–46; 1,3: 322–41; 1,4: 426–56.

Rebera, Ranjini. "Black on Thursdays." *Women's Link* (1993a): 11.

Rebera, Ranjini. "Every Thursday . . ." *Voices from the Silence* 4,1A (Spring 1993b): 11.

Reynolds, Henry. "Aborigines and European Social Hierarchy." *Aboriginal History* 7,1 (1983): 124–33.

Reynolds, Henry. "Black-White Watershed." *Australian,* 6–7 June 1992, p. 2.

Reynolds, Henry. "West Australian Justice Won't Come from Within." *Sydney Morning Herald,* 22 November 1993, p. 13.

Riley, Mark. "National Disgrace: The Ugly Faces of Australian Racism." *Sydney Morning Herald,* 13 March 1992, pp. 1, 4.

Rivett, Kenneth. "Slashing Migrant Intake Poses Problems." *Sydney Morning Herald,* 25 January 1992, p. 24.

Roberts, Greg. "Mission Impossible." *Sydney Morning Herald,* 15 February 1992, sec. 2, p. 33.

Roberts, Greg. "Case Raises Doubts on Graziers' Rights." *Sydney Morning Herald,* 28 October 1992, p. 7.

Roberts, R., Jones, R., and Smith, M. "Thermoluminescence Dating of a 50,000-year-old Human Occupation Site in Northern Australia." *Nature* 345 (10 May 1990): 153–60.

Rosendale, George. "Aboriginal Myths and Customs: Matrix for Gospel Preaching." *Lutheran Theological Journal* 22,3 (December 1988): 117–22.

Salter, Owen. "Djiniyini's Singing People: A Talk with Aboriginal Theologian Djiniyini Gondarra." *On Being* 16,5 (June 1989), pp. 8–10.

Sanders, Douglas. "The UN Working Group on Indigenous Populations." *Human Rights Quarterly* 11,3 (1989): 406–33.

Scott, Sophie. "Families Wept During Video." *Daily Telegraph Mirror,* 14 March 1992, p. 5.

Secord, Walt. "Startling Findings of Racism Survey." *Australian Jewish News,* 29 January 1993, p. 1.

See. "Racism Entrenched Even in Churches." *See,* 276, September 1991, p. 13.

Seligmann, C. G. "An Australian Bible Story." *Man* 16 (1916): 43–44.

Sider, Daphne, and Wright, Tony. "Black Australian of Year Insult, Says Jones." *Sydney Morning Herald,* 28 January 1993, p. 7.

Signy, Helen. "Title a Moral Right: Church." *Sydney Morning Herald,* 19 June 1993, p. 11.

Signy, Helen. "Blacks Worst Off, Forum Told." *Sydney Morning Herald,* 11 April 1994, p. 6.

"Sin claudicaciones ni pragmatismos." *Madres de Plaza de Mayo* 9,99 (julio 1993): 22–23.

Sindab, Jean. "Women Under Racism: An Agenda for Justice, Peace and the Integrity of Creation." *PCR Information* 26 (1990):7–24.

Skulley, Mark. "Yothu Singer May Seek Action on Bar Rebuff." *Sydney Morning Herald,* 6 March 1992, p. 2.

Society of St Vincent de Paul Australia. "The Society and Mabo." *Record* 77,3 (Spring 1993): 2.

Spalding, Ian. "No Genteel Silence." *Crux* 68,3 (June-July 1965), p. 3.

Sproull, Richard. "Mabo Fears 'Send Mine Investors Elsewhere.'" *Australian,* 28 February 1994, p. 19.

Stanner, W. E. H. "On Aboriginal Religion." *Oceania* 30,2&4 (1959); 31,2&4 (1960); 32,2 (1961); 33,4 (1963); 34,1 (1963).

Stephens, Tony. "Sharing the Pain . . . and Hope." *Sydney Morning Herald,* 14 March 1992, p. 6.

Stephens, Tony. "A Celebration of Our Hidden History." *Sydney Morning Herald,* 27 January 1993, p. 3.

Stevens, Matthew. "Moody's Backs Miners Despite Mabo Question." *Australian,* 31 January 1994, pp. 17, 24.

Stewart, Alison. "Racists, Radicals or Victims of Prejudice?" *Bulletin,* 9 August 1988, p. 40.

Sun-Herald. "Migrant Row Shadow On Our Heritage." *Sun-Herald,* 26 January 1992, p. 26.

Suter, Keith D. "Australian Aborigines and the Church." *Christian Century* 105,31 (October 26, 1988): 954–56.

Swain, Tony. "Belonging to the Emperor: An Australian Perspective on the Encyclopedia of Religion." *Australian Religion Studies Review* 2,3 (1989a): 91–99.

Swain, Tony. "Dreaming, Whites and the Australian Landscape: Some Popular Misconceptions." *Journal of Religion* 15,3 (1989b): 345–50.

Swain, Tony. "Love and Other Bullets." *Religious Traditions* 13 (1990): 68–87.

Swain, Tony. "A New Sky Hero from a Conquered Land." *History of Religions* 29,3 (1990): 195–232.

Sydney Morning Herald [SMH]. "Reflections on Nation-Building" [Editorial]. *Sydney Morning Herald,* 26 January 1988, p. 12.

SMH. "Aborigines Less Likely to Drink, Study Finds." *Sydney Morning Herald*, 26 March 1988, p. 3.

SMH. "Radio Has Racist Links, Senate Told." *Sydney Morning Herald*, 3 March 1989, p. 2.

SMH. "Redfern Raid Angers Aborigines." *Sydney Morning Herald*, 9 February 1990, p. 1.

SMH. "Avoiding the Racism Debate" [Editorial]. *Sydney Morning Herald*, 23 January 1992, p. 12.

SMH. "How the People of the Top End Will Commemorate their Blackest Day." *Sydney Morning Herald*, 25 January 1992, p. 20.

SMH. "Govt Get Tough on Refugees." *Sydney Morning Herald*, 13 February 1992, p. 1.

SMH. "Realism in Redfern" [Editorial]. *Sydney Morning Herald*, 6 March 1992, p. 12.

SMH. "Record Industry Awards List." *Sydney Morning Herald*, 7 March 1992, p. 47.

SMH. "The Refugees and the Rorters" [Editorial]. *Sydney Morning Herald*, 14 February 1992, p. 10.

SMH. "No Bar to Top Award Win for Yothu Yindi." *Sydney Morning Herald*, 7 March 1992, p. 5.

SMH. "Lessons from Black Deaths" [Editorial]. *Sydney Morning Herald*, 13 March 1992, p. 8.

SMH. "Blacks in One Australia" [Editorial]. *Sydney Morning Herald*, 14 March 1992, p. 20.

SMH. "Aboriginal Leader Harassed." *Sydney Morning Herald*, 16 March 1992, p. 3.

SMH. "Tickner May Use Powers to Stop Dam." *Sydney Morning Herald*, 17 March 1992, p. 2.

SMH. "Guard Plan for No-Go Area." *Sydney Morning Herald*, 21 March 1992, p. 6.

SMH. "Black Rights and White Guilt" [Editorial]. *Sydney Morning Herald*, 5 June 1992, p. 12.

SMH. "Australian Response to Black Deaths Criticised." *Sydney Morning Herald*, 11 July 1992, p. 9.

SMH. "Fischer and Aborigines" [Editorial]. *Sydney Morning Herald*, 14 January 1993, p. 10.

SMH. "A Label to be Proud of." *Sydney Morning Herald*, 27 January 1993, p. 1.

SMH. "End Uncertainty on Land Rights" [Editorial]. *Sydney Morning Herald*, 29 April 1993, p. 12.

SMH. "Silly Money Talk About Mabo" [Editorial]. *Sydney Morning Herald*, 15 June 1993, p. 16.

SMH. "Tim Fischer's Mabo Mayhem" [Editorial]. *Sydney Morning Herald*, 22 June 1993, p. 12.

SMH. "Bones Point to 'Myth' of Nomadic Life." *Sydney Morning Herald*, 22 September 1993, p. 9.

SMH. "Brisbane Alert to Further Violence." *Sydney Morning Herald*, 9 November 1993, p. 6.

SMH. "Politics of Aboriginal Votes." *Sydney Morning Herald*, 1 January 1994, p. 6.

SMH. "It's Black Friday." *Sydney Morning Herald*, 7 January 1994, p. 1

SMH. "$100m 'Vital for Black Health.'" *Sydney Morning Herald*, 12 March 1994, p. 4.

SMH. "Nats' Call for Aboriginal Test 'Scientific Racism.'" *Sydney Morning Herald*, 8 April 1994, p. 2.

SMH. "Warning on Outbreaks of Racism." *Sydney Morning Herald,* 16 April 1994, p. 8.

SMH. "The Point of Multiculturalism." *Sydney Morning Herald,* 8 June 1994, p. 14.

SMH. "Black Funding a 'Gigantic Fraud.'" *Sydney Morning Herald,* 27 August 1994, p. 11.

SMH. "The Aboriginal Gravy Train." *Sydney Morning Herald,* 31 August 1994, p. 18.

Tatz, Colin M. "Blueprint for Action." *Aboriginal Quarterly* 1,2 [Supplement] (1968): 12.

Tickner, Liz. "Tenure Like Land Claims: Council." *West Australian,* 1 February 1993, p. 8.

Tinker, George. "The Full Circle of Liberation: An American Indian Theology of Place." *Sojourners* (October 1992): 12, 14–17.

"The TOP Interview—Charles Harris." *Trinity Occassional Papers* 2,1 (January 1983): 13–16.

Totaro, Paola. "Reconsider Changes to Syllabus: Chadwick." *Sydney Morning Herald,* 11 July 1992, p. 2.

Treadgold, M. L. "Intercensal Change in Aboriginal Incomes, 1976–1986." *Australian Bulletin of Labour* 14,4 (1988): 592–609.

Treadgold, Tim. "Land Rights Versus Miners." *Business Review Weekly,* 7 August 1992, pp. 46–51.

Trompf, Garry W. Review of *Through Aboriginal Eyes,* by Anne Pattel-Gray. *Insights* 2,6 (July 1992):39.

Turner, Otis. "The Web of Institutional Racism." *Church & Society* 82,1 (September/October 1991): 13–27.

Ungunmerr-Baumann, Miriam Rose, and Brennan, Frank. "Reverencing the Earth in the Australian Dreaming." *The Way* (January 1989): 38–45.

Van Drimmelen, Rob. "Household Rules." *One World* 197 (July 1994): 7–9.

Van Klaveren, John. "New Bridge Links Black and White." *Crosslight* 9 (October 1992): 18–19.

Verrender, Ian. "Minorco Buys Share in Olympic Dam." *Sydney Morning Herald,* 5 November 1992, p. 31.

Viscovich, Mary. "Australia: the Bar is Colored." *Herald-Sun,* 6 March 1992, p. 12.

Voumard, Sonya. "Diversity Rejected in Poll." *Sydney Morning Herald,* 7 June 1994, p. 2.

Walker, Jamie. "Death in Custody Files Dumped." *Australian,* 25 August 1989, p. 2.

Waller, Kevin. "Redfern Cops It Sweet." *Sydney Morning Herald,* 7 March 1992, pp. 1–2.

Wallis, Jim. "For Us, Everything Is Life: Aboriginal Spirituality in Australia [Interview with the Rev. Djiniyini Gondarra]." *Sojourners* (May 1992), pp. 24–27.

Watego, Cliff. "Institutional Racism: Economics and Education." *Black Voices* 5,1 (December 1989): 9–21.

Waterford, Jack. "The Judge Who Reversed an Ancient Wrong." *Canberra Times,* 14 June 1992, p. 8. [Re: "The Mabo Case and *Terra Nullius."*]

Watson, Duncan S. "Thinking Theologically in Australia." *Trinity Occasional Papers* 9,1 (September 1990), pp. 20–27.

Weems, Renita J. "Do You See What I See? Diversity in Interpretation." *Church & Society* 82,1 (September/October 1991): 28–43.

Whitlam, [E.] Gough. "The Blight of Racism Needs Action." *National Outlook* 14,6 (August 1992): 22–25.

Williams, Graham. "The Urgent Needs of Aborigines." *Sydney Morning Herald,* National Health, 18 May 1994, p. 4s.

Williams, Graham, and Chamberlain, Paul. "NSW Jails the Most Aborigines." *Sydney Morning Herald,* 18 February 1992, p. 3.

Williams, Ramon. "40,000 March for Justice and Peace." *Journey* (March 1988): 4.

Wockner, Cindy, and Buckley, Amanda. "$200m Bid to Beat Racism." *Daily Telegraph Mirror,* 14 March 1992, pp. 1, 4.

Woods, James. "Jail Tragedy Continues." *Courier Mail* 15 July 1993, pp. 1–2.

Wootten, Hal. "99 Reasons . . . The Royal Commission into Black Deaths in Custody." *Polemic* 2,3 (1991), pp. 124–28.

Wootten, Hal. "Resolve Land Title Uncertainties Speedily" [Letter to the Editor]. *Sydney Morning Herald,* 24 October 1992, p. 26.

Wootten, Hal. "Self-Determination the Best Way Out of a Black Picture." *Australian,* 15 April 1993, p. 9.

Wootten, Hal. "Share of Australia for all Australians." *Sydney Morning Herald,* 8 November 1993, p. 11.

"World Conference on Human Rights: Vienna, Austria, June 1993." *United Nations Review* (January-February & March-April 1993): 2–3.

Zdenkowski, George. "Draconian Laws Make Scapegoats of Youth." *Sydney Morning Herald,* 12 February 1992, p. 15.

Zuel, Bernard. "Churches Examine Mabo." *Sydney Morning Herald,* 6 December 1993, p. 7.

Articles—Special Series

Bentley, Peter. "Australia Focus (I)—Church Profiles (1)." *Ecumenical Press Service* 56,14 (16–30 April 1989): 55.

Bentley, Peter. "Australia Focus (II)—Church Profiles (2)." *Ecumenical Press Service* 56,21 (1–5 July 1989): 12.

Best, Bruce. "Australia (III)—Multicultural—or not?" *One World* No. 153 (March 1990): 4–5.

Matheson, Alan. "Australia Focus (III)—Church and Discrimination." *Ecumenical Press Service* 56,22 (6–20 July 1989): 24.

Matheson, Alan. "Australia Focus (IV)—Eastern Christianity, QUARTOs." *Ecumenical Press Service* 56,30 (1–5 September 1989): 30.

Periodicals—Special Issues

Act Against Racism: A Guide for Advocates. Sydney: Human Rights and Equal Opportunity Commission, [1992], 18 pp.

Art Monthly Australia. n.d. [Issue: "Aboriginal Art in the Public Eye."]

Celebrate. 6,4 (August 1987): 1–16; Blackburn, Vic.: Collins Dove, 1987, 16 pp. [Issue: "We Belong to the Land."]

PCR Information. Geneva: World Council of Churches, Programme to Combat Racism:

No. 4/1979: Racism and the Unity of the Church.

No. 5–9/1980: Churches Responding to Racism in the 1980s.

No. 13/1981: NGO Conference on Indigenous People and the Land.

No. 15/1982: Organized, Racial Violence: New Trends; edited by Anwar Barkat.

No. 16/1983: Land Rights for Indigenous People.

No. 19/1985: Women Under Racism.

No. 26/1990: Racial Justice: An Issue of Justice, Peace and the Integrity of Creation.

No. 28/1991: Between Two Worlds: Report of a WCC Team Visit to Aboriginal Communities in Australia.

Race & Class 29,3 (Winter 1988). [Issue: Special Feature—"The Australian Bicentenary."]

Castles, Stephen; Cope, Bill; Kalantzis, Mary; Morrissey, Michael. "The Bicentenary and the Failure of Australian Nationalism."

Pettman, Jan. "Learning About Power and Powerlessness: Aborigines and White Australia's Bicentenary."

Grabosky, Peter N. "Aboriginal Deaths in Custody: the Case of John Pat."

Report on the Americas 25,4 (February 1992). [Issue: "The Black Americas 1492–1992."]

Social Alternatives.

   2,2 (August 1981). [Issue: "Black Alternatives in Australia."]

   7,1 (April 1988). [Issue: "Black Alternatives on the Bicentenial."]

   8,1 (April 1989). [Issue: "Black Assessment of the Bicentenial."]

   13,2 (August 1994). [Issue: "Mabo."]

Social Analysis No. 24 (December 1988): 1–88. [Issue: "Aborigines and the State in Australia."]

12 to 25. 2,2 (1992): 1–50. [Issue: "Building Bridges."]

Zadok Institute for Christianity and Society—Series 1 Papers

Frazer, Jill, and Preston, Noel. *Aborigines and Australian Christianity.* Parts I, II. Dickinson, A.C.T.: Zadok Centre Papers, 1987.

Harris, John. "Christianity and Aboriginal Australians—."

— Part 1: "The Earliest Christian Missions." No. S35 (December 1987): 1–12.

— Part 2: "Indifference and Compassion in the Mid-19th Century." No. S36 (March 1988): 1–12.

— Part 3: "Dispossession and Despair: The Missionary Response at the End of the 19th Century." No. S37 ([June 1988]): 1–12.

— Part 4: "Justice and Injustice at the Beginning of the 20th Century." No. S38 (September 1988): 1–12.

Periodicals—General

Aboriginal and Islander Health Worker Journal
Aboriginal Employment and Education News (Dept. of Employment, Educ. & Training)
Aboriginal Health Worker
Aboriginal History
Aboriginal Law Bulletin (University of New South Wales, Aboriginal Law Centre)
Aboriginal Quarterly
Adelaide Advertiser
AFC News (Australian Film Commission)
Alumni Papers (University of New South Wales)
Age
Archaeology & Physical Anthropology in Oceania (University of Sydney)

ATSIC News (Aboriginal and Torres Strait Islander Commission)
Australian
Australian Abo Call: The Voice of the Aborigines
Australian Aboriginal Studies: Journal of the Australian Institute of Aboriginal Studies
Australian Law Reports
Australian Law Journal Reports
Australian Quarterly
AWD Australia-New South Wales Newsletter (Action for World Development)
BIPR Bulletin (Bureau of Immigration and Population Research)
Black Issues in Higher Education
Black Voices (James Cook University of North Queensland)
Boomali Newsletter (Boomali Aboriginal Artists Co-operative)
Bulletin
Business Review Weekly
Canberra Times
CDBR Newsletter (National Committee to Defend Black Rights)
Centre for Conflict Resolution Newsletter (Macquarie University)
Commonwealth Law Reports (High Court of Australia)
Current Issues in Criminal Justice (University of Sydney, Institute of Criminology)
Daily Telegraph Mirror
Duran Duran (Aboriginal Education Council-N.S.W.)
Elimatta (Manly Warringah Aboriginal Support Group)
Environment
Ethnos (Ethnic Affairs Commission of N.S.W.)
Federal Law Reports (Federal Court of Australia)
Good Weekend
Herald-Sun
Human Rights Australia (Human Rights & Equal Opportunity Commission)
Human Rights Newsletter
Human Rights Quarterly
Insight (Australian Department of Foreign Affairs and Trade)
Journal of the Aboriginal Studies Association (Aboriginal Studies Association)
Koori Mail
Land, Rights, Laws: Issues of Native Title (AIATSIS Native Titles Research Unit)
Land Rights News (of the Northern and Central Land Councils)
National Aboriginal Conference Newsletter (National Aboriginal Conference)
National Geographic
National Social Justice Report (Australian Democrats)
Natural History
Native Title Newsletter (AIATSIS Native Titles Research Unit)
New York Times
Newcastle Aboriginal Support Group Newsletter (Newcastle Aboriginal Support Grp.)
1993 International Year of the World's Indigenous People Newsletter
Oceania (University of Sydney)

On Aboriginal Affairs (Aboriginal Affairs)
Polemic (University of Sydney Law Society)
Poverty Watch (Fair Share)
Quadrant
Race & Class (Institute of Race Relations, London)
Sage: A Scholarly Journal on Black Women (Sage Women's Educational Press)
Social Alternatives
Social Analysis
Sun-Herald
Sunday Telegraph
Sydney Morning Herald
Third World Network Features
Time
Townsville Bulletin
United Nations Review (United Nations Association)
Walking Together (Council for Aboriginal Reconciliation)
West Australian
Woomera (NSW Aboriginal Land Council Newsletter)
Yeperenye Yeye (Yipirinya School)

Periodicals—Church-Related

A-Gender (Uniting Church in Australia)
ACFOA News (Australian Council for Overseas Aid)
AECN (Asian Ecumenical Communicators Network)
Assembly Update (Uniting Church in Australia)
Auburn Report on Church and Society
Australian Friend (Religious Society of Friends (Quakers) in Australia)
Australian Religion Studies Review (Australian Assoc. for the Study of Religions)
Biblical Interpretation
Catholic Weekly (Roman Catholic Church)
CCA News (Christian Conference of Asia)
Celebrate (Roman Catholic Church)
Christian Book Newsletter
Christianity and Crisis
Church & Society (Presbyterian Church U.S.A.)
Church & State
Church Scene (Anglican Church of Australia)
Commission on Faith and Order Newsletter (Australian Council of Churches)
Compass Theology Review
Conference News (Conference of Churches of Western Australia)
Covenanting (Uniting Church in Australia)
Crosslight (Uniting Church in Australia-Victoria and Tasmania)
CTC Bulletin (Christian Conference of Asia)
Echoes: Justice, Peace and Creation News (World Council of Churches)

EcuDialogue (Presbyterian Church U.S.A., Ecumenical and Interfaith Relations)
EcuLink (National Council of the Churches of Christ in the U.S.A.)
Ecumenical & Interfaith Jottings (Australian Catholic Bishops Conference)
Ecumenical Press Service (World Council of Churches)
Ecumenical Review (World Council of Churches)
Ecustics (Conference of Churches in Aotearoa New Zealand)
Ernabella Newsletter (Australian Presbyterian Board of Missions)
Ethnic Link (Uniting Church in Australia)
Faith and Freedom
History of Religions
Horizons (Presbyterian Church U.S.A., Presbyterian Women)
In God's Image (Asian Women's Resource Centre for Culture and Theology)
In Unity (Australian Council of Churches/National Council of Churches in Australia)
Insights (Uniting Church in Australia, N.S.W.)
Interchange (Uniting Church in Australia, N.S.W., Board for Social Responsibility)
Interface (Uniting Church in Australia, N.S.W., Board of Education)
Intermesh (Scaffolding)
International Review of Mission (World Council of Churches)
Journal of Black Theology in South Africa (Black Theology Project)
Journal of Christian Education
Journal of Religion
Journal of Religious Education
Journal of the American Academy of Religion (American Academy of Religion)
Journal of the Interdenominational Theological Center (Interdenom. Theological Ctr.)
Journey (Uniting Church in Australia, Qld.)
Justice Jottings (Presbyterian Church U.S.A.)
Link (World Council of Churches, Programme to Combat Racism)
Message Stick (Uniting Aboriginal and Islander Christian Congress)
Minister's Bulletin (National Missionary Council of Australia)
Ministry (Uniting Church in Australia)
Missiology
Mission Probe (Uniting Church in Australia)
Naboth News
National Baptist (Baptist Union of Australia)
National Outlook
NATSICC News (National Aboriginal and Torres Strait Islander Catholic Council)
NCV Quarterly
Nelen Yubu (Roman Catholic Church)
Neue Zeitschrift für Missionswissenschaft
New Times (Uniting Church in Australia, S.A.)
A newsletter for Aboriginal salvationists in the Australia Southern Territory (Salvation Army)
Nungalinya News (Nungalinya Theological College)
Nungalinya Occassional Bulletins (Nungalinya Theological College)
One World (World Council of Churches)

Other Side

Pacific Journal of Theology (South Pacific Association of Theological Schools)

PCR Information (World Council of Churches, Programme to Combat Racism)

Presbyterian Life (Presbyterian Church in Australia)

Presbyterian Outlook (Presbyterian Church U.S.A.)

Presbyterian Survey (Presbyterian Church U.S.A.)

Princeton Seminary Bulletin (Princeton Theological Seminary)

Record (Society of St. Vincent de Paul, Australia)

Reformed World (World Alliance of Reformed Churches)

Religious Traditions (University of Sydney/McGill University)

RMS News (Refugee and Migrant Services, National Council of Churches in Australia)

See (Anglican Church of Australia, Dioceses of Melbourne and Bendigo)

Sharing (N.S.W. Ecumenical Council)

Sojourners (Sojourners Community)

South Pacific Journal of Mission Studies (South Pacific Assoc. for Mission Studies)

Southern Cross (Anglican Church of Australia)

SR & J Network (Uniting Church in Australia)

Stirring Times

Trinity Occasional Papers (Trinity Theological College)

Uniya (Roman Catholic Church)

Walking Together (Roman Catholic Church, Sydney Archdiocese Justice and Peace)

Western Impact (Uniting Church in Australia, W.A.)

Wiradjuri Bawamarra (Wiradjuri Christian Development Ministries)

Women in a Changing World (World Council of Churches)

Youth (World Council of Churches)

Zadok Perspectives (Zadok Institute for Christianity and Society)

Educational Curricula—Series

Aboriginal Studies R–12: Guidelines for Teachers. Adelaide: Education Department of South Australia, 1988.

Home: Years R–3. Aboriginal Studies R–12. Adelaide: Education Department of South Australia, 1988.

Ourselves and Others: Years R–3. Aboriginal Studies R–12. Adelaide: Education Department of South Australia, 1988.

Thukeri: A Ngarrindjeri Dreaming Story: Years R–3. Aboriginal Studies R–12. Adelaide: Education Department of South Australia, 1988.

Urrakurli, Wakarla and Wildu: An Adnyamathanha Dreaming Story: Years R–3. Aboriginal Studies R–12. Adelaide: Education Department of South Australia, 1988.

Winda: A Narrunga Dreaming Story: Years R–3. Aboriginal Studies R–12. Adelaide: Education Department of South Australia, 1988.

Aboriginal Dreaming Stories: Years 3–4. Aboriginal Studies R–12. Adelaide: Education Department of South Australia, 1988, 32 pp.

The Dreaming and the Environment: Years 3–4. Aboriginal Studies R–12. Adelaide: Education Department of South Australia, 1988.

Aboriginal Lifestyles Before European Settlement: Years 5–7. Aboriginal Studies R–12. Adelaide: Education Department of South Australia, 1988.

Aboriginal People and Their Communities Today: Years 5–7. Aboriginal Studies R–12. Adelaide: Education Department of South Australia, 1988.

Dreaming Trails and Culture Contact: Years 5–7. Aboriginal Studies R–12. Adelaide: Education Department of South Australia, 1988, 40 pp.

The Pitjantjatjara People—Lifestyle and Family Relationships: Years 5–7. Aboriginal Studies R–12. Adelaide: Education Department of South Australia, 1988.

Educational Curricula—General

Australian Heritage Commission. *Special Aboriginal Places.* Canberra: Australian Government Publishing Service, 1991, 17 pp.

Australian Heritage Commission. *Special Historic Places* Canberra: Australian Government Publishing Service, 1991, 23 pp.

Australian Heritage Commission. *Special Natural Places.* Canberra: Australian Government Publishing Service, 1991, 12 pp.

Australian Heritage Commission. *National Estate for Kids.* Canberra: Australian Government Publishing Service, 1991.

Australian Heritage Commission. *National Estate for Primary Schools: Teacher's Guide—A Teaching Resource about Australia's Historic, Aboriginal and Natural Heritage Places.* Middle to Upper Primary [edition]. Canberra: Australian Government Publishing Service, 1991, 99 pp.

Media Releases

"ATSIC Acting Chairperson Calls for the Establishment of a *National Land Acquisition Fund.*" Media Release, Aboriginal and Torres Strait Islander Commission, Canberra, 10 December 1992, 2 pp.

"ATSIC Applauds Government Commitment to Improved Intergovernmental Relations in Aboriginal and Torres Strait Islander Affairs." Media Release, Aboriginal and Torres Strait Islander Commission, Canberra, 8 December 1992, 2 pp.

"ATSIC Chairperson Outlines Aboriginal Agenda for the Next Decade in a Major Speech to the United Nations." Media Release, Aboriginal and Torres Strait Islander Commission, Canberra, 10 December 1992, 2 pp.

"Australia: Towards a New Partnership—A Statement by the Executive Committee of the Australian Council of Churches Marking the International Year for the World's Indigenous Peoples." Media Release, Sydney, 10 December 1992, 2 pp.

"Commonwealth Action Planned for Indigenous Year." Media Release, Office of the Minister for Aboriginal and Torres Strait Islander Affairs, Canberra, 10 December 1992, 2 pp.

"Museums in Australia and Aboriginal and Torres Strait Islander Peoples: Major Policy Released Today." Media Release, Council of Australian Museum Associations, Sydney, N.S.W., 18 May 1993.

"NSW Aboriginal Police Policy Basis for a New Partnership, Says Tickner." Media Release, Office of the Minister for Aboriginal and Torres Strait Islander Affairs, Canberra, 8 December 1992, 2 pp.

Pyne, Chris, M.P. "Time to End Mabo Myths." Media Release, Office of the Member for Sturt, 19 May 1993, 1 p.

"Religious Leaders, Royal Commissioners, in Joint Mabo Call." Media Release, Australian Council of Churches, Sydney, N.S.W., 8 July 1993, 3 pp.

Roberton, Hugh S. "Commonwealth Gives Additional £1,000,000 Social Services for Australia's Aborigines. Media Release, Canberra, A.C.T., 10 July 1959, 2 pp.

Ruddock, Philip. "Transcript: Face the Press: Coalition Immigration and Ethnic Affairs Policy." Media Release, Office of Philip Ruddock, M.P., 4 September 1992, 11 pp.

"[Untitled]." News Release, Executive of the Australian Conference of Leaders of Religious Institutes, Sydney, 9 December 1992, 1 p.

"Wisdom in PM's Speech on Indigenous Year." Media Release, Office of the Minister for Aboriginal and Torres Strait Islander Affairs, Canberra, A.C.T., 10 December 1992, 2 pp.

Addresses—Published

Addresses to the United Nations Working Group on Indigenous Populations, Geneva [Switzerland], July 1992 by the Chairperson of ATSIC, Miss Lois O'Donoghue, CBE, AM and Commissioner for Torres Strait Mr George Mye, MBE. Canberra: Aboriginal and Torres Strait Islander Commission 1991, 18 pp.

O'Donoghue, Lois. *Immigration and Australia's Indigenous People: Address by the Chairperson of the Aboriginal and Torres Strait Islander Commission, Lois O'Donoghue, CBE, AM, Bureau of Immigration Research Conference, Melbourne, 15 November 1990.* Canberra: Aboriginal and Torres Strait Islander Commission 1990, 6 pp.

O'Donoghue, Lois. *Sir Robert Garran Oration: Speech by Miss Lois O'Donoghue, CBE, AM Chairperson of the Aboriginal and Torres Strait Islander Commission, Royal Australian Institute of Public Administration, 1991 National Conference, Darwin, N.T., 11 September 1991.* Canberra: Aboriginal and Torres Strait Islander Commission 1991, 15 pp.

Addresses—Unpublished

Amjad-Ali, Charles. "Global Perspectives." Keynote Address, *Living Under the Southern Cross,* University of Western Sydney-Hawkesbury, Richmond, N.S.W., 20 January 1993.

Bellear, Sol. Speech on the Occasion of the Australian Launch of the International Year for the World's Indigenous People. Redfern, N.S.W., 10 December 1992.

Byrne, Paul. "Report on Black Deaths in Custody." Australian Academy of Forensic Sciences, 122nd Plenary Scientific Session, November 1987.

Castles, Stephen. "Outline of Issues." Address delivered at the *Summit Meeting on Racism,* Ethnic Affairs Commission of New South Wales, 8 June 1989.

Clarke, Bernard A. "Towards the 21st Century—The Challenges of Mission." *From Mission to Church* Conference, Australian Council of Churches, Commission on Mission, Sydney, N.S.W., 27 August 1993.

Clarke, Geoff. Press Conference. World Council of Churches Seventh Assembly, Canberra, A.C.T., 8 February 1991.

Cribbs, Arthur. "Racism, Population and Sustainability [Panel]." United Church of Christ General Synod/Christian Church (Disciples of Christ) General Assembly, Pre-Assembly/Synod Seminar, St. Louis, Missouri, U.S.A., 15 July 1993.

Gilbert, Kevin. Address (at Aboriginal Tent). World Council of Churches Seventh Assembly, Canberra, A.C.T., 18 February 1991.

Gregorios, Metropolitan Paulos Mar. Official Response to the Address by the Prime Minister of Australia (the Hon. R. J. L. Hawke), World Council of Churches Seventh Assembly, Canberra, A.C.T., 8 February 1991.

Habgood, John (Archbishop of York, England, U.K.). "The Role of the Churches in the International Order." The Thomas Corbishley Lecture, n.p., England, United Kingdom, 9 October 1991.

Harris, Dorothy. "Introduction to Australia and Aboriginal Issues." Address, World Council of Churches Seventh Assembly, South-East Asia Pre-Assembly Regional Meeting, Dhyana Pura Training Center, Bali, Indonesia, 1–4 May 1990.

Hasluck, Paul, M.P. "New Hope for Old Australians." Address, Wesley Church, Melbourne, Victoria, (Sunday) 14 July 1957, 9 pp.

Hasluck, Paul, M.P. "Are Our Aborigines Neglected?" Address, P.S.A. Service, The Lyceum, Sydney, New South Wales, (Sunday) 12 July 1959, 7 pp.

Hasluck, Paul, M.P. "Some Problems of Assimilation." Address, Australian and New Zealand Association for the Advancement of Science, Section F, Perth, Western Australia, (Friday) 28 August 1959, 7 pp.

Hawke, The Hon. R. J. L. (Prime Minister of Australia). Welcoming Address, World Council of Churches Seventh Assembly, Canberra, A.C.T., 8 February 1991.

Keating, The Hon. Paul J. (Prime Minister of Australia). "Commonwealth Response to the Royal Commission into Aboriginal Deaths in Custody." Canberra, A.C.T., 24 June 1992.

Keating, The Hon. Paul J. (Prime Minister of Australia). "Australian Launch of the International Year for the World's Indigenous People." Redfern, N.S.W., 10 December 1992.

Kirby, Michael. "Religious Liberty in Multicultural Australia." Address to the International Religious Liberty Association, South Pacific Division, Pacific Congress, Suva, Fiji, 9 June 1993.

O'Donoghue, Lois. Speech to the United Nations General Assembly on the Occasion of the Launch of the International Year of the World's Indigenous People, New York, U.S.A., 10 December 1992.

Partington, Gary. "Why Aboriginal Studies Won't Stop Racism." Paper presented to the *Confronting Racism* Conference, University of Technology-Sydney, 9–11 December 1993.

Pattel-Gray, Anne. "Aboriginality and the Great White Flood." Plenary Address delivered at the 6th Annual Conference, Australian Association for the Study of Religion, Sydney, N.S.W., July 1991.

Pattel-Gray, Anne. "Australian Aboriginal People." *Minutes of the Forty-First Meeting, Central Committee of the World Council of Churches, Geneva, Switzerland, 25–30 March 1990*, World Council of Churches, Geneva, Switzerland, 25–30 March 1990.

Pattel-Gray, Anne. Official Response to the Address by the Prime Minister of Australia (the Hon. R. J. L. Hawke), World Council of Churches Seventh Assembly, Canberra, A.C.T., 8 February 1991.

Pattel-Gray, Anne. "Racism, Population and Sustainability [Panel]." United Church of Christ General Synod/Christian Church (Disciples of Christ) General Assembly, Pre-Assembly/Synod Seminar, St. Louis, Missouri, U.S.A., 15 July 1993.

Pattel-Gray, Anne. "Response: The Issues We Confront [by the Rev. Graham Paulson]." *From Mission to Church* Conference, Australian Council of Churches, Commission on Mission, Sydney, N.S.W., 27 August 1993.

Paulson, Graham A. "Aboriginal Perspectives." Keynote Address, *Living Under the Southern Cross,* University of Western Sydney-Hawkesbury, Richmond, N.S.W., 19 January 1993.

Paulson, Graham A. "The Issues We Confront." *From Mission to Church* Conference, Australian Council of Churches, Commission on Mission, Sydney, N.S.W., 27 August 1993.

Shoemaker, Adam. "The Politics of *Yothu Yindi.*" Paper presented to the *Contronting Racism* Conference, University of Technology-Sydney, 9–11 December 1993.

Stanner, W. E. H. ABC Boyer Lectures, 1968.

Watson, Maureen. "Stories." Aboriginal Spirituality: Past, Present, Future—National Conference on Aboriginal Spirituality and Perceptions of Christianity, Victor Harbour, South Australia, 2–6 August 1990.

Whitlam, Gough. Opening Address, *Survival '93,* La Perouse, N.S.W., 26 January 1993.

Audio-Visual Materials—Films

Aboriginal Australia. Canberra: Aboriginal and Torres Strait Islander Commission, 1989– [Series of documentaries, short films, advertisements, etc.].

Aboriginal Studies: Windows on Indigenous Australia. Adelaide: ABC and University of South Australia, 1993 [Series for Open Learning studies].

Always Was, Always Will Be. Melbourne: Australian Film Institute, 1989, 32 mins., colour videocassette VHS-PAL/NTSC; produced and directed by Robert Bropho, Martha Ansara, *et al.*

Cop It Sweet. Sydney: ABC-TV Documentaries, 1992; produced by Jenny Brockie; aired nationally on 5 March 1992.

Cry for Justice. Sydney: Aboriginal & Islander Commission of the Australian Council of Churches, 1992, 60 mins., colour videocassette VHS-PAL/NTSC; executive directed and produced by Anne Pattel-Gray.

Darwin's Body-Snatchers. Directed by David Monaghan; aired in Britain on 8 October 1991.

Lousy Little Sixpence (1909–1930). Sydney: Ronin Films, 1982; Canberra: Sixpence Productions, 1983, 54 mins., colour videocassette VHS-PAL/U-Matic; directed by Alex Morgan and Gerry Bostock.

One Australia. n.p.: ABC Television Special, 1991; produced and directed by Christine Sammers; aired in Sydney on 23 January 1992.

One People, Sing Freedom. Sydney: ABC Television Aboriginal Programs Unit, 1988, 50 mins., colour videocassette VHS-PAL; produced by Jim Everett.

The Secret Country: The First Australians Fight Back. Great Britain: Central Independent Television, 1985, 50 mins., 16 mm. film, colour videocassette VHS-PAL; directed by John Pilger.

Special Treatment: Locking Up Aboriginal Children. Sydney: Smith Street Films, 1991, 56 mins., colour videocassette VHS-PAL; produced by Margaret Smith.

State of Shock. 1989; produced by David Bradbury.

Walking the Walk: Social Justice in Everyday Life. Sydney: Greenwich Media, 1991, 26 mins., VHS-PAL; produced by the Sydney Archdiocesan *Rerum Novarum* Organizing Committee.

Women of the Sun. Sydney: Generation Films, 1982, 60 min. (x 4), colour videocassette VHS-PAL; produced by Bob Weis, written by Hyllus Maris and Sonia Borg.
Episode 1: "Alinta—'The Flame'" [set in 1824]; Directed by James Ricketson.
Episode 2: "Maydina—'The Shadow'" [set in 1890s]; Directed by David Stevens.
Episode 3: "Nerida Anderson" [set in 1939 on a reserve]; Directed by Stephen Wallace.
Episode 4: "Lo-Arna" [set in 1981 in the city]; Directed by Geoffrey Nottage.

Audio-Visual Interviews—Sound Recording

Russell, Don. "Talk of the Nation." National Public Radio, Washington, D.C., U.S.A., 26 January 1994.

Audio-Visual Interviews—Television Programs

Nelson, Brendan. Interview, *A Current Affair,* Channel 9, 29 July 1994.
Whitlam, E. Gough. Interview, *Face the Press,* SBS-TV, 26 July 1992.

Audio-Visual Resources—Radio & Television Stations

Australian Broadcasting Commission, Aboriginal Programmes Unit; radio and television.
Central Australia Aboriginal Media Association (CAAMA); radio and television.
Imparja, Alice Springs, N.T.; television.
Radio Redfern, 88.9 FM, Sydney, N.S.W.; radio.
Townsville Aboriginal and Islander Media Association (TAIMA); radio.
Western Australia Aboriginal Media Association (WAIMA); radio.

Maps

Aboriginal Land and Population. No. 12. Second edition. Canberra: Australian Surveying and Land Information Group, 1986.
Tyndale Map. Canberra: Australian Government Publishing Service, 1974.

Oral Testimonies

Aboriginal People

A Hang, K. Adelaide, S.A., November 1992; Sydney, N.S.W., May 1994.
Allem, L. Sydney, N.S.W., November 1992; Darwin, N.T., January 1993– .
Baxter, N. Adelaide, S.A., November 1992.
Bayles, T. Sydney, N.S.W., January 1988.
Bellear, Sol. Sydney, N.S.W., December 1992–February 1993, December 1993.
Brooke, N. Townsville, Qld., December 1992; June 1994.
Broome, C. Sydney, N.S.W., September 1992; January 1993.
Broome, D. Sydney, N.S.W., September–December 1992.
Bropho, R. Perth, W.A., August 1990.
Brown, L. Sydney, N.S.W., January 1992.
Clarke, B. Sydney, N.S.W., January 1988; Adelaide, S.A., November 1992.

Collard, D. Perth, W.A., August 1991.

Collard, G. Alice Springs, N.T., May 1992.

Collins, A. Nhulunbuy, N.T., April 1991; Sydney, N.S.W., April 1992.

Corbett, H. Sydney, N.S.W., December 1993.

Delaney, I. Canberra, A.C.T., November 1992– .

Dingo, E. Sydney, N.S.W., January 1988.

Dodson, M. Sydney, N.S.W., December 1993.

Garrawurra, R. Sydney, N.S.W., February 1992.

Gilbert, K. Canberra, A.C.T., February 1991, November 1992.

Gondarra, D. Sydney, N.S.W., September 1992.

Grant, C. Sydney, N.S.W., September 1992.

Harris, C. Sydney, N.S.W., January 1988; Lismore, N.S.W., May 1992.

Higgins, L. Sydney, N.S.W., December 1993.

Hill, K. Sydney, N.S.W., November 1992; Darwin, N.T., January 1993– .

Iles, B. Winton, Queensland, June 1989.

Lacey, A. Sydney, N.S.W., November 1992; Darwin, N.T., January 1993– .

Lester, C. La Perouse, N.S.W., 1992–93.

Lester, J. La Perouse, N.S.W., 1992–93.

Lester, S. La Perouse, N.S.W., 1992–93.

Lewis, G. Umuwa, S.A., May 1992.

Malcolm, A. Sydney, N.S.W., 1991–94.

Mansell, D. Sydney, N.S.W., September 1992.

Marika, W. Nhulunbuy, N.T., April 1991; Sydney, N.S.W., September 1992.

Morrison, R. Canberra, A.C.T., February 1991; Darwin, N.T., February 1993.

Nganyingu, P. Ernabella, N.T., May 1992.

O'Donoghue, L. Canberra, A.C.T., December 1990–March 1991, November 1992.

Passi, D. Sydney, N.S.W., December 1993.

Pattel, J. Sydney, N.S.W., 1987–94.

Paulson, G. Sydney, N.S.W., June–August, December 1992, January, December 1993.

Paulson, I. Sydney, N.S.W., June–August 1992.

Rice, J. Sydney, N.S.W., December 1993.

Ross, A. Sydney, N.S.W., November 1992; Darwin, N.T., January 1993– .

Rosendale, G. Cairns, Qld., 1990; Sydney, N.S.W., February, July 1992.

Stanford, D. Perth, W.A., August 1991; Sydney, N.S.W., January 1992.

Thompson, L. Sydney, N.S.W., December 1993, January 1994.

Tilmouth, B. Canberra, A.C.T., February 1991; Alice Springs, N.T., May 1992, June 1994.

Turner, P. Canberra, A.C.T., December 1990–March 1991.

Walker, A. Sydney, N.S.W., February 1992; Tabulam, N.S.W., May 1992.

Walker, H. Sydney, N.S.W., February 1992; Tabulam, N.S.W., May 1992.

Weatherall, R. Canberra, A.C.T., February 1991; Sydney, N.S.W., 1992.

West, I. Darwin, N.T., 1987.

Whitlam, G. Sydney, N.S.W., December 1993.

Widders, T. Sydney, N.S.W., November 1992, December 1993.

Williams, A. Sydney, N.S.W., October 1992.

Yunupingu, A. Nhulunbuy, N.T., April 1991.

Yunupingu, B. Nhulunbuy, N.T., April 1991.

Yunupingu, Dh. Nhulunbuy, N.T., April 1991; Sydney, N.S.W., July 1992, March 1993.

Yunupingu, Dj. Nhulunbuy, N.T., April 1991; Sydney, N.S.W., July 1992, March 1993.

Yunupingu, G. Canberra, A.C.T., February 1991; Nhulunbuy, N.T., April 1991; Sydney, N.S.W., January 1992; Alice Springs, N.T., May 1992; Sydney, N.S.W., September 1992, August 1994.

Yunupingu, M. Nhulunbuy, N.T., April 1991; Sydney, N.S.W., September 1992.

Yunupingu, S. Gunyangara, N.T., 1991; Sydney, N.S.W., 1992–93.

Yunupingu, Y. Yirrkala, N.T., April 1991; Sydney, N.S.W., June 1992; Sydney, N.S.W., 1993.

Non-Aboriginal People

Amjad-Ali, C. Sydney, N.S.W., January 1993.

Boesak, W. Johannesburg, South Africa, 1993.

Downer, A. Sydney, N.S.W., October 1994.

Einfeld, M. Sydney, N.S.W., December 1993.

Hewson, John. Canberra, A.C.T., February 1991.

Hayden, B. Canberra, A.C.T., February 1991.

Hand, G. Canberra, A.C.T., January–February 1991.

Jackson, A. Parramatta, N.S.W., July 1992.

Jones, M. Kansas City, MO., U.S.A., 1993.

Kadiba, J. Sydney, N.S.W., July 1992.

Kopi, S. Sydney, N.S.W., January–June 1992.

Moore, T. Sydney, N.S.W., September 1994.

Mosala, I. Johannesburg, South Africa, 1993.

Ramírez, G. Sydney, New South Wales (N.S.W.), 1993–94.

Ramírez, J. Sydney, N.S.W., 1993–94.

Tickner, R. Sydney, N.S.W., 1991.

Watson, M. Alice Springs, N.T., June 1994.

Whitlam, F. Sydney, N.S.W., January 1993.

Unpublished Materials

Berndt, R. M., and Berndt, C. H. "Native Labour and Welfare in the Northern Territory." Sydney: n.p., 1946.

Brennan, Frank, and Crawford, James. *Aboriginality, Recognition and Australian Law: Where to From Here?* [Sydney, 1989], 22 pp.

Busch, R. A. "[Open Letter "to all Members of the Uniting Church"]." MacGregor, Qld.: Uniting Church in Australia Assembly, [23 July,] 1984.

Christian, Deborah. 'Aboriginal Independent Churches.' Unpublished MS, University of Sydney, 1983.

Corowa, Dennis. "Reflections on the Invasion of Australia: A Paper Presented at the National Meeting of UAICC, Sydney, 6 November 1990," 4 pp.

Eva Valley Statement. Eva Valley, Northern Territory, 5 August 1993, 2 pp.

312   *The Great White Flood: Racism in Australia*

Gill, David M. "The Morning After: Living With the Consequences of Canberra '91." *Report to the Australian Council of Churches (Executive Committee Minutes)*. Australian Council of Churches, Sydney, Australia, 1991, Document No. 7.1b, p. 3.

Habgood, John. "The Role of the Churches in the International Order." The Thomas Corbishley Lecture, n.p., England, U.K., 9 October 1991. [Habgood is Archbishop of York, England, U.K.]

Kling, Margaret Jane. "A Case Study: Women and Health." San José, El Salvador: Jesuit Refugee Service, [1988]. [Unpublished paper.]

Morgan, Hugh M. Letter to Robert Tickner (Minister for Aboriginal and Torres Strait Islander Affairs) and Lois O'Donoghue (Chairperson ATSIC), 28 January 1993.

National Council of Churches in Australia [In-formation]. Preparatory Documents, 1992–.

Newcomb, Steven T. Letter to Pope John Paul II from the Indigenous Law Institute, 4 May 1993, 2 pp.

TIB [Thursdays in Black]. *Thursdays in Black: Demanding a World Without Rape and Violence*. Flyer. n.p.: n.p., [1992].

Tickner, Robert, MP. Unpublished correspondence regarding ecclesial endorsements of the (then-proposed) Council for Aboriginal Reconciliation. Archives of the Australian Council of Churches, Aboriginal & Islander Commission, 1991b.

Windt, Uri, et al. *Content Analysis of NSW Primary School Social Studies Textbooks with Respect to the Development of Racial Attitudes in Children*. Sydney: Unpublished study, Department of Sociology, University of New South Wales, 1970.